The Editors

DEBORAH ESCH, Associate Professor of English at the University of Toronto, received her Ph.D. in Comparative Literature from Yale University. She has also taught at Princeton and Stanford. Author of *In the Event: Reading Journalism, Reading Theory* and co-editor of *Critical Encounters*, she has also published extensively on literary and cultural theory.

JONATHAN WARREN, Assistant Professor of English at York University, received his Ph.D. from the University of Toronto. His articles have appeared in *Early Modern Literary Studies*, *Studies in Twentieth Century Literature*, and the *Henry James Review*.

THE TURN OF THE SCREW

AUTHORITATIVE TEXT
CONTEXTS
CRITICISM

SECOND EDITION

W. W. NORTON & COMPANY, INC.

Also Publishes

THE NORTON ANTHOLOGY OF AFRICAN AMERICAN LITERATURE
edited by Henry Louis Gates Jr. and Nellie Y. McKay et al.

THE NORTON ANTHOLOGY OF AMERICAN LITERATURE
edited by Nina Baym et al.

THE NORTON ANTHOLOGY OF CONTEMPORARY FICTION
edited by R. V. Cassill and Joyce Carol Oates

THE NORTON ANTHOLOGY OF ENGLISH LITERATURE
edited by M. H. Abrams and Stephen Greenblatt et al.

THE NORTON ANTHOLOGY OF LITERATURE BY WOMEN
edited by Sandra M. Gilbert and Susan Gubar

THE NORTON ANTHOLOGY OF MODERN POETRY
edited by Richard Ellmann and Robert O'Clair

THE NORTON ANTHOLOGY OF POETRY
edited by Margaret Ferguson et al.

THE NORTON ANTHOLOGY OF SHORT FICTION
edited by R. V. Cassill and Richard Bausch

THE NORTON ANTHOLOGY OF WORLD MASTERPIECES
edited by Sarah Lawall et al.

THE NORTON FACSIMILE OF THE FIRST FOLIO OF SHAKESPEARE
prepared by Charlton Hinman

THE NORTON INTRODUCTION TO LITERATURE
edited by Jerome Beaty and J. Paul Hunter

THE NORTON INTRODUCTION TO THE SHORT NOVEL
edited by Jerome Beaty

THE NORTON READER
edited by Linda H. Peterson, John C. Brereton, and Joan E. Hartman

THE NORTON SAMPLER
edited by Thomas Cooley

THE NORTON SHAKESPEARE, BASED ON THE OXFORD EDITION
edited by Stephen Greenblatt et al.

For a complete list of Norton Critical Editions, visit us
on the World Wide Web at
www.wwnorton.com/college/english/nce/welcome.htm

A NORTON CRITICAL EDITION

Henry James

THE TURN OF THE SCREW

AUTHORITATIVE TEXT

CONTEXTS

CRITICISM

SECOND EDITION

Edited by

DEBORAH ESCH
UNIVERSITY OF TORONTO
and
JONATHAN WARREN
YORK UNIVERSITY

First Edition edited by

ROBERT KIMBROUGH
UNIVERSITY OF WISCONSIN

W • W • NORTON & COMPANY • *New York* • *London*

The text of this book is composed in Electra with the display set in Bernhard Modern. Composition by PennSet, Inc. Manufacturing by Maple-Vail Book Group. Book design by Antonina Krass. Cover illustration: "Miles and the Governess" by Charles Demuth.

Library of Congress Cataloging-in-Publication Data
James, Henry, 1843–1916.
The turn of the screw : authoritative text, contexts, criticism / Henry James. — 2nd ed. / edited by Deborah Esch and Jonathan Warren.
p. cm. — (A Norton critical edition)
Includes bibliographical references.

ISBN 0-393-95904-X (pbk.)

1. Governesses—England—Fiction. 2. James, Henry, 1843–1916. Turn of the screw. 3. Governesses in literature. I. Esch, Deborah, 1954– . II. Warren, Jonathan. III. Title.
PS2116.T8 1998
813'.4—dc21 98-31635
CIP

W. W. Norton & Company, Inc., 500 Fifth Avenue, New York, N.Y. 10110
www.wwnorton.com
W. W. Norton & Company Ltd., Castle House, 75/76 Wells Street, London W1T 3QT

5 6 7 8 9 0

Contents

Criticism

Preface to the Second Edition

In his own critical preface to the volume of the New York Edition that includes *The Turn of the Screw,* Henry James makes a remarkable claim for the tale: "this perfectly independent and irresponsible little fiction rejoices, beyond any rival on a like ground, in a conscious provision of prompt retort to the sharpest question that may be addressed to it. For it has the small strength—if I should n't say rather the unattackable ease—of a perfect homogeneity, of being, to the very last grain of its virtue, all of a kind; the very kind, as it happens, least apt to be baited by earnest criticism, the only sort of criticism of which account need be taken."

In the century since its initial publication in 1898, *The Turn of the Screw* has generated a range of earnest critical responses, from journalistic reviews to major theoretical essays. Strikingly, as a number of readers have noted, many of the analytical tools and strategies brought to bear in interpreting and evaluating the text are not only anticipated in James's preface, but they are figured within the tale itself: for the critics, as for the governess, the characters and events around which the narrative turns, and turns again, evoke a profound unease in the face of epistemological as well as ethical uncertainty, and hence a tendency to impose univocal order and sense on language that strongly resists such acts of force.

The criticism that has emerged around James's tale is often as much a record of efforts to quell that anxiety as it is an attempt to understand a story that consistently defies such efforts. Indeed, this impulse to subdue the narrative is the key feature of *The Turn of the Screw*'s vast secondary literature: it establishes itself as a tendency early on, orients the major scholarship on the tale throughout most of the past century, and instigates the countermoves of later readers. Contemporary reviewers' exclamations of moral alarm were the first in a proliferation not only of sweeping denunciations of the tale's evil—a number of early responses condemn James's story for its iniquity with vigor—but of readings that seek to quiet the tale's insistent troubling of interpretive calm and complacency. The confidence of these early expressions of outrage—and, indeed, the contemporaneous commendations of artistic success—established the interpretive matrix for the tale's first major critical controversy. With evident faith in the possibility of a conclusive answer, James's most influential early readers addressed the text in terms of a strict binarism: Are the ghosts real, or are they figments of the governess's vexed imagination? Ironically, the critics' readiness to embrace such a stark opposition of possibilities—one that apparently permits a single correct answer to the most earnest of queries—mirrors the stance of the hapless governess. As one early review, provided in this edition, notes: "instead of watching the drama, one becomes part of it."

Yet the critical trajectory in this case, far from simply reenacting the tendentious interpretative maneuvers of the governess, in fact traces a very Jamesian circuit that is inseparable from the rhetorical turns that characterize his writing. If some prominent earlier critics of *The Turn of the Screw* sought to impose inflexible and polarized models of understanding, that rigidity has, over time, come to show more respect for the specificity of James's language: to heed, for example the attestation in the tale's introductory chapter that "the story *won't* tell . . . not in any literal, vulgar way," and to take some account of James's claim in the preface that "my values are positively all blanks save so far as an excited horror, a promoted pity, a created expertness . . . proceed to read into them more or less fantastic figures." The dilemma of the governess's reliability has gradually yielded to less preclusive points of departure that acknowledge the range of meanings afforded by James's prefatory insistence that the governess, if unendowed with conventional "signs and marks, features and humours," still retains irrefutable "authority." In response to the suggestion that the governess is "n't sufficiently characterised," James resolutely disowns any obligation to try "clumsily . . . for more," to invest her with a further capacity to "deal with her own mystery." James ironically encourages others to bother, as they surely have, with a difficulty that, for himself, he thought intelligently neglected. If James reserves the longed-for marks and signs, his withholding is *also* a kind of provision of such features. His haze, if it obscures, is, nonetheless, "blest golden."

A few early reviewers acclaim the tale's beauty with an interpretive vocabulary that anticipates the latest phase in the text's critical reception. Rather than castigating James for an immoral theme or fretting about ascertaining the final truth of the tale, critics such as Henry Harland, whose review in the *Academy* is provided in this edition, surmised that to understand the enigmas of *The Turn of the Screw* one must appreciate the nature of the puzzle. For Harland, *The Turn of the Screw* is "an instance, illustrative of the rest of life" that James presents "not as an anecdote, but, tacitly, as an illustration." In these terms the tale is the very opposite of perverse: neither a cunning experiment nor a detached incident, it is rather an example and a diagram of sorts. Its inexorable ambiguities mark it not as the extreme case, but as the normal one. James's values are blanks: as Droch observes, "while his art is present in every sentence, the artist is absolutely obliterated." James foregoes the pretence of mastery, providing neither certain caution nor encouragement. Yet, by absenting such sure directives from the text, James instead opens up generative gaps, productive of an authority divorced from the determinations of signs and marks, features and humors in which only the naive put their trust. Despite the urging of generations of critics that we do so, we fill in these gaps at our peril: like the governess, we only long to succumb to the sedative allure of a master upon whom we have been forbidden to call. *The Turn of the Screw* is an extended evocation of a longing for an authority that is not there and an anatomy of the variety of possible forms capitulations to longing may take. By seeing beauty in yearning, where others found reason to shudder or contend, Harland anticipated the latest phase in the criticism of James's tale. *The Turn of the Screw* is a typical Jamesian instance in which any impulse to defuse interpretive anxiety is rewarded with multiplied worries. For James, "our doubt is our passion and our passion is our task."

This Norton Critical Edition of *The Turn of the Screw* provides James's New York Edition text as established by Robert Kimbrough in 1966 followed by a textual history and a full section of textual notes. For this second edition, the contexts, criticism, and bibliography sections have been thoroughly revised and updated. The contexts section begins with a selection of James's own writings on the subjects of the ghost story and supernatural. The second grouping of materials provides excerpts from James's notebooks and letters on *The Turn of the Screw* in particular, ending with the preface to the volume of the New York Edition that includes the tale. An illustrations section reproduces four paintings by Charles Demuth (the fifth appears in color on the cover) inspired by the tale and constituting a form of textual criticism. "Other Possible Sources" provides four essays that discover potential origins for the tale that expand James's own account of its provenance. Criticism is divided chronologically into three groupings. The first provides a selection of reviews and other early reactions to *The Turn of the Screw*. The second is a sample of the major critical voices in the middle part of the century. The selections for the third section, "1970–Present," acknowledge the range of ways that the tale has served as a focal text in recent theoretical considerations of James and of narrative more generally. A chronology and selected bibliography conclude the edition.

In producing this second edition, we have relied on Robert Kimbrough's established text as well as the example he set with the first edition. We are grateful to have had such helpful guidance. We are indebted to Carol Bemis for her patient and valuable editorial support.

Deborah Esch and Jonathan Warren

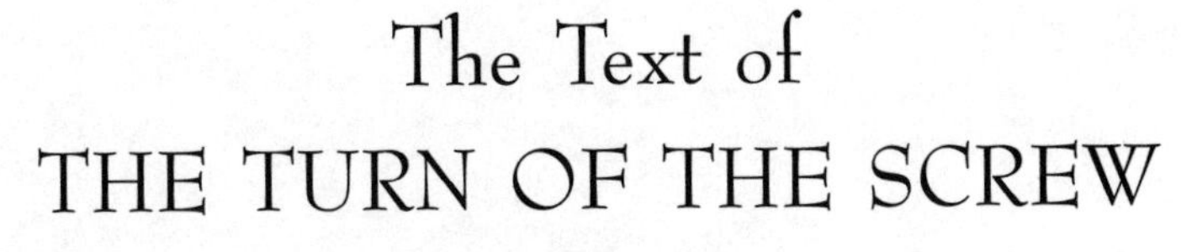

The Text of THE TURN OF THE SCREW

The Turn of the Screw

The story had held us, round the fire, sufficiently breathless, but except the obvious remark that it was gruesome, as on Christmas Eve in an old house a strange tale should essentially be, I remember no comment uttered till somebody happened to note it as the only case he had met in which such a visitation had fallen on a child. The case, I may mention, was that of an apparition in just such an old house as had gathered us for the occasion—an appearance, of a dreadful kind, to a little boy sleeping in the room with his mother and waking her up in the terror of it; waking her not to dissipate his dread and soothe him to sleep again, but to encounter also herself, before she had succeeded in doing so, the same sight that had shocked him. It was this observation that drew from Douglas—not immediately, but later in the evening—a reply that had the interesting consequence to which I call attention. Some one else told a story not particularly effective, which I saw he was not following. This I took for a sign that he had himself something to produce and that we should only have to wait. We waited in fact till two nights later; but that same evening, before we scattered, he brought out what was in his mind.

"I quite agree—in regard to Griffin's ghost, or whatever it was—that its appearing first to the little boy, at so tender an age, adds a particular touch. But it's not the first occurrence of its charming kind that I know to have been concerned with a child. If the child gives the effect another turn of the screw, what do you say to *two* children—?"

"We say of course," somebody exclaimed, "that two children give two turns! Also that we want to hear about them."

I can see Douglas there before the fire, to which he had got up to present his back, looking down at this converser with his hands in his pockets. "Nobody but me, till now, has ever heard. It 's quite too horrible." This was naturally declared by several voices to give the thing the utmost price, and our friend, with quiet art, prepared his triumph by turning his eyes over the rest of us and going on: "It 's beyond everything. Nothing at all that I know touches it."

"For sheer terror?" I remember asking.

He seemed to say it was n't so simple as that; to be really at a loss how to qualify it. He passed his hand over his eyes, made a little wincing grimace. "For dreadful—dreadfulness!"

"Oh how delicious!" cried one of the women.

He took no notice of her; he looked at me, but as if, instead of me, he saw what he spoke of. "For general uncanny ugliness and horror and pain."

"Well then," I said, "just sit right down and begin."

He turned round to the fire, gave a kick to a log, watched it an instant. Then as he faced us again: "I can't begin. I shall have to send to town." There was a unanimous groan at this, and much reproach; after which, in his preoccupied way, he explained. "The story 's written. It 's in a locked drawer—it has not been out for years. I could write to my man and enclose the key; he could send down the packet as he finds it." It was to me in particular that he appeared to propound this—appeared almost to appeal for aid not to hesitate. He had broken a thickness of ice, the formation of many a winter; had had his reasons for a long silence. The others resented postponement, but it was just his scruples that charmed me. I adjured him to write by the first post and to agree with us for an early hearing; then I asked him if the experience in question had been his own. To this his answer was prompt. "Oh thank God, no!"

"And is the record yours? You took the thing down?"

"Nothing but the impression. I took that *here*"—he tapped his heart. "I 've never lost it."

"Then your manuscript—?"

"Is in old faded ink and in the most beautiful hand." He hung fire again. "A woman's. She has been dead these twenty years. She sent me the pages in question before she died." They were all listening now, and of course there was somebody to be arch, or at any rate to draw the inference. But if he put the inference by without a smile it was also without irritation. "She was a most charming person, but she was ten years older than I. She was my sister's governess," he quietly said. "She was the most agreeable woman I 've ever known in her position; she 'd have been worthy of any whatever. It was long ago, and this episode was long before. I was at Trinity, and I found her at home on my coming down the second summer. I was much there that year—it was a beautiful one; and we had, in her off-hours, some strolls and talks in the garden—talks in which she struck me as awfully clever and nice. Oh yes; don't grin: I liked her extremely and am glad to this day to think she liked me too. If she had n't she would n't have told me. She had never told any one. It was n't simply that she said so, but that I knew she had n't. I was sure; I could see. You'll easily judge why when you hear."

"Because the thing had been such a scare?"

He continued to fix me. "You'll easily judge," he repeated: "*you* will."

I fixed him too. "I see. She was in love."

He laughed for the first time. "You *are* acute. Yes, she was in love. That is she *had* been. That came out—she could n't tell her story without its coming out. I saw it, and she saw I saw it; but neither of us spoke of it. I remember the time and the place—the corner of the lawn, the shade of the great beeches and the long hot summer afternoon. It was n't a scene for a shudder; but oh—!" He quitted the fire and dropped back into his chair.

"You 'll receive the packet Thursday morning?" I said.

"Probably not till the second post."

"Well then; after dinner—"

"You 'll all meet me here?" He looked us round again. "Is n't anybody going?" It was almost the tone of hope.

"Everybody will stay!"

"*I* will—and *I* will!" cried the ladies whose departure had been fixed. Mrs. Griffin, however, expressed the need for a little more light. "Who was it she was in love with?"

"The story will tell," I took upon myself to reply.

"Oh I can't wait for the story!"

"The story *won't* tell," said Douglas; "not in any literal vulgar way."

"More 's the pity then. That 's the only way I ever understand."

"Won't *you* tell, Douglas?" somebody else required.

He sprang to his feet again. "Yes—to-morrow. Now I must go to bed. Good-night." And, quickly catching up a candlestick, he left us slightly bewildered. From our end of the great brown hall we heard his step on the stair; whereupon Mrs. Griffin spoke. "Well, if I don't know who she was in love with I know who *he* was."

"She was ten years older," said her husband.

"*Raison de plus*[1]—at that age! But it 's rather nice, his long reticence."

"Forty years!" Griffin put in.

"With this outbreak at last."

"The outbreak," I returned, "will make a tremendous occasion of Thursday night"; and every one so agreed with me that in the light of it we lost all attention for everything else. The last story, however incomplete and like the mere opening of a serial, had been told; we handshook and "candlestuck," as somebody said, and went to bed.

I knew the next day that a letter containing the key had, by the first post, gone off to his London apartments; but in spite of—or perhaps just on account of—the eventual diffusion of this knowledge we quite let him alone till after dinner, till such an hour of the evening in fact as might best accord with the kind of emotion on which our hopes were fixed. Then he became as communicative as we could desire, and indeed gave us his best reason for being so. We had it from him again

1. All the more reason.

before the fire in the hall, as we had had our mild wonders of the previous night. It appeared that the narrative he had promised to read us really required for a proper intelligence a few words of prologue. Let me say here distinctly, to have done with it, that this narrative, from an exact transcript of my own made much later, is what I shall presently give. Poor Douglas, before his death—when it was in sight—committed to me the manuscript that reached him on the third of these days and that, on the same spot, with immense effect, he began to read to our hushed little circle on the night of the fourth. The departing ladies who had said they would stay did n't, of course, thank heaven, stay: they departed, in consequence of arrangements made, in a rage of curiosity, as they professed, produced by the touches with which he had already worked us up. But that only made his little final auditory more compact and select, kept it, round the hearth, subject to a common thrill.

The first of these touches conveyed that the written statement took up the tale at a point after it had, in a manner, begun. The fact to be in possession of was therefore that his old friend, the youngest of several daughters of a poor country parson, had at the age of twenty, on taking service for the first time in the schoolroom, come up to London, in trepidation, to answer in person an advertisement that had already placed her in brief correspondence with the advertiser. This person proved, on her presenting herself for judgment at a house in Harley Street that impressed her as vast and imposing—this prospective patron proved a gentleman, a bachelor in the prime of life, such a figure as had never risen, save in a dream or an old novel, before a fluttered anxious girl out of a Hampshire vicarage. One could easily fix his type; it never, happily, dies out. He was handsome and bold and pleasant, off-hand and gay and kind. He struck her, inevitably, as gallant and splendid, but what took her most of all and gave her the courage she afterwards showed was that he put the whole thing to her as a favour, an obligation he should gratefully incur. She figured him as rich, but as fearfully extravagant—saw him all in a glow of high fashion, of good looks, of expensive habits, of charming ways with women. He had for his town residence a big house filled with the spoils of travel and the trophies of the chase; but it was to his country home, an old family place in Essex, that he wished her immediately to proceed.[2]

He had been left, by the death of his parents in India, guardian to a small nephew and a small niece, children of a younger, a military brother whom he had lost two years before. These children were, by the strangest of chances for a man in his position—a lone man without the right sort of experience or a grain of patience—very heavy on his hands. It had all been a great worry and, on his own part doubtless, a series of blunders, but he immensely pitied the poor chicks and had

2. Harley Street was a fashionable residential area at the "time" of the story; Hampshire lies SW of London; Essex, NE.

done all he could; had in particular sent them down to his other house, the proper place for them being of course the country, and kept them there from the first with the best people he could find to look after them, parting even with his own servants to wait on them and going down himself, whenever he might, to see how they were doing. The awkward thing was that they had practically no other relations and that his own affairs took up all his time. He had put them in possession of Bly, which was healthy and secure, and had placed at the head of their little establishment—but below-stairs only—an excellent woman, Mrs. Grose, whom he was sure his visitor would like and who had formerly been maid to his mother. She was now housekeeper and was also acting for the time as superintendent to the little girl, of whom, without children of her own, she was by good luck extremely fond. There were plenty of people to help, but of course the young lady who should go down as governess would be in supreme authority. She would also have, in holidays, to look after the small boy, who had been for a term at school—young as he was to be sent, but what else could be done?—and who, as the holidays were about to begin, would be back from one day to the other. There had been for the two children at first a young lady whom they had had the misfortune to lose. She had done for them quite beautifully—she was a most respectable person—till her death, the great awkwardness of which had, precisely, left no alternative but the school for little Miles. Mrs. Grose, since then, in the way of manners and things, had done as she could for Flora; and there were, further, a cook, a housemaid, a dairywoman, an old pony, an old groom and an old gardener, all likewise thoroughly respectable.

So far had Douglas presented his picture when some one put a question. "And what did the former governess die of? Of so much respectability?"

Our friend's answer was prompt. "That will come out. I don't anticipate."

"Pardon me—I thought that was just what you *are* doing."

"In her successor's place," I suggested, "I should have wished to learn if the office brought with it—"

"Necessary danger to life?" Douglas completed my thought. "She did wish to learn, and she did learn. You shall hear to-morrow what she learnt. Meanwhile of course the prospect struck her as slightly grim. She was young, untried, nervous: it was a vision of serious duties and little company, of really great loneliness. She hesitated—took a couple of days to consult and consider. But the salary offered much exceeded her modest measure, and on a second interview she faced the music, she engaged." And Douglas, with this, made a pause that, for the benefit of the company, moved me to throw in—

"The moral of which was of course the seduction exercised by the splendid young man. She succumbed to it."

He got up and, as he had done the night before, went to the fire, gave a stir to a log with his foot, then stood a moment with his back to us. "She saw him only twice."

"Yes, but that's just the beauty of her passion."

A little to my surprise, on this, Douglas turned round to me. "It *was* the beauty of it. There were others," he went on, "who had n't succumbed. He told her frankly all his difficulty—that for several applicants the conditions had been prohibitive. They were somehow simply afraid. It sounded dull—it sounded strange; and all the more so because of his main condition."

"Which was—?"

"That she should never trouble him—but never, never: neither appeal nor complain nor write about anything; only meet all questions herself, receive all moneys from his solicitor, take the whole thing over and let him alone. She promised to do this, and she mentioned to me that when, for a moment, disburdened, delighted, he held her hand, thanking her for the sacrifice, she already felt rewarded."

"But was that all her reward?" one of the ladies asked.

"She never saw him again."

"Oh!" said the lady; which, as our friend immediately again left us, was the only other word of importance contributed to the subject till, the next night, by the corner of the hearth, in the best chair, he opened the faded red cover of a thin old-fashioned gilt-edged album. The whole thing took indeed more nights than one, but on the first occasion the same lady put another question. "What 's your title?"

"I have n't one."

"Oh *I* have!" I said. But Douglas, without heeding me, had begun to read with a fine clearness that was like a rendering to the ear of the beauty of his author's hand.[3]

I

I remember the whole beginning as a succession of flights and drops, a little see-saw of the right throbs and the wrong. After rising, in town, to meet his appeal I had at all events a couple of very bad days—found all my doubts bristle again, felt indeed sure I had made a mistake. In this state of mind I spent the long hours of bumping swinging coach that carried me to the stopping-place at which I was to be met by a vehicle from the house. This convenience, I was told, had been ordered, and I found, toward the close of the June afternoon, a commodious fly in waiting for me. Driving at that hour, on a lovely day, through a country the summer sweetness of which served as a friendly welcome, my fortitude revived and, as we turned into the avenue, took

3. The first of twelve installments that ran in *Collier's Weekly* in 1898 ended here (see Textual History).

a flight that was probably but a proof of the point to which it had sunk. I suppose I had expected, or had dreaded, something so dreary that what greeted me was a good surprise. I remember as a thoroughly pleasant impression the broad clear front, its open windows and fresh curtains and the pair of maids looking out; I remember the lawn and the bright flowers and the crunch of my wheels on the gravel and the clustered tree-tops over which the rooks circled and cawed in the golden sky. The scene had a greatness that made a different affair from my own scant home, and there immediately appeared at the door, with a little girl in her hand, a civil person who dropped me as decent a curtsey as if I had been the mistress or a distinguished visitor. I had received in Harley Street a narrower notion of the place, and that, as I recalled it, made me think the proprietor still more of a gentleman, suggested that what I was to enjoy might be a matter beyond his promise.

I had no drop again till the next day, for I was carried triumphantly through the following hours by my introduction to the younger of my pupils. The little girl who accompanied Mrs. Grose affected me on the spot as a creature too charming not to make it a great fortune to have to do with her. She was the most beautiful child I had ever seen, and I afterwards wondered why my employer had n't made more of a point to me of this. I slept little that night—I was too much excited; and this astonished me too, I recollect, remained with me, adding to my sense of the liberality with which I was treated. The large impressive room, one of the best in the house, the great state bed, as I almost felt it, the figured full draperies, the long glasses in which, for the first time, I could see myself from head to foot, all struck me—like the wonderful appeal of my small charge—as so many things thrown in. It was thrown in as well, from the first moment, that I should get on with Mrs. Grose in a relation over which, on my way, in the coach, I fear I had rather brooded. The one appearance indeed that in this early outlook might have made me shrink again was that of her being so inordinately glad to see me. I felt within half an hour that she was so glad—stout simple plain clean wholesome woman—as to be positively on her guard against showing it too much. I wondered even then a little why she should wish *not* to show it, and that, with reflexion, with suspicion, might of course have made me uneasy.

But it was a comfort that there could be no uneasiness in a connexion with anything so beatific as the radiant image of my little girl, the vision of whose angelic beauty had probably more than anything else to do with the restlessness that, before morning, made me several times rise and wander about my room to take in the whole picture and prospect; to watch from my open window the faint summer dawn, to look at such stretches of the rest of the house as I could catch, and to listen, while in the fading dusk the first birds began to twitter, for the possible recurrence of a sound or two, less natural and not without but within, that I had fancied I heard. There had been a moment when I believed I recognised, faint and far, the cry of a child; there had been another when I found myself just consciously starting as at the passage, before my door, of a light footstep. But these fancies were not marked enough not to be thrown off, and it is only in the light, or the gloom, I should rather say, of other and subsequent matters that they now come back to me. To watch, teach, "form" little Flora would too evidently be the making of a happy and useful life. It had been agreed between us downstairs that after this first occasion I should have her as a matter of course at night, her small white bed being already arranged, to that end, in my room. What I had undertaken was the whole care of her, and she had remained just this last time with Mrs. Grose only as an effect of our consideration for my inevitable strangeness and her natural timidity. In spite of this timidity—which the child herself, in the oddest way in the world, had been perfectly frank and brave about, allowing it, without a sign of uncomfortable consciousness, with the deep sweet serenity indeed of one of Raphael's holy infants,[4] to be discussed, to be imputed to her and to determine us—I felt quite sure she would presently like me. It was part of what I already liked Mrs. Grose herself for, the pleasure I could see her feel in my admiration and wonder as I sat at supper with four tall candles and with my pupil, in a high chair and a bib, brightly facing me between them over bread and milk. There were naturally things that in Flora's presence could pass between us only as prodigious and gratified looks, obscure and roundabout allusions.

"And the little boy—does he look like her? Is he too so very remarkable?"

One would n't, it was already conveyed between us, too grossly flatter a child. "Oh Miss, *most* remarkable. If you think well of this one!"—and she stood there with a plate in her hand, beaming at our companion, who looked from one of us to the other with placid heavenly eyes that contained nothing to check us.

"Yes; if I do—?"

"You *will* be carried away by the little gentleman!"

"Well, that, I think, is what I came for—to be carried away. I 'm afraid, however," I remember feeling the impulse to add, "I 'm rather easily carried away. I was carried away in London!"

I can still see Mrs. Grose's broad face as she took this in. "In Harley Street?"

"In Harley Street."

"Well, Miss, you 're not the first—and you won't be the last."

4. Raphael (1483–1520), Italian painter in the High Renaissance, renowned for his religious works.

"Oh I 've no pretensions," I could laugh, "to being the only one. My other pupil, at any rate, as I understand, comes back to-morrow?"

"Not to-morrow—Friday, Miss. He arrives, as you did, by the coach, under care of the guard,[5] and is to be met by the same carriage."

I forthwith wanted to know if the proper as well as the pleasant and friendly thing would n't therefore be that on the arrival of the public conveyance I should await him with his little sister; a proposition to which Mrs. Grose assented so heartily that I somehow took her manner as a kind of comforting pledge—never falsified, thank heaven!—that we should on every question be quite at one. Oh she was glad I was there!

What I felt the next day was, I suppose, nothing that could be fairly called a reaction from the cheer of my arrival; it was probably at the most only a slight oppression produced by a fuller measure of the scale, as I walked round them, gazed up at them, took them in, of my new circumstances. They had, as it were, an extent and mass for which I had not been prepared and in the presence of which I found myself, freshly, a little scared not less than a little proud. Regular lessons, in this agitation, certainly suffered some wrong; I reflected that my first duty was, by the gentlest arts I could contrive, to win the child into the sense of knowing me. I spent the day with her out of doors; I arranged with her, to her great satisfaction, that it should be she, she only, who might show me the place. She showed it step by step and room by room and secret by secret, with droll delightful childish talk about it and with the result, in half an hour, of our becoming tremendous friends. Young as she was I was struck, throughout our little tour, with her confidence and courage, with the way, in empty chambers and dull corridors, on crooked staircases that made me pause and even on the summit of an old machicolated square tower[6] that made me dizzy, her morning music, her disposition to tell me so many more things than she asked, rang out and led me on. I have not seen Bly since the day I left it, and I dare say that to my present older and more informed eyes it would show a very reduced importance. But as my little conductress, with her hair of gold and her frock of blue, danced before me round corners and pattered down passages, I had the view of a castle of romance inhabited by a rosy sprite, such a place as would somehow, for diversion of the young idea, take all colour out of story-books and fairy-tales. Was n't it just a story-book over which I had fallen a-doze and a-dream? No; it was a big ugly antique but convenient house, embodying a few features of a building still older, half-displaced and half-utilised, in which I had the fancy of our being almost as lost as a handful of passengers in a great drifting ship. Well, I was strangely at the helm!

5. Mail guard.
6. Designed like a castle turret with firing apertures, or battlements.

II

This came home to me when, two days later, I drove over with Flora to meet, as Mrs. Grose said, the little gentleman; and all the more for an incident that, presenting itself the second evening, had deeply disconcerted me. The first day had been, on the whole, as I have expressed, reassuring; but I was to see it wind up to a change of note. The postbag that evening—it came late—contained a letter for me which, however, in the hand of my employer, I found to be composed but of a few words enclosing another, addressed to himself, with a seal still unbroken. "This, I recognise, is from the head-master, and the head-master 's an awful bore. Read him please; deal with him; but mind you don't report. Not a word. I 'm off!" I broke the seal with a great effort—so great a one that I was a long time coming to it; took the unopened missive at last up to my room and only attacked it just before going to bed. I had better have let it wait till morning, for it gave me a second sleepless night. With no counsel to take, the next day, I was full of distress; and it finally got so the better of me that I determined to open myself at least to Mrs. Grose.

"What does it mean? The child's dismissed his school."

She gave me a look that I remarked at the moment; then, visibly, with a quick blankness, seemed to try to take it back. "But are n't they all—?"

"Sent home—yes. But only for the holidays. Miles may never go back at all."

Consciously, under my attention, she reddened. "They won't take him?"

"They absolutely decline."

At this she raised her eyes, which she had turned from me; I saw them fill with good tears. "What has he done?"

I cast about; then I judged best simply to hand her my document—which, however, had the effect of making her, without taking it, simply put her hands behind her. She shook her head sadly. "Such things are not for me, Miss."

My counsellor could n't read! I winced at my mistake, which I attentuated as I could, and opened the letter again to repeat it to her; then, faltering in the act and folding it up once more, I put it back in my pocket. "Is he really *bad*?"

The tears were still in her eyes. "Do the gentlemen say so?"

"They go into no particulars. They simply express their regret that it should be impossible to keep him. That can have but one meaning." Mrs. Grose listened with dumb emotion; she forbore to ask me what this meaning might be; so that, presently, to put the thing with some coherence and with the mere aid of her presence to my own mind, I went on: "That he 's an injury to the others."

At this, with one of the quick turns of simple folk, she suddenly flamed up. "Master Miles!—*him* an injury?"

There was such a flood of good faith in it that, though I had not yet seen the child, my very fears made me jump to the absurdity of the idea. I found myself, to meet my friend the better, offering it, on the spot, sarcastically. "To his poor little innocent mates!"

"It's too dreadful," cried Mrs. Grose, "to say such cruel things! Why he's scarce ten years old."

"Yes, yes; it would be incredible."

She was evidently grateful for such a profession. "See him, Miss, first. *Then* believe it!" I felt forthwith a new impatience to see him; it was the beginning of a curiosity that, all the next hours, was to deepen almost to pain. Mrs. Grose was aware, I could judge, of what she had produced in me, and she followed it up with assurance. "You might as well believe it of the little lady. Bless her," she added the next moment—"*look* at her!"

I turned and saw that Flora, whom, ten minutes before, I had established in the schoolroom with a sheet of white paper, a pencil and a copy of nice "round O's," now presented herself to view at the open door. She expressed in her little way an extraordinary detachment from disagreeable duties, looking at me, however, with a great childish light that seemed to offer it as a mere result of the affection she had conceived for my person, which had rendered necessary that she should follow me. I needed nothing more than this to feel the full force of Mrs. Grose's comparison, and, catching my pupil in my arms, covered her with kisses in which there was a sob of atonement.

None the less, the rest of the day, I watched for further occasion to approach my colleague, especially as, toward evening, I began to fancy she rather sought to avoid me. I overtook her, I remember, on the staircase; we went down together and at the bottom I detained her, holding her there with a hand on her arm. "I take what you said to me at noon as a declaration that *you 've* never known him to be bad."

She threw back her head; she had clearly by this time, and very honestly, adopted an attitude. "Oh never known him—I don't pretend *that*!"

I was upset again. "Then you *have* known him—?"

"Yes indeed, Miss, thank God!"

On reflexion I accepted this. "You mean that a boy who never is—?"

"Is no boy for *me*!"

I held her tighter. "You like them with the spirit to be naughty?" Then, keeping pace with her answer, "So do I!" I eagerly brought out. "But not to the degree to contaminate—"

"To contaminate?"—my big word left her at a loss.

I explained it. "To corrupt."

She stared, taking my meaning in; but it produced in her an odd laugh. "Are you afraid he 'll corrupt *you?*" She put the question with such a fine bold humour that with a laugh, a little silly doubtless, to match her own, I gave way for the time to the apprehension of ridicule.

But the next day, as the hour for my drive approached, I cropped up in another place. "What was the lady who was here before?"

"The last governess? She was also young and pretty—almost as young and almost as pretty, Miss, even as you."

"Ah then I hope her youth and her beauty helped her!" I recollect throwing off. "He seems to like us young and pretty!"

"Oh he *did*," Mrs. Grose assented: "it was the way he liked every one!" She had no sooner spoken indeed than she caught herself up. "I mean that 's *his* way—the master's."

I was struck. "But of whom did you speak first?"

She looked blank, but she coloured. "Why of *him*."

"Of the master?"

"Of who else?"

There was so obviously no one else that the next moment I had lost my impression of her having accidentally said more than she meant; and I merely asked what I wanted to know. "Did *she* see anything in the boy—?"

"That was n't right? She never told me."

I had a scruple, but I overcame it. "Was she careful—particular?"

Mrs. Grose appeared to try to be conscientious. "About some things—yes."

"But not about all?"

Again she considered. "Well, Miss—she 's gone. I won't tell tales."

"I quite understand your feeling," I hastened to reply; but I thought it after an instant not opposed to this concession to pursue: "Did she die here?"

"No—she went off."

I don't know what there was in this brevity of Mrs. Grose's that struck me as ambiguous. "Went off to die?" Mrs. Grose looked straight out of the window, but I felt that, hypothetically, I had a right to know what young persons engaged for Bly were expected to do. "She was taken ill, you mean, and went home?"

"She was not taken ill, so far as appeared, in this house. She left it, at the end of the year, to go home, as she said, for a short holiday, to which the time she had put in had certainly given her a right. We had then a young woman—a nursemaid who had stayed on and who was a good girl and clever; and *she* took the children altogether for the interval. But our young lady never came back, and at the very moment I was expecting her I heard from the master that she was dead."

I turned this over. "But of what?"

"He never told me! But please, Miss," said Mrs. Grose, "I must get to my work."[7]

III

Her thus turning her back on me was fortunately not, for my just preoccupations, a snub that could check the growth of our mutual esteem. We met, after I had brought home little Miles, more intimately than ever on the ground of my stupefaction, my general emotion: so monstrous was I then ready to pronounce it that such a child as had now been revealed to me should be under an interdict. I was a little late on the scene of his arrival, and I felt, as he stood wistfully looking out for me before the door of the inn at which the coach had put him down, that I had seen him on the instant, without and within, in the great glow of freshness, the same positive fragrance of purity, in which I had from the first moment seen his little sister. He was incredibly beautiful, and Mrs. Grose had put her finger on it: everything but a sort of passion of tenderness for him was swept away by his presence. What I then and there took him to my heart for was something divine that I have never found to the same degree in any child—his indescribable little air of knowing nothing in the world but love. It would have been impossible to carry a bad name with a greater sweetness of innocence, and by the time I had got back to Bly with him I remained merely bewildered—so far, that is, as I was not outraged—by the sense of the horrible letter locked up in one of the drawers of my room. As soon as I could compass a private word with Mrs. Grose I declared to her that it was grotesque.

She promptly understood me. "You mean the cruel charge—?"

"It does n't live an instant. My dear woman, *look* at him!"

She smiled at my pretension to have discovered his charm. "I assure you, Miss, I do nothing else! What will you say then?" she immediately added.

"In answer to the letter?" I had made up my mind. "Nothing at all."

"And to his uncle?"

I was incisive. "Nothing at all."

"And to the boy himself?"

I was wonderful. "Nothing at all."

She gave with her apron a great wipe to her mouth. "Then I 'll stand by you. We 'll see it out."

"We 'll see it out!" I ardently echoed, giving her my hand to make it a vow.

She held me there a moment, then whisked up her apron again with her detached hand. "Would you mind, Miss, if I used the freedom—"

7. Second weekly installment ended here.

"To kiss me? No!" I took the good creature in my arms and after we had embraced like sisters felt still more fortified and indignant.

This at all events was for the time: a time so full that as I recall the way it went it reminds me of all the art I now need to make it a little distinct. What I look back at with amazement is the situation I accepted. I had undertaken, with my companion, to see it out, and I was under a charm apparently that could smooth away the extent and the far and difficult connexions of such an effort. I was lifted aloft on a great wave of infatuation and pity. I found it simple, in my ignorance, my confusion and perhaps my conceit, to assume that I could deal with a boy whose education for the world was all on the point of beginning. I am unable even to remember at this day what proposal I framed for the end of his holidays and the resumption of his studies. Lessons with me indeed, that charming summer, we all had a theory that he was to have; but I now feel that for weeks the lessons must have been rather my own. I learnt something—at first certainly—that had not been one of the teachings of my small smothered life; learnt to be amused, and even amusing, and not to think for the morrow. It was the first time, in a manner, that I had known space and air and freedom, all the music of summer and all the mystery of nature. And then there was consideration—and consideration was sweet. Oh it was a trap—not designed but deep—to my imagination, to my delicacy, perhaps to my vanity; to whatever in me was most excitable. The best way to picture it all is to say that I was off my guard. They gave me so little trouble—they were of a gentleness so extraordinary. I used to speculate—but even this with a dim disconnectedness—as to how the rough future (for all futures are rough!) would handle them and might bruise them. They had the bloom of health and happiness; and yet, as if I had been in charge of a pair of little grandees, of princes of the blood, for whom everything, to be right, would have to be fenced about and ordered and arranged, the only form that in my fancy the after-years could take for them was that of a romantic, a really royal extension of the garden and the park. It may be of course above all that what suddenly broke into this gives the previous time a charm of stillness—that hush in which something gathers or crouches. The change was actually like the spring of a beast.

In the first weeks the days were long; they often, at their finest, gave me what I used to call my own hour, the hour when, for my pupils, tea-time and bed-time having come and gone, I had before my final retirement a small interval alone. Much as I liked my companions this hour was the thing in the day I liked most; and I liked it best of all when, as the light faded—or rather, I should say, the day lingered and the last calls of the last birds sounded, in a flushed sky, from the old trees—I could take a turn into the grounds and enjoy, almost with a sense of property that amused and flattered me, the beauty and dignity of the place. It was a pleasure at these moments to feel myself tranquil and justified; doubtless perhaps also to reflect that by my discretion, my quiet good sense and general high propriety, I was giving pleasure—if he ever thought of it!—to the person to whose pressure I had yielded. What I was doing was what he had earnestly hoped and directly asked of me, and that I *could*, after all, do it proved even a greater joy than I had expected. I dare say I fancied myself in short a remarkable young woman and took comfort in the faith that this would more publicly appear. Well, I needed to be remarkable to offer a front to the remarkable things that presently gave their first sign.

It was plump, one afternoon, in the middle of my very hour: the children were tucked away and I had come out for my stroll. One of the thoughts that, as I don't in the least shrink now from noting, used to be with me in these wanderings was that it would be as charming as a charming story suddenly to meet some one. Some one would appear there at the turn of a path and would stand before me and smile and approve. I did n't ask more than that—I only asked that he should *know*; and the only way to be sure he knew would be to see it, and the kind light of it, in his handsome face. That was exactly present to me—by which I mean the face was—when, on the first of these occasions, at the end of a long June day, I stopped short on emerging from one of the plantations and coming into view of the house. What arrested me on the spot—and with a shock much greater than any vision had allowed for—was the sense that my imagination had, in a flash, turned real. He did stand there!—but high up, beyond the lawn and at the very top of the tower to which, on that first morning, little Flora had conducted me. This tower was one of a pair—square incongruous crenellated structures[8]—that were distinguished, for some reason, though I could see little difference, as the new and the old. They flanked opposite ends of the house and were probably architectural absurdities, redeemed in a measure indeed by not being wholly disengaged nor of a height too pretentious, dating, in their gingerbread antiquity, from a romantic revival that was already a respectable past. I admired them, had fancies about them, for we could all profit in a degree, especially when they loomed through the dusk, by the grandeur of their actual battlements; yet it was not at such an elevation that the figure I had so often invoked seemed most in place.

It produced in me, this figure, in the clear twilight, I remember, two distinct gasps of emotion, which were, sharply, the shock of my first and that of my second surprise. My second was a violent perception of the mistake of my first: the man who met my eyes was not the person I had precipitately supposed. There came to me thus a bewilderment of vision of which, after these years, there is no living view that I can

8. See note 6, above. The towers are furnished with battlements, indented parapets for the original purpose of defending against assailants, and later simply as decoration.

hope to give. An unknown man in a lonely place is a permitted object of fear to a young woman privately bred; and the figure that faced me was—a few more seconds assured me—as little any one else I knew as it was the image that had been in my mind. I had not seen it in Harley Street—I had not seen it anywhere. The place moreover, in the strangest way in the world, had on the instant and by the very fact of its appearance become a solitude. To me at least, making my statement here with a deliberation with which I have never made it, the whole feeling of the moment returns. It was as if, while I took in, what I did take in, all the rest of the scene had been stricken with death. I can hear again, as I write, the intense hush in which the sounds of evening dropped. The rooks stopped cawing in the golden sky and the friendly hour lost for the unspeakable minute all its voice. But there was no other change in nature, unless indeed it were a change that I saw with a stranger sharpness. The gold was still in the sky, the clearness in the air, and the man who looked at me over the battlements was as definite as a picture in a frame. That's how I thought, with extraordinary quickness, of each person he might have been and that he was n't. We were confronted across our distance quite long enough for me to ask myself with intensity who then he was and to feel, as an effect of my inability to say, a wonder that in a few seconds more became intense.

The great question, or one of these, is afterwards, I know, with regard to certain matters, the question of how long they have lasted. Well, this matter of mine, think what you will of it, lasted while I caught at a dozen possibilities, none of which made a difference for the better, that I could see, in there having been in the house—and for how long, above all?—a person of whom I was in ignorance. It lasted while I just bridled a little with the sense of how my office seemed to require that there should be no such ignorance and no such person. It lasted while this visitant, at all events—and there was a touch of the strange freedom, as I remember, in the sign of familiarity of his wearing no hat—seemed to fix me, from his position, with just the question, just the scrutiny through the fading light, that his own presence provoked. We were too far apart to call to each other, but there was a moment at which, at shorter range, some challenge between us, breaking the hush, would have been the right result of our straight mutual stare. He was in one of the angles, the one away from the house, very erect, as it struck me, and with both hands on the ledge. So I saw him as I see the letters I form on this page; then, exactly, after a minute, as if to add to the spectacle, he slowly changed his place—passed, looking at me hard all the while, to the opposite corner of the platform. Yes, it was intense to me that during this transit he never took his eyes from me, and I can see at this moment the way his hand, as he went, moved from one of the crenellations to the next. He stopped at the other corner, but less long, and even as he turned away still markedly fixed me. He turned away; that was all I knew.[9]

IV

It was not that I did n't wait, on this occasion, for more, since I was as deeply rooted as shaken. Was there a "secret" at Bly—a mystery of Udolpho or an insane, an unmentionable relative kept in unsuspected confinement?[1] I can't say how long I turned it over, or how long, in a confusion of curiosity and dread, I remained where I had had my collision; I only recall that when I re-entered the house darkness had quite closed in. Agitation, in the interval, certainly had held me and driven me, for I must, in circling about the place, have walked three miles; but I was to be later on so much more overwhelmed that this mere dawn of alarm was a comparatively human chill. The most singular part of it in fact—singular as the rest had been—was the part I became, in the hall, aware of in meeting Mrs. Grose. This picture comes back to me in the general train—the impression, as I received it on my return, of the wide white panelled space, bright in the lamplight and with its portraits and red carpet, and of the good surprised look of my friend, which immediately told me she had missed me. It came to me straightway, under her contact, that, with plain heartiness, mere relieved anxiety at my appearance, she knew nothing whatever that could bear upon the incident I had there ready for her. I had not suspected in advance that her comfortable face would pull me up, and I somehow measured the importance of what I had seen by my thus finding myself hesitate to mention it. Scarce anything in the whole history seems to me so odd as this fact that my real beginning of fear was one, as I may say, with the instinct of sparing my companion. On the spot, accordingly, in the pleasant hall and with her eyes on me, I, for a reason that I could n't then have phrased, achieved an inward revolution—offered a vague pretext for my lateness and, with the plea of the beauty of the night and of the heavy dew and wet feet, went as soon as possible to my room.

Here it was another affair; here, for many days after, it was a queer affair enough. There were hours, from day to day—or at least there were moments, snatched even from clear duties—when I had to shut myself up to think. It was n't so much yet that I was more nervous than I could bear to be as that I was remarkably afraid of becoming so; for the truth I had now to turn over was simply and clearly the truth that I could arrive at no account whatever of the visitor with whom I had

9. Third weekly installment and "Part First" ended here.
1. *The Mysteries of Udolpho* (1794) by Anne Radcliffe (1764–1823), a ghost novel in which the heroine is carried off to a lonely castle in the Apennines; the alternative describes the situation which confronts the governess-heroine of Charlotte Brontë's *Jane Eyre* (1847).

been so inexplicably and yet, as it seemed to me, so intimately concerned. It took me little time to see that I might easily sound, without forms of enquiry and without exciting remark, any domestic complication. The shock I had suffered must have sharpened all my senses; I felt sure, at the end of three days and as the result of mere closer attention, that I had not been practised upon by the servants nor made the object of any "game." Of whatever it was that I knew nothing was known around me. There was but one sane inference: some one had taken a liberty rather monstrous. That was what, repeatedly, I dipped into my room and locked the door to say to myself. We had been, collectively, subject to an intrusion; some unscrupulous traveller, curious in old houses, had made his way in unobserved, enjoyed the prospect from the best point of view and then stolen out as he came. If he had given me such a bold hard stare, that was but a part of his indiscretion. The good thing, after all, was that we should surely see no more of him.

This was not so good a thing, I admit, as not to leave me to judge that what, essentially, made nothing else much signify was simply my charming work. My charming work was just my life with Miles and Flora, and through nothing could I so like it as through feeling that to throw myself into it was to throw myself out of my trouble. The attraction of my small charges was a constant joy, leading me to wonder afresh at the vanity of my original fears, the distaste I had begun by entertaining for the probable grey prose of my office. There was to be no grey prose, it appeared, and no long grind; so how could work not be charming that presented itself as daily beauty? It was all the romance of the nursery and the poetry of the schoolroom. I don't mean by this of course that we studied only fiction and verse; I mean that I can express no otherwise the sort of interest my companions inspired. How can I describe that except by saying that instead of growing deadly used to them—and it 's a marvel for a governess: I call the sisterhood to witness!—I made constant fresh discoveries. There was one direction, assuredly, in which these discoveries stopped: deep obscurity continued to cover the region of the boy's conduct at school. It had been promptly given me, I have noted, to face that mystery without a pang. Perhaps even it would be nearer the truth to say that—without a word—he himself had cleared it up. He had made the whole charge absurd. My conclusion bloomed there with the real rose-flush of his innocence: he was only too fine and fair for the little horrid unclean school-world, and he had paid a price for it. I reflected acutely that the sense of such individual differences, such superiorities of quality, always, on the part of the majority—which could include even stupid sordid head-masters—turns infallibly to the vindictive.

Both the children had a gentleness—it was their only fault, and it never made Miles a muff[2]—that kept them (how shall I express it?) almost impersonal and certainly quite unpunishable. They were like those cherubs of the anecdote who had—morally at any rate—nothing to whack![3] I remember feeling with Miles in especial as if he had had, as it were, nothing to call even an infinitesimal history. We expect of a small child scant enough "antecedents," but there was in this beautiful little boy something extraordinarily sensitive, yet extraordinarily happy, that, more than in any creature of his age I have seen, struck me as beginning anew each day. He had never for a second suffered. I took this as a direct disproof of his having really been chastised. If he had been wicked he would have "caught" it, and I should have caught it by the rebound—I should have found the trace, should have felt the wound and the dishonour. I could reconstitute nothing at all, and he was therefore an angel. He never spoke of his school, never mentioned a comrade or a master; and I, for my part, was quite too much disgusted to allude to them. Of course I was under the spell, and the wonderful part is that, even at the time, I perfectly knew I was. But I gave myself up to it; it was an antidote to any pain, and I had more pains than one. I was in receipt in these days of disturbing letters from home, where things were not going well. But with this joy of my children what things in the world mattered? That was the question I used to put to my scrappy retirements. I was dazzled by their loveliness.

There was a Sunday—to get on—when it rained with such force and for so many hours that there could be no procession to church; in consequence of which, as the day declined, I had arranged with Mrs. Grose that, should the evening show improvement, we would attend together the late service. The rain happily stopped, and I prepared for our walk, which, through the park and by the good road to the village, would be a matter of twenty minutes. Coming downstairs to meet my colleague in the hall, I remembered a pair of gloves that had required three stitches and that had received them—with a publicity perhaps not edifying—while I sat with the children at their tea, served on Sundays, by exception, in that cold clean temple of mahogany and brass, the "grown-up" dining-room. The gloves had been dropped there, and I turned in to recover them. The day was grey enough, but the afternoon light still lingered, and it enabled me, on crossing the threshold, not only to recognise, on a chair near the wide window, then closed, the articles I wanted, but to become aware of a person on the other side of the window and looking straight in. One step into the room had sufficed; my vision was instantaneous; it was all there. The person looking straight in was the person who had already appeared to me. He

2. The *Oxford English Dictionary* defines "muff" as "one without skill or aptitude for some particular work or pursuit," hence, one clumsy, awkward, or ridiculous.
3. The ethereal nature of angels has long been the basis for countless anecdotes.

appeared thus again with I won't say greater distinctness, for that was impossible, but with a nearness that represented a forward stride in our intercourse and made me, as I met him, catch my breath and turn cold. He was the same—he was the same, and seen, this time, as he had been seen before, from the waist up, the window, though the dining-room was on the ground floor, not going down to the terrace on which he stood. His face was close to the glass, yet the effect of this better view was, strangely, just to show me how intense the former had been. He remained but a few seconds—long enough to convince me he also saw and recognised; but it was as if I had been looking at him for years and had known him always. Something, however, happened this time that had not happened before; his stare into my face, through the glass and across the room, was as deep and hard as then, but it quitted me for a moment during which I could still watch it, see it fix successively several other things. On the spot there came to me the added shock of a certitude that it was not for me he had come. He had come for some one else.

The flash of this knowledge—for it was knowledge in the midst of dread—produced in me the most extraordinary effect, starting, as I stood there, a sudden vibration of duty and courage. I say courage because I was beyond all doubt already far gone. I bounded straight out of the door again, reached that of the house, got in an instant upon the drive and, passing along the terrace as fast as I could rush, turned a corner and came full in sight. But it was in sight of nothing now—my visitor had vanished. I stopped, almost dropped, with the real relief of this; but I took in the whole scene—I gave him time to reappear. I call it time, but how long was it? I can't speak to the purpose to-day of the duration of these things. That kind of measure must have left me: they could n't have lasted as they actually appeared to me to last. The terrace and the whole place, the lawn and the garden beyond it, all I could see of the park, were empty with a great emptiness. There were shrubberies and big trees, but I remember the clear assurance I felt that none of them concealed him. He was there or was not there: not there if I did n't see him. I got hold of this; then, instinctively, instead of returning as I had come, went to the window. It was confusedly present to me that I ought to place myself where he had stood. I did so; I applied my face to the pane and looked, as he had looked, into the room. As if, at this moment, to show me exactly what his range had been, Mrs. Grose, as I had done for himself just before, came in from the hall. With this I had the full image of a repetition of what had already occurred. She saw me as I had seen my own visitant; she pulled up short as I had done; I gave her something of the shock that I had received. She turned white, and this made me ask myself if I had blanched as much. She stared, in short, and retreated just on *my* lines, and I knew she had then passed out and come round to me and that

I should presently meet her. I remained where I was, and while I waited I thought of more things than one. But there 's only one I take space to mention. I wondered why *she* should be scared.

V

Oh she let me know as soon as, round the corner of the house, she loomed again into view. "What in the name of goodness is the matter—?" She was now flushed and out of breath.

I said nothing till she came quite near. "With me?" I must have made a wonderful face. "Do I show it?"

"You 're as white as a sheet. You look awful."

I considered; I could meet on this, without scruple, any degree of innocence. My need to respect the bloom of Mrs. Grose's had dropped, without a rustle, from my shoulders, and if I wavered for the instant it was not with what I kept back. I put out my hand to her and she took it; I held her hard a little, liking to feel her close to me. There was a kind of support in the shy heave of her surprise. "You came for me for church, of course, but I can't go."

"Has anything happened?"

"Yes. You must know now. Did I look very queer?"

"Through this window? Dreadful!"

"Well," I said, "I've been frightened." Mrs. Grose's eyes expressed plainly that *she* had no wish to be, yet also that she knew too well her place not to be ready to share with me any marked inconvenience. Oh it was quite settled that she *must* share! "Just what you saw from the dining-room a minute ago was the effect of that. What *I* saw—just before—was much worse."

Her hand tightened. "What was it?"

"An extraordinary man. Looking in."

"What extraordinary man?"

"I have n't the least idea."

Mrs. Grose gazed round us in vain. "Then where is he gone?"

"I know still less."

"Have you see him before?"

"Yes—once. On the old tower."

She could only look at me harder. "Do you mean he 's a stranger?"

"Oh very much!"

"Yet you did n't tell me?"

"No—for reasons. But now that you 've guessed—"

Mrs. Grose's round eyes encountered this charge. "Ah I have n't guessed!" she said very simply. "How can I if *you* don't imagine?"

"I don't in the very least."

"You've seen him nowhere but on the tower?"

"And on this spot just now."

Mrs. Grose looked round again. "What was he doing on the tower?"

"Only standing there and looking down at me."

She thought a minute. "Was he a gentleman?"

I found I had no need to think. "No." She gazed in deeper wonder. "No."

"Then nobody about the place? Nobody from the village?"

"Nobody—nobody. I did n't tell you, but I made sure."

She breathed a vague relief: this was, oddly, so much to the good. It only went indeed a little way. "But if he is n't a gentleman—"

"What *is* he? He's a horror."

"A horror?"

"He 's—God help me if I know *what* he is!"

Mrs. Grose looked round once more; she fixed her eyes on the duskier distance and then, pulling herself together, turned to me with full inconsequence. "It 's time we should be at church."

"Oh I 'm not fit for church!"

"Won't it do you good?"

"It won't do *them*—!" I nodded at the house.

"The children?"

"I can't leave them now."

"You 're afraid—"

I spoke boldly "I 'm afraid of *him*."

Mrs. Grose's large face showed me, at this, for the first time, the faraway faint glimmer of a consciousness more acute: I somehow made out in it the delayed dawn of an idea I myself had not given her and that was as yet quite obscure to me. It comes back to me that I thought instantly of this as something I could get from her; and I felt it to be connected with the desire she presently showed to know more. "When was it—on the tower?"

"About the middle of the month. At this same hour."

"Almost at dark," said Mrs. Grose.

"Oh no, not nearly. I saw him as I see you."

"Then how did he get in?"

"And how did he get out?" I laughed. "I had no opportunity to ask him! This evening, you see," I pursued, "he has not been able to get in."

"He only peeps?"

"I hope it will be confined to that!" She had now let go my hand; she turned away a little. I waited an instant; then I brought out: "Go to church. Goodbye. I must watch."

Slowly she faced me again. "Do you fear for them?"

We met in another long look. "Don't *you*?" Instead of answering she came nearer to the window and, for a minute, applied her face to the glass. "You see how he could see," I meanwhile went on.

She did n't move. "How long was he here?"

"Till I came out. I came to meet him."

Mrs. Grose at last turned round, and there was still more in her face. "*I* could n't have come out."

"Neither could I!" I laughed again. "But I did come. I 've my duty."

"So have I mine," she replied; after which she added: "What 's he like?"

"I've been dying to tell you. But he 's like nobody."

"Nobody?" she echoed.

"He has no hat." Then seeing in her face that she already, in this, with a deeper dismay, found a touch of picture, I quickly added stroke to stroke. "He has red hair, very red, close-curling, and a pale face, long in shape, with straight good features and little rather queer whiskers that are as red as his hair. His eyebrows are somehow darker; they look particularly arched and as if they might move a good deal. His eyes are sharp, strange—awfully; but I only know clearly that they 're rather small and very fixed. His mouth 's wide, and his lips are thin, except for his little whiskers he 's quite clean-shaven. He gives me a sort of sense of looking like an actor."

"An actor!" It was impossible to resemble one less, at least, than Mrs. Grose at that moment.

"I 've never seen one, but so I suppose them. He 's tall, active, erect," I continued, "but never—no, never!—a gentleman."

My companion's face had blanched as I went on; her round eyes started and her mild mouth gaped. "A gentleman?" she gasped, confounded, stupefied: "a gentleman *he*?"

"You know him then?"

She visibly tried to hold herself. "But he *is* handsome?"

I saw the way to help her. "Remarkably!"

"And dressed—?"

"In somebody's clothes. They 're smart, but they 're not his own."

She broke into a breathless affirmative groan. "They 're the master's!"

I caught it up. "You *do* know him?"

She faltered but a second. "Quint!" she cried.

"Quint?"

"Peter Quint—his own man, his valet, when he was here!"

"When the master was?"

Gaping still, but meeting me, she pieced it all together. "He never wore his hat, but he did wear—well, there were waistcoats missed! They were both here—last year. Then the master went, and Quint was alone."

I followed, but halting a little. "Alone?"

"Alone with *us*." Then as from a deeper depth, "In charge," she added.

"And what became of him?"

She hung fire so long that I was still more mystified. "He went too," she brought out at last.

"Went where?"

Her expression, at this, became extraordinary. "God knows where! He died."

"Died?" I almost shrieked.

She seemed fairly to square herself, plant herself more firmly to express the wonder of it. "Yes. Mr. Quint's dead."[4]

VI

It took of course more than that particular passage to place us together in presence of what we had now to live with as we could, my dreadful liability to impressions of the order so vividly exemplified, and my companion's knowledge henceforth—a knowledge half consternation and half compassion—of that liability. There had been this evening, after the revelation that left me for an hour so prostrate—there had been for either of us no attendance on any service but a little service of tears and vows, of prayers and promises, a climax to the series of mutual challenges and pledges that had straightway ensued on our retreating together to the schoolroom and shutting ourselves up there to have everything out. The result of our having everything out was simply to reduce our situation to the last rigour of its elements. She herself had seen nothing, not the shadow of a shadow, and nobody in the house but the governess was in the governess's plight; yet she accepted without directly impugning my sanity the truth as I gave it to her, and ended by showing me on this ground an awestricken tenderness, a deference to my more than questionable privilege, of which the very breath has remained with me as that of the sweetest of human charities.

What was settled between us accordingly that night was that we thought we might bear things together; and I was not even sure that in spite of her exemption it was she who had the best of the burden. I knew at this hour, I think, as well as I knew later, what I was capable of meeting to shelter my pupils; but it took me some time to be wholly sure of what my honest comrade was prepared for to keep terms with so stiff an agreement. I was queer company enough—quite as queer as the company I received; but as I trace over what we went through I see how much common ground we must have found in the one idea that, by good fortune, *could* steady us. It was the idea, the second movement, that led me straight out, as I may say, of the inner chamber of my dread. I could take the air in the court, at least, and there Mrs. Grose could join me. Perfectly can I recall now the particular way strength

4. Fourth weekly installment ended here.

came to me before we separated for the night. We had gone over and over every feature of what I had seen.

"He was looking for some one else, you say—some one who was not you?"

"He was looking for little Miles." A portentous clearness now possessed me. "*That 's* whom he was looking for."

"But how do you know?"

"I know, I know, I know!" My exaltation grew. "And *you* know, my dear!"

She did n't deny this, but I required, I felt, not even so much telling as that. She took it up again in a moment. "What if *he* should see him?"

"Little Miles? That's what he wants!"

She looked immensely scared again. "The child?"

"Heaven forbid! The man. He wants to appear to *them*." That he might was an awful conception, and yet somehow I could keep it at bay; which moreover, as we lingered there, was what I succeeded in practically proving. I had an absolute certainty that I should see again what I had already seen, but something within me said that by offering myself bravely as the sole subject of such experience, by accepting, by inviting, by surmounting it all, I should serve as an expiatory victim and guard the tranquillity of the rest of the household. The children in special I should thus fence about and absolutely save. I recall one of the last things I said that night to Mrs. Grose.

"It does strike me that my pupils have never mentioned—!"

She looked at me hard as I musingly pulled up. "His having been here and the time they were with him?"

"The time they were with him, and his name, his presence, his history, in any way. They 've never alluded to it."

"Oh the little lady does n't remember. She never heard or knew."

"The circumstances of his death?" I thought with some intensity. "Perhaps not. But Miles would remember—Miles would know."

"Ah don't try him!" broke from Mrs. Grose.

I returned her the look she had given me. "Don't be afraid." I continued to think. "It *is* rather odd."

"That he has never spoken of him?"

"Never by the least reference. And you tell me they were 'great friends.'"

"Oh it was n't *him*!" Mrs. Grose with emphasis declared. "It was Quint's own fancy. To play with him, I mean—to spoil him." She paused a moment; then she added: "Quint was much too free."

This gave me, straight from my vision of his face—*such* a face!—a sudden sickness of disgust. "Too free with *my* boy?"

"Too free with every one!"

I forbore for the moment to analyse this description further than by the reflexion that a part of it applied to several of the members of the household, of the half-dozen maids and men who were still of our small colony. But there was everything, for our apprehension, in the lucky fact that no discomfortable legend, no perturbation of scullions, had ever, within any one's memory, attached to the kind old place. It had neither bad name nor ill fame, and Mrs. Grose, most apparently, only desired to cling to me and to quake in silence. I even put her, the very last thing of all, to the test. It was when, at midnight, she had her hand on the schoolroom door to take leave. "I *have it* from you then—for it 's of great importance—that he was definitely and admittedly bad?"

"Oh not admittedly. *I* knew it—but the master did n't."

"And you never told him?"

"Well, he did n't like tale-bearing—he hated complaints. He was terribly short with anything of that kind, and if people were all right to *him*—"

"He would n't be bothered with more?" This squared well enough with my impression of him: he was not a trouble-loving gentleman, nor so very particular perhaps about some of the company he himself kept. All the same, I pressed my informant. "I promise you *I* would have told!"

She felt my discrimination. "I dare say I was wrong. But really I was afraid."

"Afraid of what?"

"Of things that man could do. Quint was so clever—he was so deep."

I took this in still more than I probably showed. "You were n't afraid of anything else? Not of his effect—?"

"His effect?" she repeated with a face of anguish and waiting while I faltered.

"On innocent little precious lives. They were in your charge."

"No, they were n't in mine!" she roundly and distressfully returned. "The master believed in him and placed him here because he was supposed not to be quite in health and the country air so good for him. So he had everything to say. Yes"—she let me have it—"even about *them*."

"Them—that creature?" I had to smother a kind of howl. "And you could bear it?"

"No. I could n't—and I can't now!" And the poor woman burst into tears.

A rigid control, from the next day, was, as I have said, to follow them; yet how often and how passionately, for a week, we came back together to the subject! Much as we had discussed it that Sunday night, I was, in the immediate later hours in especial—for it may be imagined whether I slept—still haunted with the shadow of something she had not told me. I myself had kept back nothing, but there was a word Mrs. Grose had kept back. I was sure moreover by morning that this was not from a failure of frankness, but because on every side there were fears. It seems to me indeed, in raking it all over, that by the time the morrow's sun was high I had restlessly read into the facts before us almost all the meaning they were to receive from subsequent and more cruel occurrences. What they gave me above all was just the sinister figure of the living man—the dead one would keep a while!—and of the months he had continuously passed at Bly, which, added up, made a formidable stretch. The limit of this evil time had arrived only when, on the dawn of a winter's morning, Peter Quint was found, by a labourer going to early work, stone dead on the road from the village: a catastrophe explained—superficially at least—by a visible wound to his head; such a wound as might have been produced (and as, on the final evidence, *had* been) by a fatal slip, in the dark and after leaving the public-house, on the steepish icy slope, a wrong path altogether, at the bottom of which he lay. The icy slope, the turn mistaken at night and in liquor, accounted for much—practically, in the end and after the inquest and boundless chatter, for everything; but there had been matters in his life, strange passages and perils, secret disorders, vices more than suspected, that would have accounted for a good deal more.

I scarce know how to put my story into words that shall be a credible picture of my state of mind; but I was in these days literally able to find a joy in the extraordinary flight of heroism the occasion demanded of me. I now saw that I had been asked for a service admirable and difficult; and there would be a greatness in letting it be seen—oh in the right quarter!—that I could succeed where many another girl might have failed. It was an immense help to me—I confess I rather applaud myself as I look back!—that I saw my response so strongly and so simply. I was there to protect and defend the little creatures in the world the most bereaved and the most loveable, the appeal of whose helplessness had suddenly become only too explicit, a deep constant ache of one's own engaged affection. We were cut off, really, together; we were united in our danger. They had nothing but me, and I—well, I had *them*. It was in short a magnificent chance. This chance presented itself to me in an image richly material. I was a screen—I was to stand before them. The more I saw the less they would. I began to watch them in a stifled suspense, a disguised tension, that might well, had it continued too long, have turned to something like madness. What saved me, as I now see, was that it turned to another matter altogether. It did n't last as suspense—it was superseded by horrible proofs. Proofs, I say, yes—from the moment I really took hold.

This moment dated from an afternoon hour that I happened to spend in the grounds with the younger of my pupils alone. We had left Miles indoors, on the red cushion of a deep window-seat; he had wished to finish a book, and I had been glad to encourage a purpose so laudable in a young man whose only defect was a certain ingenuity of restless-

wants to shield kids from outside

ness. His sister, on the contrary, had been alert to come out, and I strolled with her half an hour, seeking the shade, for the sun was still high and the day exceptionally warm. I was aware afresh with her, as we went, of how, like her brother, she contrived—it was the charming thing in both children—to let me alone without appearing to drop me and to accompany me without appearing to oppress. They were never importunate and yet never listless. My attention to them all really went to seeing them amuse themselves immensely without me: this was a spectacle they seemed actively to prepare and that employed me as an active admirer. I walked in a world of their invention—they had no occasion whatever to draw upon mine; so that my time was taken only with being for them some remarkable person or thing that the game of the moment required and that was merely, thanks to my superior, my exalted stamp, a happy and highly distinguished sinecure. I forget what I was on the present occasion; I only remember that I was something very important and very quiet and that Flora was playing very hard. We were on the edge of the lake, and, as we had lately begun geography, the lake was the Sea of Azof.[5]

Suddenly, amid these elements, I became aware that on the other side of the Sea of Azof we had an interested spectator. The way this knowledge gathered in me was the strangest thing in the world—the strangest, that is, except the very much stranger in which it quickly merged itself. I had sat down with a piece of work—for I was something or other that could sit—on the old stone bench which overlooked the pond; and in this position I began to take in with certitude and yet without direct vision the presence, a good way off, of a third person. The old trees, the thick shrubbery, made a great and pleasant shade, but it was all suffused with the brightness of the hot still hour. There was no ambiguity in anything; none whatever at least in the conviction I from one moment to another found myself forming as to what I should see straight before me and across the lake as a consequence of raising my eyes. They were attached at this juncture to the stitching in which I was engaged, and I can feel once more the spasm of my effort not to move them till I should so have steadied myself as to be able to make up my mind what to do. There was an alien object in view—a figure whose right of presence I instantly and passionately questioned. I recollect counting over perfectly the possibilities, reminding myself that nothing was more natural for instance than the appearance of one of the men about the place, or even of a messenger, a postman or a tradesman's boy, from the village. That reminder had as little effect on my practical certitude as I was conscious—still even without looking—of its having upon the character and attitude of our visitor. Nothing was

5. A long, narrow, shallow, windy inland sea, connecting with the Black Sea.

more natural than that these things should be the other things they absolutely were not.

Of the positive identity of the apparition I would assure myself as soon as the small clock of my courage should have ticked out the right second; meanwhile, with an effort that was already sharp enough, I transferred my eyes straight to little Flora, who, at the moment, was about ten yards away. My heart had stood still for an instant with the wonder and terror of the question whether she too would see; and I held my breath while I waited for what a cry from her, what some sudden innocent sign either of interest or of alarm, would tell me. I waited, but nothing came; then in the first place—and there is something more dire in this, I feel, than in anything I have to relate—I was determined by a sense that within a minute all spontaneous sounds from her had dropped; and in the second by the circumstance that also within the minute she had, in her play, turned her back to the water. This was her attitude when I at last looked at her—looked with the confirmed conviction that we were still, together, under direct personal notice. She had picked up a small flat piece of wood which happened to have in it a little hole that had evidently suggested to her the idea of sticking in another fragment that might figure as a mast and make the thing a boat. This second morsel, as I watched her, she was very markedly and intently attempting to tighten in its place. My apprehension of what she was doing sustained me so that after some seconds I felt I was ready for more. Then I again shifted my eyes—I faced what I had to face.

VII

I got hold of Mrs. Grose as soon after this as I could; and I can give no intelligible account of how I fought out the interval. Yet I still hear myself cry as I fairly threw myself into her arms: "They *know*—it 's too monstrous: they know, they know!"

"And what on earth—?" I felt her incredulity as she held me.

"Why all that *we* know—and heaven knows what more besides!" Then as she released me I made it out to her, made it out perhaps only now with full coherency even to myself. "Two hours ago, in the garden"—I could scarce articulate—"Flora *saw*!"

Mrs. Grose took it as she might have taken a blow in the stomach. "She has told you?" she panted.

"Not a word—that 's the horror. She kept it to herself! The child of eight, *that* child!" Unutterable still for me was the stupefaction of it.

Mrs. Grose of course could only gape the wider. "Then how do you know?"

"I was there—I saw with my eyes: saw she was perfectly aware."

"Do you mean aware of *him*?"

"No—of *her*." I was conscious as I spoke that I looked prodigious things, for I got the slow reflexion of them in my companion's face. "Another person—this time; but a figure of quite as unmistakeable horror and evil: a woman in black, pale and dreadful—with such an air also, and such a face!—on the other side of the lake. I was there with the child—quiet for the hour; and in the midst of it she came."

"Came how—from where?"

"From where they come from! She just appeared and stood there—but not so near."

"And without coming nearer?"

"Oh for the effect and the feeling she might have been as close as you!"

My friend, with an odd impulse, fell back a step. "Was she some one you 've never seen?"

"Never. But some one the child has. Some one *you* have." Then to show how I had thought it all out: "My predecessor—the one who died."

"Miss Jessel?"

"Miss Jessel. You don't believe me?" I pressed.

She turned right and left in her distress. "How can you be sure?"

This drew from me, in the state of my nerves, a flash of impatience. "Then ask Flora—*she* 's sure!" But I had no sooner spoken than I caught myself up. "No, for God's sake *don't*! She'll say she is n't—she 'll lie!"

Mrs. Grose was not too bewildered instinctively to protest. "Ah how *can* you?"

"Because I 'm clear. Flora does n't want me to know."

"It 's only then to spare you."

"No, no—there are depths, depths! The more I go over it the more I see in it, and the more I see in it the more I fear. I don't know what I *don't* see, what I *don't* fear!"

Mrs. Grose tried to keep up with me. "You mean you 're afraid of seeing her again?"

"Oh no; that 's nothing—now!" Then I explained. "It's of *not* seeing her."

But my companion only looked wan. "I don't understand."

"Why, it 's that the child may keep it up—and that the child assuredly *will*—without my knowing it."

At the image of this possibility Mrs. Grose for a moment collapsed, yet presently to pull herself together again as from the positive force of the sense of what, should we yield an inch, there would really be to give way to. "Dear, dear—we must keep our heads! And after all, if she does n't mind it—!" She even tried a grim joke. "Perhaps she likes it!"

"Like *such* things—a scrap of an infant!"

"Is n't it just a proof of her blest innocence?" my friend bravely enquired.

She brought me, for the instant, almost round. "Oh we must clutch at *that*—we must cling to it! If it is n't a proof of what you say, it 's a proof of—God knows what! For the woman 's a horror of horrors."

Mrs. Grose, at this, fixed her eyes a minute on the ground; then at last raising them. "Tell me how you know," she said.

"Then you admit it 's what she was?" I cried.

"Tell me how you know," my friend simply repeated.

"Know? By seeing her! By the way she looked."

"At you, do you mean—so wickedly?"

"Dear me, no—I could have borne that. She gave me never a glance. She only fixed the child."

Mrs. Grose tried to see it. "Fixed her?"

"Ah with such awful eyes!"

She stared at mine as if they might really have resembled them. "Do you mean of dislike?"

"God help us, no. Of something much worse."

"Worse than dislike?"—this left her indeed at a loss.

"With a determination—indescribable. With a kind of fury of intention."

I made her turn pale. "Intention?"

"To get hold of her." Mrs. Grose—her eyes just lingering on mine—gave a shudder and walked to the window; and while she stood there looking out I completed my statement. "*That* 's what Flora knows."

After a little she turned round. "The person was in black, you say?"

"In mourning—rather poor, almost shabby. But—yes—with extraordinary beauty." I now recognised to what I had at last, stroke by stroke, brought the victim of my confidence, for she quite visibly weighed this. "Oh handsome—very, very," I insisted; "wonderfully handsome. But infamous."

She slowly came back to me. "Miss Jessel—*was* infamous." She once more took my hand in both her own, holding it as tight as if to fortify me against the increase of alarm I might draw from this disclosure. "They were both infamous," she finally said.

So for a little we faced it once more together: and I found absolutely a degree of help in seeing it now so straight. "I appreciate," I said, "the great decency of your not having hitherto spoken: but the time has certainly come to give me the whole thing." She appeared to assent to this, but still only in silence; seeing which I went on: "I must have it now. Of what did she die? Come, there was something between them."

"There was everything."

"In spite of the difference—?"

"Oh of their rank, their condition"—she brought it woefully out. "*She* was a lady."

I turned it over; I again saw. "Yes—she was a lady."

"And he so dreadfully below," said Mrs. Grose.

I felt that I doubtless need n't press too hard, in such company, on the place of a servant in the scale; but there was nothing to prevent an acceptance of my companion's own measure of my predecessor's abasement. There was a way to deal with that, and I dealt; the more readily for my full vision—on the evidence—of our employer's late clever good-looking "own" man; impudent, assured, spoiled, depraved. "The fellow was a hound."

Mrs. Grose considered as if it were perhaps a little a case for a sense of shades. "I 've never seen one like him. He did what he wished."

"With *her*?"

"With them all."

It was as if now in my friend's own eyes Miss Jessel had again appeared. I seemed at any rate for an instant to trace their evocation of her as distinctly as I had seen her by the pond; and I brought out with decision: "It must have been also what *she* wished!"

Mrs. Grose's face signified that it had been indeed, but she said at the same time: "Poor woman—she paid for it!"

"Then you do know what she died of?" I asked.

"No—I know nothing. I wanted not to know; I was glad enough I did n't; and I thanked heaven she was well out of this!"

"Yet you had then your idea—"

"Of her real reason for leaving? Oh yes—as to that. She could n't have stayed. Fancy it here—for a governess! And afterwards I imagined—and I still imagine. And what I imagine is dreadful."

"Not so dreadful as what *I* do," I replied; on which I must have shown her—as I was indeed but too conscious—a front of miserable defeat. It brought out again all her compassion for me, and at the renewed touch of her kindness my power to resist broke down. I burst, as I had the other time made her burst, into tears; she took me to her motherly breast, where my lamentation overflowed. "I don't do it!" I sobbed in despair; "I don't save or shield them! It's far worse than I dreamed. They 're lost."[6]

VIII

What I had said to Mrs. Grose was true enough: there were in the matter I had put before her depths and possibilities that I lacked resolution to sound; so that when we met once more in the wonder of it we were of a common mind about the duty of resistance to extravagant fancies. We were to keep our heads if we should keep nothing else—difficult indeed as that might be in the face of all that, in our prodigious experience, seemed least to be questioned. Late that night, while the

6. Fifth weekly installment and "Part Second" ended here.

house slept, we had another talk in my room; when she went all the way with me as to its being beyond doubt that I had seen exactly what I had seen. I found that to keep her thoroughly in the grip of this I had only to ask her how, if I had "made it up," I came to be able to give, of each of the persons appearing to me, a picture disclosing, to the last detail, their special marks—a portrait on the exhibition of which she had instantly recognised and named them. She wished, of course —small blame to her!—to sink the whole subject; and I was quick to assure her that my own interest in it had now violently taken the form of a search for the way to escape from it. I closed with her cordially on the article of the likelihood that with recurrence—for recurrence we took for granted—I should get used to my danger; distinctly professing that my personal exposure had suddenly become the least of my discomforts. It was my new suspicion that was intolerable; and yet even to this complication the later hours of the day had brought a little ease.

On leaving her, after my first outbreak, I had of course returned to my pupils, associating the right remedy for my dismay with that sense of their charm which I had already recognised as a resource I could positively cultivate and which had never failed me yet. I had simply, in other words, plunged afresh into Flora's special society and there become aware—it was almost a luxury!—that she could put her little conscious hand straight upon the spot that ached. She had looked at me in sweet speculation and then had accused me to my face of having "cried." I had supposed the ugly signs of it brushed away; but I could literally—for the time at all events—rejoice, under this fathomless charity, that they had not entirely disappeared. To gaze into the depths of blue of the child's eyes and pronounce their loveliness a trick of premature cunning was to be guilty of a cynicism in preference to which I naturally preferred to abjure my judgement and, so far as might be, my agitation. I could n't abjure for merely wanting to, but I could repeat to Mrs. Grose—as I did there, over and over, in the small hours—that with our small friends' voices in the air, their pressure on one's heart and their fragrant faces against one's cheek, everything fell to the ground but their incapacity and their beauty. It was a pity that, somehow, to settle this once for all, I had equally to re-enumerate the signs of subtlety that, in the afternoon, by the lake, had made a miracle of my show of self-possession. It was a pity to be obliged to re-investigate the certitude of the moment itself and repeat how it had come to me as a revelation that the inconceivable communion I then surprised must have been for both parties a matter of habit. It was a pity I should have had to quaver out again the reasons for my not having, in my delusion, so much as questioned that the little girl saw our visitant even as I actually saw Mrs. Grose herself, and that she wanted, by just so much as she did thus see, to make me suppose she did n't, and at the same time, without showing anything, arrive at a guess as to whether I myself did! It was a pity I needed to recapitulate the portentous little activities by which she sought to divert my attention—the perceptible increase of movement, the greater intensity of play, the singing, the gabbling of nonsense and the invitation to romp.

Yet if I had not indulged, to prove there was nothing in it, in this review, I should have missed the two or three dim elements of comfort that still remained to me. I should n't for instance have been able to asseverate to my friend that I was certain—which was so much to the good—that *I* at least had not betrayed myself. I should n't have been prompted, by stress of need, by desperation of mind—I scarce know what to call it—to invoke such further aid to intelligence as might spring from pushing my colleague fairly to the wall. She had told me, bit by bit, under pressure, a great deal; but a small shifty spot on the wrong side of it all still sometimes brushed my brow like the wing of a bat; and I remember how on this occasion—for the sleeping house and the concentration alike of our danger and our watch seemed to help—I felt the importance of giving the last jerk to the curtain. "I don't believe anything so horrible," I recollect saying; "no, let us put it definitely, my dear, that I don't. But if I did, you know, there 's a thing I should require now, just without sparing you the least bit more—oh not a scrap, come!—to get out of you. What was it you had in mind when, in our distress, before Miles came back, over the letter from his school, you said, under my insistence, that you did n't pretend for him he had n't literally *ever* been 'bad'? He has *not*, truly, 'ever,' in these weeks that I myself have lived with him and so closely watched him; he has been an imperturbable little prodigy of delightful loveable goodness. Therefore you might perfectly have made the claim for him if you had not, as it happened, seen an exception to take. What was your exception, and to what passage in your personal observation of him did you refer?"

It was a straight question enough, but levity was not our note, and in any case I had before the grey dawn admonished us to separate got my answer. What my friend had had in mind proved immensely to the purpose. It was neither more nor less than the particular fact that for a period of several months Quint and the boy had been perpetually together. It was indeed the very appropriate item of evidence of her having ventured to criticise the propriety, to hint at the incongruity, of so close an alliance, and even to go so far on the subject as a frank overture to Miss Jessel would take her. Miss Jessel had, with a very high manner about it, requested her to mind her business, and the good woman had on this directly approached little Miles. What she had said to him, since I pressed, was that *she* liked to see young gentlemen not forget their station.

I pressed again, of course, the closer for that. "You reminded him that Quint was only a base menial?"

"As you might say! And it was his answer, for one thing, that was bad."

"And for another thing?" I waited. "He repeated your words to Quint?"

"No, not that. It's just what he *would n't*!" she could still impress on me. "I was sure, at any rate," she added, "that he did n't. But he denied certain occasions."

"What occasions?"

"When they had been about together quite as if Quint were his tutor—and a very grand one—and Miss Jessel only for the little lady. When he had gone off with the fellow, I mean, and spent hours with him."

"He then prevaricated about it—he said he had n't?" Her assent was clear enough to cause me to add in a moment: "I see. He lied."

"Oh!" Mrs. Grose mumbled. This was a suggestion that it did n't matter; which indeed she backed up by a further remark. "You see, after all, Miss Jessel did n't mind. She did n't forbid him."

I considered. "Did he put that to you as a justification?"

At this she dropped again. "No, he never spoke of it."

"Never mentioned her in connexion with Quint?"

She saw, visibly flushing, where I was coming out. "Well, he did n't show anything. He denied," she repeated; "he denied."

Lord, how I pressed her now! "So that you could see he knew what was between the two wretches?"

"I don't know—I don't know!" the poor woman wailed.

"You do know, you dear thing," I replied; "only you have n't my dreadful boldness of mind, and you keep back, out of timidity and modesty and delicacy, even the impression that in the past, when you had, without my aid, to flounder about in silence, most of all made you miserable. But I shall get it out of you yet! There was something in the boy that suggested to you," I continued, "his covering and concealing their relation."

"Oh he could n't prevent—"

"Your learning the truth? I dare say! But, heavens," I fell, with vehemence, a-thinking, "what it shows that they must, to that extent, have succeeded in making of him!"

"Ah nothing that 's not nice *now*!" Mrs. Grose lugubriously pleaded.

"I don't wonder you looked queer," I persisted, "when I mentioned to you the letter from his school!"

"I doubt if I looked as queer as you!" she retorted with homely force. "And if he was so bad then as that comes to, how is he such an angel now?"

"Yes indeed—and if he was a fiend at school! How, how, how? Well," I said in my torment, "you must put it to me again, though I shall not be able to tell you for some days. Only put it to me again!" I cried in a way that made my friend stare. "There are directions in which I must n't for the present let myself go." Meanwhile I returned to her first example—the one to which she had just previously referred—of the boy's happy capacity for an occasional slip. "If Quint—on your remonstrance at the time you speak of—was a base menial, one of the things Miles said to you, I find myself guessing, was that you were another." Again her admission was so adequate that I continued: "And you forgave him that?"

"Would n't *you*?"

"Oh yes!" And we exchanged there, in the stillness, a sound of the oddest amusement. Then I went on: "At all events, while he was with the man—"

"Miss Flora was with the woman. It suited them all!"

It suited me too, I felt, only too well; by which I mean that it suited exactly the particular deadly view I was in the very act of forbidding myself to entertain. But I so far succeeded in checking the expression of this view that I will throw, just here, no further light on it than may be offered by the mention of my final observation to Mrs. Grose. "His having lied and been impudent are, I confess, less engaging specimens than I had hoped to have from you of the outbreak in him of the little natural man. Still," I mused, "they must do, for they make me feel more than ever that I must watch."

It made me blush, the next minute, to see in my friend's face how much more unreservedly she had forgiven him than her anecdote struck me as pointing out to my own tenderness any way to do. This was marked when, at the schoolroom door, she quitted me. "Surely you don't accuse *him*—"

"Of carrying on an intercourse that he conceals from me? Ah remember that, until further evidence, I now accuse nobody." Then before shutting her out to go by another passage to her own place, "I must just wait," I wound up.

IX

I waited and waited, and the days took as they elasped something from my consternation. A very few of them, in fact, passing, in constant sight of my pupils, without a fresh incident, sufficed to give to grievous fancies and even to odious memories a kind of brush of the sponge. I have spoken of the surrender to their extraordinary childish grace as a thing I could actively promote in myself, and it may be imagined if I neglected now to apply at this source for whatever balm it would yield. Stranger than I can express certainly, was the effort to struggle against my new lights. It would doubtless have been a greater tension still, however, had it not been so frequently successful. I used to wonder how my little charges could help guessing that I thought strange things about them; and the circumstance that these things only made them more interesting was not by itself a direct aid to keeping them in the dark. I trembled lest they should see that they *were* so immensely more interesting. Putting things at the worst, at all events, as in meditation I so often did, any clouding of their innocence could only be—blameless and foredoomed as they were—a reason the more for taking risks. There were moments when I knew myself to catch them up by an irresistible impulse and press them to my heart. As soon as I had done so I used to wonder—"What will they think of that? Does n't it betray too much?" It would have been easy to get into a sad wild tangle about how much I might betray; but the real account, I feel, of the hours of peace I could still enjoy was that the immediate charm of my companions was a beguilement still effective even under the shadow of the possibility that it was studied. For if it occurred to me that I might occasionally excite suspicion by the little outbreaks of my sharper passion for them, so too I remember asking if I might n't see a queerness in the traceable increase of their own demonstrations.

They were at this period extravagantly and preternaturally fond of me; which, after all, I could reflect, was no more than a graceful response in children perpetually bowed down over and hugged. The homage of which they were so lavish succeeded in truth for my nerves quite as well as if I never appeared to myself, as I may say, literally to catch them at a purpose in it. They had never, I think, wanted to do so many things for their poor protectress; I mean—though they got their lessons better and better, which was naturally what would please her most—in the way of diverting, entertaining, surprising her; reading her passages, telling her stories, acting her charades, pouncing out at her, in disguises, as animals and historical characters, and above all astonishing her by the "pieces" they had secretly got by heart and could interminably recite. I should never get to the bottom—were I to let myself go even now—of the prodigious private commentary, all under still more private correction, with which I in these days overscored their full hours. They had shown me from the first a facility for everything, a general faculty which, taking a fresh start, achieved remarkable flights. They got their little tasks as if they loved them; they indulged, from the mere exuberance of the gift, in the most unimposed little miracles of memory. They not only popped out at me as tigers and as Romans, but as Shakespeareans, astronomers and navigators. This was so singularly the case that it had presumably much to do with the fact as to which, at the present day, I am at a loss for a different explanation: I allude to my unnatural composure on the subject of another school for Miles. What I remember is that I was content for the time not to open the question, and that contentment must have sprung from the sense of his perpetually striking show of cleverness. He was too clever for a bad governess, for a parson's daughter, to spoil; and the strangest if not the brightest thread in the pensive embroidery I just spoke of was the impression I might have got, if I had dared to work it out, that he was under some influence operating in his small intellectual life as a tremendous incitement.

If it was easy to reflect, however, that such a boy could postpone school, it was at least as marked that for such a boy to have been "kicked out" by a school-master was a mystification without end. Let me add that in their company now—and I was careful almost never to be out of it—I could follow no scent very far. We lived in a cloud of music and affection and success and private theatricals. The musical sense in each of the children was of the quickest, but the elder in especial had a marvellous knack of catching and repeating. The schoolroom piano broke into all gruesome fancies; and when that failed there were confabulations in corners, with a sequel of one of them going out in the highest spirits in order to "come in" as something new. I had had brothers myself, and it was no revelation to me that little girls could be slavish idolaters of little boys. What surpassed everything was that there was a little boy in the world who could have for the inferior age, sex and intelligence so fine a consideration. They were extraordinarily at one, and to say that they never either quarrelled or complained is to make the note of praise coarse for their quality of sweetness. Sometimes perhaps indeed (when I dropped into coarseness) I came across traces of little understandings between them by which one of them should keep me occupied while the other slipped away. There is a naïf side, I suppose, in all diplomacy; but if my pupils practised upon me it was surely with the minimum of grossness. It was all in the other quarter that, after a lull, the grossness broke out.

I find that I really hang back; but I must take my horrid plunge. In going on with the record of what was hideous at Bly I not only challenge the most liberal faith—for which I little care; but (and this is another matter) I renew what I myself suffered, I again push my dreadful way through it to the end. There came suddenly an hour after which, as I look back, the business seems to me to have been all pure suffering; but I have at least reached the heart of it, and the straightest road out is doubtless to advance. One evening—with nothing to lead up or prepare it—I felt the cold touch of the impression that had breathed on me the night of my arrival and which, much lighter then as I have mentioned, I should probably have made little of in memory had my subsequent sojourn been less agitated. I had not gone to bed; I sat reading by a couple of candles. There was a roomful of old books at Bly—last-century fiction some of it, which, to the extent of a distinctly deprecated renown, but never to so much as that of a stray specimen, had reached the sequestered home and appealed to the unavowed curiosity of my youth. I remember that the book I had in my hand was

Fielding's "Amelia";[7] also that I was wholly awake. I recall further both a general conviction that it was horribly late and a particular objection to looking at my watch. I figure finally that the white curtain draping, in the fashion of those days, the head of Flora's little bed, shrouded, as I had assured myself long before, the perfection of childish rest. I recollect in short that though I was deeply interested in my author I found myself, at the turn of a page and with his spell all scattered, looking straight up from him and hard at the door of my room. There was a moment during which I listened, reminded of the faint sense I had had, the first night, of there being something undefinably astir in the house, and noted the soft breath of the open casement just move the half-drawn blind. Then, with all the marks of a deliberation that must have seemed magnificent had there been any one to admire it, I laid down my book, rose to my feet and, taking a candle, went straight out of the room and, from the passage, on which my light made little impression, noiselessly closed and locked the door.

I can say now neither what determined nor what guided me, but I went straight along the lobby, holding my candle high, till I came within sight of the tall window that presided over the great turn of the staircase. At this point I precipitately found myself aware of three things. They were practically simultaneous, yet they had flashes of succession. My candle, under a bold flourish, went out, and I perceived, by the uncovered window, that the yielding dusk of earliest morning rendered it unnecessary. Without it, the next instant, I knew that there was a figure on the stair. I speak of sequences, but I require no lapse of seconds to stiffen myself for a third encounter with Quint. The apparition had reached the landing halfway up and was therefore on the spot nearest the window, where, at sight of me, it stopped short and fixed me exactly as it had fixed me from the tower and from the garden. He knew me as well as I knew him; and so, in the cold faint twilight, with a glimmer in the high glass and another on the polish of the oak stair below, we faced each other in our common intensity. He was absolutely, on this occasion, a living detestable dangerous presence. But that was not the wonder of wonders; I reserve this distinction for quite another circumstance: the circumstance that dread had unmistakeably quitted me and that there was nothing in me unable to meet and measure him.

I had plenty of anguish after that extraordinary moment, but I had, thank God, no terror. And he knew I had n't—I found myself at the end of an instant magnificently aware of this. I felt, in a fierce rigour of confidence, that if I stood my ground a minute I should cease—for the time at least—to have him to reckon with; and during the minute,

7. *Amelia* (1751) by Henry Fielding (1707–1754), a novel about an all-good, long-suffering heroine.

accordingly, the thing was as human and hideous as a real interview: hideous just because it *was* human, as human as to have met alone, in the small hours, in a sleeping house, some enemy, some adventurer, some criminal. It was the dead silence of our long gaze at such close quarters that gave the whole horror, huge as it was, its only note of the unnatural. If I had met a murderer in such a place and at such an hour we still at least would have spoken. Something would have passed, in life, between us; if nothing had passed one of us would have moved. The moment was so prolonged that it would have taken but little more to make me doubt if even *I* were in life. I can't express what followed it save by saying that the silence itself—which was indeed in a manner an attestation of my strength—became the element into which I saw the figure disappear; in which I definitely saw it turn, as I might have seen the low wretch to which it had once belonged turn on receipt of an order, and pass, with my eyes on the villainous back that no hunch could have more disfigured, straight down the staircase and into the darkness in which the next bend was lost.[8]

X

I remained a while at the top of the stair, but with the effect presently of understanding that when my visitor had gone, he had gone: then I returned to my room. The foremost thing I saw there by the light of the candle I had left burning was that Flora's little bed was empty; and on this I caught my breath with all the terror that, five minutes before, I had been able to resist. I dashed at the place in which I had left her lying and over which—for the small silk counterpane and the sheets were disarranged—the white curtains had been deceivingly pulled forward; then my step, to my unutterable relief, produced an answering sound: I noticed an agitation of the window-blind, and the child, ducking down, emerged rosily from the other side of it. She stood there in so much of her candour and so little of her night-gown, with her pink bare feet and the golden glow of her curls. She looked intensely grave, and I had never had such a sense of losing an advantage acquired (the thrill of which had just been so prodigious) as on my consciousness that she addressed me with a reproach—"You naughty: where *have* you been?" Instead of challenging her own irregularity I found myself arraigned and explaining. She herself explained, for that matter, with the loveliest eagerest simplicity. She had known suddenly, as she lay there, that I was out of the room, and had jumped up to see what had become of me. I had dropped, with the joy of her reappearance, back into my chair—feeling then, and then only, a little faint; and she had pattered straight over to me, thrown herself upon my knee, given herself to be held with the flame of the candle full in the wonderful little face that

8. Sixth weekly installment ended here.

was still flushed with sleep. I remember closing my eyes an instant, yieldingly, consciously, as before the excess of something beautiful that shone out of the blue of her own. "You were looking for me out of the window?" I said. "You thought I might be walking in the grounds?"

"Well, you know, I thought some one was"—she never blanched as she smiled out that at me.

Oh how I looked at her now! "And did you see any one?"

"Ah *no*!" she returned almost (with the full privilege of childish inconsequence) resentfully, though with a long sweetness in her little drawl of the negative.

At that moment, in the state of my nerves, I absolutely believed she lied; and if I once more closed my eyes it was before the dazzle of the three or four possible ways in which I might take this up. One of these for a moment tempted me with such singular force that, to resist it, I must have gripped my little girl with a spasm that, wonderfully, she submitted to without a cry or a sign of fright. Why not break out at her on the spot and have it all over?—give it to her straight in her lovely little lighted face? "You see, you see, you *know* that you do and that you already quite suspect I believe it; therefore why not frankly confess it to me, so that we may at least live with it together and learn perhaps, in the strangeness of our fate, where we are and what it means?" This solicitation dropped, alas, as it came: if I could immediately have succumbed to it I might have spared myself—well, you'll see what. Instead of succumbing I sprang again to my feet, looked at her bed and took a helpless middle way. "Why did you pull the curtain over the place to make me think you were still there?"

Flora luminously considered; after which, with her little divine smile: "Because I don't like to frighten you!"

"But if I had, by your idea, gone out—?"

She absolutely declined to be puzzled; she turned her eyes to the flame of the candle as if the question were as irrelevant, or at any rate as impersonal, as Mrs. Marcet[9] or nine-times-nine. "Oh but you know," she quite adequately answered, "that you might come back, you dear, and that you *have*!" And after a little, when she had got into bed, I had, a long time, by almost sitting on her for the retention of her hand, to show how I recognised the pertinence of my return.

You may imagine the general complexion, from that moment, of my nights. I repeatedly sat up till I did n't know when; I selected moments when my room-mate unmistakeably slept, and, stealing out, took noiseless turns in the passage. I even pushed as far as to where I had last met Quint. But I never met him there again, and I may as well say at once that I on no other occasion saw him in the house. I just missed, on the staircase, nevertheless, a different adventure. Looking down it

9. Jane Marcet (1769–1858) was the author of elementary children's texts and popularized accounts of the social and natural sciences.

from the top I once recognised the presence of a woman seated on one of the lower steps with her back presented to me, her body half-bowed and her head, in an attitude of woe, in her hands. I had been there but an instant, however, when she vanished without looking round at me. I knew, for all that, exactly what dreadful face she had to show; and I wondered whether, if instead of being above I had been below, I should have had the same nerve for going up that I had lately shown Quint. Well, there continued to be plenty of call for nerve. On the eleventh night after my latest encounter with that gentleman—they were all numbered now—I had an alarm that perilously skirted it and that indeed, from the particular quality of its unexpectedness, proved quite my sharpest shock. It was precisely the first night during this series that, weary with vigils, I had conceived I might again without laxity lay myself down at my old hour. I slept immediately and, as I afterwards knew, till about one o'clock; but when I woke it was to sit straight up, as completely roused as if a hand had shaken me. I had left a light burning, but it was now out, and I felt an instant certainty that Flora had extinguished it. This brought me to my feet and straight, in the darkness, to her bed, which I found she had left. A glance at the window enlightened me further, and the striking of a match completed the picture.

The child had again got up—this time blowing out the taper, and had again, for some purpose of observation or response, squeezed in behind the blind and was peering out into the night. That she now saw—as she had not, I had satisfied myself, the previous time—was proved to me by the fact that she was disturbed neither by my re-illumination nor by the haste I made to get into slippers and into a wrap. Hidden, protected, absorbed, she evidently rested on the sill—the casement opened forward—and gave herself up. There was a great still moon to help her, and this fact had counted in my quick decision. She was face to face with the apparition we had met at the lake, and could now communicate with it as she had not then been able to do. What I, on my side, had to care for was, without disturbing her, to reach, from the corridor, some other window turned to the same quarter. I got to the door without her hearing me; I got out of it, closed it and listened, from the other side, for some sound from her. While I stood in the passage I had my eyes on her brother's door, which was but ten steps off and which, indescribably, produced in me a renewal of the strange impulse that I lately spoke of as my temptation. What if I should go straight in and march to *his* window?—what if, by risking to his boyish bewilderment a revelation of my motive, I should throw across the rest of the mystery the long halter of my boldness?

This thought held me sufficiently to make me cross to his threshold and pause again. I preternaturally listened; I figured to myself what might portentously be; I wondered if his bed were also empty and he also secretly at watch. It was a deep soundless minute, at the end of which my impulse failed. He was quiet; he might be innocent; the risk was hideous; I turned away. There was a figure in the grounds—a figure prowling for a sight, the visitor with whom Flora was engaged; but it was n't the visitor most concerned with my boy. I hesitated afresh, but on other grounds and only a few seconds; then I had made my choice. There were empty rooms enough at Bly, and it was only a question of choosing the right one. The right one suddenly presented itself to me as the lower one—though high above the gardens—in the solid corner of the house that I have spoken of as the old tower. This was a large square chamber, arranged with some state as a bedroom, the extravagant size of which made it so inconvenient that it had not for years, though kept by Mrs. Grose in exemplary order, been occupied. I had often admired it and I knew my way about in it; I had only, after just faltering at the first chill gloom of its disuse, to pass across it and unbolt in all quietness one of the shutters. Achieving this transit I uncovered the glass without a sound and, applying my face to the pane, was able, the darkness without being much less than within, to see that I commanded the right direction. Then I saw something more. The moon made the night extraordinarily penetrable and showed me on the lawn a person, diminished by distance, who stood there motionless as if fascinated, looking up to where I had appeared—looking, that is, not so much straight at me as at something that was apparently above me. There was clearly another person above me—there was a person on the tower; but the presence on the lawn was not in the least what I had conceived and had confidently hurried to meet. The presence on the lawn—I felt sick as I made it out—was poor little Miles himself.

XI

It was not till late next day that I spoke to Mrs. Grose; the rigour with which I kept my pupils in sight making it often difficult to meet her privately: the more as we each felt the importance of not provoking—on the part of the servants quite as much as on that of the children—any suspicion of a secret flurry or of a discussion of mysteries. I drew a great security in this particular from her mere smooth aspect. There was nothing in her fresh face to pass on to others the least of my horrible confidences. She believed me, I was sure, absolutely: if she had n't I don't know what would have become of me, for I could n't have borne the strain alone. But she was a magnificent monument to the blessing of a want of imagination, and if she could see in our little charges nothing but their beauty and amiability, their happiness and cleverness, she had no direct communication with the sources of my trouble. If they had been at all visibly blighted or battered she would doubtless have grown, on tracing it back, haggard enough to match them; as matters stood, however, I could feel her, when she surveyed them with her large white arms folded and the habit of serenity in all her look, thank the Lord's mercy that if they were ruined the pieces would still serve. Flights of fancy gave place, in her mind, to a steady fireside glow, and I had already begun to perceive how, with the development of the conviction that—as time went on without a public accident—our young things could, after all, look out for themselves, she addressed her greatest solicitude to the sad case presented by their deputy-guardian. That, for myself, was a sound simplification: I could engage that, to the world, my face should tell no tales, but it would have been, in the conditions, an immense added worry to find myself anxious about hers.

At the hour I now speak of she had joined me, under pressure, on the terrace, where, with the lapse of the season, the afternoon sun was now agreeable; and we sat there together while before us and at a distance, yet within call if we wished, the children strolled to and fro in one of their most manageable moods. They moved slowly, in unison, below us, over the lawn, the boy, as they went, reading aloud from a story-book and passing his arm round his sister to keep her quite in touch. Mrs. Grose watched them with positive placidity; then I caught the suppressed intellectual creak with which she conscientiously turned to take from me a view of the back of the tapestry. I had made her a receptacle of lurid things, but there was an odd recognition of my superiority—my accomplishments and my function—in her patience under my pain. She offered her mind to my disclosures as, had I wished to mix a witch's broth and propose it with assurance, she would have held out a large clean saucepan. This had become thoroughly her attitude by the time that, in my recital of the events of the night, I reached the point of what Miles had said to me when, after seeing him, at such a monstrous hour, almost on the very spot where he happened now to be, I had gone down to bring him in; choosing then, at the window, with a concentrated need of not alarming the house, rather that method than any noisier process. I had left her meanwhile in little doubt of my small hope of representing with success even to her actual sympathy my sense of the real splendour of the little inspiration with which, after I had got him into the house, the boy met my final articulate challenge. As soon as I appeared in the moonlight on the terrace he had come to me as straight as possible; on which I had taken his hand without a word and led him, through the dark spaces, up the staircase where Quint had so hungrily hovered for him, along the lobby where I had listened and trembled, and so to his forsaken room.

Not a sound, on the way, had passed between us, and I had wondered—oh *how* I had wondered!—if he were groping about in his dreadful little mind for something plausible and not too grotesque. It would tax his invention certainly, and I felt, this time, over his real embarrassment, a curious thrill of triumph. It was a sharp trap for any game hitherto successful. He could play no longer at perfect propriety, nor could he pretend to it; so how the deuce would he get out of the scrape? There beat in me indeed, with the passionate throb of this question, an equal dumb appeal as to how the deuce *I* should. I was confronted at last, as never yet, with all the risk attached even now to sounding my own horrid note. I remember in fact that as we pushed into his little chamber, where the bed had not been slept in at all and the window, uncovered to the moonlight, made the place so clear that there was no need of striking a match—I remember how I suddenly dropped, sank upon the edge of the bed from the force of the idea that he must know how he really, as they say, "had" me. He could do what he liked, with all his cleverness to help him, so long as I should continue to defer to the old tradition of the criminality of those caretakers of the young who minister to superstitions and fears. He "had" me indeed, and in a cleft stick; for who would ever absolve me, who would consent that I should go unhung, if, by the faintest tremor of an overture, I were the first to introduce into our perfect intercourse an element so dire? No, no: it was useless to attempt to convey to Mrs. Grose, just as it is scarcely less so to attempt to suggest here, how, during our short stiff brush there in the dark, he fairly shook me with admiration. I was of course thoroughly kind and merciful; never, never yet had I placed on his small shoulders hands of such tenderness as those with which, while I rested against the bed, I held him there well under fire. I had no alternative but, in form at least, to put it to him.

"You must tell me now—and all the truth. What did you go out for? What were you doing there?"

I can still see his wonderful smile, the whites of his beautiful eyes and the uncovering of his clear teeth, shine to me in the dusk. "If I tell you why, will you understand?" My heart, at this, leaped into my mouth. *Would* he tell me why? I found no sound on my lips to press it, and I was aware of answering only with a vague repeated grimacing nod. He was gentleness itself, and while I wagged my head at him he stood there more than ever a little fairy prince. It was his brightness indeed that gave me a respite. Would it be so great if he were really going to tell me? "Well," he said at last, "just exactly in order that you should do this."

"Do what?"

"Think me—for a change—*bad*!" I shall never forget the sweetness and gaiety with which he brought out the word, nor how, on top of it, he bent forward and kissed me. It was practically the end of everything. I met his kiss and I had to make, while I folded him for a minute in my arms, the most stupendous effort not to cry. He had given exactly the account of himself that permitted least my going behind it, and it was only with the effect of confirming my acceptance of it that, as I presently glanced about the room, I could say—

"Then you did n't undress at all?"

He fairly glittered in the gloom. "Not at all. I sat up and read."

"And when did you go down?"

"At midnight. When I'm bad I *am* bad!"

"I see, I see—it's charming. But how could you be sure I should know it?"

"Oh I arranged that with Flora." His answers rang out with a readiness! "She was to get up and look out."

"Which is what she did do." It was I who fell into the trap!

"So she disturbed you, and, to see what she was looking at, you also looked—you saw."

"While you," I concurred, "caught your death in the night air!"

He literally bloomed so from this exploit that he could afford radiantly to assent. "How otherwise should I have been bad enough?" he asked. Then, after another embrace, the incident and our interview closed on my recognition of all the reserves of goodness that, for his joke, he had been able to draw upon.

XII

The particular impression I had received proved in the morning light, I repeat, not quite successfully presentable to Mrs. Grose, though I re-enforced it with the mention of still another remark that he had made before we separated. "It all lies in half a dozen words," I said to her, "words that really settle the matter. 'Think, you know, what I *might* do!' He threw that off to show me how good he is. He knows down to the ground what he 'might do.' That 's what he gave them a taste of at school."

"Lord, you do change!" cried my friend.

"I don't change—I simply make it out. The four, depend upon it, perpetually meet. If on either of these last nights you had been with either child you 'd clearly have understood. The more I 've watched and waited the more I 've felt that if there were nothing else to make it sure it would be made so by the systematic silence of each. *Never,* by a slip of the tongue, have they so much as alluded to either of their old friends, any more than Miles has alluded to his expulsion. Oh yes, we may sit here and look at them, and they may show off to us there to their fill; but even while they pretend to be lost in their fairy-tale they 're steeped in their vision of the dead restored to them. He 's not reading to her," I declared; "they 're talking of *them*—they 're talking horrors! I go on, I know, as if I were crazy; and it 's a wonder I 'm not.

What I 've seen would have made *you* so; but it has only made me more lucid, made me get hold of still other things."

My lucidity must have seemed awful, but the charming creatures who were victims of it, passing and repassing in their interlocked sweetness, gave my colleague something to hold on by; and I felt how tight she held as, without stirring in the breath of my passion, she covered them still with her eyes. "Of what other things have you got hold?"

"Why of the very things that have delighted, fascinated and yet, at bottom, as I now so strangely see, mystified and troubled me. Their more than earthly beauty, their absolutely unnatural goodness. It 's a game," I went on: "It 's a policy and a fraud!"

"On the part of little darlings—?"

"As yet mere lovely babies? Yes, mad as that seems!" The very act of bringing it out really helped me to trace it—follow it all up and piece it all together. "They have n't been good—they 've only been absent. It has been easy to live with them because they 're simply leading a life of their own. They 're not mine—they 're not ours. They 're his and they 're hers!"

"Quint's and that woman's?"

"Quint's and that woman's. They want to get to them."

Oh how, at this, poor Mrs. Grose appeared to study them! "But for what?"

"For the love of all the evil that, in those dreadful days, the pair put into them. And to ply them with that evil still, to keep up the work of demons, is what brings the others back."

"Laws!" said my friend under her breath. The exclamation was homely, but it revealed a real acceptance of my further proof of what, in the bad time—for there had been a worse even than this!—must have occurred. There could have been no such justification for me as the plain assent of her experience to whatever depth of depravity I found credible in our brace of scoundrels. It was in obvious submission of memory that she brought out after a moment: "They *were* rascals! But what can they now do?" she pursued.

"Do?" I echoed so loud that Miles and Flora, as they passed at their distance, paused an instant in their walk and looked at us. "Don't they do enough?" I demanded in a lower tone, while the children, having smiled and nodded and kissed hands to us, resumed their exhibition. We were held by it a minute; then I answered: "They can destroy them!" At this my companion did turn, but the appeal she launched was a silent one, the effect of which was to make me more explicit. "They don't know as yet quite how—but they 're trying hard. They 're seen only across, as it were, and beyond—in strange places and on high places, the top of towers, the roof of houses, the outside of windows, the further edge of pools; but there 's a deep design, on either side, to shorten the distance and overcome the obstacle: so the success of the tempters is only a question of time. They 've only to keep to their suggestions of danger."

"For the children to come?"

"And perish in the attempt!" Mrs. Grose slowly got up, and I scrupulously added: "Unless, of course, we can prevent!"

Standing there before me while I kept my seat she visibly turned things over. "Their uncle must do the preventing. He must take them away."

"And who 's to make him?"

She had been scanning the distance, but she now dropped on me a foolish face. "You, Miss."

"By writing to him that his house is poisoned and his little nephew and niece mad?"

"But if they *are*, Miss?"

"And if I am myself, you mean? That 's charming news to be sent him by a person enjoying his confidence and whose prime undertaking was to give him no worry."

Mrs. Grose considered, following the children again. "Yes, he do hate worry. That was the great reason—"

"Why those fiends took him in so long? No doubt, though his indifference must have been awful. As I 'm not a fiend, at any rate, I should n't take him in."

My companion, after an instant and for all answer, sat down again and grasped my arm. "Make him at any rate come to you."

I stared. "To *me*?" I had a sudden fear of what she might do. " 'Him'?"

"He ought to *be* here—he ought to help."

I quickly rose and I think I must have shown her a queerer face than ever yet. "You see me asking him for a visit?" No, with her eyes on my face she evidently could n't. Instead of it even—as a woman reads another—she could see what I myself saw: his derision, his amusement, his contempt for the breakdown of my resignation at being left alone and for the fine machinery I had set in motion to attract his attention to my slighted charms. She did n't know—no one knew—how proud I had been to serve him and to stick to our terms; yet she none the less took the measure, I think, of the warning I now gave her. "If you should so lose your head as to appeal to him for me—"

She was really frightened. "Yes, Miss?"

"I would leave, on the spot, both him and you."[1]

1. Seventh weekly installment and "Part Third" ended approximately here (see Textual Notes).

XIII

It was all very well to join them, but speaking to them proved quite as much as ever an effort beyond my strength—offered, in close quarters, difficulties as insurmountable as before. This situation continued a month, and with new aggravations and particular notes, the note above all, sharper and sharper, of the small ironic consciousness on the part of my pupils. It was not, I am as sure to-day as I was sure then, my mere infernal imagination: it was absolutely traceable that they were aware of my predicament and that this strange relation made, in a manner, for a long time, the air in which we moved. I don't mean that they had their tongues in their cheeks or did anything vulgar, for that was not one of their dangers: I do mean, on the other hand, that the element of the unnamed and untouched became, between us, greater than any other, and that so much avoidance could n't have been made successful without a great deal of tacit arrangement. It was as if, at moments, we were perpetually coming into sight of subjects before which we must stop short, turning suddenly out of alleys that we perceived to be blind, closing with a little bang that made us look at each other—for, like all bangs, it was something louder than we had intended—the doors we had indiscreetly opened. All roads lead to Rome, and there were times when it might have struck us that almost every branch of study or subject of conversation skirted forbidden ground. Forbidden ground was the question of the return of the dead in general and of whatever, in especial, might survive, for memory, of the friends little children had lost. There were days when I could have sworn that one of them had, with a small invisible nudge, said to the other: "She thinks she'll do it this time—but she *won't*!" To "do it" would have been to indulge for instance—and for once in a way—in some direct reference to the lady who had prepared them for my discipline. They had a delightful endless appetite for passages in my own history to which I had again and again treated them; they were in possession of everything that had ever happened to me, had had, with every circumstance, the story of my smallest adventures and of those of my brothers and sisters and of the cat and the dog at home, as well as many particulars of the whimsical bent of my father, of the furniture and arrangement of our house and of the conversation of the old women of our village. There were things enough, taking one with another, to chatter about, if one went very fast and knew by instinct when to go round. They pulled with an art of their own the strings of my invention and my memory; and nothing else perhaps, when I thought of such occasions afterwards, gave me so the suspicion of being watched from under cover. It was in any case over *my* life, *my* past and *my* friends alone that we could take anything like our ease; a state of affairs that led them sometimes without the least pertinence to break out into sociable reminders. I was invited—with no visible connexion—to repeat afresh Goody Gosling's celebrated *mot*[2] or to confirm the details already supplied as to the cleverness of the vicarage pony.

It was partly at such junctures as these and partly at quite different ones that, with the turn my matters had now taken, my predicament, as I have called it, grew most sensible. The fact that the days passed for me without another encounter ought, it would have appeared, to have done something toward soothing my nerves. Since the light brush, that second night on the upper landing, of the presence of a woman at the foot of the stair, I had seen nothing, whether in or out of the house, that one had better not have seen. There was many a corner round which I expected to come upon Quint, and many a situation that, in a merely sinister way, would have favoured the appearance of Miss Jessel. The summer had turned, the summer had gone; the autumn had dropped upon Bly and had blown out half our lights. The place, with its grey sky and withered garlands, its bared spaces and scattered dead leaves, was like a theatre after the performance—all strewn with crumpled playbills. There were exactly states of the air, conditions of sound and of stillness, unspeakable impressions of the *kind* of ministering moment, that brought back to me, long enough to catch it, the feeling of the medium in which, that June evening out of doors, I had had my first sight of Quint, and in which too, at those other instants, I had, after seeing him through the window, looked for him in vain in the circle of shrubbery. I recognised the signs, the portents—I recognised the moment, the spot. But they remained unaccompanied and empty, and I continued unmolested; if unmolested one could call a young woman whose sensibility had, in the most extraordinary fashion, not declined but deepened. I had said in my talk with Mrs. Grose on that horrid scene of Flora's by the lake—and had perplexed her by so saying—that it would from that moment distress me much more to lose my power than to keep it. I had then expressed what was vividly in my mind: the truth that, whether the children really saw or not—since, that is, it was not yet definitely proved—I greatly preferred, as a safeguard, the fulness of my own exposure. I was ready to know the very worst that was to be known. What I had then had an ugly glimpse of was that my eyes might be sealed just while theirs were most opened. Well, my eyes *were* sealed, it appeared, at present—a consummation for which it seemed blasphemous not to thank God. There was, alas, a difficulty about that: I would have thanked him with all my soul had I not had in a proportionate measure this conviction of the secret of my pupils.

How can I retrace to-day the strange steps of my obsession? There were times of our being together when I would have been ready to

2. The allusion here is unexplained; does James mean a favorite Mother Goose rhyme or, perhaps, the witticism of one of the governess's former neighbors?

swear that, literally, in my presence, but with my direct sense of it closed, they had visitors who were known and were welcome. Then it was that, had I not been deterred by the very chance that such an injury might prove greater than the injury to be averted, my exaltation would have broken out. "They 're here, they 're here, you little wretches," I would have cried, "and you can't deny it now!" The little wretches denied it with all the added volume of their sociability and their tenderness, just in the crystal depths of which—like the flash of a fish in a stream—the mockery of their advantage peeped up. The shock had in truth sunk into me still deeper than I knew on the night when, looking out either for Quint or for Miss Jessel under the stars, I had seen there the boy over whose rest I watched and who had immediately brought in with him—had straightway there turned on me—the lovely upward look with which, from the battlements above us, the hideous apparition of Quint had played. If it was a question of a scare my discovery on this occasion had scared me more than any other, and it was essentially in the scared state that I drew my actual conclusions. They harassed me so that sometimes, at odd moments, I shut myself up audibly to rehearse—it was at once a fantastic relief and a renewed despair—the manner in which I might come to the point. I approached it from one side and the other while, in my room, I flung myself about, but I always broke down in the monstrous utterance of names. As they died away on my lips I said to myself that I should indeed help them to represent something infamous if by pronouncing them I should violate as rare a little case of instinctive delicacy as any schoolroom probably had ever known. When I said to myself: "*They* have the manners to be silent, and you, trusted as you are, the baseness to speak!" I felt myself crimson and covered my face with my hands. After these secret scenes I chattered more than ever, going on volubly enough till one of our prodigious palpable hushes occurred—I can call them nothing else—the strange dizzy lift or swim (I try for terms!) into a stillness, a pause of all life, that had nothing to do with the more or less noise we at the moment might be engaged in making and that I could hear through any intensified mirth or quickened recitation or louder strum of the piano. Then it was that the others, the outsiders, were there. Though they were not angels they "passed," as the French say, causing me, while they stayed, to tremble with the fear of their addressing to their younger victims some yet more infernal message or more vivid image than they had thought good enough for myself.

What it was least possible to get rid of was the cruel idea that, whatever I had seen, Miles and Flora saw *more*—things terrible and unguessable and that sprang from dreadful passages of intercourse in the past. Such things naturally left on the surface, for the time, a chill that we vociferously denied we felt; and we had all three, with repetition, got into such splendid training that we went each time, to mark the close of the incident, almost automatically through the very same movements. It was striking of the children at all events to kiss me inveterately with a wild irrelevance and never to fail—one or the other—of the precious question that had helped us through many a peril. "When do you think he *will* come? Don't you think we *ought* to write?"—there was nothing like that enquiry, we found by experience, for carrying off an awkwardness. "He" of course was their uncle in Harley Street; and we lived in much profusion of theory that he might at any moment arrive to mingle in our circle. It was impossible to have given less encouragement than he had administered to such a doctrine, but if we had not had the doctrine to fall back upon we should have deprived each other of some of our finest exhibitions. He never wrote to them—that may have been selfish, but it was a part of the flattery of his trust of myself; for the way in which a man pays his highest tribute to a woman is apt to be but by the more festal celebration of one of the sacred laws of his comfort. So I held that I carried out the spirit of the pledge given not to appeal to him when I let our young friends understand that their own letters were but charming literary exercises. They were too beautiful to be posted; I kept them myself; I have them all to this hour. This was a rule indeed which only added to the satiric effect of my being plied with the supposition that he might at any moment be among us. It was exactly as if our young friends knew how almost more awkward than anything else that might be for me. There appears to me moreover as I look back no note in all this more extraordinary than the mere fact that, in spite of my tension and of their triumph, I never lost patience with them. Adorable they must in truth have been, I now feel, since I did n't in these days hate them! Would exasperation, however, if relief had longer been postponed, finally have betrayed me? It little matters, for relief arrived. I call it relief though it was only the relief that a snap brings to a strain or the burst of a thunderstorm to a day of suffocation. It was at least change, and it came with a rush.

XIV

Walking to church a certain Sunday morning, I had little Miles at my side and his sister, in advance of us and at Mrs. Grose's, well in sight. It was a crisp clear day, the first of its order for some time; the night had brought a touch of frost and the autumn air, bright and sharp, made the church-bells almost gay. It was an odd accident of thought that I should have happened at such a moment to be particularly and very gratefully struck with the obedience of my little charges. Why did they never resent my inexorable, my perpetual society? Something or other had brought nearer home to me that I had all but pinned the boy to my shawl, and that in the way our companions were marshalled before me I might have appeared to provide against some danger of rebellion. I was like a gaoler with an eye to possible surprises and escapes. But all this belonged—I mean their magnificent little surrender—just to the special array of the facts that were most abysmal. Turned out for Sunday by his uncle's tailor, who had had a free hand and a notion of pretty waistcoats and of his grand little air, Miles's whole title to independence, the rights of his sex and situation, were so stamped upon him that if he had suddenly struck for freedom I should have had nothing to say. I was by the strangest of chances wondering how I should meet him when the revolution unmistakeably occurred. I call it a revolution because I now see how, with the word he spoke, the curtain rose on the last act of my dreadful drama and the catastrophe was precipitated. "Look here, my dear, you know," he charmingly said, "when in the world, please, am I going back to school?"

Transcribed here the speech sounds harmless enough, particularly as uttered in the sweet, high, casual pipe with which, at all interlocutors, but above all at his eternal governess, he threw off intonations as if he were tossing roses. There was something in them that always made one "catch," and I caught at any rate now so effectually that I stopped as short as if one of the trees of the park had fallen across the road. There was something new, on the spot, between us, and he was perfectly aware I recognised it, though to enable me to do so he had no need to look a whit less candid and charming than usual. I could feel in him how he already, from my at first finding nothing to reply, perceived the advantage he had gained. I was so slow to find anything that he had plenty of time, after a minute, to continue with his suggestive but inconclusive smile: "You know, my dear, that for a fellow to be with a lady *always*—!" His "my dear" was constantly on his lips for me, and nothing could have expressed more the exact shade of the sentiment with which I desired to inspire my pupils than its fond familiarity. It was so respectfully easy.

But oh how I felt that at present I must pick my own phrases! I remember that, to gain time, I tried to laugh, and I seemed to see in the beautiful face with which he watched me how ugly and queer I looked. "And always with the same lady?" I returned.

He neither blenched nor winked. The whole thing was virtually out between us. "Ah of course she 's a jolly 'perfect' lady; but after all I 'm a fellow, don't you see? who 's—well, getting on."

I lingered there with him an instant ever so kindly. "Yes, you 're getting on." Oh but I felt helpless!

I have kept to this day the heartbreaking little idea of how he seemed to know that and to play with it. "And you can't say I 've not been awfully good, can you?"

I laid my hand on his shoulder, for though I felt how much better it would have been to walk on I was not yet quite able. "No, I can't say that, Miles."

"Except just that one night, you know—!"

"That one night?" I could n't look as straight as he.

"Why when I went down—went out of the house."

"Oh yes. But I forget what you did it for."

"You forget?"—he spoke with the sweet extravagance of childish reproach. "Why it was just to show you I could!"

"Oh yes—you could."

"And I can again."

I felt I might perhaps after all succeed in keeping my wits about me. "Certainly. But you won't."

"No, not *that* again. It was nothing."

"It was nothing," I said. "But we must go on."

He resumed our walk with me, passing his hand into my arm. "Then when *am* I going back?"

I wore, in turning it over, my most responsible air. "Were you very happy at school?"

He just considered. "Oh I 'm happy enough anywhere!"

"Well then," I quavered, "if you 're just as happy here—!"

"Ah but that is n't everything! Of course *you* know a lot—"

"But you hint that you know almost as much?" I risked as he paused.

"Not half I want to!" Miles honestly professed. "But it is n't so much that."

"What is it then?"

"Well—I want to see more life."

"I see; I see." We had arrived within sight of the church and of various persons, including several of the household of Bly, on their way to it and clustered about the door to see us go in. I quickened our step; I wanted to get there before the question between us opened up much further; I reflected hungrily that he would have for more than an hour to be silent; and I thought with envy of the comparative dusk of the pew and of the almost spiritual help of the hassock on which I might bend my knees. I seemed literally to be running a race with some confusion to which he was about to reduce me, but I felt he had got in first when, before we had even entered the churchyard, he threw out—

"I want my own sort!"

It literally made me bound forward. "There are n't many of your own sort, Miles!" I laughed. "Unless perhaps dear little Flora!"

"You really compare me to a baby girl?"

This found me singularly weak. "Don't you then *love* our sweet Flora?"

"If I did n't—and you too; if I did n't—!" he repeated as if retreating for a jump, yet leaving his thought so unfinished that, after we had come into the gate, another stop, which he imposed on me by the pressure of his arm, had become inevitable. Mrs. Grose and Flora had passed into the church, the other worshippers had followed and we were, for the minute, alone among the old thick graves. We had paused, on the path from the gate, by a low oblong table-like tomb.

"Yes, if you did n't—?"

He looked, while I waited, about at the graves. "Well, you know what!" But he did n't move, and he presently produced something that made me drop straight down on the stone slab as if suddenly to rest. "Does my uncle think what *you* think?"

I markedly rested. "How do you know what I think?"

"Ah well, of course I don't; for it strikes me you never tell me. But I mean does *he* know?"

"Know what, Miles?"

"Why the way I 'm going on."

I recognised quickly enough that I could make, to this enquiry, no answer that would n't involve something of a sacrifice of my employer. Yet it struck me that we were all, at Bly, sufficiently sacrificed to make that venial. "I don't think your uncle much cares."

Miles, on this, stood looking at me. "Then don't you think he can be made to?"

"In what way?"

"Why by his coming down."

"But who 'll get him to come down?"

"*I* will!" the boy said with extraordinary brightness and emphasis. He gave me another look charged with that expression and then marched off alone into church.

XV

The business was practically settled from the moment I never followed him. It was a pitiful surrender to agitation, but my being aware of this had somehow no power to restore me. I only sat there on my tomb and read into what our young friend had said to me the fulness of its meaning; by the time I had grasped the whole of which, I had also embraced, for absence, the pretext that I was ashamed to offer my pupils and the rest of the congregation such an example of delay. What I said to myself above all was that Miles had got something out of me and that the gage of it for him would be just this awkward collapse. He had got out of me that there was something I was much afraid of, and that he should probably be able to make use of my fear to gain, for his own purpose, more freedom. My fear was of having to deal with the intolerable question of the grounds of his dismissal from school, since that was really but the question of the horrors gathered behind. That his uncle should arrive to treat with me of these things was a solution that, strictly speaking, I ought now to have desired to bring on; but I could so little face the ugliness and the pain of it that I simply procrastinated and lived from hand to mouth. The boy, to my deep discomposure, was immensely in the right, was in a position to say to me: "Either you clear up with my guardian the mystery of this interruption of my studies, or you cease to expect me to lead with you a life that 's so unnatural for a boy." What was so unnatural for the particular boy I was concerned with was this sudden revelation of a consciousness and a plan.

That was what really overcame me, what prevented my going in. I walked round the church, hesitating, hovering; I reflected that I had already, with him, hurt myself beyond repair. Therefore I could patch up nothing and it was too extreme an effort to squeeze beside him into the pew: he would be so much more sure than ever to pass his arm into mine and make me sit there for an hour in close mute contact with his commentary on our talk. For the first minute since his arrival I wanted to get away from him. As I paused beneath the high cast window and listened to the sounds of worship I was taken with an impulse that might master me, I felt, and completely, should I give it the least encouragement. I might easily put an end to my ordeal by getting away altogether. Here was my chance; there was no one to stop me; I could give the whole thing up—turn my back and bolt. It was only a question of hurrying again, for a few preparations, to the house which the attendance at church of so many of the servants would practically have left unoccupied. No one, in short, could blame me if I should just drive desperately off. What was it to get away if I should get away only till dinner? That would be in a couple of hours, at the end of which—I had the acute prevision—my little pupils would play at innocent wonder about my non-appearance in their train.

"What *did* you do, you naughty bad thing? Why in the world, to worry us so—and take our thoughts off too, don't you know?—did you desert us at the very door?" I could n't meet such questions nor, as they asked them, their false little lovely eyes; yet it was all so exactly what I should have to meet that, as the prospect grew sharp to me, I at last let myself go.

I got, so far as the immediate moment was concerned, away; I came straight out of the churchyard and, thinking hard, retraced my steps through the park. It seemed to me that by the time I reached the house I had made up my mind to cynical flight. The Sunday stillness both of the approaches and of the interior, in which I met no one, fairly stirred me with a sense of opportunity. Were I to get off quickly this way I should get off without a scene, without a word. My quickness would have to be remarkable, however, and the question of a conveyance was the great one to settle. Tormented, in the hall, with difficulties and obstacles, I remember sinking down at the foot of the staircase—suddenly collapsing there on the lowest step and then, with a revulsion, recalling that it was exactly where, more than a month before, in the darkness of night and just so bowed with evil things, I had seen the spectre of the most horrible of women. At this I was able to straighten myself; I went the rest of the way up; I made, in my turmoil, for the schoolroom, where there were objects belonging to me that I should have to take. But I opened the door to find again, in a flash, my eyes unsealed. In the presence of what I saw I reeled straight back upon resistance.

Seated at my own table in the clear noonday light I saw a person whom, without my previous experience, I should have taken at the first blush for some housemaid who might have stayed at home to look after the place and who, availing herself of rare relief from observation and of the schoolroom table and my pens, ink and paper, had applied herself to the considerable effort of a letter to her sweetheart. There was an effort in the way that, while her arms rested on the table, her hands, with evident weariness, supported her head; but at the moment I took this in I had already become aware that, in spite of my entrance, her attitude strangely persisted. Then it was—with the very act of its announcing itself—that her identity flared up in a change of posture. She rose, not as if she had heard me, but with an indescribable grand melancholy of indifference and detachment, and, within a dozen feet of me, stood there as my vile predecessor. Dishonoured and tragic, she was all before me; but even as I fixed and, for memory, secured it, the awful image passed away. Dark as midnight in her black dress, her haggard beauty and her unutterable woe, she had looked at me long enough to appear to say that her right to sit at my table was as good as mine to sit at hers. While these instants lasted indeed I had the extraordinary chill of a feeling that it was I who was the intruder. It was as a wild protest against it that, actually addressing her—"You terrible miserable woman!"—I heard myself break into a sound that, by the open door, rang through the long passage and the empty house. She looked at me as if she heard me, but I had recovered myself and cleared the air. There was nothing in the room the next minute but the sunshine and the sense that I must stay.[3]

XVI

I had so perfectly expected the return of the others to be marked by a demonstration that I was freshly upset at having to find them merely dumb and discreet about my desertion. Instead of gaily denouncing and caressing me they made no allusion to my having failed them, and I was left, for the time, on perceiving that she too said nothing, to study Mrs. Grose's odd face. I did this to such purpose that I made sure they had in some way bribed her to silence; a silence that, however, I would engage to break down on the first private opportunity. This opportunity

3. Eighth weekly installment ended here.

came before tea: I secured five minutes with her in the housekeeper's room, where, in the twilight, amid a smell of lately-baked bread, but with the place all swept and garnished, I found her sitting in pained placidity before the fire. So I see her still, so I see her best: facing the flame from her straight chair in the dusky shining room, a large clean picture of the "put away"—of drawers closed and locked and rest without a remedy.

"Oh yes, they asked me to say nothing; and to please them—so long as they were there—of course I promised. But what had happened to you?"

"I only went with you for the walk," I said. "I had then to come back to meet a friend."

She showed her surprise. "A friend—*you*?"

"Oh yes, I 've a couple!" I laughed. "But did the children give you a reason?"

"For not alluding to your leaving us? Yes; they said you 'd like it better. *Do* you like it better?"

My face had made her rueful. "No, I like it worse!" But after an instant I added: "Did they say why I should like it better?"

"No; Master Miles only said 'We must do nothing but what she likes!' "

"I wish indeed he would! And what did Flora say?"

"Miss Flora was too sweet. She said 'Oh of course, of course!'—and I said the same."

I thought a moment. "You were too sweet too—I can hear you all. But none the less, between Miles and me, it 's now all out."

"All out?" My companion stared. "But what, Miss?"

"Everything. It doesn't matter. I 've made up my mind. I came home, my dear," I went on, "for a talk with Miss Jessel."

I had by this time formed the habit of having Mrs. Grose literally well in hand in advance of my sounding that note; so that even now, as she bravely blinked under the signal of my word, I could keep her comparatively firm. "A talk! Do you mean she spoke?"

"It came to that. I found her, on my return, in the schoolroom."

"And what did she say?" I can hear the good woman still, and the candour of her stupefaction.

"That she suffers the torments—!"

It was this, of a truth, that made her, as she filled out my picture, gape. "Do you mean," she faltered "—of the lost?"

"Of the lost. Of the damned. And that 's why, to share them—" I faltered myself with the horror of it.

But my companion, with less imagination, kept me up. "To share them—?"

"She wants Flora." Mrs. Grose might, as I gave it to her, fairly have fallen away from me had I not been prepared. I still held her there, to show I was. "As I 've told you, however, it does n't matter."

"Because you 've made up your mind? But to what?"

"To everything."

"And what do you call 'everything'?"

"Why to sending for their uncle."

"Oh Miss, in pity do," my friend broke out.

"Ah but I will, I *will*! I see it 's the only way. What 's 'out,' as I told you, with Miles is that if he thinks I 'm afraid to—and has ideas of what he gains by that—he shall see he 's mistaken. Yes, yes; his uncle shall have it here from me on the spot (and before the boy himself if necessary) that if I 'm to be reproached with having done nothing again about more school—"

"Yes, Miss—" my companion pressed me.

"Well, there 's that awful reason."

There were now clearly so many of these for my poor colleague that she was excusable for being vague. "But—a—which?"

"Why the letter from his old place."

"You 'll show it to the master?"

"I ought to have done so on the instant."

"Oh no!" said Mrs. Grose with decision.

"I 'll put it before him," I went on inexorably, "that I can't undertake to work the question on behalf of a child who has been expelled—"

"For we 've never in the least known what!" Mrs. Grose declared.

"For wickedness. For what else—when he 's so clever and beautiful and perfect? Is he stupid? Is he untidy? Is he infirm? Is he ill-natured? He 's exquisite—so it can be only *that*; and that would open up the whole thing. After all," I said, "it 's their uncle's fault. If he left here such people—!"

"He did n't really in the least know them. The fault 's mine." She had turned quite pale.

"Well, you shan't suffer," I answered.

"The children shan't!" she emphatically returned.

I was silent a while; we looked at each other. "Then what am I to tell him?"

"You need n't tell him anything. *I 'll* tell him."

I measured this. "Do you mean you 'll write—?" Remembering she could n't, I caught myself up. "How do you communicate?"

"I tell the bailiff. *He* writes."

"And should you like him to write our story?"

My question had a sarcastic force that I had not fully intended, and it made her after a moment inconsequently break down. The tears were again in her eyes. "Ah Miss, *you* write!"

"Well—to-night," I at last returned; and on this we separated.

XVII

I went so far, in the evening, as to make a beginning. The weather had changed back, a great wind was abroad, and beneath the lamp, in my room, with Flora at peace beside me, I sat for a long time before a blank sheet of paper and listened to the lash of the rain and the batter of the gusts. Finally I went out, taking a candle; I crossed the passage and listened a minute at Miles's door. What, under my endless obsession, I had been impelled to listen for was some betrayal of his not being at rest, and I presently caught one, but not in the form I had expected. His voice tinkled out. "I say, you there—come in." It was gaiety in the gloom!

I went in with my light and found him in bed, very wide awake but very much at his ease. "Well, what are *you* up to?" he asked with a grace of sociability in which it occurred to me that Mrs. Grose, had she been present, might have looked in vain for proof that anything was "out."

I stood over him with my candle. "How did you know I was there?"

"Why of course I heard you. Did you fancy you made no noise? You 're like a troop of cavalry!" he beautifully laughed.

"Then you were n't asleep?"

"Not much! I lie awake and think."

I had put my candle, designedly, a short way off, and then, as he held out his friendly old hand to me, had sat down on the edge of his bed. "What is it," I asked, "that you think of?"

"What in the world, my dear, but *you*?"

"Ah the pride I take in your appreciation does n't insist on that! I had so far rather you slept."

"Well, I think also, you know, of this queer business of ours."

I marked the coolness of his firm little hand. "Of what queer business, Miles?"

"Why the way you bring me up. And all the rest!"

I fairly held my breath a minute, and even from my glimmering taper there was light enough to show how he smiled up at me from his pillow. "What do you mean by all the rest?"

"Oh you know, you know!"

I could say nothing for a minute, though I felt as I held his hand and our eyes continued to meet that my silence had all the air of admitting his charge and that nothing in the whole world of reality was perhaps at that moment so fabulous as our actual relation. "Certainly you shall go back to school," I said, "if it be that that troubles you. But not to the old place—we must find another, a better. How could I know it did trouble you, this question, when you never told me so, never spoke of it at all?" His clear listening face, framed in its smooth whiteness, made him for the minute as appealing as some wistful patient in a children's hospital; and I would have given, as the resemblance came to me, all I possessed on earth really to be the nurse or the sister of charity who might have helped to cure him. Well, even as it was I perhaps might help! "Do you know you've never said a word to me about your school—I mean the old one; never mentioned it in any way?"

He seemed to wonder; he smiled with the same loveliness. But he clearly gained time; he waited, he called for guidance. "Have n't I?" It was n't for *me* to help him—it was for the thing I had met!

Something in his tone and the expression of his face, as I got this from him, set my heart aching with such a pang as it had never yet known; so unutterably touching was it to see his little brain puzzled and his little resources taxed to play, under the spell laid on him, a part of innocence and consistency. "No, never—from the hour you came back. You 've never mentioned to me one of your masters, one of your comrades, nor the least little thing that ever happened to you at school. Never, little Miles—no never—have you given me an inkling of anything that *may* have happened there. Therefore you can fancy how much I 'm in the dark. Until you came out, that way, this morning, you had since the first hour I saw you scarce even made a reference to anything in your previous life. You seemed so perfectly to accept the present." It was extraordinary how my absolute conviction of his secret precocity—or whatever I might call the poison of an influence that I dared but half-phrase—made him, in spite of the faint breath of his inward trouble, appear as accessible as an older person, forced me to treat him as an intelligent equal. "I thought you wanted to go on as you are."

It struck me that at this he just faintly coloured. He gave, at any rate, like a convalescent slightly fatigued, a languid shake of his head. "I don't—I don't. I want to get away."

"You 're tired of Bly?"

"Oh no, I like Bly."

"Well then—?"

"Oh *you* know what a boy wants!"

I felt I did n't know so well as Miles, and I took temporary refuge. "You want to go to your uncle?"

Again, at this, with his sweet ironic face, he made a movement on the pillow. "Ah you can't get off with that!"

I was silent a little, and it was I now, I think, who changed colour. "My dear, I don't want to get off!"

"You can't even if you do. You can't, you can't!"—he lay beautifully staring. "My uncle must come down and you must completely settle things."

"If we do," I returned with some spirit, "you may be sure it will be to take you quite away."

"Well, don't you understand that that 's exactly what I 'm working for? You 'll have to *tell* him—about the way you 've let it all drop: you'll have to tell him a tremendous lot!"

The exultation with which he uttered this helped me somehow for the instant to meet him rather more. "And how much will *you*, Miles, have to tell him? There are things he 'll ask you!"

He turned it over. "Very likely. But what things?"

"The things you 've never told me. To make up his mind what to do with you. He can't send you back—"

"I don't want to go back!" he broke in. "I want a new field."

He said it with admirable serenity, with positive unimpeachable gaiety; and doubtless it was that very note that most evoked for me the poignancy, the unnatural childish tragedy, of his probable reappearance at the end of three months with all this bravado and still more dishonour. It overwhelmed me now that I should never be able to bear that, and it made me let myself go. I threw myself upon him and in the tenderness of my pity I embraced him. "Dear little Miles, dear little Miles—!"

My face was close to his, and he let me kiss him, simply taking it with indulgent good humour. "Well, old lady?"

"Is there nothing—nothing at all that you want to tell me?"

He turned off a little, facing round toward the wall and holding up his hand to look at as one had seen sick children look. "I've told you —I told you this morning."

Oh I was sorry for him! "That you just want me not to worry you?"

He looked round at me now as if in recognition of my understanding him; then ever so gently, "To let me alone," he replied.

There was even a strange little dignity in it, something that made me release him, yet, when I had slowly risen, linger beside him. God knows *I* never wished to harass him, but I felt that merely, at this, to turn my back on him was to abandon or, to put it more truly, lose him. "I 've just begun a letter to your uncle," I said.

"Well then, finish it!"

I waited a minute. "What happened before?"

He gazed up at me again. "Before what?"

"Before you came back. And before you went away."

For some time he was silent, but he continued to meet my eyes. "What happened?"

It made me, the sound of the words, in which it seemed to me I caught for the very first time a small faint quaver of consenting consciousness—it made me drop on my knees beside the bed and seize once more the chance of possessing him. "Dear little Miles, dear little Miles, if you *knew* how I want to help you! It 's only that, it 's nothing but that, and I 'd rather die than give you a pain or do you a wrong—I 'd rather die than hurt a hair of you. Dear little Miles"—oh I brought it out now even if I *should* go too far—"I just want you to help me to save you!" But I knew in a moment after this that I had gone too far. The answer to my appeal was instantaneous, but it came in the form of an extraordinary blast and chill, a gust of frozen air and a shake of the room as great as if, in the wild wind, the casement had crashed in. The boy gave a loud high shriek which, lost in the rest of the shock of sound, might have seemed, indistinctly, though I was so close to him, a note either of jubilation or of terror. I jumped to my feet again and was conscious of darkness. So for a moment we remained, while I stared about me and saw the drawn curtains unstirred and the window still tight. "Why the candle 's out!" I then cried.

"It was I who blew it, dear!" said Miles.

XVIII

The next day, after lessons, Mrs. Grose found a moment to say to me quietly: "Have you written, Miss?"

"Yes—I've written." But I did n't add—for the hour—that my letter, sealed and directed, was still in my pocket. There would be time enough to send it before the messenger should go to the village. Meanwhile there had been on the part of my pupils no more brilliant, more exemplary morning. It was exactly as if they had both had at heart to gloss over any recent little friction. They performed the dizziest feats of arithmetic, soaring quite out of *my* feeble range, and perpetrated, in higher spirits than ever, geographical and historical jokes. It was conspicuous of course in Miles in particular that he appeared to wish to show how easily he could let me down. This child, to my memory, really lives in a setting of beauty and misery that no words can translate; there was a distinction all his own in every impulse he revealed; never was a small natural creature, to the uninformed eye all frankness and freedom, a more ingenious, a more extraordinary little gentleman. I had perpetually to guard against the wonder of contemplation into which my initiated view betrayed me; to check the irrelevant gaze and discouraged sigh in which I constantly both attacked and renounced the enigma of what such a little gentleman could have done that deserved a penalty. Say that, by the dark prodigy I knew, the imagination of all evil *had* been opened up to him: all the justice within me ached for the proof that it could ever have flowered into an act.

He had never at any rate been such a little gentleman as when, after our early dinner on this dreadful day, he came round to me and asked if I should n't like him for half an hour to play to me. David playing to Saul could never have shown a finer sense of the occasion.[4] It was literally a charming exhibition of tact, of magnanimity, and quite tantamount to his saying outright: "The true knights we love to read about

4. 1 Samuel 16.14–23.

never push an advantage too far. I know what you mean now: you mean that—to be let alone yourself and not followed up—you 'll cease to worry and spy upon me, won't keep me so close to you, will let me go and come. Well, I 'come,' you see—but I don't go! There 'll be plenty of time for that. I do really delight in your society and I only want to show you that I contended for a principle." It may be imagined whether I resisted this appeal or failed to accompany him again, hand in hand, to the schoolroom. He sat down at the old piano and played as he had never played; and if there are those who think he had better have been kicking a football I can only say that I wholly agree with them. For at the end of a time that under his influence I had quite ceased to measure I started up with a strange sense of having literally slept at my post. It was after luncheon, and by the schoolroom fire, and yet I had n't really in the least slept; I had only done something much worse—I had forgotten. Where all this time was Flora? When I put the question to Miles he played on a minute before answering, and then could only say: "Why, my dear, how do *I* know?"—breaking moreover into a happy laugh which immediately after, as if it were a vocal accompaniment, he prolonged into incoherent extravagant song.

I went straight to my room, but his sister was not there; then, before going downstairs, I looked into several others. As she was nowhere about she would surely be with Mrs. Grose, whom in the comfort of that theory I accordingly proceeded in quest of. I found her where I had found her the evening before, but she met my quick challenge with blank scared ignorance. She had only supposed that, after the repast, I had carried off both the children; as to which she was quite in her right, for it was the very first time I had allowed the little girl out of my sight without some special provision. Of course now indeed she might be with the maids, so that the immediate thing was to look for her without an air of alarm. This we promptly arranged between us; but when, ten minutes later and in pursuance of our arrangement, we met in the hall, it was only to report on either side that after guarded enquiries we had altogether failed to trace her. For a minute there, apart from observation, we exchanged mute alarms, and I could feel with what high interest my friend returned me all those I had from the first given her.

"She 'll be above," she presently said—"in one of the rooms you have n't searched."

"No; she 's at a distance." I had made up my mind. "She has gone out."

Mrs. Grose stared. "Without a hat?"

I naturally also looked volumes. "Is n't that woman always without one?"

"She 's with *her*?"

"She 's with *her*!" I declared. "We must find them."

My hand was on my friend's arm, but she failed for the moment, confronted with such an account of the matter, to respond to my pressure. She communed, on the contrary, where she stood, with her uneasiness. "And where 's Master Miles?"

"Oh *he 's* with Quint. They 'll be in the schoolroom."

"Lord, Miss!" My view, I was myself aware—and therefore I suppose my tone—had never yet reached so calm an assurance.

"The trick 's played," I went on; "they 've successfully worked their plan. He found the most divine little way to keep me quiet while she went off."

" 'Divine'?" Mrs. Grose bewilderedly echoed.

"Infernal then!" I almost cheerfully rejoined. "He has provided for himself as well. But come!"

She had helplessly gloomed at the upper regions. "You leave him—?"

"So long with Quint? Yes—I don't mind that now."

She always ended at these moments by getting possession of my hand, and in this manner she could at present still stay me. But after gasping an instant at my sudden resignation, "Because of your letter?" she eagerly brought out.

I quickly, by way of answer, felt for my letter, drew it forth, held it up, and then, freeing myself, went and laid it on the great hall-table. "Luke will take it," I said as I came back. I reached the house-door and opened it; I was already on the steps.

My companion still demurred: the storm of the night and the early morning had dropped, but the afternoon was damp and grey. I came down to the drive while she stood in the doorway. "You go with nothing on?"

"What do I care when the child has nothing? I can't wait to dress," I cried, "and if you must do so I leave you. Try meanwhile yourself upstairs."

"With *them*?" Oh on this the poor woman promptly joined me![5]

XIX

We went straight to the lake, as it was called at Bly, and I dare say rightly called, though it may have been a sheet of water less remarkable than my untravelled eyes supposed it. My acquaintance with sheets of water was small, and the pool of Bly, at all events on the few occasions of my consenting, under the protection of my pupils, to affront its surface in the old flat-bottomed boat moored there for our use, had impressed me both with its extent and its agitation. The usual place of embarkation was half a mile from the house, but I had an intimate conviction that, wherever Flora might be, she was not near home. She

5. Ninth weekly installment and "Part Fourth" ended here.

had not given me the slip for any small adventure, and, since the day of the very great one that I had shared with her by the pond, I had been aware, in our walks, of the quarter to which she most inclined. This was why I had now given to Mrs. Grose's steps so marked a direction—a direction making her, when she perceived it, oppose a resistance that showed me she was freshly mystified. "You 're going to the water, Miss?—you think she's *in*—?"

"She may be, though the depth is, I believe, nowhere very great. But what I judge most likely is that she 's on the spot from which, the other day, we saw together what I told you."

"When she pretended not to see—?"

"With that astounding self-possession! I 've always been sure she wanted to go back alone. And now her brother has managed it for her."

Mrs. Grose still stood where she had stopped. "You suppose they really *talk* of them?"

I could meet this with an assurance! "They say things that, if we heard them, would simply appal us."

"And if she *is* there—?"

"Yes?"

"Then Miss Jessel is?"

"Beyond a doubt. You shall see."

"Oh thank you!" my friend cried, planted so firm that, taking it in, I went straight on without her. By the time I reached the pool, however, she was close behind me, and I knew that, whatever, to her apprehension, might befall me, the exposure of sticking to me struck her as her least danger. She exhaled a moan of relief as we at last came in sight of the greater part of the water without a sight of the child. There was no trace of Flora on that nearer side of the bank where my observation of her had been most startling, and none on the opposite edge, where, save for a margin of some twenty yards, a thick copse came down to the pond. This expanse, oblong in shape, was so narrow compared to its length that, with its ends out of view, it might have been taken for a scant river. We looked at the empty stretch, and then I felt the suggestion in my friend's eyes. I knew what she meant and I replied with a negative headshake.

"No, no; wait! She has taken the boat."

My companion stared at the vacant mooring-place and then again across the lake. "Then where is it?"

"Our not seeing it is the strongest of proofs. She has used it to go over, and then has managed to hide it."

"All alone—that child?"

"She 's not alone, and at such times she 's not a child: she 's an old, old woman." I scanned all the visible shore while Mrs. Grose took again, into the queer element I offered her, one of her plunges of submission; then I pointed out that the boat might perfectly be in a small refuge formed by one of the recesses of the pool, an indentation masked, for the hither side, by a projection of the bank and by a clump of trees growing close to the water.

"But if the boat 's there, where on earth 's *she*?" my colleague anxiously asked.

"That's exactly what we must learn." And I started to walk further.

"By going all the way round?"

"Certainly, far as it is. It will take us but ten minutes, yet it 's far enough to have made the child prefer not to walk. She went straight over."

"Laws!" cried my friend again: the chain of my logic was ever too strong for her. It dragged her at my heels even now, and when we had got halfway round—a devious tiresome process, on ground much broken and by a path choked with overgrowth—I paused to give her breath. I sustained her with a grateful arm, assuring her that she might hugely help me; and this started us afresh, so that in the course of but few minutes more we reached a point from which we found the boat to be where I had supposed it. It had been intentionally left as much as possible out of sight and was tied to one of the stakes of a fence that came, just there, down to the brink and that had been an assistance to disembarking. I recognised, as I looked at the pair of short thick oars, quite safely drawn up, the prodigious character of the feat for a little girl; but I had by this time lived too long among wonders and had panted to too many livelier measures. There was a gate in the fence, through which we passed, and that brought us after a trifling interval more into the open. Then "There she is!" we both exclaimed at once.

Flora, a short way off, stood before us on the grass and smiled as if her performance had now become complete. The next thing she did, however, was to stoop straight down and pluck—quite as if it were all she was there for—a big ugly spray of withered fern. I at once felt sure she had just come out of the copse. She waited for us, not herself taking a step, and I was conscious of the rare solemnity with which we presently approached her. She smiled and smiled, and we met; but it was all done in a silence by this time flagrantly ominous. Mrs. Grose was the first to break the spell: she threw herself on her knees and, drawing the child to her breast, clasped in a long embrace the little tender yielding body. While this dumb convulsion lasted I could only watch it—which I did the more intently when I saw Flora's face peep at me over our companion's shoulder. It was serious now—the flicker had left it; but it strengthened the pang with which I at that moment envied Mrs. Grose the simplicity of *her* relation. Still, all this while, nothing more passed between us save that Flora had let her foolish fern again drop to the ground. What she and I had virtually said to each other was that pretexts were useless now. When Mrs. Grose finally got up she kept the child's hand, so that the two were still before me; and the singular reticence of our communion was even more marked in the frank look she addressed me. "I 'll be hanged," it said, "if *I 'll* speak!"

It was Flora who, gazing all over me in candid wonder, was the first. She was struck with our bareheaded aspect. "Why where are your things?"

"Where yours are, my dear!" I promptly returned.

She had already got back her gaiety and appeared to take this as an answer quite sufficient. "And where 's Miles?" she went on.

There was something in the small valour of it that quite finished me: these three words from her were, in a flash like the glitter of a drawn blade, the jostle of the cup that my hand for weeks and weeks had held high and full to the brim and that now, even before speaking, I felt overflow in a deluge. "I 'll tell you if you 'll tell *me*—" I heard myself say, then heard the tremor in which it broke.

"Well, what?"

Mrs. Grose's suspense blazed at me, but it was too late now, and I brought the thing out handsomely. "Where, my pet, is Miss Jessel?"

XX

Just as in the churchyard with Miles, the whole thing was upon us. Much as I had made of the fact that this name had never once, between us, been sounded, the quick smitten glare with which the child's face now received it fairly likened my breach of the silence to the smash of a pane of glass. It added to the interposing cry, as if to stay the blow, that Mrs. Grose at the same instant uttered over my violence—the shriek of a creature scared, or rather wounded, which, in turn, within a few seconds, was completed by a gasp of my own. I seized my colleague's arm. "She 's there, she 's there!"

Miss Jessel stood before us on the opposite bank exactly as she had stood the other time, and I remember, strangely, as the first feeling now produced in me, my thrill of joy at having brought on a proof. She was there, so I was justified; she was there, so I was neither cruel nor mad. She was there for poor scared Mrs. Grose, but she was there most for Flora; and no moment of my monstrous time was perhaps so extraordinary as that in which I consciously threw out to her—with the sense that, pale and ravenous demon as she was, she would catch and understand it—an inarticulate message of gratitude. She rose erect on the spot my friend and I had lately quitted, and there was n't in all the long reach of her desire an inch of her evil that fell short. This first vividness of vision and emotion were things of a few seconds, during which Mrs. Grose's dazed blink across to where I pointed struck me as showing that she too at last saw, just as it carried my own eyes precipitately to the child. The revelation then of the manner in which Flora was affected startled me in truth far more than it would have done to find her also merely agitated, for direct dismay was of course not what I had expected. Prepared and on her guard as our pursuit had actually made her, she would repress every betrayal; and I was therefore at once shaken by my first glimpse of the particular one for which I had not allowed. To see her, without a convulsion of her small pink face, not even feign to glance in the direction of the prodigy I announced, but only, instead of that, turn at *me* an expression of hard still gravity, an expression absolutely new and unprecedented and that appeared to read and accuse and judge me—this was a stroke that somehow converted the little girl herself into a figure portentous. I gaped at her coolness even though my certitude of her thoroughly seeing was never greater than at that instant, and then, in the immediate need to defend myself, I called her passionately to witness. "She 's there, you little unhappy thing—there, there, *there*, and you know it as well as you know me!" I had said shortly before to Mrs. Grose that she was not at these times a child, but an old, old woman, and my description of her could n't have been more strikingly confirmed than in the way in which, for all notice of this, she simply showed me, without an expressional concession or admission, a countenance of deeper and deeper, of indeed suddenly quite fixed reprobation. I was by this time—if I can put the whole thing at all together—more appalled at what I may properly call her manner than at anything else, though it was quite simultaneously that I became aware of having Mrs. Grose also, and very formidably, to reckon with. My elder companion, the next moment, at any rate, blotted out everything but her own flushed face and her loud shocked protest, a burst of high disapproval. "What a dreadful turn, to be sure, Miss! Where on earth do you see anything?"

I could only grasp her more quickly yet, for even while she spoke the hideous plain presence stood undimmed and undaunted. It had already lasted a minute, and it lasted while I continued, seizing my colleague, quite thrusting her at it and presenting her to it, to insist with my pointing hand. "You don't see her exactly as *we* see?—you mean to say you don't now—*now*? She 's as big as a blazing fire! Only look, dearest woman, *look*—!" She looked, just as I did, and gave me, with her deep groan of negation, repulsion, compassion—the mixture with her pity of her relief at her exemption—a sense, touching to me even then, that she would have backed me up if she had been able. I might well have needed that, for with this hard blow of the proof that her eyes were hopelessly sealed I felt my own situation horribly crumble, I felt—I *saw*—my livid predecessor press, from her position, on my defeat, and I took the measure, more than all, of what I should have from this instant to deal with in the astounding little attitude of Flora. Into this attitude Mrs. Grose immediately and violently entered, breaking, even while there pierced through my sense of ruin a prodigious private triumph, into breathless reassurance.

"She is n't there, little lady, and nobody 's there—and you never see nothing, my sweet! How can poor Miss Jessel—when poor Miss Jessel 's dead and buried? *We* know, don't we love?"—and she appealed, blundering in, to the child. "It 's all a mere mistake and a worry and a joke—and we 'll go home as fast as we can!"

Our companion, on this, had responded with a strange quick primness of propriety, and they were again, with Mrs. Grose on her feet, united, as it were, in shocked opposition to me. Flora continued to fix me with her small mask of disaffection, and even at that minute I prayed God to forgive me for seeming to see that, as she stood there holding tight to our friend's dress, her incomparable childish beauty had suddenly failed, had quite vanished. I 've said it already—she was literally, she was hideously hard; she had turned common and almost ugly. "I don't know what you mean. I see nobody. I see nothing. I never *have*. I think you 're cruel. I don't like you!" Then, after this deliverance, which might have been that of a vulgarly pert little girl in the street, she hugged Mrs. Grose more closely and buried in her skirts the dreadful little face. In this position she launched an almost furious wail. "Take me away, take me away—oh take me away from *her*!"

"From *me*?" I panted.

"From you—from you!" she cried.

Even Mrs. Grose looked across at me dismayed; while I had nothing to do but communicate again with the figure that, on the opposite bank, without a movement, as rigidly still as if catching, beyond the interval, our voices, was as vividly there for my disaster as it was not there for my service. The wretched child had spoken exactly as if she had got from some outside source each of her stabbing little words, and I could therefore, in the full despair of all I had to accept, but sadly shake my head at her. "If I had ever doubted all my doubt would at present have gone. I 've been living with the miserable truth, and now it has only too much closed round me. Of course I 've lost you: I 've interfered, and you 've seen, under *her* dictation"—with which I faced, over the pool again, our infernal witness—"the easy and perfect way to meet it. I 've done my best, but I 've lost you. Good-bye." For Mrs. Grose I had an imperative, an almost frantic "Go, go!" before which, in infinite distress, but mutely possessed of the little girl and clearly convinced, in spite of her blindness, that something awful had occurred and some collapse engulfed us, she retreated, by the way we had come, as fast as she could move.

Of what first happened when I was left alone I had no subsequent memory. I only knew that at the end of, I suppose, a quarter of an hour, an odorous dampness and roughness, chilling and piercing my trouble, had made me understand that I must have thrown myself, on my face, to the ground and given way to a wildness of grief. I must have lain there long and cried and wailed, for when I raised my head the day was almost done. I got up and looked a moment, through the twilight, at the grey pool and its blank haunted edge, and then I took, back to the house, my dreary and difficult course. When I reached the gate in the fence the boat, to my surprise, was gone, so that I had a fresh reflexion to make on Flora's extraordinary command of the situation. She passed that night, by the most tacit and, I should add, were not the word so grotesque a false note, the happiest of arrangements, with Mrs. Grose. I saw neither of them on my return, but on the other hand I saw, as by an ambiguous compensation, a great deal of Miles. I saw—I can use no other phrase—so much of him that it fairly measured more than it had ever measured. No evening I had passed at Bly was to have had the portentous quality of this one; in spite of which—and in spite also of the deeper depths of consternation that had opened beneath my feet—there was literally, in the ebbing actual, an extraordinarily sweet sadness. On reaching the house I had never so much as looked for the boy; I had simply gone straight to my room to change what I was wearing and to take in, at a glance, much material testimony to Flora's rupture. Her little belongings had all been removed. When later, by the schoolroom fire, I was served with tea by the usual maid, I indulged, on the article of my other pupil, in no enquiry whatever. He had his freedom now—he might have it to the end! Well, he did have it; and it consisted—in part at least—of his coming in at about eight o'clock and sitting down with me in silence. On the removal of the tea-things I had blown out the candles and drawn my chair closer: I was conscious of a mortal coldness and felt as if I should never again be warm. So when he appeared I was sitting in the glow with my thoughts. He paused a moment by the door as if to look at me; then —as if to share them—came to the other side of the hearth and sank into a chair. We sat there in absolute stillness; yet he wanted, I felt, to be with me.[6]

XXI

Before a new day, in my room, had fully broken, my eyes opened to Mrs. Grose, who had come to my bedside with worse news. Flora was so markedly feverish that an illness was perhaps at hand; she had passed a night of extreme unrest, a night agitated above all by fears that had for their subject not in the least her former but wholly her present governess. It was not against the possible re-entrance of Miss Jessel on the scene that she protested—it was conspicuously and passionately against mine. I was at once on my feet, and with an immense deal to ask; the more that my friend had discernibly now girded her loins to

6. Tenth weekly installment ended here.

meet me afresh. This I felt as soon as I had put to her the question of her sense of the child's sincerity as against my own. "She persists in denying to you that she saw, or has ever seen, anything?"

My visitor's trouble truly was great. "Ah Miss, it is n't a matter on which I can push her! Yet it is n't either, I must say, as if I much needed to. It has made her, every inch of her, quite old."

"Oh I see her perfectly from here. She resents, for all the world like some high little personage, the imputation on her truthfulness and, as it were, her respectability. 'Miss Jessel indeed—*she*!' Ah she 's 'respectable,' the chit! The impression she gave me there yesterday was, I assure you, the very strangest of all: it was quite beyond any of the others. I *did* put my foot in it! She 'll never speak to me again."

Hideous and obscure as it all was, it held Mrs. Grose briefly silent; then she granted my point with a frankness which, I made sure, had more behind it. "I think indeed, Miss, she never will. She do have a grand manner about it!"

"And that manner"—I summed it up—"is practically what 's the matter with her now."

Oh that manner, I could see in my visitor's face, and not a little else besides! "She asks me every three minutes if I think you 're coming in."

"I see—I see." I too, on my side, had so much more than worked it out. "Has she said to you since yesterday—except to repudiate her familiarity with anything so dreadful—a single other word about Miss Jessel?"

"Not one, Miss. And of course, you know," my friend added, "I took it from her by the lake that just then and there at least there *was* nobody."

"Rather! And naturally you take it from her still."

"I don't contradict her. What else can I do?"

"Nothing in the world! You 've the cleverest little person to deal with. They 've made them—their two friends, I mean—still cleverer even than nature did; for it was wondrous material to play on! Flora has now her grievance, and she'll work it to the end."

"Yes, Miss; but to *what* end?"

"Why that of dealing with me to her uncle. She 'll make me out to him the lowest creature—!"

I winced at the fair show of the scene in Mrs. Grose's face; she looked for a minute as if she sharply saw them together. "And him who thinks so well of you!"

"He has an odd way—it comes over me now," I laughed, "—of proving it! But that does n't matter. What Flora wants of course is to get rid of me."

My companion bravely concurred. "Never again to so much as look at you."

"So that what you 've come to me now for," I asked, "is to speed me on my way?" Before she had time to reply, however, I had her in check. "I 've a better idea—the result of my reflexions. My going *would* seem the right thing, and on Sunday I was terribly near it. Yet that won't do. It 's *you* who must go. You must take Flora."

My visitor, at this, did speculate. "But where in the world—?"

"Away from here. Away from *them*. Away, even most of all, now, from me. Straight to her uncle."

"Only to tell on you—?"

"No, not 'only'! To leave me, in addition, with my remedy."

She was still vague. "And what *is* your remedy?"

"Your loyalty, to begin with. And then Miles's."

She looked at me hard. "Do you think he—?"

"Won't, if he has the chance, turn on me? Yes, I venture still to think it. At all events I want to try. Get off with his sister as soon as possible and leave me with him alone." I was amazed, myself, at the spirit I had still in reserve, and therefore perhaps a trifle the more disconcerted at the way in which, in spite of this fine example of it, she hesitated. "There 's one thing, of course," I went on: "they must n't, before she goes, see each other for three seconds." Then it came over me that, in spite of Flora's presumable sequestration from the instant of her return from the pool, it might already be too late. "Do you mean," I anxiously asked, "that they *have* met?"

At this she quite flushed. "Ah, Miss, I 'm not such a fool as that! If I 've been obliged to leave her three or four times, it has been each time with one of the maids, and at present, though she 's alone, she 's locked in safe. And yet—and yet!" There were too many things.

"And yet what?"

"Well, are you so sure of the little gentleman?"

"I 'm not sure of anything but *you*. But I have, since last evening, a new hope. I think he wants to give me an opening. I do believe that—poor little exquisite wretch!—he wants to speak. Last evening, in the firelight and the silence, he sat with me for two hours as if it were just coming."

Mrs. Grose looked hard through the window at the grey gathering day. "And did it come?"

"No, though I waited and waited I confess it did n't, and it was without a breach of the silence, or so much as a faint allusion to his sister's condition and absence, that we at last kissed for goodnight. All the same," I continued, "I can't, if her uncle sees her, consent to his seeing her brother without my having given the boy—and most of all because things have got so bad—a little more time."

My friend appeared on this ground more reluctant than I could quite understand. "What do you mean by more time?"

"Well, a day or two—really to bring it out. He 'll then be on *my* side—of which you see the importance. If nothing comes I shall only fail, and you at the worst have helped me by doing on your arrival in town whatever you may have found possible." So I put it before her, but she continued for a little so lost in other reasons that I came again to her aid. "Unless indeed," I wound up, "you really want *not* to go."

I could see it, in her face, at last clear itself: she put out her hand to me as a pledge. "I 'll go—I 'll go. I 'll go this morning."

I wanted to be very just. "If you *should* wish still to wait I 'd engage she should n't see me."

"No, no: it 's the place itself. She must leave it." She held me a moment with heavy eyes, then brought out the rest. "Your idea 's the right one. I myself, Miss—"

"Well?"

"I can't stay."

The look she gave me with it made me jump at possibilities. "You mean that, since yesterday, you *have* seen—?"

She shook her head with dignity. "I 've *heard*—!"

"Heard?"

"From that child—horrors! There!" she sighed with tragic relief. "On my honour, Miss, she says things—!" But at this evocation she broke down; she dropped with a sudden cry upon my sofa and, as I had seen her do before, gave way to all the anguish of it.

It was quite in another manner that I for my part let myself go. "Oh thank God!"

She sprang up again at this, drying her eyes with a groan. " 'Thank God'?"

"It so justifies me!"

"It does that, Miss!"

I could n't have desired more emphasis, but I just waited "She 's so horrible?"

I saw my colleague scarce knew how to put it. "Really shocking."

"And about me?"

"About you, Miss—since you must have it. It 's beyond everything, for a young lady; and I can't think wherever she must have picked up—"

"The appalling language she applies to me? I can then!" I broke in with a laugh that was doubtless significant enough.

It only in truth left my friend still more grave. "Well, perhaps I ought to also—since I 've heard some of it before! Yet I can't bear it," the poor woman went on while with the same movement she glanced, on my dressing-table, at the face of my watch. "But I must go back."

I kept her, however. "Ah if you can't bear it—!"

"How can I stop[7] with her, you mean? Why just *for* that: to get her away. Far from this," she pursued, "far from *them*—"

"She may be different? she may be free?" I seized her almost with joy. "Then in spite of yesterday you *believe*—"

"In such doings?" Her simple description of them required, in the light of her expression, to be carried no further, and she gave me the whole thing as she had never done. "I believe."

Yes, it was a joy, and we were still shoulder to shoulder: if I might continue sure of that I should care but little what else happened. My support in the presence of disaster would be the same as it had been in my early need of confidence, and if my friend would answer for my honesty I would answer for all the rest. On the point of taking leave of her, none the less, I was to some extent embarrassed. "There 's one thing of course—it occurs to me—to remember. My letter giving the alarm will have reached town before you."

I now felt still more how she had been beating about the bush and how weary at last it had made her. "Your letter won't have got there. Your letter never went."

"What then became of it?"

"Goodness knows! Master Miles—"

"Do you mean *he* took it?" I gasped.

She hung fire, but she overcame her reluctance. "I mean that I saw yesterday, when I came back with Miss Flora, that it was n't where you had put it. Later in the evening I had the chance to question Luke, and he declared that he had neither noticed nor touched it." We could only exchange, on this, one of our deeper mutual soundings, and it was Mrs. Grose who first brought up the plumb with an almost elate "You see!"

"Yes, I see that if Miles took it instead he probably will have read it and destroyed it."

"And don't you see anything else?"

I faced her a moment with a sad smile. "It strikes me that by this time your eyes are open even wider than mine."

They proved to be so indeed, but she could still almost blush to show it. "I make out now what he must have done at school." And she gave, in her simple sharpness, an almost droll disillusioned nod. "He stole!"

I turned it over—I tried to be more judicial. "Well—perhaps."

She looked as if she found me unexpectedly calm. "He stole *letters*!"

She could n't know my reasons for a calmness after all pretty shallow; so I showed them off as I might. "I hope then it was to more purpose than in this case! The note, at all events, that I put on the table yesterday," I pursued, "will have given him so scant an advantage—for it contained only the bare demand for an interview—that he 's already

7. Stay.

much ashamed of having gone so far for so little, and that what he had on his mind last evening was precisely the need of confession." I seemed to myself for the instant to have mastered it, to see it all. "Leave us, leave us"—I was already, at the door, hurrying her off. "I 'll get it out of him. He 'll meet me. He 'll confess. If he confesses he 's saved. And if he 's saved—"

"Then *you* are?" The dear woman kissed me on this, and I took her farewell. "I 'll save you without him!" she cried as she went.

XXII

Yet it was when she had got off—and I missed her on the spot—that the great pinch really came. If I had counted on what it would give me to find myself alone with Miles I quickly recognised that it would give me at least a measure. No hour of my stay in fact was so assailed with apprehensions as that of my coming down to learn that the carriage containing Mrs. Grose and my younger pupil had already rolled out of the gates. Now I *was*, I said to myself, face to face with the elements, and for much of the rest of the day, while I fought my weakness, I could consider that I had been supremely rash. It was a tighter place still than I had yet turned round in; all the more that, for the first time, I could see in the aspect of others a confused reflexion of the crisis. What had happened naturally caused them all to stare; there was too little of the explained, throw out whatever we might, in the suddenness of my colleague's act. The maids and the men looked blank; the effect of which on my nerves was an aggravation until I saw the necessity of making it a positive aid. It was in short by just clutching the helm that I avoided total wreck; and I dare say that, to bear up at all, I became that morning very grand and very dry. I welcomed the consciousness that I was charged with much to do, and I caused it to be known as well that, left thus to myself, I was quite remarkably firm. I wandered with that manner, for the next hour or two, all over the place and looked, I have no doubt, as if I were ready for any onset. So, for the benefit of whom it might concern, I paraded with a sick heart.

The person it appeared least to concern proved to be, till dinner, little Miles himself. My perambulations had given me meanwhile no glimpse of him, but they had tended to make more public the change taking place in our relation as a consequence of his having at the piano, the day before, kept me, in Flora's interest, so beguiled and befooled. The stamp of publicity had of course been fully given by her confinement and departure, and the change itself was now ushered in by our non-observance of the regular custom of the schoolroom. He had already disappeared when, on my way down, I pushed open his door, and I learned below that he had breakfasted—in the presence of a couple of the maids—with Mrs. Grose and his sister. He had then gone out, as he said, for a stroll; than which nothing, I reflected, could better have expressed his frank view of the abrupt transformation of my office. What he would now permit this office to consist of was yet to be settled: there was at the least a queer relief—I mean for myself in especial—in the renouncement of one pretension. If so much had sprung to the surface I scarce put it too strongly in saying that what had perhaps sprung highest was the absurdity of our prolonging the fiction that I had anything more to teach him. It sufficiently stuck out that, by tacit little tricks in which even more than myself he carried out the care for my dignity, I had had to appeal to him to let me off straining to meet him on the ground of his true capacity. He had at any rate his freedom now; I was never to touch it again: as I had amply shown, moreover, when, on his joining me in the schoolroom the previous night, I uttered, in reference to the interval just concluded, neither challenge nor hint. I had too much, from this moment, my other ideas. Yet when he at last arrived the difficulty of applying them, the accumulations of my problem, were brought straight home to me by the beautiful little presence on which what had occurred had as yet, for the eye, dropped neither stain nor shadow.

To mark, for the house, the high state I cultivated I decreed that my meals with the boy should be served, as we called it, downstairs; so that I had been awaiting him in the ponderous pomp of the room outside the window of which I had had from Mrs. Grose, that first scared Sunday, my flash of something it would scarce have done to call light. Here at present I felt afresh—for I had felt it again and again—how my equilibrium depended on the success of my rigid will, the will to shut my eyes as tight as possible to the truth that what I had to deal with was, revoltingly, against nature. I could only get on at all by taking "nature" into my confidence and my account, by treating my monstrous ordeal as a push in a direction unusual, of course, and unpleasant, but demanding after all, for a fair front, only another turn of the screw of ordinary human virtue. No attempt, none the less, could well require more tact than just this attempt to supply, one's self, *all* the nature. How could I put even a little of that article into a suppression of reference to what had occurred? How on the other hand could I make a reference without a new plunge into the hideous obscure? Well, a sort of answer, after a time, had come to me, and it was so far confirmed as that I was met, incontestably, by the quickened vision of what was rare in my little companion. It was indeed as if he had found even now—as he had so often found at lessons—still some other delicate way to ease me off. Was n't there light in the fact which, as we shared our solitude, broke out with a specious glitter it had never yet quite worn?—the fact that (opportunity aiding, precious opportunity which had now come) it would be preposterous, with a child so endowed, to forego the help one might wrest from absolute intelligence? What had his intelligence been given him for but to save him? Might n't one, to reach his mind, risk the stretch of a stiff arm across his character? It was as if, when we were face to face in the dining-room, he had literally shown me the way. The roast mutton was on the table and I had dispensed with attendance. Miles, before he sat down, stood a moment with his hands in his pockets and looked at the joint, on which he seemed on the point of passing some humorous judgement. But what he presently produced was: "I say, my dear, is she really very awfully ill?"

"Little Flora? Not so bad but that she 'll presently be better. London will set her up. Bly had ceased to agree with her. Come here and take your mutton."

He alertly obeyed me, carried the plate carefully to his seat and, when he was established, went on. "Did Bly disagree with her so terribly all at once?"

"Not so suddenly as you might think. One had seen it coming on."

"Then why did n't you get her off before?"

"Before what?"

"Before she became too ill to travel."

I found myself prompt. "She 's *not too* ill to travel; she only might have become so if she had stayed. This was just the moment to seize. The journey will dissipate the influence"—oh I was grand!—"and carry it off."

"I see, I see"—Miles, for that matter, was grand too. He settled to his repast with the charming little "table manner" that, from the day of his arrival, had relieved me of all grossness of admonition. Whatever he had been expelled from school for, it was n't for ugly feeding. He was irreproachable, as always, today; but was unmistakably more conscious. He was discernibly trying to take for granted more things than he found, without assistance, quite easy; and he dropped into peaceful silence while he felt his situation. Our meal was of the briefest—mine a vain pretence, and I had the things immediately removed. While this was done Miles stood again with his hands in his little pockets and his back to me—stood and looked out of the wide window through which, that other day, I had seen what pulled me up. We continued silent while the maid was with us—as silent, it whimsically occurred to me, as some young couple who, on their wedding-journey, at the inn, feel shy in the presence of the waiter. He turned round only when the waiter had left us. "Well—so we 're alone!"[8]

XXIII

"Oh more or less." I imagine my smile was pale. "Not absolutely. We should n't like that!" I went on.

"No—I suppose we should n't. Of course we 've the others."

8. Eleventh weekly installment ended here.

"We 've the others—we 've indeed the others," I concurred.

"Yet even though we have them," he returned, still with his hands in his pockets and planted there in front of me, "they don't much count, do they?"

I made the best of it, but I felt wan. "It depends on what you call 'much'!"

"Yes"—with all accommodation—"everything depends!" On this, however, he faced to the window again and presently reached it with his vague restless cogitating step. He remained there a while with his forehead against the glass, in contemplation of the stupid shrubs I knew and the dull things of November. I had always my hypocrisy of "work," behind which I now gained the sofa. Steadying myself with it there as I had repeatedly done at those moments of torment that I have described as the moments of my knowing the children to be given to something from which I was barred, I sufficiently obeyed my habit of being prepared for the worst. But an extraordinary impression dropped on me as I extracted a meaning from the boy's embarrassed back—none other than the impression that I was not barred now. This inference grew in a few minutes to sharp intensity and seemed bound up with the direct perception that it was positively *he* who was. The frames and squares of the great window were a kind of image, for him, of a kind of failure. I felt that I saw him, in any case, shut in or shut out. He was admirable but not comfortable: I took it in with a throb of hope. Was n't he looking through the haunted pane for something he could n't see?—and was n't it the first time in the whole business that he had known such a lapse? The first, the very first: I found it a splendid portent. It made him anxious, though he watched himself; he had been anxious all day and, even while in his usual sweet little manner he sat at table, had needed all his small strange genius to give it a gloss. When he at last turned round to meet me it was almost as if this genius had succumbed. "Well, I think I 'm glad Bly agrees with *me*!"

"You 'd certainly seem to have seen, these twenty-four hours, a good deal more of it than some time before. I hope," I went on bravely, "that you've been enjoying yourself."

"Oh yes, I 've been ever so far; all round about—miles and miles away. I 've never been so free."

He had really a manner of his own, and I could only try to keep up with him. "Well, do you like it?"

He stood there smiling; then at last he put into two words—"Do *you*?"—more discrimination than I had ever heard two words contain. Before I had time to deal with that, however, he continued as if with the sense that this was an impertinence to be softened. "Nothing could be more charming than the way you take it, for of course, if we 're alone together now it 's you that are alone most. But I hope," he threw in, "you don't particularly mind!"

"Having to do with you?" I asked. "My dear child, how can I help minding? Though I 've renounced all claim to your company—you 're so beyond me—I at least greatly enjoy it. What else should I stay on for?"

He looked at me more directly, and the expression of his face, graver now, struck me as the most beautiful I had ever found in it. "You stay on just for *that*?"

"Certainly. I stay on as your friend and from the tremendous interest I take in you till something can be done for you that may be more worth your while. That need n't surprise you." My voice trembled so that I felt it impossible to suppress the shake. "Don't you remember how I told you, when I came and sat on your bed the night of the storm, that there was nothing in the world I would n't do for you?"

"Yes, yes!" He, on his side, more and more visibly nervous, had a tone to master; but he was so much more successful than I that, laughing out through his gravity, he could pretend we were pleasantly jesting. "Only that, I think, was to get me to do something for *you*!"

"It was partly to get you to do something," I conceded. "But, you know, you did n't do it."

"Oh yes," he said with the brightest superficial eagerness, "you wanted me to tell you something."

"That 's it. Out, straight out. What you have on your mind, you know."

"Ah then is *that* what you 've stayed over for?"

He spoke with a gaiety through which I could still catch the finest little quiver of resentful passion; but I can't begin to express the effect upon me of an implication of surrender even so faint. It was as if what I had yearned for had come at last only to astonish me. "Well, yes—I may as well make a clean breast of it. It was precisely for that."

He waited so long that I supposed it for the purpose of repudiating the assumption on which my action had been founded; but what he finally said was: "Do you mean now—here?"

"There could n't be a better place or time." He looked round him uneasily, and I had the rare—oh the queer!—impression of the very first symptom I had seen in him of the approach of immediate fear. It was as if he were suddenly afraid of me—which struck me indeed as perhaps the best thing to make him. Yet in the very pang of the effort I felt it vain to try sternness, and I heard myself the next instant so gentle as to be almost grotesque. "You want so to go out again?"

"Awfully!" He smiled at me heroically, and the touching little bravery of it was enhanced by his actually flushing with pain. He had picked up his hat, which he had brought in, and stood twirling it in a way that gave me, even as I was just nearly reaching port, a perverse horror of what I was doing. To do it in *any* way was an act of violence, for what did it consist of but the obtrusion of the idea of grossness and guilt on a small helpless creature who had been for me a revelation of the possibilities of beautiful intercourse? Was n't it base to create for a being so exquisite a mere alien awkwardness? I suppose I now read into our situation a clearness it could n't have had at the time, for I seem to see our poor eyes already lighted with some spark of a prevision of the anguish that was to come. So we circled about with terrors and scruples, fighters not daring to close. But it was for each other we feared! That kept us a little longer suspended and unbruised. "I 'll tell you everything," Miles said—"I mean I 'll tell you anything you like. You 'll stay on with me, and we shall both be all right, and I *will* tell you—I *will*. But not now."

"Why not now?"

My insistence turned him from me and kept him once more at his window in a silence during which, between us, you might have heard a pin drop. Then he was before me again with the air of a person for whom, outside, some one who had frankly to be reckoned with was waiting. "I have to see Luke."

I had not yet reduced him to quite so vulgar a lie, and I felt proportionately ashamed. But, horrible as it was, his lies made up my truth. I achieved thoughtfully a few loops of my knitting. "Well then go to Luke, and I 'll wait for what you promise. Only in return for that satisfy, before you leave me, one very much smaller request."

He looked as if he felt he had succeeded enough to be able still a little to bargain. "Very much smaller—?"

"Yes, a mere fraction of the whole. Tell me"—oh my work preoccupied me, and I was off-hand!—"if, yesterday afternoon, from the table in the hall, you took, you know, my letter."

XXIV

My grasp of how he received this suffered for a minute from something that I can describe only as a fierce split of my attention—a stroke that at first, as I sprang straight up, reduced me to the mere blind movement of getting hold of him, drawing him close and, while I just fell for support against the nearest piece of furniture, instinctively keeping him with his back to the window. The appearance was full upon us that I had already had to deal with here: Peter Quint had come into view like a sentinel before a prison. The next thing I saw was that, from outside, he had reached the window, and then I knew that, close to the glass and glaring in through it, he offered once more to the room his white face of damnation. It represents but grossly what took place within me at the sight to say that on the second my decision was made; yet I believe that no woman so overwhelmed ever in so short a time recovered her command of the *act*. It came to me in the very horror of the immediate presence that the act would be, seeing and facing what I saw and faced, to keep the boy himself unaware. The inspiration—I can call it by no other name—was that I felt how voluntarily, how transcendently, I *might*. It was like fighting with a demon for a human soul, and when I had fairly so appraised it I saw how the human soul—held out, in the tremor of my hands, at arms' length—had a perfect dew of sweat on a lovely childish forehead. The face that was close to mine was as white as the face against the glass, and out of it presently came a sound, not low nor weak, but as if from much further away, that I drank like a waft of fragrance.

"Yes—I took it."

At this, with a moan of joy, I enfolded, I drew him close; and while I held him to my breast, where I could feel in the sudden fever of his little body the tremendous pulse of his little heart, I kept my eyes on the thing at the window and saw it move and shift its posture. I have likened it to a sentinel, but its slow wheel, for a moment, was rather the prowl of a baffled beast. My present quickened courage, however, was such that, not too much to let it through, I had to shade, as it were, my flame. Meanwhile the glare of the face was again at the window, the scoundrel fixed as if to watch and wait. It was the very confidence that I might now defy him, as well as the positive certitude, by this time, of the child's unconsciousness, that made me go on. "What did you take it for?"

"To see what you said about me."

"You opened the letter?"

"I opened it."

My eyes were now, as I held him off a little again, on Miles's own face, in which the collapse of mockery showed me how complete was the ravage of uneasiness. What was prodigious was that at last, by my success, his sense was sealed and his communication stopped: he knew that he was in presence, but knew not of what, and knew still less that I also was and that I did know. And what did this strain of trouble matter when my eyes went back to the window only to see that the air was clear again and—by my personal triumph—the influence quenched? There was nothing there. I felt that the cause was mine and that I should surely get *all*. "And you found nothing!"—I let my elation out.

He gave the most mournful, thoughtful little headshake. "Nothing."

"Nothing, nothing!" I almost shouted in my joy.

"Nothing, nothing," he sadly repeated.

I kissed his forehead; it was drenched. "So what have you done with it?"

"I 've burnt it."

"Burnt it?" It was now or never. "Is that what you did at school?"

Oh what this brought up! "At school?"

"Did you take letters?—or other things?"

"Other things?" He appeared now to be thinking of something far off and that reached him only through the pressure of his anxiety. Yet it did reach him. "Did I *steal*?"

I felt myself redden to the roots of my hair as well as wonder if it were more strange to put to a gentleman such a question or to see him take it with allowances that gave the very distance of his fall in the world. "Was it for that you might n't go back?"

The only thing he felt was rather a dreary little surprise. "Did you know I might n't go back?"

"I know everything."

He gave me at this the longest and strangest look. "Everything?"

"Everything. Therefore *did* you—?" But I could n't say it again.

Miles could, very simply. "No. I did n't steal."

My face must have shown him I believed him utterly; yet my hands—but it was for pure tenderness—shook him as if to ask him why, if it was all for nothing, he had condemned me to months of torment. "What then did you do?"

He looked in vague pain all round the top of the room and drew his breath, two or three times over, as if with difficulty. He might have been standing at the bottom of the sea and raising his eyes to some faint green twilight. "Well—I said things."

"Only that?"

"They thought it was enough!"

"To turn you out for?"

Never, truly, had a person "turned out" shown so little to explain it as this little person! He appeared to weigh my question, but in a manner quite detached and almost helpless. "Well, I suppose I ought n't."

"But to whom did you say them?"

He evidently tried to remember, but it dropped—he had lost it. "I don't know!"

He almost smiled at me in the desolation of his surrender, which was indeed practically, by this time, so complete that I ought to have left it there. But I was infatuated—I was blind with victory, though even then the very effect that was to have brought him so much nearer was already that of added separation. "Was it to every one?" I asked.

"No; it was only to—" But he gave a sick little headshake. "I don't remember their names."

"Were they then so many?"

"No—only a few. Those I liked."

Those he liked? I seemed to float not into clearness, but into a darker obscure, and within a minute there had come to me out of my very pity the appalling alarm of his being perhaps innocent. It was for the instant confounding and bottomless, for if he *were* innocent what then on earth was I? Paralysed, while it lasted, by the mere brush of the question, I let him go a little, so that, with a deep-drawn sigh, he turned away from me again; which, as he faced toward the clear window, I suffered, feeling that I had nothing now there to keep him from. "And did they repeat what you said?" I went on after a moment.

He was soon at some distance from me, still breathing hard and again with the air, though now without anger for it, of being confined against his will. Once more, as he had done before, he looked up at the dim day as if, of what had hitherto sustained him, nothing was left but an unspeakable anxiety. "Oh yes," he nevertheless replied—"they must have repeated them. To those *they* liked," he added.

There was somehow less of it than I had expected; but I turned it over. "And these things came round—?"

"To the masters? Oh yes!" he answered very simply. "But I did n't know they 'd tell."

"The masters? They did n't—they 've never told. That 's why I ask you."

He turned to me again his little beautiful fevered face. "Yes, it was too bad."

"Too bad?"

"What I suppose I sometimes said. To write home."

I can't name the exquisite pathos of the contradiction given to such a speech by such a speaker; I only know that the next instant I heard myself throw off with homely force: "Stuff and nonsense!" But the next after that I must have sounded stern enough. "What *were* these things?"

My sternness was all for his judge, his executioner; yet it made him avert himself again, and that movement made *me*, with a single bound and an irrepressible cry, spring straight upon him. For there again, against the glass, as if to blight his confession and stay his answer, was the hideous author of our woe—the white face of damnation. I felt a sick swim at the drop of my victory and all the return of my battle, so that the wildness of my veritable leap only served as a great betrayal. I saw him, from the midst of my act, meet it with a divination, and on the perception that even now he only guessed, and that the window was still to his own eyes free, I let the impulse flame up to convert the climax of his dismay into the very proof of his liberation. "No more, no more, no more!" I shrieked to my visitant as I tried to press him against me.

"Is she *here*?" Miles panted as he caught with his sealed eyes the direction of my words. Then as his strange "she" staggered me and, with a gasp, I echoed it, "Miss Jessel, Miss Jessel!" he with sudden fury gave me back.

I seized, stupefied, his supposition—some sequel to what we had done to Flora, but this made me only want to show him that it was better still than that. "It 's not Miss Jessel! But it 's at the window—straight before us. It 's *there*—the coward horror, there for the last time!"

At this, after a second in which his head made the movement of a baffled dog's on a scent and then gave a frantic little shake for air and light, he was at me in a white rage, bewildered, glaring vainly over the place and missing wholly, though it now, to my sense, filled the room like the taste of poison, the wide overwhelming presence. "It 's *he*?"

I was so determined to have all my proof that I flashed into ice to challenge him. "Whom do you mean by 'he'?"

"Peter Quint—you devil!" His face gave again, round the room, its convulsed supplication. "*Where?*"

They are in my ears still, his supreme surrender of the name and his tribute to my devotion. "What does he matter now, my own?—what will he *ever* matter? I have you," I launched at the beast, "but he has lost you for ever!" Then for the demonstration of my work, "There, *there*!" I said to Miles.

But he had already jerked straight round, stared, glared again, and seen but the quiet day. With the stroke of the loss I was so proud of he uttered the cry of a creature hurled over an abyss, and the grasp with which I recovered him might have been that of catching him in his fall. I caught him, yes, I held him—it may be imagined with what a passion; but at the end of a minute I began to feel what it truly was that I held. We were alone with the quiet day, and his little heart, dispossessed, had stopped.[9]

9. Last weekly installment and "Part Fifth" ended here.

The Text

Textual History

During Henry James's life, *The Turn of the Screw* was published in five authorized forms: as a serial in *Collier's Weekly* early in 1898, as the first of two tales in separate English and American books in October 1898, as the second of four tales in a volume of the New York Edition in 1908 (see Textual Notes, below), and as the first volume of *The Uniform Tales of Henry James* published by Martin Secker in London, April 1915, but on the "distinct understanding, please, that he conform *literatim* and punctuation to [the New York Edition] text. It is vital that he adhere to that authentic punctuation—to the last comma or rather, more essentially, no-comma."[1] Collation indicates that Secker did adhere, for the few variants are clearly accidental. As a result this last volume will not be considered here or in the Textual Notes which follow.

James's composition of the tale fell between two major publications—*What Maisie Knew*, which was serialized in *The Chap Book* from January 15 to August 1, 1897, and *In the Cage*, which was begun early in 1898 after James moved from London to Lamb House in Rye, and which appeared in August. After finishing *Maisie* (there is evidence that he was still at work on it during the summer), he wrote the short *John Delavoy*, which was printed in November 1897, in America (but was not published until 1898), thus leaving the fall of 1897 open for work on *The Turn of the Screw*.

October and November are the logical months because as late as September 25, James wrote to A. C. Benson without mentioning the tale, yet in the spring of 1898 he wrote Benson (see below, pp. 113–14) that the "germ" of the narrative was based on a story told to James by Benson's father (see Notebook entry of January 1895, below, p. 112) and that he had written the tale in the fall of 1897.[2] If James had started the story in September he surely would have acknowledged the source in the first letter. By October 28, 1897, however, when James contracted with Blackwood's to write his *William Whetmore Story and His Friends* he said that he was too busy to undertake it at present. The only other James items of this time

1. Unpublished letter, Henry James to his agent J. B. Pinker, September 11, 1914, in the Yale University Library. Quoted by Leon Edel and Dan H. Laurence, *A Bibliography of Henry James* (London: Rupert Hart-Davis, second edition, revised, 1961), p. 155. (The editors are indebted to this volume for many of the facts which follow.)
2. In December 1897, James mentioned that fall had been lingering since mid-October, and in December 1898, he said that for the past several years summer had been extending itself right through September.

are a very few short notes and essays; thus, in all probability he was then at work on *The Turn of the Screw.*

By the end of November he had finished, for on December 1 he wrote to his sister-in-law (see letter to Alice James, pp. 112–13) that he had not answered her last letter because for a "long time" he had been hard at work on "my little book" which "I *have*, at last, finished." Even though he went on to say that he was ready to start another book, this present reference must be to *The Turn of the Screw*; the editors at *Collier's* had to have time to plan and set the illustrated serial version, and James took time amid his preparations for his move to the country after Christmas to revise a typescript of the serial version as the basis for separate book publication by Heinemann in England. On January 27, 1898, the first installment of the serial appeared in America, and an edition of *The Turn of the Screw* was deposited in the British Museum for purposes of copyright in England, but was, in fact, never published. The plates for pages 3–169 of this edition which contain the entire tale were used, however, in the first English edition of *The Two Magics*, the only difference being that the words "THE END" were removed from page 169 when another story, *Covering End*, was added in the spring of 1898 to complete the book. Because of the finished nature of this January deposit copy,[3] and because James made no changes in the text of *The Turn of the Screw* before the October publication of *The Two Magics*, his preparation of the story for Heinemann (and Macmillan, see below) must have been completed in December.

No one can ever say with any assurance why and when James ever wrote a story. As his Notebooks show, he mulled over "germs" or ideas for various periods of time, long and short, some coming into fruition, singly or variously grafted, and some remaining dormant. In this case, the Contexts section shows that James had always been interested in the ghost story and that in January 1895, in the aftermath of his retreat from the theater and return to fiction, he recorded the "germ" of *The Turn of the Screw*, but there are no indications that he played with the idea in any way before the fall of 1897, at which time James was approached for a story by Robert Collier who had left college in June to join his father on *Collier's Weekly*. On the one hand, Collier wanted to raise the tone of this popular magazine and sought out Henry James who was beginning to be thought of as a writer of more importance than merely "the author of *Daisy Miller*"; on the other hand, James knew the level of the audience of *Collier's* (he had been negotiating the year before with Clement King Shorter to do a "thrilling" love story for the popular *London Illustrated News* and could well have turned to his Notebook for a sensational idea, here the ghost-story told to him by Archbishop Benson.

No manuscript of the story exists, for by 1897 James was regularly dictating to a typist, this time to a Scotsman (see below, pp. 157–58), and few

3. Because the description of this edition by Edel and Laurence (see note 1, above) does not agree with the deposit copy that Robert Kimbrough examined, perhaps a fuller description of this copy is in order: pp. ii + 169 + 7 [blank]: contents: [i-ii], half-title: The Turn of the Screw, verso blank: [1–2], title page all in black: The Turn of / The Screw / By Henry James / [acorn design, as on title page of *The Two Magics*] / London: William Heinemann / *All rights reserved* MDCCCXCVIII, verso blank: [3]–169, corrected pages; [170–176], all blank.

publishers then bothered to keep typescript "copy." Nevertheless, the consistency of American spelling in the first three editions affords sufficient evidence to allow the assertion that all three are based primarily on the same typescript, the one which he sent to Collier. When he mailed it off, James retained a copy which he revised slightly for his book publishers, then had identical copies made, for the first English and American editions differ only with regard to a few commas and in hyphenation practice even though they were set separately (transatlantic distribution was expressly forbidden). Thus, technically, we have three editions in 1898, but only two versions. Then, because the New York Edition has behind it probably a corrected copy of the English edition (hyphenation affords the only evidence), the same typescript may be said to lie behind all three of the major versions. Nowhere along the line did James rewrite or recast whole passages or chapters.

Even though there is a consistency of thrust running through the three versions (all texts follow the same chapter divisions), there are clear differences among the three. The periodical version, in addition to being divided into a frame and twenty-four chapters, has twelve installments and five "Parts." In the *Two Magics* version, these parts are removed, small inconsistencies are cleared up, an early naming of Miss Jessel is suppressed, the ending of one chapter is deleted, the atmosphere of suspense is heightened, Flora's age is raised, and more focus is placed on the governess. But the major revisions appear in the 1908 New York version. Here James seemed intent on shifting the center of attention away from the details of action observed by the governess to the reactions felt by the governess. By removing commas (see the letter quoted above) he came closer to approximating the stream of her consciousness. By increasing the use of the possessive pronoun "my" and by replacing verbs of perception and thought with those of feeling and intuition (see book by Cranfill and Clark, below in Bibliography), James draws us intimately into the course of her narrative. The effect is more vital and vivid than that created by either of the earlier versions. For both textual and aesthetic reasons, the text of the New York Edition was chosen as the copy text of the present Norton Critical Edition.

Textual Notes

The following records mostly various major changes which James made in wording, but some variant spelling and punctuation have been recorded in order to support conclusions given above in the note on Textual History. Words in boldface give the reading of the Norton–New York Edition text for which variants from earlier editions are given. Ellipses are used in readings of any length taken from the present text. The numbers preceding an entry give the page and line numbers of the Norton text from which the reading is taken. Variant readings are given in regular type below a boldface entry, and each separate reading is preceded by an italicized capital letter identifying the text. The letters and the texts for which they stand are as follows:

P the periodical text published in twelve installments in *Collier's Weekly*, from vol. XX, no. 17 (January 27, 1898) to vol. XXI, no. 2 (April 16, 1898).
E the first English edition published by William Heinemann in *The Two Magics: The Turn of the Screw* [and] *Covering End*, October 5, 1898.
A the first American edition published by The Macmillan Company, *The Two Magics*, in October 1898 (probably also on the 5th).
N *The Novels and Tales of Henry James*, New York Edition, vol. XII (*The Aspern Papers*; *The Turn of the Screw*; *The Liar*; *The Two Faces*), published in New York by Charles Scribner's Sons and issued in London by Macmillan and Company in 1908.

The texts following an entry are given in the chronological order of their revision. Texts not referred to in a given entry—and not noted earlier as lacking the passage in question—agree with the New York Edition reading. Editorial comment on variants is given in italic type, and emendations in the New York Edition have been marked with an asterisk. Occasionally words common to variant readings have been added at the beginning or end of an entry to help identify the variant.

1.1 The story
P between the title and the first line PART FIRST
1.4 note it as
P remark that it was
E A say that it was
1.11 shocked
P E A shaken
1.22 been concerned with
P E A involved
1.24 two children
P E A they
1.27 this converser
P E A his interlocutor
2.34 summer. I
N omits the period which all texts have
4.9 night of the fourth
P night—it was almost the whole!—of the fourth
4.31 figured
P E A conceived
4.37 his
P E A their
5.21 quite
P both
5.32 "Pardon
P E A "Excuse
6.23–25 The whole thing took indeed more nights than one, but on the first occasion the same lady
P Then the same lady
6.29 author's hand
P first installment ends here
6.33 all my doubts bristle
P E A myself doubtful
6.40–7.1 took a flight
P E A encountered a reprieve
7.18–19 affected me on the spot as a creature too charming not to make it a great fortune
P E A appeared to me on the spot a creature so charming as to make it a great fortune
7.21–22 had n't made more of a point to me of this.
P E A had not told me more of her.
7.27–28 wonderful appeal
P E A extraordinary charm
7.32 that of her being so inordinately
P E A the clear circumstance of her being so
7.33 felt
P E A perceived
8.30 it was already conveyed between us, too grossly
Omitted from P E and A
9.5–8 I forthwith wanted ° ° ° Mrs. Grose assented
P E A I expressed that the proper, as well as the pleasant and friendly thing would be therefore that on the arrival of the public conveyance I should be in waiting for him with his little sister; an idea

in which Mrs. Grose concurred *no comma after* proper *in E and A*

9.17–18 Regular lessons, in this agitation, certainly suffered some wrong;

P E A Lessons, in this agitation, certainly suffered some delay;

9.31–32 to my present older and more informed eyes it would show a very reduced importance.

P E A to my older and more informed eyes it would now appear sufficiently contracted.

10.5 to a change of note

P E A in keen apprehension

10.34 the

P E A my

12.4 apprehension of ridicule.

P danger of absurdity.

12.7 she was also young and pretty—

P Oh, Miss Jessel—that was her name—was also young and pretty;

13.2 my work."

P second installment ends here

14.15 weeks

P a considerable time,

14.30–31 fenced about and ordered and arranged,

P inclosed and protected

E A enclosed and protected,

15.4 yielded.

P E A responded.

16.41–42 it was intense to me that

P E A I had the sharpest sense that, *comma only in P*

16.44 crenellations

P E A crenelations

17.2 I knew.

P third installment and first part end here

17.3 It was not

P between the running title and the roman numeral PART SECOND

18.9 monstrous.

P E A gross.

18.20–21 through nothing could I so like it [*my work*] as through feeling that to throw myself into it was to throw myself out of my trouble.

P nothing so made me like it as precisely to feel that I could throw myself into it in trouble.

E A through nothing could I so like it as through feeling that I could throw myself into it in trouble.

19.5 nothing to call even an infinitesimal

P E A no

19.6 scant enough "antecedents,"

P no long one,

E A a scant one

19.12–13 trace, should have felt the wound and the dishonour.

P E A trace.

19.13 could reconstitute

P E A found

20.27 to-day

A today

24.8–9 express the wonder of it. "Yes. Mr. Quint's dead."

P articulate the wonder of it. "Yes. Yes. Quint is dead."

E A utter the wonder of it. "Yes. Mr. Quint is dead."

24.9 Mr. Quint's dead."

P fourth installment ends here

24.19 the schoolroom

P Mrs. Grose's room

24.35 stiff an agreement.

P E A comprising a contact.

25.22 the rest of the household.

P E A companions.

25.29 way. They 've never alluded to it."

P E A way." *omit the rest*

26.4 scullions,

P the kitchen,

26.9 the schoolroom

P my

26.19 informant.

P E A interlocutress.

27.31 engaged affection.

P E A committed heart.

27.36 tension

P E A excitement

27.39–40 proofs. Proofs, and say, yes—from the moment I really took hold.

P facts. Facts and say, yes—from the moment I really read them.

27.45 a certain ingenuity of

P E A an occasional excess of the

28.19 amid these elements,

P amid these circumstances

E A in these circumstances

28.35–36 an alien object in view—a figure

P a third person in view—a person

29.34 articulate

P produce it

29.38 eight
P six
30.37 understand."
P E A understand you."
31.8 was?"
P was!"
31.34 disclosure.
P admission.
32.14–15 now in my friend's own eyes Miss Jessel had again appeared.
P Miss Jessel had again appeared in my friend's remembering eyes.
32.34 They 're lost!"
P fifth installment and second part end here
32.35 What I had said
P between the running title and the roman numeral PART THIRD
33.1 had another talk in my room; when
P had, in the schoolroom, another talk, and then she
33.3 I found that to keep her thoroughly in the grip of this
P To hold her perfectly in the pinch of this, I found,
E To hold her perfectly in the pinch of that, I found,
A To hold her perfectly in the pinch of that, I found
34.13–14 but a small shifty spot on the wrong side of
P but the blur of a little dumb spot behind
34.31 straight question enough,
P E A dreadfully austere inquiry,
34.39–40 high manner about it,
P strange manner,
E A most strange manner,
36.30 her
P my
36.38 balm
Omitted from P
37.7–38 when I knew myself to catch them up by an irresistible impulse and press
P E A when, by an irresistible impulse, I found myself catching them up and pressing
37.38 as Shakespeareans,
P masqueraded with brilliancy as Shakespeareans,
38.28 horrid
Omitted from P E and A
38.31–32 dreadful
Omitted from P E and A
40.14 low wretch
P base varlet
40.17 bend was lost.
P sixth installment ends here
42.13 vigils,
P E A watching,
42.30 still moon
P glitter of starlight
43.19 The moon
P Thick stars
44.4–5 Flights of fancy gave place, in her mind, to a steady fireside glow,
P The place of the imagination was taken up by her ample kindness,
44.11 worry
P E A strain
45.10 window, uncovered to the moonlight
P windows bare to the constellations,
45.35 fairy
Omitted from P
48.13–14 his house is poisoned and his little nephew and niece mad?"
P I have the honor to inform him that they see the dead come back?"
48.40 him and you."
P continues him and you."

Then what's your remedy?" she asked as I watched the children.

I continued, without answering, to watch them. "I would leave *them*," and went on.

"But what *is* your remedy?" she persisted.

It seemed, after all, to have come to me then and there. "To speak to them." And I joined them.

seventh installment and third part end here.
49.1 It was all
P between the running title and the roman numeral PART FOURTH
49.28 the lady who
P the lady—never once named—who
49.34 whimsical bent
P eccentric habits
E A eccentric nature
50.3 pony
P jackdaw.
51.16–17 it was essentially in the scared state that I drew my actual conclusions.
P E A it was in the condition of nerves

produced by it that I made my actual inductions

55.30 of which, I

All texts omit the comma

57.33 must stay.

P eighth installment ends here

58.6–7 picture of the "put away"—of drawers closed and locked and rest without remedy.

P image of cupboards closed and diligence vaguely baffled.

E A image of the *etc. as in* N

59.44 to-night

A tonight

65.3 where she stood,

P E A on the spot

65.32 promptly joined me!

P ninth installment and fourth part end here

65.33 We went

P between the running title and the roman numeral PART FIFTH

67.13 halfway

P E half way

A half-way

68.10–11 words from her were, in a flash . . . blade, the jostle

N lacks the punctuation of P E and A

69.10–11 a figure portentous. I gaped at her coolness even though my certitude of her thoroughly seeing was never greater

P E A the very presence that could make me quail. I quailed even though my certitude that she thoroughly saw was never greater

69.14 know it as well as you know

P E A see her as well as you see

70.9 disaffection

P E A reprobation

71.11–12 fairly measured more than it had ever measured.

P E A was as if it were more than it had ever been.

71.19 Her little belongings had all been removed.

Omitted from P

71.31 with me.

P tenth installment ends here

76.5 He'll meet me. He'll confess.

Omitted from P

77.16 arrived the difficulty

P arrived for our main repast the difficulty

78.2 a stiff arm across

P a rude long arm across

E A an angular arm over

78.27 expelled

P E A driven

78.38 waiter

P maid

78.39 alone!"

P eleventh installment ends here

82.31 success,

P triumph

82.39 little headshake.

P little melancholy headshake.

84.37–38 shrieked to my visitant as I tried to press him against me.

P E A shrieked, as I tried to press him against me, to my visitant

85.14 work,

P triumph,

CONTEXTS

James, the Ghost Story, and the Supernatural

HENRY JAMES

To Thomas Sergeant Perry†

["*So Much for Cora*"]

New-York, Sunday [1 November 1863]

Dear Sargy,

* * * I went to listen to the preaching of Mrs. Cora V. L. Hatch.[1] She holds forth in a kind of underground lecture room in Astor Place. The assemblage, its subterraneous nature, the dim lights, the hard-working, thoughtful physiognomies of everyone present quite realised my idea of the meetings of the early Christians in the Catacombs, although the only proscription under which the Hatch disciples labour is the necessity of paying 10 cents at the door. Three individuals from the audience formed themselves into a committee to select a subject for Cora to discuss—and they were marshalled out of the room by a kind of fat showman, who, as I wittily suggested, was probably Mr. Chorus V. L. Hatch.[2] They chose: "the Evidence of the continued existence of the Spirit after death." For some moments Cora remained motionless; probably, as Bob Temple said, "silently invoking her maker." Then she began to speak. Well, the long and short of it is, that the whole thing was a string of such arrant platitudes, that after about an hour of it, when there seemed to be no signs of a let-up we turned and fled. So much for Cora. * * *

Yours very truly,
H.J.

† From *Letters* edited by Leon Edel. Vol 1, 1843–1875, pp. 43–48. Reprinted by permission of the publisher from *The Letters of Henry James* by Leon Edel (ed.), Cambridge, Mass.: Harvard University Press, Copyright © 1974, 1984 by Leon Edel, editorial material, and © 1974, 1984 Alexander James, James copyrighted material. T. S. Perry (1845–1928), critic and essayist, was a close boyhood friend and schoolmate. He first met James in Newport in 1858. He became a lifelong friend to the James boys.

1. A "trance" lecturer.
2. A foreshadowing of the secular preaching James would satirize a quarter of a century later in *The Bostonians* [*Edel's note*].

A Review†

["*Mysteries* * * * *at Our Own Doors*"]

* * * People talk of novels with a purpose; and from this class of works, both by her patrons and her enemies, Miss Braddon's tales are excluded. But what novel ever betrayed a more resolute purpose than the production of what we may call Miss Braddon's second manner? Her purpose was at any hazard to make a hit, to catch the public ear. It was a difficult task, but audacity could accomplish it. Miss Braddon accordingly resorted to extreme measures, and created the sensation novel. It is to this audacity, this courage of despair, as manifested in her later works, that we have given the name of pluck. In these works it has settled down into a quiet determination not to let her public get ahead of her. A writer who has suddenly leaped into a popularity greatly disproportionate to his merit, can only retain his popularity by observing a strictly respectful attitude to his readers. This has been Miss Braddon's attitude, and she has maintained it with unwearied patience. She has been in her way a disciple as well as a teacher. She has kept up with the subtle innovations to which her art, like all others, is subject, as well as with the equally delicate fluctuations of the public taste. The result has been a very obvious improvement in her style.

She has been preceded in the same path by Mr. Wilkie Collins, whose "Woman in White", with its diaries and letters and its general ponderosity, was a kind of nineteenth century version of "Clarissa Harlowe."[1] Mind, we say a nineteenth century version. To Mr. Collins belongs the credit of having introduced into fiction those most mysterious of mysteries, the mysteries which are at our own doors. This innovation gave a new impetus to the literature of horrors. It was fatal to the authority of Mrs. Radcliffe and her ever-lasting castle in the Apennines.[2] What are the Apennines to us, or we to the Apennines? Instead of the terrors of "Udolpho", we were treated to the terrors of the cheerful country-house and the busy London lodgings. And there is no doubt that these were infinitely the more terrible. Mrs. Radcliffe's mysteries were romances pure and simple; while those of Mr. Wilkie Collins were stern reality. The supernatural, which Mrs. Radcliffe constantly implies, though she generally saves her conscience, at the elev-

† From a review of *Aurora Floyd*, by M. E. Braddon, *The Nation*, I (November 9, 1865), 593. Mary Elizabeth Braddon (1837–1915) became famous with her first sensationalist novel, *Lady Audley's Secret* (1862).

1. Wilkie Collins (1824–1889) wrote *Woman in White* in 1860, one of the earliest complicated, lengthy novels of detection. Samuel Richardson (1689–1761) published his seven-volume novel *Clarissa Harlowe* over two years, 1747–48. Both novels are presented from shifting points of view.
2. Anne Radcliffe (1764–1823), early writer of horror stories with rationalized conclusions; her most famous was *The Mysteries of Udolpho* (1794).

enth hour, by explaining it away, requires a powerful imagination in order to be as exciting as the natural, as Mr. Collins and Miss Braddon, without any imagination at all, know how to manage it. A good ghost-story, to be half as terrible as a good murder-story, must be connected at a hundred points with the common objects of life. The best ghost-story probably ever written—a tale published some years ago in *Blackwood's Magazine*[3]—was constructed with an admirable understanding of this principle. Half of its force was derived from its prosaic, commonplace, daylight accessories. Less delicately terrible, perhaps, than the vagaries of departed spirits, but to the full as *interesting*, as the modern novel reader understands the word, are the numberless possible forms of human malignity. Crime, indeed, has always been a theme for dramatic poets; but with the old poets its dramatic interest lay in the fact that it compromised the criminal's moral repose. Whence else is the interest of *Orestes* and *Macbeth*? With Mr. Collins and Miss Braddon (our modern Euripides and Shakespeare) the interest of crime is in the fact that it compromises the criminal's personal safety. The play is a tragedy, not in virtue of an avenging diety, but in virtue of a preventive system of law; not through the presence of a company of fairies, but through that of an admirable organization of police detectives. Of course, the nearer the criminal and the detective are brought home to the reader, the more lively his "sensation." They are brought home to the reader by a happy choice of probable circumstances; and it is through their skill in the choice of these circumstances—their thorough going realism—that Mr. Collins and Miss Braddon have become famous. * * *

We have said that although Mr. Collins anticipated Miss Braddon in the work of devising domestic mysteries adapted to the wants of a sternly prosaic age, she was yet the founder of the sensation novel. Mr. Collins's productions deserve a more respectable name. They are massive and elaborate constructions—monuments of mosaic work, for the proper mastery of which it would seem, at first, that an index and note-book were required. They are not so much works of art as works of science. To read "The Woman in White", requires very much the same intellectual effort as to read Motley or Froude.[4] We may say, therefore, that Mr. Collins being to Miss Braddon what Richardson is to Miss Austen,[5] we date the novel of domestic mystery from the former lady, for the same reason that we date the novel of domestic tranquillity from the latter. Miss Braddon began by a skilful combination of bigamy, arson, murder, and insanity. These phenomena are all represented in the deeds of Lady Audley. The novelty lay in the heroine being, not a

3. Noted for its horror, mystery stories, especially in the middle decades of the nineteenth century.
4. John Lathrop Motley, American (1814–1877), and James Anthony Froude, Englishman (1818–1894), were both celebrated historians of the grand style.
5. Jane Austen (1775–1817), whose *Pride and Prejudice* (1813) fits James's description.

picturesque Italian of the fourteenth century, but an English gentlewoman of the current year, familiar with the use of the railway and the telegraph. The intense probability of the story is constantly reiterated. Modern England—the England of to-day's newspaper—crops up at every step. * * *

A Notebook Entry†

["*Subject for a Ghost-Story*"]

January 22d [1879]. Subject for a ghost-story.

Imagine a door—either walled-up, or that has been long locked—at which there is an occasional knocking—a knocking which—as the other side of the door is inaccessible—can only be ghostly. The occupant of the house or room, containing the door, has long been familiar with the sound; and, regarding it as ghostly, has ceased to heed it particularly—as the ghostly presence remains on the other side of the door, and never reveals itself in other ways. But this person may be imagined to have some great and constant trouble; and it may be observed by another person, relating the story, that the knocking increases with each fresh manifestation of the trouble. He breaks open the door and the trouble ceases—as if the spirit had desired to be admitted, that it might interpose, redeem and protect.

A Notebook Entry††

["*Another Theme of the Same Kind*"]

A young girl, unknown to herself, is followed, constantly, by a figure which other persons see. She is perfectly unconscious of it—but there is a dread that she may cease to be so. The figure is that of a young man—and there is a theory that the day that she falls in love, she may suddenly perceive it. Her mother dies, and the narrator of the story then discovers, by finding an old miniature among her letters and papers, that the figure is that of a young man whom she has jilted in her youth, and who therefore committed suicide. The girl *does* fall in love, and sees the figure. She accepts her lover, and never sees it again!

† From *The Complete Notebooks of Henry James* edited by Leon Edel and Lyall H. Powers (NY: Oxford UP, 1987), 10; copyright © 1987 by Leon Edel and Lyall H. Powers. Reprinted by permission of Oxford University Press. See below, Preface to *The Altar of the Dead*, pp. 103–07.

†† From *The Complete Notebooks of Henry James* edited by Leon Edel and Lyall H. Powers (NY: Oxford UP, 1987), 10; copyright © 1987 by Leon Edel and Lyall H. Powers. Reprinted by permission of Oxford University Press. Entry undated, but follows the previous one.

To Violet Paget [Vernon Lee]†

["*Not the* Class *of Fiction I Myself Most Cherish*"]

34 De Vere Gardens W.
April 27*th* 1890

Dear Miss Paget.

Your gruesome, graceful, *genialisch* "Hauntings"[1] came to me a good bit since; but, pleasure-stirring as was the gift, I have, to thank you for it, been able to control what George Eliot would have called my "emotive" utterance until I should have had the right hour to reassimilate the very special savour of the work. This I have done within a day or two and the ingenious tales, full of imagination and of Italy are *there* —diffused through my intellectual being and within reach of my introspective—or introactive—hand. (My organism will strike you as mixed, as well as my metaphor—and what I mainly mean is that I *possess* the eminently psychical stories as well as the material volume.) I have enjoyed again, greatly, the bold, aggressive speculative fancy of them * * * The supernatural story, the subject wrought in fantasy, is not the *class* of fiction I myself most cherish (prejudiced as you may have perceived me in favour of a close connotation, or close observation, of the real—or whatever one may call it—the familiar, the inevitable). But that only makes my enjoyment of your artistry more of a subjection. * * * Believe me, dear Miss Paget, your most truly,

Henry James

To Francis Boott††

["*I See Ghosts Everywhere*"]

Torquay
October 11*th* [1895]

My dear Francis.

This is but a p.s. of three lines to the letter I posted to you yesterday; after doing which I became aware that I hadn't alluded to poor

† From *Letters* edited by Leon Edel. Vol 3, 1883–1895, pp. 276–78. Reprinted by permission of the publisher from *The Letters of Henry James* by Leon Edel (ed.), Cambridge, Mass.: Harvard University Press, Copyright © 1974, 1984 Leon Edel, editorial material, and © 1974, 1984 Alexander James, James copyrighted material. Paget (1856–1935) was an essayist, a novelist, and a prolific travel writer.

1. A volume containing four of Vernon Lee's ghost stories, published in 1890 [*Edel's note*].

†† From *Letters* edited by Leon Edel. Vol. 4, 1895–1916, pp. 23–24. Reprinted by permission of the publisher from *The Letters of Henry James* by Leon Edel (ed.), Cambridge, Mass.: Harvard University Press, Copyright © 1974, 1984 Leon Edel, editorial material, and © 1974, 1984 Alexander James, James copyrighted material. Boott (1813–1904), an old friend to the James family, heir to New England textile mills, and an amateur composer, was the father of

W. W. Story's death, the news of which I had just seen in the *Times*. I make up the omission rather on general grounds of aesthetic decorum than on that of supposing his departure affects you much—for I believe you didn't like him, or any feature of Casa Story. I feel a certain sense of historic mutation in the thought that Casa Story is no more: it had been for so long, and went back so far: it had seen so much and so many come and go. You it had seen go, hadn't it?—but not very often come! I saw poor W.W. in Rome sixteen months ago and he was the ghost, only, of his old clownship—very silent and vague and gentle. It was very sad and the Barberini very empty and shabby.[1] What will become of that great unsettled population of statues, which his children don't love nor covet? There were hundreds of them in his studio, and they will be loose upon the world. * * * How ghostly must Newport be! But I see ghosts everywhere. You are the only solid substance. Yours, my dear Francis, *da capo*,

Henry James

To Bernard Shaw†

[*"The Imagination * * * Leads a Life of Its Own"*]

Lamb House, Rye
20th Jan: 1909.

My dear Bernard Shaw

* * * I do such things because I happen to be a man of imagination and taste, extremely interested in life, and because the imagination, thus, from the moment direction and motive play upon it from all sides, absolutely enjoys and insists on and incurably leads a life of its own, for which just this vivacity itself is its warrant. You surely haven't done all your own so interesting work without learning what it is for the imagination to *play* with an idea—an idea about life—under a happy obsession, for all it is worth. Half the beautiful things that the benefac-

---

James's close friend Elizabeth "Lizzie" Boott (1846–1888). Leon Edel has proposed that Francis Boott served as a figure for Gilbert Osmond in *The Portrait of a Lady*, and his daughter as a model for Pansy. According to Edel, the father and daughter also influenced James's characterization of Adam and Maggie Verver in *The Golden Bowl*. See Edel, *Henry James*, vol. 1, 254 and vol. 4, 211.

1. During all the years of his Roman residence Story occupied a ducal apartment in the Palazzo Barberini [*Editors*].

† From *Letters* edited by Leon Edel. Vol. 4, 1895–1916, pp. 378–79. Reprinted by permission of the publisher from *The Letters of Henry James* by Leon Edel (ed.), Cambridge, Mass.: Harvard University Press, Copyright © 1974, 1984 Leon Edel, editorial material, and © 1974, 1984 Alexander James, James copyrighted material. Shaw had suggested that James's play *The Saloon* (from the story "Owen Wingrave," see next item) would be more logical if the hero at the end "killed" the ghost, instead of the way James ordered it.

tors of the human species have produced would surely be wiped out if you don't allow this adventurous and speculative imagination its rights. You simplify too much, by the same token, when you limit the field of interest to what you call the scientific—your employment of which term in such a connection even greatly, I confess, confounds and bewilders me. * * *

Believe me your most truely,
Henry James

From a Preface†

*["The Question * * * of the 'Supernatural' "]*

* * * I fear I can defend such doings but under the plea of my amusement in them—an amusement I of course hoped others might succeed in sharing.[1] But so comes in exactly the principle under the wide strong wing of which several such matters are here harvested; things of a type that might move me, had I space, to a pleading eloquence. Such compositions as "The Jolly Corner," printed here not for the first time, but printed elsewhere only as I write and after my quite ceasing to expect it; "The Friends of the Friends," to which I here change the colourless title of "The Way It Came" (1896), "Owen Wingrave" (1893), "Sir Edmund Orme" (1891), "The Real Right Thing" (1900), would obviously never have existed but for that love of "a story as a story" which had from far back beset and beguiled their author. To this passion, the vital flame at the heart of any sincere attempt to lay a scene and launch a drama, he flatters himself he has never been false; and he will indeed have done his duty but little by it if he has failed to let it, whether robustly or quite insidiously, fire his fancy and rule his scheme. He has consistently felt it (the appeal to wonder and terror and curiosity and pity and to the delight of fine recognitions, as well as to the joy, perhaps sharper still, of the mystified state) the very source of wise counsel and the very law of charming effect. He has revelled in the creation of alarm and suspense and surprise and relief, in all the arts that practise, with a scruple for nothing but any lapse of application, on the credulous soul of the candid or, immeasurably better, on the seasoned spirit of the cunning, reader. He has built, rejoicingly, on that blest faculty of wonder just named, in the latent eagerness of which the novelist so finds, throughout, his best warrant that he can but pin his faith and

† From the Preface to *The Altar of the Dead * * * and other Tales*, volume XVII, *The Novels and Tales of Henry James*, The New York Edition (New York: Charles Scribner's Sons, 1909) xv–xxi.

1. James is defending his right to "dramatise," or simply present objectively his stories (as in the letter to Shaw, above).

attach his car to it, rest in fine his monstrous weight and his queer case on it, as on a strange passion planted in the heart of man for his benefit, a mysterious provision made for him in the scheme of nature. He has seen this particular sensibility, the need and the love of wondering and the quick response to any pretext for it, as the beginning and the end of his affair—thanks to the innumerable ways in which that chord may vibrate. His prime care has been to master those most congruous with his own faculty, to make it vibrate as finely as possible—or in other words to the production of the interest appealing most (by its kind) to himself. This last is of course the particular clear light by which the genius of representation ever best proceeds—with its beauty of adjustment to any strain of attention whatever. Essentially, meanwhile, excited wonder must have a subject, must face in a direction, must be, increasingly, *about* something. Here comes in then the artist's bias and his range—determined, these things, by his own fond inclination. About what, good man, does he himself most wonder?—for upon that, whatever it may be, he will naturally most abound. Under that star will he gather in what he shall most seek to represent; so that if you follow thus his range of representation you will know how, you will see where, again, good man, he for himself most aptly vibrates.

All of which makes a desired point for the little group of compositions here placed together; the point that, since the question has ever been before me but of wondering and, with all achievable adroitness, of causing to wonder, so the whole fairy-tale side of life has used, for its tug at my sensibility, a cord all its own. When we want to wonder there's no such good ground for it as the wonderful—premising indeed always, by an induction as prompt, that this element can but be at best, to fit its different cases, a thing of appreciation. What is wonderful in one set of conditions may quite fail of its spell in another set; and, for that matter, the peril of the unmeasured strange, in fiction, being the silly, just as its strength, when it saves itself, is the charming, the wind of interest blows where it lists, the surrender of attention persists where it can. The ideal, obviously, on these lines, is the straight fairy-tale, the case that has purged in the crucible all its *bêtises*[2] while keeping all its grace. It may seem odd, in a search for the amusing, to try to steer wide of the silly by hugging close the "supernatural"; but one man's amusement is at the best (we have surely long had to recognise) another's desolation; and I am prepared with the confession that the "ghost-story," as we for convenience call it, has ever been for me the most possible form of the fairy-tale. It enjoys, to my eyes, this honour by being so much the neatest—neat with that neatness without which *representation*, and therewith beauty, drops. One's working of the spell is of

2. Absurdities.

course—decently and effectively—but by the represented thing, and the grace of the more or less closely represented state is the measure of any success; a truth by the general smug neglect of which it 's difficult not be struck. To begin to wonder, over a case, I must begin to believe—to begin to give out (that is to attend) I must begin to take in, and to enjoy *that* profit I must begin to see and hear and feel. This would n't seem, I allow, the general requirement—as appears from the fact that so many persons profess delight in the picture of marvels and prodigies which by any, even the easiest, critical measure *is* no picture; in the recital of wonderful horrific or beatific things that are neither represented nor, so far as one makes out, seen as representable: a weakness not invalidating, round about us, the most resounding appeals to curiosity. The main condition of interest—that of some appreciable rendering of sought effects—is absent from them; so that when, as often happens, one is asked how one "likes" such and such a "story" one can but point responsively to the lack of material for a judgement.

The apprehension at work, we thus see, would be of certain projected conditions, and its first need therefore is that these appearances be constituted in some other and more colourable fashion than by the author's answering for them on his more or less gentlemanly honour. This is n't enough; *give* me your elements, *treat* me your subject, one has to say—I must wait till then to tell you how I like them. I might "rave" about them all were they given and treated; but there is no basis of opinion in such matters without a basis of vision, and no ground for that, in turn, without some communicated closeness of truth. There are portentous situations, there are prodigies and marvels and miracles as to which this communication, whether by necessity or by chance, works comparatively straight—works, by our measure, to some convincing consequence; there are others as to which the report, the picture, the plea, answers no tithe of the questions we would put. Those questions *may* perhaps then, by the very nature of the case, be unanswerable—though often again, no doubt, the felt vice is but in the quality of the provision made for them: on any showing, my own instinct, even in the service of great adventures, is all for the best *terms* of things; all for ground on which touches and tricks may be multiplied, the greatest number of questions answered, the greatest appearance of truth conveyed. With the preference I have noted for the "neat" evocation—the image, of any sort, with fewest attendant vaguenesses and cheapnesses, fewest loose ends dangling and fewest features missing, the image kept in fine the most susceptible of intensity—with this predilection, I say, the safest arena for the play of moving accidents and mighty mutations and strange encounters, or whatever odd matters, is the field, as I may call it, rather of their second than of their first exhibition. By which, to avoid obscurity, I mean nothing more cryptic than I feel myself show them best by showing almost exclusively the way they are felt, by recognising as their main interest some impression strongly made by them and intensely received. We but too probably break down. I have ever reasoned, when we attempt the prodigy, the appeal to mystification, in itself; with its "objective" side too emphasised the report (it is ten to one) will practically run thin. We want it clear, goodness knows, but we also want it thick, and we get the thickness in the human consciousness that entertains and records, that amplifies and interprets it. That indeed, when the question is (to repeat) of the "supernatural," constitutes the only thickness we do get; here prodigies, when they come straight, come with an effect imperilled; they keep all their character, on the other hand, by looming through some other history—the indispensable history of somebody's *normal* relation to something. It 's in such connexions as these that they most interest, for what we are then mainly concerned with is their imputed and borrowed dignity. Intrinsic values they have none—as we feel for instance in such a matter as the would-be portentous climax of Edgar Poe's "Arthur Gordon Pym," where the indispensable history is absent, where the phenomena evoked, the moving accidents, coming straight, as I say, are immediate and flat, and the attempt is all at the horrific in itself. The result is that, to my sense, the climax fails—fails because it stops short, and stops short for want of connexions. There *are* no connexions; not only, I mean, in the sense of further statement, but of our own further relation to the elements, which hang in the void: whereby we see the effect lost, the imaginative effort wasted.

I dare say, to conclude, that whenever, in quest, as I have noted, of the amusing, I have invoked the horrific, I have invoked it, in such air as that of "The Turn of the Screw," that of "The Jolly Corner," that of "The Friends of the Friends," that of "Sir Edmund Orme," that of "The Real Right Thing," in earnest aversion to waste and from the sense that in art economy is always beauty. The apparitions of Peter Quint and Miss Jessel, in the first of the tales just named, the elusive presence nightly "stalked" through the New York house by the poor gentleman in the second, are matters as to which in themselves, really, the critical challenge (essentially nothing ever but the spirit of fine attention) may take a hundred forms—and a hundred felt or possibly proved infirmities is too great a number. Our friends' respective minds about them, on the other hand, are a different matter—challengeable, and repeatedly, if you like, but never challengeable without some consequent further stiffening of the whole texture. Which proposition involves, I think, a moral. The moving accident, the rare conjunction, whatever it be, does n't make the story—in the sense that the story is our excitement, our amusement, our thrill and our suspense; the human emotion and the human attestation, the clustering human conditions we expect presented, only make it. The extraordinary is most extraordinary in that it happens to you and me, and it 's of value (of value for others) but so far as visibly brought home to us. At any rate, odd though it may sound to pretend that one feels on safer ground in tracing such an adventure as that of the hero of "The Jolly Corner" than in pursuing a bright career among pirates or detectives, I allow that composition to pass as the measure or limit, on my own part, of any achievable comfort in the "adventure-story"; and this not because I may "render"—well, what my poor gentleman attempted and suffered in the New York house—better than I may render detectives or pirates or other splendid desperadoes, though even here too there would be something to say; but because the spirit engaged with the forces of violence interests me most when I can think of it as engaged most deeply, most finely and most "subtly" (precious term!). For then it is that, as with the longest and firmest prongs of consciousness, I grasp and hold the throbbing subject; *there* it is above all that I find the steady light of the picture.

After which attempted demonstration I drop with scant grace perhaps to the admission here of a general vagueness on the article of my different little origins. I have spoken of these in three or four connexions, but ask myself to no purpose, I fear, what put such a matter as "Owen Wingrave" or as "The Friends of the Friends," such a fantasy as "Sir Edmund Orme," into my head.[3] The habitual teller of tales finds these things in old note-books—which however but shifts the burden a step; since how, and under what inspiration, did they first wake up in these rude cradles? One's notes, as all writers remember, sometimes explicitly mention, sometimes indirectly reveal, and sometimes wholly dissimulate, such clues and such obligations. The search for these last indeed, through faded or pencilled pages, is perhaps one of the sweetest of our more pensive pleasures. Then we chance on some idea we *have* afterwards treated; then, greeting it with tenderness, we wonder at the first form of a motive that was to lead us so far and to show, no doubt, to eyes not our own, for so other; then we heave the deep sigh of relief over all that is never, thank goodness, to be done again. * * *

3. The germ of "Sir Edmund Orme" seems to be the journal entry of January 22, 1879, above, p. 100.

Dictated Notes for *The Ivory Tower*†

[*"The Pressure and the Screw"*]

* * * Of course I myself see *all* my stuff—I mean see it in each case —as an action; but there are degrees and proportions and *kinds* of plasticity—and everything isn't theatrically (using the term scientifically and, ah, so non-vulgarly!) workable to what I call the peculiar and special and ideal tune. At the same time one doesn't know—ideally— till one has got into real close quarters with one's proposition by absolutely ciphering it out, by absolutely putting to the proof and to the test what it will give. What then do I see my K.B. case, under the pressure and the screw, as susceptible of giving? *Any* way I want to see; but *if* the way that has begun to glimmer and flush before me does appear to justify itself, what infinite *concomitant* advantages and blessings and inspirations will then be involved in it! Porphyro grows faint really as he thinks of them.

Dictated Notes for *The Ivory Tower*††

[*"My Poor Blest Old Genius"*]

* * * Thus just these first little wavings of the oh so tremulously passionate little old want (now!) make for me, I feel, a sort of promise of richness and beauty and variety: a sort of portent of the happy presence of the elements. The good days of last August and even my broken September and my better October come back to me with their gage of divine possibilities, and I welcome these to my arms, I press them with unutterable tenderness. I seem to emerge from these recent bad days —the fruit of blind accident (Jan. 1910)—and the prospect clears and flushes, and my poor blest old Genius pats me so admirably and lov-

† From *The Complete Notebooks of Henry James* edited by Leon Edel and Lyall H. Powers (NY: Oxford UP, 1987), 259. Copyright © 1987 by Leon Edel and Lyall H. Powers. Reprinted by permission of Oxford University Press. James's notes for his "K.B. case" are the preliminary sketches for *The Ivory Tower*, an uncompleted ten-part novel. "K.B." refers to Katherine De Kay (Mrs. Arthur) Bronson. A native of New York and Newport, Bronson often entertained James at her Venetian home. Bronson's "situation" was the germ for James's cogitations. She may be the inspiration for Mrs. Prest in *The Aspern Papers* (see *The Complete Notebooks of Henry James*, edited by Leon Edel and Lyall H. Powers [New York: Oxford University Press, 1987], 222 n24).

†† From *The Complete Notebooks of Henry James* edited by Leon Edel and Lyall H. Powers (NY: Oxford UP, 1987), 268. Copyright © 1987 by Leon Edel and Lyall H. Powers. Reprinted by permission of Oxford University Press. James invokes his muse for the last time in the extended notebook entry from which this excerpt is drawn. In his planning, James discovers a form of curative to the health problems that burdened him after a nervous breakdown in 1909. On James's health at this time, see Edel, *Henry James*, vol. 5, 434–42.

ingly on the back that I turn. I screw round, and bend my lips to passionately, in my gratitude, kiss its hand. * * *

To Theodate Pope Riddle†

["Beneath Comment or Criticism"]

105, Pall Mall, S.W.
January 12*th* 1912

My dear Theodate.[1]

I return you the dreadful document,[2] pronouncing it without hesitation the most abject and impudent, the hollowest, vulgarest, and basest rubbish I could possibly conceive. Utterly empty and illiterate, without substance or sense, a mere babble of platitudinous phrases, it is beneath comment or criticism, in short beneath contempt. The *commonness* of it simply nauseates—it seems to have been given to those people to invent, richly, new kinds and degrees of commonness, to open up new oceans or vast dismal deserts of it. And that these are those for whom such lucubrations represent a series of *values*, and who spend their time and invite others to spend theirs over them, makes me wonder * * * But I'm not, my dear Theodate, * * * expressing myself with resentment—only with a bewildered sense of strangeness through which I look at you as over the abyss of oddity of your *asking* about that thing to which I hate to accord the dignity even of sending it safely back to you!

Affectionate old friend,
Henry James

Dictated Notes for *The Sense of the Past*††

["The Ideal Thing for Dramatic Interest"]

* * * The ideal thing for dramatic interest and sharpness would be that there is just one matter in which, just one point at which, just one link

† From *Letters* edited by Leon Edel. Vol. 4, 1895–1916, pp. 599–600. Reprinted by permission of the publisher from *The Letters of Henry James* by Leon Edel (ed.), Cambridge, Mass.: Harvard University Press, Copyright © 1974, 1984 Leon Edel, editorial material, and © 1974, 1984 Alexander James, James copyrighted materials.

1. HJ met Theodate Pope Riddle during his 1905 trip to the United States and saw her again during the visit of 1910–1911. She was an architect and had built Avon Old Farms at Farmington, Connecticut, where HJ enjoyed inspecting her collection of impressionist paintings [*Edel's note*].
2. The document was a report of a séance in which it was claimed William James had tried to communicate with his family [*Edel's note*].

†† From *The Complete Notebooks of Henry James* edited by Leon Edel and Lyall H. Powers (NY: Oxford UP, 1987), 517. Reprinted by permission of the publisher.

with his other identity by which he betrays himself,[1] gives himself away, testifies supremely to his alienism, abnormalism, the nature of his identity in fine; the ideal thing would be that, I say, and that it should be definite and visible, absolutely catchable-in-the-act, enough for her to seize it, come into possession of it, and yet not merely terrify or horrify her: affect her in short, on the contrary, with but a finer yearningness of interest.[2] The ideal, as I say, would be that this fact or circumstance should be tremendously right from the tone of the "Screw" point of view, should be intensely in the note of that tone, should be a concrete and definite thing. Find it, find it; get it right and it will be the making of the story. It must consist of something he has to do, some condition he has to execute, some moment he has to traverse, or rite or sacrifice he has to perform—say even some liability he has to face and the occurrence of which depends somehow on the state in which he keeps himself. I seem to see it, it glimmers upon me; though I didn't think of it at first—I hadn't originally got as far as it—it hovers before me though in the form of the only thing it *can* be. When I call it a liability I seem to catch it by the tip of the tail; seem to get a sort of sense of what it *may* in a manner be. Let me figure it out a bit, and under gentle, or rather patiently firm, direct pressure it will come out. He is liable then say to glimpses of vision of the other man, the one portrayed in the picture and whom he had had the portentous passage with before going to the Ambassador, he is liable, put it, to recurrences of a sense of that presence—which thus, instead of being off in the boundless vast of the modern, that is of the Future, as he has described its being to the Ambassador, *does* seem to him at times to hover and to menace; only not to the appearance or effect of reassuring or relieving him, but only to that of really quite mocking and not pitying him, of showing him to himself as "sold," horribly sold.

1. James refers to Ralph Pendrel, the protagonist of *The Sense of the Past,* an American who inherits a London house and, entering it, is ensnared within his own ancestral past. James began the novel in early 1900 but put it aside until 1914, when he penned the extensive notes from which this excerpt is taken. The novel remains incomplete. See Edel, *Henry James,* vol. 4, 328–36.
2. The girl to whom James refers is a figure in Pendrel's past who seems to glean his secret.

James on *The Turn of the Screw*

A Notebook Entry†

[*"Idea of a Servant Suspected"*]

March 16th [1892]. Idea of a servant suspected of doing the mean things—the base things people in London take for granted servants do —reading of letters, diaries, peeping, spying, etc.; turning out utterly innocent and incapable of these things—and turning the tables of scorn on the master or mistress, at a moment when, much depending on it, they are (the servant is) supposed to have committed all the little baseness.

A Notebook Entry††

[*"Grose"*]

Names. Hanmer — Meldrum — Synge — Grundle — Adwick — Blanchett—Sansom—Saunt—Highmore—Hannington (or place)—Medley (house)—Myrtle—Saxon—Yule—Chalkley—Grantham—Farange—Grose — Corfe — Lebus — Glasspoole (or place) — Bedfont, Redfont (places?)—Vereker—Gainer—Gayner—Shum—Oswald—Gonville—Mona (girl)—Mark—Floyer—Minton—Panton—Summervale—Chidley—Shirley—Dreever—Trendle—Stannace—Housefield—Longworth —Langsom—Nettlefold—Nettlefield—Beaumorris—Delacoombe—Treston — Mornington — Warmington — Harmer — Oldfield — Horsefield — Eastmead.

† From *The Complete Notebooks of Henry James* edited by Leon Edel and Lyall H. Powers (New York: Oxford UP, 1987), 65–66.

†† From *The Complete Notebooks of Henry James*, edited by Leon Edel and Lyall H. Powers (New York: Oxford University Press, 1987), 108. An entry placed between those of November 18, 1894, and January 12, 1895.

A Notebook Entry†

["Note Here the Ghost-Story"]

Saturday, January 12th, 1895. Note here the ghost-story told me at Addington (evening of Thursday 10th), by the Archbishop of Canterbury: the mere vague, undetailed, faint sketch of it—being all he had been told (very badly and imperfectly), by a lady who had no art of relation, and no clearness: the story of the young children (indefinite number and age) left to the care of servants in an old country-house, through the death, presumably, of parents. The servants, wicked and depraved, corrupt and deprave the children; the children are bad, full of evil, to a sinister degree. The servants *die* (the story vague about the way of it) and their apparitions, figures, return to haunt the house *and* children, to whom they seem to beckon, whom they invite and solicit, from across dangerous places, the deep ditch of a sunk fence, etc.—so that the children may destroy themselves, lose themselves, by responding, by getting into their power. So long as the children are kept from them, they are not lost; but they try and try and try, these evil presences, to get hold of them. It is a question of the children 'coming over to where they are.' It is all obscure and imperfect, the picture, the story, but there is a suggestion of strangely gruesome effect in it. The story to be told—tolerably obviously—by an outside spectator, observer.

To Alice [Mrs. William] James††

["Finished My Little Book"]

Dictated.

34 De Vere Gardens, W.
1st December, 1897

Dearest Alice,

It's too hideous and horrible, this long time that I have not written you and that your last beautiful letter, placed, for reminder, well within sight, has converted all my emotion on the subject into a constant, chronic blush. The reason has been that I have been driving very hard for another purpose this inestimable aid to expression, and that, as I have a greater loathing than ever for the mere manual act, I haven't,

† From *The Complete Notebooks of Henry James*, edited by Leon Edel and Lyall H. Powers (New York: Oxford University Press, 1987), 109. Copyright © 1987 by Leon Edel and Lyall H. Powers. Reprinted by permission of Oxford University Press.

†† From *Letters* edited by Leon Edel. Vol. 4, 1895–1916, pp. 61–65. Reprinted by permission of the publisher from *The Letters of Henry James* by Leon Edel (ed.), Cambridge, Mass.: Harvard University Press, Copyright © 1974, 1984 Leon Edel, editorial material, and © 1974, 1984 Alexander James, James copyrighted material. Alice was the wife of William James.

on the one side, seen my way to inflict on you a written letter, or on the other had the virtue to divert, till I should have finished my little book, to another stream any of the valued and expensive industry of my amanuensis. I *have*, at last, finished my little book—that is *a* little book, and so have two or three mornings of breathing-time before I begin another. * * *

Henry James.

To A. C. Benson†

[*"Of the Ghostly and Ghastly"*]

34 De Vere Gardens, W.
March 11th, 1898.

My dear Arthur,

I suppose that in the mysterious scheme of providence and fate such an inspiration as your charming note—out of the blue!—of a couple of days ago, is intended somehow to make up to me for the terror with which my earlier—in fact *all* my past—productions inspire me, and for the insurmountable aversion I feel to looking at them again or to considering them in any way. This morbid state of mind is really a blessing in disguise—for it has for happy consequences that such an incident as your letter becomes thereby extravagantly pleasant and gives me a genial glow. All thanks and benedictions—I shake your hand very hard—or *would* do so if I could attribute to you anything so palpable, personal and actual *as* a hand. Yet I shall never write a sequel to the *P. of an L.*[1]—admire my euphonic indefinite article. It's all too faint and far away—too ghostly and ghastly—and I have bloodier things *en tête*.[2] I can do better than that!

But à propos, precisely, of the ghostly and ghastly, I have a little confession to make to you that has been on my conscience these three months and that I hope will excite in your generous breast nothing but tender memories and friendly sympathies.

On one of those two memorable—never to be obliterated—winter nights that I spent at the sweet Addington, your father, in the drawing-room by the fire, where we were talking a little, in the spirit of recreation, of such things, repeated to me the few meagre elements of a small and gruesome spectral story that had been told *him* years before and that he could only give the dimmest account of—partly because he had forgotten details and partly—and much more—because there

† From *The Letters of Henry James* edited by Percy Lubbock. Vol. 1 (London: Macmillan, 1920), 285–87. A. C. Benson (1862–1925), genteel man of letters, son of the just deceased Archbishop of Canterbury.

1. James's *The Portrait of a Lady* (1881).
2. In mind.

had *been* no details and no coherency in the tale as he received it, from a person who also but half knew it. The vaguest essence only was there—some dead servants and some children. This essence *struck* me and I made a note of it (of a most scrappy kind) on going home. There the note remained till this autumn, when, struck with it afresh, I wrought it into a fantastic fiction which, first intended to be of the briefest, finally became a thing of some length and is now being "serialised" in an American periodical. It will appear late in the spring (chez Heinemann) in a volume with *one* other story, and then I will send it to you. In the meanwhile please think of the *doing* of the thing on my part as having sprung from that kind old evening at Addington —quite gruesomely as my unbridled imagination caused me to see the inevitable development of the subject. It was all worth mentioning to you. I am very busy and very decently fit and very much yours, always, my dear Arthur,

Henry James.

To Paul Bourget†

["A *Little Volume Just Published*"]

Dictated

Lamb House, Rye.
19th August, 1898.

Mon cher Ami,

* * * I ordered my year-old "Maisie" the other day to be sent to you, and I trust she will by this time have safely arrived—in spite of some ambiguity in the literation of the name of your villa as, with your letter in my hand, I earnestly meditate upon it. I have also despatched to Madame Paul myself a little volume just published[1]—a poor little pot-boiling study of nothing at all, *qui ne tire pas à conséquence*.[2] It is but a monument to my fatal technical passion, which prevents my ever giving up anything I have begun. So that when something that I have supposed to be a subject turns out on trial really to be none, *je m'y acharne d'autant plus*,[3] for mere superstition—superstitious fear, I mean, of the consequences and omens of weakness. The small book in question is really but an exercise in the art of not appearing to one's

† From *The Letters of Henry James* edited by Percy Lubbock. Vol. 1 (London: Macmillan, 1920), 293–98. Paul Bourget (1852–1935), French essayist and novelist, whom James first met in 1884.

1. Probably refers to *In the Cage*, which James wrote after *The Turn of the Screw*, but which was published in August, two months before *The Two Magics*. Much of what James says here may well be applied to *The Turn of the Screw*.
2. Which is really inconsequential.
3. I persist all the more.

self to fail. You will say it is rather cruel that for such exercises the public also should have to pay. Well, Madame Paul and you get your *exemplaire*[4] for nothing. * * *

Henry James.

To Dr. Waldstein†

["That Wanton Little Tale"]

Lamb House, Rye.
Oct: 21st, 1898.

Dear Sir,

Forgive my neglect, under great pressure of occupation, of your so interesting letter of 12th. I have since receiving it had complicated calls on my time. That the *Turn of the Screw* has been suggestive and significant to you—in any degree—it gives me great pleasure to hear; and I can only thank you very kindly for the impulse of sympathy that made you write. I am only afraid, perhaps, that my conscious intention strikes you as having been larger than I deserve it should be thought. It is the intention so primarily, with me, always, of the artist, the *painter*, that *that* is what I most, myself, feel in it—and the lesson, the idea—ever—conveyed is only the one that deeply lurks in any vision prompted by life. And as regards a presentation of things so fantastic as in that wanton little Tale, I can only rather blush to see real substance read into them—I mean for the generosity of the reader. *But*, of course, where there *is* life, there's truth, and the truth was at the back of my head. The poet is always justified when he is not a humbug; always grateful to the justifying commentator. My bogey-tale dealt with things so hideous that I felt that to save it at all it needed some infusion of beauty or prettiness, and the beauty of the pathetic was the only attainable—was indeed inevitable. But ah, the exposure indeed, the helpless plasticity of childhood that isn't dear or sacred to *some*body! That *was* my little tragedy—over which you show a wisdom for which I thank you again. Believe me, thus, my dear Sir, yours most truly,

Henry James.

4. Copy.
† From *Letters* edited by Leon Edel. Vol. 4, 1895–1916, p. 84. Reprinted by permission of the publisher from *The Letters of Henry James* by Leon Edel (ed.), Cambridge, Mass.: Harvard University Press, Copyright © 1974, 1984 Leon Edel, editorial material, and © 1974, 1984 Alexander James, James copyrighted material. Louis Waldstein, M.D. (1853–1915), author of *The Subconscious Self and Its Relation to Education and Health*, London, 1897.

To H. G. Wells†

["The Thing Is Essentially a Pot-Boiler"]

Lamb House, Rye.
Dec. 9th, 1898.

My dear H. G. Wells,

Your so liberal and graceful letter is to my head like coals of fire—so repeatedly for all these weeks have I had feebly to suffer frustrations in the matter of trundling over the marsh to ask for your news and wish for your continued amendment. The shortening days and the deepening mud have been at the bottom of this affair. I never get out of the house till 3 o'clock, when night is quickly at one's heels. I would have taken a regular day—I mean started in the a.m.—but have been so ridden, myself, by the black care of an unfinished and *running* (galloping, leaping and bounding,) serial that parting with a day has been like parting with a pound of flesh.[1] I am still a neck ahead, however, and *this* week will see me through; I accordingly hope very much to be able to turn up on one of the ensuing days. I will sound a horn, so that you yourself be not absent on the chase. Then I will express more articulately my appreciation of your various signs of critical interest, as well as assure you of my sympathy in your own martyrdom. What will you have? It's all a grind and a bloody battle—as well as a considerable lark, and the difficulty itself is the refuge from the vulgarity. Bless your heart, I think I could easily say worse of the T. of the S., the young woman, the spooks, the style, the everything, than the worst any one else could manage. One knows the most damning things about one's self. Of course I had, about my young woman, to take a very sharp line. The grotesque business I had to make her picture and the childish psychology I had to make her trace and present, were, for me at least, a very difficult job, in which absolute lucidity and logic, a singleness of effect, were imperative. Therefore I had to rule out subjective complications of her own—play of tone etc.; and keep her impersonal save for the most obvious and indispensable little note of neatness, firmness and courage—without which she wouldn't have had her data. But the thing is essentially a pot-boiler and a *jeu d'esprit*.

† From *Letters* edited by Leon Edel. Vol. 4, 1895–1916, pp. 85–87. Reprinted by permission of the publisher from *The Letters of Henry James* by Leon Edel (ed.), Cambridge, Mass.: Harvard University Press, Copyright © 1974, 1984 Leon Edel, editorial material, and © 1974, 1984 Alexander James, James copyrighted material. H. G. Wells (1866–1946), at this time a friend and neighbor of James. Later they were to fall out, Wells cruelly parodying James's stories like *The Turn of the Screw* in *Boon* (London, 1915).

1. *The Awkward Age* began in *Harper's Weekly* on October 1, 1898, and ran through January 7, 1899.

With the little play,[2] the absolute creature of its conditions, I had simply to make up a deficit and take a small *revanche*.[3] For three moral years had the actress for whom it was written (utterly to try to *fit*) persistently failed to produce it, and I couldn't wholly waste my labour. The B.P.[4] won't read a play with the mere names of the speakers—so I simply paraphrased these and added such indications as might be the equivalent of decent acting—a history and an evolution that seem to me moreover explicatively and sufficiently smeared all over the thing. The moral is of course Don't write one-act plays. But I didn't mean thus to sprawl. I envy your hand your needle pointed fingers. As you don't say that you're *not* better I prepare myself to be greatly struck with the same, and with kind regards to your wife.

Believe me yours ever,

Henry James

To F. W. H. Myers†

["*The T. of the S. Is a Very Mechanical Matter*"]

Lamb House, Rye.
Dec. 19th, 1898.

My dear Myers,

I don't know what you will think of my unconscionable delay to acknowledge your letter of so many, so very many days ago, nor exactly how I can make vivid to you the nature of my hindrances and excuses. I have, in truth, been (until some few days since) intensely and anxiously busy, finishing, under pressure, a long job that had from almost the first—I mean from long before I had reached the end—begun to be (loathsome name and fact!) "serialized"—so that the printers were at my heels and I had to make a sacrifice of my correspondence *utterly*—to keep the sort of cerebral freshness required for not losing my head or otherwise collapsing. But I won't expatiate. Please believe my silence has been wholly involuntary. And yet, now that I *am* writing I scarce know what to say to you on the subject on which you wrote,

2. *Covering End*, the second work in *The Two Magics*, was originally a one-act play that James wrote for Ellen Terry. In 1908 James recast the story into a three-act play under the title *The High Bid*, which ran successfully.
3. Revenge.
4. British Public.
† From *Letters* edited by Leon Edel. Vol. 4, 1895–1916, pp. 87–88. Reprinted by permission of the publisher from *The Letters of Henry James* by Leon Edel (ed.), Cambridge, Mass.: Harvard University Press, F. W. H. Myers (1843–1901), minor poet and man of letters, one of the founders of the Society of Psychical Research, of which William James was once president.

especially as I'm afraid I don't quite *understand* the principal question you put to me about "The Turn of the Screw." However, that scantily matters; for in truth I am afraid I have on some former occasions rather awkwardly signified to you that I somehow can't pretend to give any coherent account of my small inventions "after the fact." There they are—the fruit, at best, of a very imperfect ingenuity and with all the imperfections thereof on their heads. The one thing and another that are questionable and ambiguous in them I mostly take to be conditions of their having got themselves pushed through at all. The *T. of the* S. is a very mechanical matter, I honestly think—an inferior, a merely *pictorial*, subject and rather a shameless pot-boiler. The thing that, as I recall it, I most wanted not to fail of doing, under penalty of extreme platitude, was to give the impression of the communication to the children of the most infernal imaginable evil and danger—the condition, on their part, of being as *exposed* as we can humanly conceive children to be. This was my artistic knot to untie, to put any sense of logic into the thing, and if I had known any way of producing *more* the image of their contact and condition I should assuredly have been proportionately eager to resort to it. I evoked the worst I could, and only feel tempted to say, as in French: "Excusez du peu!"[1]

I am living so much down here that I fear I am losing hold of some of my few chances of occasionally seeing you. The charming old humble-minded "quaintness" and quietness of this little brown hilltop city lays a spell upon me. I send you and your wife and all your house all the greetings of the season and am, my dear Myers, yours very constantly,

Henry James.

To W. D. Howells†

[*"Another Duplex Book Like the 'Two Magics'"*]

Lamb House, Rye.
29th June, 1900.

My dear Howells,

* * * I brood with mingled elation and depression on your ingenious, your really inspired, suggestion that I shall give you a ghost, and that my ghost shall be "international." I say inspired because, singularly

1. Bear with it.

† From *Letters* edited by Leon Edel. Vol. 4, 1895–1916, pp. 149–52. Reprinted by permission of the publisher from *The Letters of Henry James* by Leon Edel (ed.), Cambridge, Mass.: Harvard University Press, Copyright © 1974, 1984 Leon Edel, editorial material, and © 1974, 1984 Alexander James, James copyrighted material. William Dean Howells (1837–1920), James's lifelong friend, had written asking for a ghost story for the *Atlantic Monthly*.

enough, I set to work some months ago at an international ghost, and on just this scale, 50,000 words; entertaining for a little the highest hopes of him. He was to have been wonderful and beautiful; he was to have been called (perhaps too metaphysically) "The Sense of the Past"; and he was to have been supplied to a certain Mr. Doubleday who was then approaching me—had then approached me. . . . The outstretched arm, however, alas, was drawn in again, or lopped off, or otherwise paralysed and negatived, and I was left with my little project—intrinsically, I hasten to add, and most damnably difficult—on my hands. * * *

I'm not even sure that the international ghost is what will most bear being worried out—though, again, in another particular, the circumstances, combining with your coincident thought, seemed pointed by the finger of providence. What——wanted was two Tales—both tales of "terror" and making another duplex book like the "Two Magics." Accordingly I had had (dreadful deed!) to puzzle out more or less a second, a different piece of impudence of the same general type. But I had only, when the project collapsed, caught hold of the tip of the tail of this other monster—whom I now mention because his tail seemed to show him as necessarily still more interesting than No. 1. If I can at all recapture *him*, or anything like him, I will do my best to sit down to him and "mount" him with due neatness. In short, I will do what I can. If I can't be terrible, I shall nevertheless still try to be international. The difficulties are that it's difficult to be terrible save in the short piece and international save in the long. But trust me.[1] * * *

Henry James.

A Notebook Entry†

["*Something as Simple as* The Turn of the Screw"]

Lamb House, August 9th, 1900.

I've a great desire to see if I can worry out, as I've worried out before, some possible *alternative* to the 50,000 words story as to which I've been corresponding with Howells, and as to which I've again attacked —been attacking—*The Sense of the Past*. I fumble, I yearn, *je tâtonne*,[1]

1. James' never did finish *The Sense of the Past*, although he returned to it in the last years of his life (see p. 109, n. 1). Even though he and Howells agreed in August to drop the project, James's interest in the "international" theme led directly to his masterpiece, *The Ambassadors* (1903). Indeed, in this and in the following selections, one can sense James moving away from the ghost story.

† From *The Complete Notebooks of Henry James* edited by Leon Edel and Lyall H. Powers (New York: Oxford University Press, 1987), 189–91;

1. I grope.

a good deal for an alternative to *that* idea, which proves in execution so damnably difficult and so complex. I don't mind, God knows, the mere difficulty, however damnable; but it's fatal to find one's self in for a subject that one can't possibly treat, or hope, or begin, to treat, in the space, and that can only betray one, as regards that, after one is expensively launched. The ideal is something as simple as *The Turn of the Screw*, only different and less grossly and merely apparitional. I was rather taken with Howells's suggestion of an 'international ghost'—I kindle, I vibrate, respond to suggestion, imaginatively, so almost unfortunately, so generously and precipitately, easily. The formula, for so short a thing, rather caught me up—the more that, as the thing *has* to be but the 50,000, the important, the serious, the sincere things I have in my head are all too ample for it. And then there was the remarkable coincidence of my having begun *The Sense of the Past*, of its being really 'international,' which seemed in a small way the finger of providence. But I'm afraid the finger of providence is pointing me astray.

* * * I *had* a vague sense, last autumn when I was so deludedly figuring out *The S. of the P.* for 'Doubleday,' that, as a no. 2 thing (in 'Terror') for the same volume, there dwelt a possibility in something expressive of the peculiarly acute Modern, the current polyglot, the American-experience-abroad line. I saw something; it glimmered on me; but I didn't in my then uncertainty, follow it up. *Is* there anything to follow up? *Vedremo bene.*[2] I want something *simpler* than *The S. of the P.*, but I don't want anything, if may be, of less dignity, as it were. *The S. of the P.* rests on an idea—and it's only the idea that can give me the situation. *The Advertiser*[3] is an idea—a beautiful one, if one could happily fantasticate it. Perhaps one *can*—I must see, I must, precisely, sound that little depth. Remember this is the kind of sacred process in which *½ a dozen days*, a WEEK, of depth, of stillness, are but all too well spent. THAT kind of control of one's nerves, command of one's coolness, is the real economy. The *fantasticated* is, for this job, my probable formula, and I know what I mean by it as differentiated from the type, the squeezed sponge, of *The T. of the S.* 'Terror' *peut bien en être*,[4] and all the effective *malaise*,[5] above all, the case demands. Ah, things swim before me, *caro mio*, and I only need to sit tight, to keep my place and fix my eyes, to see them float past me in the current into which I can cast my little net and make my little haul. Hasn't one got hold of, doesn't one make out, rather, something in the general glimmer of the notion of what the quasi-grotesque Europeo-American situation, in the way the gruesome, may, *pushed to the full and right expression of its grotesqueness*, has to give? That general formula haunts

2. Well, we'll wait and see.
3. This was the name which James gave in his notebooks to a story line that he toyed with but never incorporated into a tale or novel.
4. Could be part of it.
5. Impending sense of disaster.

me, and as a *morality* as well as a terror, an idea as well as a ghost. Here truly *is* the tip of a tail to catch, a trail, a scent, a latent light to follow up. * * *

To W. D. Howells†

["A *Little 'Tale of Terror'* "]

Lamb House, Rye,
August 9, 1900

My dear Howells,

* * * Lending myself as much as possible to your suggestion of a little "tale of terror" that should be also international, I took straight up again the idea I spoke to you of having already, some months ago, tackled and, for various reasons, laid aside. I have been attacking it again with intensity and on the basis of a simplification that would make it easier, and have done for it, thus, 110 pages of type. The upshot of this, alas, however, is that though this second start is, if I—or if *you* —like, magnificent, it seriously confronts me with the element of *length*; showing me, I fear, but too vividly, that, do what I will for compression, I shall not be able to squeeze my subject into 50,000 words. It will make, even if it doesn't, for difficulty, still beat me, 70,000 or 80,000—dreadful to say; and that faces me as an excessive addition to the ingredient of "risk" we speak of. On the other hand I am not sure that I can hope to substitute for this particular affair *another* affair of "terror" which will be expressible in the 50,000; and that for an especial reason. This reason is that, above all when one has done the thing, already, as I have rather repeatedly, it is not easy to concoct a "ghost" of any freshness. The want of ease is extremely marked, moreover, if the thing is to be done on a certain scale of length. One might still toss off a spook or two more if it were a question only of the "short-story" dimension; but prolongation and extension constitute a strain which the mere apparitional—discounted, also, as by my past dealings with it—doesn't do enough to mitigate. * * *

My one chance is yet, I admit, to try to attack the same (the subject) from still another quarter, at still another angle, that I make out as a possible one and which may keep it squeezable and short. If this experiment fails, I fear I shall have to "chuck" the supernatural and the high fantastic. I have just finished, as it happens, a fine flight (of eighty thousand words) into the high fantastic, which has rather depleted me,

† From *Letters* edited by Leon Edel. Vol. 4, 1895–1916, pp. 157–62. Reprinted by permission of the publisher from *The Letters of Henry James* by Leon Edel (ed.), Cambridge, Mass.: Harvard University Press,

or at any rate affected me as discharging my obligations in that quarter. But I believe I mentioned to you in my last "The Sacred Fount"—this has been "sold" to Methuen here, and by this time, probably, to somebody else in the U.S.[1]—but, alas, not to be serialized (as to which indeed it is inapt)—as to the title of which kindly preserve silence. The *vraie vérité*, the fundamental truth lurking behind all the rest, is furthermore, no doubt, that preoccupied with half a dozen things of the altogether human order now fermenting in my brain, I don't care for "terror" (terror, that is, without "pity") so much as I otherwise might. This would seem to make it simple for me to say to you: "Hang it, if I can't pull off my Monster on *any* terms, I'll just do for you a neat little *human*—and not the less international—fifty-thousander consummately addressed to your more cheerful department; do for you, in other words, an admirable short novel of manners, thrilling too in its degree, but definitely ignoring the bugaboo."

Henry James.

To W. D. Howells

["*A Story of the '8 to 10 Thousand Words'* "]†

Lamb House, Rye.
December 11th, 1902.

My dear Howells,

* * * I am melted at your reading *en famille The Sacred Fount*, which you will, I fear, have found chaff in the mouth and which is one of several things of mine, in these last years, that have paid the penalty of having been conceived only as the "short story" that (alone, apparently) I could hope to work off somewhere (which I mainly failed of,) and then *grew* by a rank force of its own into something of which the idea had, modestly, never been to be a book. That is essentially the case with the S. F., planned, like The Spoils of Poynton, What Maisie Knew, The Turn of the Screw, and various others, as a story of the "8 to 10 thousand words"!! and then having accepted its bookish necessity or destiny in consequence of becoming already, at the start, 20,000, accepted it ruefully and blushingly, moreover, since, *given the tenuity of the idea*, the larger quantity of treatment hadn't been aimed at. I remember how I would have "chucked" *The Sacred Fount* at the 15th thousand word, if in the first place I could have afforded to "waste" 15,000, and if in the second I were not always ridden by a superstitious

1. To Charles Scribner's Sons, their first James novel.

† From *Letters* edited by Leon Edel. Vol. 4, 1895–1916, pp. 250–52.

terror of not finishing, for finishing's and for the precedent's sake, what I have begun. I am a fair coward about *dropping*, and the book in question, I fear, is, more than anything else, a monument to that superstition. When, if it meets my eye, I say to myself, "You know you might not have finished it," I make the remark not in natural reproach, but, I confess, in craven relief. * * *

Yours always and ever,
Henry James.

Preface to the New York Edition†

["*An Exercise of the Imagination*"]

* * * That particular challenge[1] at least "The Turn of the Screw" does n't incur; and this perfectly independent and irresponsible little fiction rejoices, beyond any rival on a like ground, in a conscious provision of prompt retort to the sharpest question that may be addressed to it. For it has the small strength—if I should n't say rather the unattackable ease—of a perfect homogeneity, of being, to the very last grain of its virtue, all of a kind; the very kind, as happens, least apt to be baited by earnest criticism, the only sort of criticism of which account need be taken. To have handled again this so full-blown flower of high fancy is to be led back by it to easy and happy recognitions. Let the first of these be that of the starting-point itself—the sense, all charming again, of the circle, one winter afternoon, round the hall-fire of a grave old country-house where (for all the world as if to resolve itself promptly and obligingly into convertible, into "literary" stuff) the talk turned, on I forget what homely pretext, to apparitions and night-fears, to the marked and sad drop in the general supply, and still more in the general quality, of such commodities. The good, the really effective and heart-shaking ghost-stories (roughly so to term them) appeared all to have been told, and neither new crop nor new type in any quarter awaited us. The new type indeed, the mere modern "psychical" case, washed clean of all queerness as by exposure to a flowing laboratory tap, and equipped with credentials vouching for this—the new type clearly promised little, for the more it was respectably certified the less it seemed of a nature to rouse the dear old sacred terror. Thus it was, I remember, that amid our lament for a beautiful lost form, our distinguished host expressed the wish that he might but have recovered for us one of the scantest of fragments of this form at its best. He had never

† From the Preface to *The Aspern Papers; The Turn of the Screw; The Liar; the Two Faces*, volume XII, *The Novels and Tales of Henry James*, The New York Edition, pp. xiv–xxii;

1. James concluded his remarks on *The Aspern Papers* by claiming that if he had had the time and opportunity he "could have perfectly 'worked out' Jeffrey Aspern."

forgotten the impression made on him as a young man by the withheld glimpse, as it were, of a dreadful matter that had been reported years before, and with as few particulars, to a lady with whom he had youthfully talked. The story would have been thrilling could she but have found herself in better possession of it, dealing as it did with a couple of small children in an out-of-the-way place, to whom the spirits of certain "bad" servants, dead in the employ of the house, were believed to have appeared with the design of "getting hold" of them. This was all, but there had been more, which my friend's old converser had lost the thread of: she could only assure him of the wonder of the allegations as she had anciently heard them made. He himself could give us but this shadow of a shadow—my own appreciation of which, I need scarcely say, was exactly wrapped up in that thinness. On the surface there was n't much, but another grain, none the less, would have spoiled the precious pinch addressed to its end as neatly as some modicum extracted from an old silver snuff-box and held between finger and thumb. I was to remember the haunted children and the prowling servile spirits as a "value," of the disquieting sort, in all conscience sufficient; so that when, after an interval, I was asked for something seasonable by the promoters of a periodical dealing in the time-honoured Christmas-tide toy, I bethought myself at once of the vividest little note for sinister romance that I had ever jotted down.

Such was the private source of "The Turn of the Screw"; and I wondered, I confess, why so fine a germ, gleaming there in the wayside dust of life, had never been deftly picked up. The thing had for me the immense merit of allowing the imagination absolute freedom of hand, of inviting it to act on a perfectly clear field, with no "outside" control involved, no pattern of the usual or the true or the terrible "pleasant" (save always of course the high pleasantry of one's very form) to consort with. This makes in fact the charm of my second reference, that I find here a perfect example of an exercise of the imagination unassisted, unassociated—playing the game, making the score, in the phrase of our sporting day, off its own bat. To what degree the game was worth playing I need n't attempt to say: the exercise I have noted strikes me now, I confess, as the interesting thing, the imaginative faculty acting with the *whole* of the case on its hands. The exhibition involved is in other words a fairy-tale pure and simple—save indeed as to its springing not from an artless and measureless, but from a conscious and cultivated credulity. Yet the fairy-tale belongs mainly to either of two classes, the short and sharp and single, charged more or less with the compactness of anecdote (as to which let the familiars of our childhood, Cinderella and Blue-Beard and Hop o' my Thumb and Little Red Riding Hood and many of the gems of the Brothers Grimm directly testify), or else the long and loose, the copious, the various, the endless, where, dramatically speaking, roundness is quite sacrificed—sacrificed to fulness, sacrificed to exuberance, if one will: witness at hazard almost any one of the Arabian Nights. The charm of all these things for the distracted modern mind is in the clear field of experience, as I call it, over which we are thus led to roam; an annexed but independent world in which nothing is right save as we rightly imagine it. We have to do *that*, and we do it happily for the short spurt and in the smaller piece, achieving so perhaps beauty and lucidity; we flounder, we lose breath, on the other hand—that is we fail, not of continuity, but of an agreeable unity, of the "roundness" in which beauty and lucidity largely reside—when we go in, as they say, for great lengths and breadths. And this, oddly enough, not because "keeping it up" is n't abundantly within the compass of the imagination appealed to in certain conditions, but because the finer interest depends just on *how* it is kept up.

Nothing is so easy as improvisation, the running on and on of invention; it is sadly compromised, however, from the moment its stream breaks bounds and gets into flood. Then the waters may spread indeed, gathering houses and herds and crops and cities into their arms and wrenching off, for our amusement, the whole face of the land—only violating by the same stroke our sense of the course and the channel, which is our sense of the uses of a stream and the virtue of a story. Improvisation, as in the Arabian Nights, may keep on terms with encountered objects by sweeping them in and floating them on its breast; but the great effect it so loses—that of keeping on terms with itself. This is ever, I intimate, the hard thing for the fairy-tale; but by just so much as it struck me as hard did it in "The Turn of the Screw" affect me as irresistibly prescribed. To improvise with extreme freedom and yet at the same time without the possibility of ravage, without the hint of a flood; to keep the stream, in a word, on something like ideal terms with itself; that was here my definite business. The thing was to aim at absolute singleness, clearness and roundness, and yet to depend on an imagination working freely, working (call it) with extravagance; by which law it would n't be thinkable except as free and would n't be amusing except as controlled. The merit of the tale, as it stands, is accordingly, I judge, that it has struggled successfully with its dangers. It is an excursion into chaos while remaining, like Blue-Beard and Cinderella, but an anecdote—though an anecdote amplified and highly emphasised and returning upon itself; as, for that matter, Cinderella and Blue-Beard return. I need scarcely add after this that it is a piece of ingenuity pure and simple, of cold artistic calculation, an *amusette*[2] to catch those not easily caught (the "fun" of the capture of the merely witless being ever but small), the jaded, the disillusioned, the fastidious. Otherwise expressed, the study is of a conceived "tone," the tone of suspected and felt trouble, of an inordinate and incalculable sore—the

2. A piece of child's play.

tone of tragic, yet of exquisite, mystification. To knead the subject of my young friend's, the suppositious narrator's, mystification thick, and yet strain the expression of it so clear and fine that beauty would result: no side of the matter so revives for me as that endeavour. Indeed if the artistic value of such an experiment be measured by the intellectual echoes it may again, long after, set in motion, the case would make in favour of this little firm fantasy—which I seem to see draw behind it today a train of associations. I ought doubtless to blush for thus confessing them so numerous that I can but pick among them for reference. I recall for instance a reproach made me by a reader capable evidently, for the time, of some attention, but not quite capable of enough, who complained that I had n't sufficiently "characterised" my young woman engaged in her labyrinth; had n't endowed her with signs and marks, features and humours, had n't in a word invited her to deal with her own mystery as well as with that of Peter Quint, Miss Jessel and the hapless children. I remember well, whatever the absurdity of its now coming back to me, my reply to that criticism—under which one's artistic, one's ironic heart shook for the instant almost to breaking. "You indulge in that stricture at your ease, and I don't mind confiding to you that—strange as it may appear!—one has to choose ever so delicately among one's difficulties, attaching one's self to the greatest, bearing hard on those and intelligently neglecting the others. If one attempts to tackle them all one is certain to deal completely with none; whereas the effectual dealing with a few casts a blest golden haze under cover of which, like wanton mocking goddesses in clouds, the others find prudent to retire. It was 'déjà très-joli,'[3] in 'The Turn of the Screw,' please believe, the general proposition of our young woman's keeping crystalline her record of so many intense anomalies and obscurities—by which I don't of course mean her explanation of them, a different matter; and I saw no way, I feebly grant (fighting, at the best too, periodically, for every grudged inch of my space) to exhibit her in relations other than those; one of which, precisely, would have been her relation to her own nature. We have surely as much of her own nature as we can swallow in watching it reflect her anxieties and inductions. It constitutes no little of a character indeed, in such conditions, for a young person, as she says, 'privately bred,' that she is able to make her particular credible statement of such strange matters. She has 'authority,' which is a good deal to have given her, and I could n't have arrived at so much had I clumsily tried for more."

For which truth I claim part of the charm latent on occasion in the extracted reasons of beautiful things—putting for the beautiful always, in a work of art, the close, the curious, the deep. Let me place above all, however, under the protection of that presence the side by which

3. Nicely established.

this fiction appeals most to consideration: its choice of its way of meeting its gravest difficulty. There were difficulties not so grave: I had for instance simply to renounce all attempt to keep the kind and degree of impression I wished to produce on terms with the to-day so copious psychical record of cases of apparitions. Different signs and circumstances, in the reports, mark these cases; different things are done—though on the whole very little appears to be—by the persons appearing; the point is, however, that some things are never done at all: this negative quantity is large—certain reserves and proprieties and immobilities consistently impose themselves. Recorded and attested "ghosts" are in other words as little expressive, as little dramatic, above all as little continuous and conscious and responsive, as is consistent with their taking the trouble—and an immense trouble they find it, we gather—to appear at all. Wonderful and interesting therefore at a given moment, they are inconceivable figures in an *action*—and "The Turn of the Screw" was an action, desperately, or it was nothing. I had to decide in fine between having my apparitions correct and having my story "good"—that is producing my impression of the dreadful, my designed horror. Good ghosts, speaking by book, make poor subjects, and it was clear that from the first my hovering prowling blighting presences, my pair of abnormal agents, would have to depart altogether from the rules. They would be agents in fact; there would be laid on them the dire duty of causing the situation to reek with an air of Evil. Their desire and their ability to do so, visibly measuring meanwhile their effect, together with their observed and described success—this was exactly my central idea; so that, briefly, I cast my lot with pure romance, the appearances conforming to the true type being so little romantic.

This is to say, I recognise again, that Peter Quint and Miss Jessel are not "ghosts" at all, as we now know the ghost, but goblins, elves, imps, demons as loosely constructed as those of the old trials for witchcraft; if not, more pleasingly, fairies of the legendary order, wooing their victims forth to see them dance under the moon. Not indeed that I suggest their reducibility to any form of the pleasing pure and simple; they please at the best but through having helped me to express my subject all directly and intensely. Here it was—in the use made of them—that I felt a high degree of art really required; and here it is that, on reading the tale over, I find my precautions justified. The essence of the matter was the villainy of motive in the evoked predatory creatures; so that the result would be ignoble—by which I mean would be trivial—were this element of evil but feebly or inanely suggested. Thus arose on behalf of my idea the lively interest of a possible suggestion and process of *adumbration*; the question of how best to convey that sense of the depths of the sinister without which my fable would so woefully limp. Portentous evil—how was I to save that, as an intention on the part of my demon-spirits, from the drop, the comparative vulgarity, inevitably attending, throughout the whole range of possible brief illustration, the offered example, the imputed vice, the cited act, the limited deplorable presentable instance? To bring the bad dead back to life for a second round of badness is to warrant them as indeed prodigious, and to become hence as shy of specifications as of a waiting anti-climax. One had seen, in fiction, some grand form of wrong-doing, or better still of wrong-being, imputed, seen it promised and announced as by the hot breath of the Pit—and then, all lamentably, shrink to the compass of some particular brutality, some particular immorality, some particular infamy portrayed: with the result, alas, of the demonstration's falling sadly short. If *my* bad things, for "The Turn of the Screw," I felt, should succumb to this danger, if they should n't seem sufficiently bad, there would be nothing for me but to hang an artistic head lower than I had ever known occasion to do.

The view of that discomfort and the fear of that dishonour, it accordingly must have been, that struck the proper light for my right, though by no means easy, short cut. What, in the last analysis, had I to give the sense of? Of their being, the haunting pair, capable, as the phrase is, of everything—that is of exerting, in respect to the children, the very worst action small victims so conditioned might be conceived as subject to. What would *be* then, on reflexion, this utmost conceivability?—a question to which the answer all admirably came. There is for such a case no eligible *absolute* of the wrong; it remains relative to fifty other elements, a matter of appreciation, speculation, imagination—these things moreover quite exactly in the light of the spectator's, the critic's, the reader's experience. Only make the reader's general vision of evil intense enough, I said to myself—and that already is a charming job—and his own experience, his own imagination, his own sympathy (with the children) and horror (of their false friends) will supply him quite sufficiently with all the particulars. Make him *think* the evil, make him think it for himself, and you are released from weak specifications. This ingenuity I took pains—as indeed great pains were required—to apply; and with a success apparently beyond my liveliest hope. Droll enough at the same time, I must add, some of the evidence—even when most convincing—of this success. How can I feel my calculation to have failed, my wrought suggestion not to have worked, that is, on my being assailed, as has befallen me, with the charge of a monstrous emphasis, the charge of all indecently expatiating? There is not only from beginning to end of the matter not an inch of expatiation, but my values are positively all blanks save so far as an excited horror, a promoted pity, a created expertness—on which punctual effects of strong causes no writer can ever fail to plume himself—proceed to read into them more or less fantastic figures. Of high interest to the author meanwhile—and by the same stroke a theme for the moralist—the artless resentful reaction of the entertained person who has abounded in the sense of the situation. He visits his abundance, morally, on the artist—who has but clung to an ideal of faultlessness. Such indeed, for this latter, are some of the observations by which the prolonged strain of that clinging may be enlivened! * * *

Illustrations

The American painter Charles Demuth (1883–1935) executed five watercolor illustrations of *The Turn of the Screw* between 1917 and 1918. Four are provided on the following pages. The fifth, "Miles and the Governess," appears on the cover of this Norton Critical Edition. Black-and-white reproductions of four of Demuth's paintings ("At a House in Harley Street" was not included) appeared with Edna Kenton's "Henry James to the Ruminant Reader" in 1924 (excerpted in this edition on pp. 169–70). For a reasonable assessment of the Demuth paintings *as criticism*, see Robin P. Hoople, *Distinguished Discord: Discontinuity and Pattern in the Critical Tradition of "The Turn of the Screw"* (Lewisburg: Bucknell University Press, 1997), 107–27. Hoople also provides an overview of the critics on the subject of the Demuth paintings. Charles Demuth also executed illustrations of two other James stories, "The Beast in the Jungle" and "The Real Thing."

Charles Demuth, "At a House in Harley Street." 1918.
Watercolor and pencil on paper, 8 × 11" (20.3 × 27.9 cm).
The Museum of Modern Art, New York: Gift of Abby Aldrich Rockefeller. Photograph © 1998 the Museum of Modern Art. Reproduced by permission.

Charles Demuth, "The Governess First Sees the Ghost of Peter Quint."
Philadelphia Museum of Art: Gift of Frank and Alice Osborn. Reproduced by permission.

Charles Demuth, "Flora and the Governess."
Philadelphia Museum of Art: Gift of Frank and Alice Osborn. Reproduced by permission.

Charles Demuth, "The Governess, Mrs. Grose and the Children."
Philadelphia Museum of Art: Gift of Frank and Alice Osborn. Reproduced by permission.

Other Possible Sources for *The Turn of the Screw*

ROBERT LEE WOLFF

The Genesis of "The Turn of the Screw"†

* * *

It is now time to call the reader's attention to the striking picture, herewith reproduced. Entitled "The Haunted House" and drawn by T. Griffiths,[1] it depicts two children, a boy and a girl, looking in terror across a lake at a house with a tower. From one window of the house there shines a ghostly light, which is reflected in the water; the children are standing under a great tree, and the shrubbery around the lake is very thick. It is needless to point out that there are many of these scenic elements in "The Turn of the Screw," although of course in the story the children never are together on the far side of the lake. Haunted house with tower, lake, frightened little boy and girl—how attractive it would be to prove that Henry James saw this picture before he wrote "The Turn of the Screw," and that to its vivid pictorial impression he was able, perhaps subconsciously, to add whatever nucleus of anecdote had been supplied by Archbishop Benson.

Fortunately the proof is simple. The picture appears in the special Christmas number for 1891 of *Black and White*,[2] a weekly illustrated London review. It does not illustrate any story; it is simply included as an artistic effort, to please the reader of the magazine, according to a

† From *American Literature*, XIII (March 1941): 1–8. Copyright 1941. Reprinted with the permission of Duke University Press.

1. About T. Griffiths I have been able to find very little information. Listed in Ulrich Thieme and Felix Becker, *Allgemeines Lexikon der Bildenden Künstler* (Leipzig, 1922), XV, 29, as Tom Griffiths, he is said to have come from Leeds, and to have exhibited regularly in the Royal Academy showings from 1871 to 1904. The London exhibitions in which he showed pictures are listed in Algernon Graves, *Dictionary of Artists Who Have Contributed to the Principal London Exhibitions from 1760–1893* (London, 1895), p. 113; and the titles of his Academy pictures are listed in the same author's *The Royal Academy Exhibitors 1709–1904* (London, 1905), III, 325. In 1879, for example, his picture was called "*Dark and more dark the shades of evening grow*," Wordsworth. The annual programs of the Academy name his pictures, but never reproduce them. [The picture is reproduced between pages six and seven of Wolff's original article. *Editors.*]
2. II., 39.

custom followed by many illustrated magazines of the period, notably this one. In the same number there appears for the first time Henry James's story "Sir Edmund Orme."[3] Thus it is impossible to imagine that James did not see this number of *Black and White*[4]—in fact, it will be proved beyond a doubt that he did—and so the probability that he also saw this picture is established as extremely strong. If he saw it, it almost surely served him as a source for the setting of "The Turn of the Screw."

That he forgot entirely about this picture, at least in his conscious mind, is very probable, but that his subconscious mind may very well have remembered it, is indicated by no fewer than three suggestive passages in his writings.[5]

* * *

It seems entirely probable, then, that at Christmas time, 1891, Henry James saw Tom Griffiths's picture called "The Haunted House," the memory of which disappeared into the well; that in January, 1895, he heard a fragment of a story from Archbishop Benson, the memory of which likewise disappeared into the well; and that, early in 1898, the idea of the picture and the idea of the anecdote emerged from the reservoir, fused by the shaping imagination, the anecdote having supplied the ideas for the plot, and the picture those for the setting of "The Turn of the Screw."

3. *Ibid.*, pp. 8–15. Complete files of *Black and White* are to be found in the United States only in the Library of Congress and the Yale University Library. Volume II, with this special Christmas number presumably included, is also in the Public Library in Seattle, Washington (*Union List of Serials in the Libraries of the United States and Canada*, ed. Winifred Gregory, New York, 1927, p. 245).
   Although the editor's name is never mentioned in the pages of *Black and White* itself, he was James Nicoll Dunn, who had already been connected with the *Dundee Adventurer*, *The Scotsman*, the *National Observer*, and the *Pall Mall Gazette*, and who later edited the *Morning Post* and the *Manchester Courier* (T. H. S. Escott, *Masters of English Journalism*, London, 1991, pp. 302–303).
4. *Black and White* was published weekly in London from Feb. 6, 1891, to Jan. 13, 1913, when it was merged with the *Sphere*. Besides "Sir Edmund Orme," James also contributed, in its first year, "Brooksmith," which appeared in the number for May 2, pp. 417–422. Among other contributors during this first year were Robert Louis Stevenson ("The Bottle Imp" and "The South Seas"), Rudyard Kipling ("Brugglesmith" and "Children of the Zodiac"), Thomas Hardy ("To Please His Wife"), J. M. Barrie ("Is It a Man?"), and Bret Harte (several contributions).
5. Wolff refers to James's 1898 letters to F. W. H. Myers (see pp. 117–18) and Dr. Louis Waldstein (see p. 115). The Myers letter calls *The Turn of the Screw* "pictorial"; the Waldstein letter asserts James's painterly intentions. In his volume XVII Preface to the New York Edition of *Sir Edmund Orme,* James recalls seeing the number of *Black and White* in which "The Haunted House" appeared [*Editors*].

FRANCIS X. ROELLINGER

Psychical Research and "The Turn of the Screw"†

* * * One possible and very likely source of inspiration, first mentioned many years ago by the late Dorothy Scarborough, has apparently escaped serious notice.[1] In support of her contention that the publications of the Society for Psychical Research were a fountainhead for writers of ghost stories at the turn of the century, Miss Scarborough asserted that "Henry James based his ghost story, 'The Turn of the Screw,' on an incident reported to the Psychical Society [*sic*], of a spectral old woman corrupting the mind of a child."[2] No authority is given for this interesting assertion, which, in the light of evidence that has appeared since Miss Scarborough wrote, now seems erroneous. If James did not "base" his story on the published reports of the Society, they might nevertheless have been a logical source of suggestions for the development of Benson's anecdote. For many reasons, the omission of an investigation of this possibility is remarkable. James's interest in psychical phenomena is well known to his readers, and is the subject of frequent mention in the recollections of his friends. Although he was not a member of the Society, founded in 1882, several friends were active in its affairs, two of them—F. W. H. Myers and Edmund Gurney—being founders. William James was a corresponding member from 1884 to 1889, vice president from 1890 to 1893, and president from 1894 to 1896. A report on the proceedings of a general meeting of the Society on October 31, 1890, states that "the paper by Professor William James . . . on 'Observations of Certain Phenomena of Trance' was read by his brother, Henry James."[3] William James directed the American section of the "Census of Hallucinations" conducted by the

† From *American Literature*, XX (January, 1949), 401–412. Copyright 1949. Reprinted with the permission of Duke University Press.

1. Between the publication of Wolff's and Roellinger's articles, James's previously unpublished notebook entry of January 1895 (see p. 112) confirmed the status of the Benson anecdote as the tale's source. Roellinger notes that the anecdote provided James with an important but faint sketch. He argues, in support of Wolff, that James may have also drawn from other sources [*Editors*].
2. *The Supernatural Element in Modern English Fiction* (New York, 1917), p. 204. Before I came upon this remark in Miss Scarborough's book, Mr. John Bronson Friend, of Shelburne, Massachusetts, had called my attention to the possibility of a relation between the reports of the Society and James's story. I am heavily indebted to Mr. Friend for provocation and for many valuable suggestions for this essay.
3. "Proceedings of the General Meeting," *Proceedings of the Society for Psychical Research*, VI, 660 (1889–1890). This publication is hereinafter referred to as *P.S.P.R.*

Society from 1889 to 1894.[4] The findings of the Census were made known not only through its own publications, but through reprints and summaries in magazines, in texts such as William James's *Principles of Psychology*, and in such collections as Frank E. Podmore's *Studies in Psychical Research*, and Andrew Lang's *Book of Dreams and Ghosts*, all of which appeared shortly before "The Turn of the Screw" was written.[5]

That James had read and studied the reports of the Society is evident from the Preface.[6] * * * For readers today who approach the story with preconceptions still largely derived from the familiar phantoms of Gothic fiction, it is important to realize that the ghosts of "The Turn of the Screw" are conceived to a surprising extent in terms of the cases reported to the Society. From the point of view of this emphasis the story becomes an interesting *tour de force*, an attempt to re-create what James refers to as "a beautiful lost form," and to rouse, as he puts it, "the dear old sacred horror" without departing any more than artistically necessary from the then current knowledge of psychical phenomena. * * *

* * *

In the majority of cases reported to the Society, the ghost does not appear at any known fixed time of day or year. It is usually seen distinctly "in all kinds of light, from broad daylight to the faint light of dawn." It is described in detail, and appears "in such clothes as are now, or have recently been, worn by living persons." It is seen "on looking round, as a human being might be," or it seems "to come in at the door." It rarely makes noises: "to hear its footsteps, for instance, seems to be unusual." Sudden death, "often either murder or suicide, appears to be connected with the cause of the apparition" in many cases. Percipients are not limited by sex, age, or profession. If several persons are together when the ghost appears, "it will sometimes be seen by all and sometimes not, and failure to see it is not always merely the result of not directing attention to it."[7]

The ghosts of "The Turn of the Screw" conform precisely to the second of these generic types. They do not appear at any fixed time of

4. The "Census" was conducted by collecting answers to a widely distributed questionnaire. There were 410 collectors (members of the Society and their friends), 17,000 informants, most of whom were "educated persons." Further assistance in the inquiry was obtained "by a special appeal to psychologists made by Professor Sidgwick in *Mind*, and through articles by him and other members of the Committee published in various more popular periodicals (*Nineteenth Century, New Review, Murray's Magazine, Review of Reviews*)." See "Report on the Census of Hallucinations," *P.S.P.R.*, X, 25–422 (1894).
5. According to the letter to A. C. Benson [see pp. 113–14 of this Norton Critical Edition], the story was written in the fall of 1897.
6. Roellinger refers to James's New York Edition preface and its use of terminology and apparition accounts drawn from the Society's reports. Roellinger argues that James may have used the Preface to adhere more explicitly to contemporary scientific discourse on ghosts than he had in the tale [*Editors*].
7. *P.S.P.R.*, II, 139 (1884); III, 144, 145 (1885).

day or year. They are so distinctly seen that the governess is able to give a detailed description of both to the housekeeper, who recognizes them at once. Six of the eight apparitions occur in daylight. Quint appears in the cast-off clothes of his master, and Miss Jessel in a black dress. The governess usually comes upon them suddenly and unexpectedly, on coming into view of the house, on entering a room or turning down a stair. They are silent, they never speak, they only look. The cause of death is not definitely stated in either case, but circumstances lend themselves to the interpretation that Quint was murdered and that Miss Jessel committed suicide. A remarkable feature of the story, stressed in the prologue, is that the percipients are children; although rare in fiction, it is common in the reports, ten such cases appearing in the first three volumes. On one occasion the governess directs the attention of Mrs. Grose to the apparition of Miss Jessel, but the housekeeper is unable to see it. In short, James eschews the incredible ghosts of sensational fiction for the more plausible and so-called "veridical" apparitions of the reports. He even employs, to good effect and despite his strenuous disclaimer, the mysterious absence of any apparent object or intelligent mystery until the governess begins to develop her theory that they have come "to get hold" of the children. But neither the governess nor the reader is ever positive of the correctness of this theory. * * *

Although these striking parallels do not prove conclusively that James drew upon the reports, they do show that he constructed his apparitions much more in terms of the "mere modern 'psychical' case" than perhaps he himself realized or was willing to admit. Ideas regarding psychical phenomena were much in the air throughout the eighties and nineties; it was no accident that among Archbishop Benson's guests on that January night "the talk turned . . . to apparitions and night-fears." The reports are not mentioned in the notebooks, but the remarks in the Preface are ample evidence that James had taken careful note of them. One wonders how Benson's case escaped the Census of Hallucinations: it would not have been surprising to find it there, for the name of "Mrs. Benson, Lambeth Palace," appears on the lists of associates and members of the Society from 1883 to 1896.

Shortly after the publication of "The Turn of the Screw," F. W. H. Myers wrote to James, apparently asking him several questions about the story, and James belatedly replied:

> I scarce know what to say to you on the subject on which you wrote, especially as I'm afraid I don't quite *understand* the principal question you put to me about "The Turn of the Screw." However, that scantily matters; for in truth I am afraid I have on some former occasions rather awkwardly signified to you that I

somehow can't pretend to give any coherent account of my small inventions "after the fact."[8]

The reply is obviously evasive, for the entry in the notebooks and the discussion in the Preface are very coherent accounts of this particular invention, both before and after the fact. It would be interesting to know what "principal question" this authority on psychical research addressed to the creator of the ghosts of "The Turn of the Screw."

OSCAR CARGILL

The Turn of the Screw and Alice James†

* * * It apparently did not occur to any of Wilson's critics that James might have an adequate motive for disguising his purpose in the tale; neither they nor Wilson referred to Alice James, though her tragic story provides an explanation for the "ambiguity" of both the commentary and the tale itself.[1] James's "strategy" consisted in overlaying his real story with another which might, with plausibility, be construed as a ghost story. The limitations of that "strategy" are, however, that it temporarily confounds the acute and perceptive and, like life, rewards the

8. *The Letters of Henry James*, ed. Percy Lubbock (New York, 1920) [pp. 117–18 of this Norton Critical Edition].

† [From *PMLA*, LXXVIII (June, 1963), 238–49. Reprinted by permission of the Modern Language Association of America. Page references to this Norton Critical Edition are given in brackets after the author's original citations of the first American edition of the tale.]

Invited in 1956 to contribute to that outstanding undergraduate quarterly, *The Chicago Review*, and having the previous winter noted the parallels between *The Turn of the Screw* and "The Case of Miss Lucy R.," I wrote the sketch "Henry James as Freudian Pioneer," *C.R.*, X (Summer 1956), 13–29. When Gerald Willen asked my permission to reprint this sketch in his *A Casebook on Henry James's "The Turn of the Screw"* (New York, 1960), pp. 223–238, I wished greatly to revise the sketch but I yielded my wishes when he indicated this would hold up his publication. I had previously recognized that I must repudiate the sketch (which I now do) and provide a more adequate statement. These points are not made in *C.R.*: that (1) W. J. knew the Freud-Breuer book the year after its publication and was sufficiently impressed to talk about it; (2) the Prologue is essential to the story—the climax, in fact, and the governess has been altered from villainess to heroine; (3) the special significance of the narrators Griffin and Douglas, with Douglas as lover; (4) analysis of the governess' "trauma," an explanation of why Miles was actually dismissed from school, and new causes for the governess' state; (5) the important Saul-David allusion; (6) the reader's alternatives in interpretation suggested by the setting of *Jane Eyre* against *The Mysteries of Udolpho*; (7) Fielding's *Amelia* introduced as an illuminating source; (8) the suggestion that the story might have been written for Clement Shorter; and (9) there are more extensive parallels between the *Journal of Alice James* and *The Turn of the Screw*. Earlier forms of this essay were presented at the first Fales lecture, New York Univ., and at colloquia at Brown and Duke Universities.

1. Edmund Wilson's "The Ambiguity of Henry James" appears on pp. 170–73 of this Norton Critical Edition [*Editors*].

obtuse and conventional. Thanks to it, *The Turn of the Screw* continues to be misread as "a pure ghost story."[2]

For a proper reading some of the difficulties that James himself interposed must be skirted or eliminated. The chief of these seems to be James's indication that the primary source of his inspiration was the fragment of a ghost story given him by a friend.[3] * * *

One thing is clear, if James got his anecdote from Archbishop Benson, he did not mean us to take it as the *only* source of his story. He specifically labels it "the private source." Might there not have been public sources, i.e., things in print, available to everyone? Has it been properly noticed that James confesses to *many* "intellectual echoes" in recalling the creation of the tale? He adds further, "To knead the subject of my young friend's, the supposititious narrator's mystification thick . . . I seem to see draw behind it today a train of associations . . . so numerous I can but pick among them for reference."[4] Not all of these possibilities can be investigated here, but one of them can hardly be neglected—the direct influence of Sigmund Freud.

Wilson's provocative paper should have led the author or others to the writings of Freud for a source for *The Turn of the Screw*. While

2. Leon Edel, who reprinted *The Turn of the Screw* in *The Ghostly Tales of Henry James* (New Brunswick, N. J., 1948), pp. 425–550, finds no anomaly in approaching the story as "a ghostly tale, pure and simple," examining the governess "as a deeply fascinating psychological case," and finding the tale "a projection of H. J.'s own haunted state." In "Hugh Walpole and Henry James: The Fantasy of the 'Killer and the Slain'," *American Imago*, VIII (Dec. 1951), 3–21, however, he supplies an extreme Freudian reading to the relation of the governess and Miles, but in his introduction to Harold C. Goddard's "A Pre-Freudian Reading of *The Turn of the Screw*," *Nineteenth-Century Fiction*, XII (June 1957), [pp. 161–68 of this Norton Critical Edition], he is more positive that "James wrote a ghost story . . . [but] offered sufficient data to permit the diagnosis that she [the governess] is mentally disturbed."
3. Cargill details how the Benson anecdote was established as a source. See James's notebook entry on p. 112 and his letter to A. C. Benson on pp. 113–14 [*Editors*].
4. [Henry James, *The Art of the Novel: Critical Prefaces*. (New York and London: Charles Scribner's Sons, 1934)], pp. 170, 173. Leon Edel notes parallels to *Jane Eyre*, mentioned by the governess, but not by title, at the beginning of her narrative (p. 42): "the Jane Eyre who came to a lonely house, had a housekeeper for company and an orphan as her charge, and who fell in love with her employer." *The Ghostly Tales*, p. 431. In this connection we should note, I think, the way in which the governess, "rooted, . . . shaken," refers to Jane Eyre: "Was there a secret at Bly—a mystery of Udolpho or an insane, an unmentionable relative kept in an unsuspected confinement?" James is posing, is he not, the dilemma which confronts the reader as well as the governess—he must choose between a supernatural explanation, such as confronts the reader of *The Mysteries of Udolpho* or a natural one such as is given him in *Jane Eyre*: a mad woman?

Edel, very importantly to my mind, suggests a source for the specter on the tower from a description by James in the *Nation* (25 July 1872) of Haddon Hall, which he had reached, past "rook-haunted elms" along "a meadow path by the Wye," rhyming with Bly: "The twilight deepened, the ragged battlements and the low broad oriels glanced duskily from the foliage, the rooks wheeled and clamoured in the glowing sky; and if there had been a ghost on the premises I certainly ought to have seen it. In fact I did see it, as we see ghosts nowadays" (p. 433).

Robert Lee Wolff in "The Genesis of 'The Turn of the Screw'," *American Literature*, XIII (Mar. 1941), [pp. 133–34 of this Norton Critical Edition], calls attention to the fact in the Christmas number of *Black and White*, which contained James's tale "Sir Edmund Orme," "there is a drawing depicting two children, a boy and a girl, looking in terror across a lake at a house with a tower." This is possibly the suggestion for "the sea of Azof" (p. 69).

most critics would concede that an author of genius could in his characterizations anticipate a later scientific elucidation of behavior, none has held that James in his study of the governess combined the perceptions of genius with some actual technical knowledge. The date of the story, 1898, seems too early,[5] save for the remote possibility that there might be something relevant in that early publication of Doctors Breuer and Freud—*Studien über Hysterie*—in 1895. But indeed here *is* included a case of the greatest relevancy, one which supplies more important elements than Archbishop Benson's anecdote, "The Case of Miss Lucy R."[6]

* * *

There is one over-all resemblance between "The Case of Miss Lucy R." and the story of the governess of Bly: they are both presented as reports or case histories, within a frame, for unlike most of James's stories, *The Turn of the Screw* is a tale with an elaborate portico. As we have seen, a man named Douglas produces a document which is the governess' story. It is Douglas who tells us that the governess began her adventure by falling in love in the single interview that she had with her future employer—as did Lucy R. This instant infatuation, decidedly not typical of James's stories, may be taken as a sign of susceptibility or abnormality. The employer is rich and handsome and of an old Essex family, he is the uncle of orphaned children—not two girls, but a niece and a nephew—whom he has neither the experience nor the patience to minister to personally. Like Miss Lucy's master, this new master gives the governess a sense of commission and trust in the interview, a factor in her infatuation (pp. 10–15) [4–6].

And as for the governess' "case"—the story within the story of *The Turn of the Screw*—that has special points of resemblance also with "The Case of Miss Lucy R." The valet and the former governess may be seen as trying to possess little Miles and Flora in their protectress' disturbed fancy as did the kissing male and female visitors the children of the Vienna manufacturer—hint enough for James to differentiate the sexless "bad servants" of Archbishop Benson's anecdote. In the episode of the children's retaining Miss Lucy's letter at a crucial time may well be the germ of the whole elaborate business with letters in *The Turn of the Screw*: the governess retains a letter from Miles's school saying his return is not desired, she prevents Mrs. Grose from engaging to get

5. ". . . Freudian psychology was something Henry James could not have been consciously dealing with." N. Bryllion Fagin. "Another Reading of *The Turn of the Screw*," MLN, LXVI (Mar. 1941), p. 198. Fagin appears to have been the first to suggest that the tale is an "allegory of good and evil."
6. Sigmund Freud, *Selected Papers on Hysteria and Other Psychoneuroses*, tr. A. A. Brill, 3rd ed. (Washington, D.C., 1920), pp. 14–30. In another case, that of "Mrs. Emmy von N.," a boy is frightened to death.

a letter written to the master describing conditions at Bly, and the empty letter which she herself prepares and which is stolen and destroyed by Miles.

In Miss Lucy's fear that others would discern her feelings is the governess' dread that Miles will reveal them to his uncle and a hint of the suspicion with which the other servants at Bly regard her (pp. 190–191) [76] after Mrs. Grose departs with the ill little Flora for London —thereby saving the child's mind, if not her life (pp. 180, 195) [72, 78]. On the other hand, the governess early reveals her love for the master to Mrs. Grose with the same candor that had surprised Freud in Lucy R. (p. 21) [8–9]. Whether James was influenced by Freud's analysis of Lucy's difficulties with her sense of smell or not, his governess has a peculiarly keen organ—she notes the smell of lately baked bread in the housekeeper's room (p. 143) [58], the "fragrance and purity about the children" (pp. 32, 82) [13, 33], and even the talk of little Miles, just before his death, comes to her "like a waft of fragrance" (p. 205) [82]. The impatience of the children's uncle (which the governess seems to dread throughout her adventure) derives from the impetuosity of the Vienna manufacturer as certainly as the governess' characterization as a rural parson's daughter comes from the Glasgow mother of Miss Lucy, a suggestion redolent of Presbyterianism.

Most important of all, James's governess experiences what Freud defines as a traumatic experience—similar to the rebuke of Miss Lucy —shortly after coming to Bly. After accepting the post with both trepidation and hope, she passes two sleepless nights in London, is possessed by anxiety on her way down to Bly, is unable to sleep the first night there, and then has a "second [really a fourth] sleepless night." While she is in this exhausted condition, she receives from her employer an unopened letter which announces Miles's dismissal from school. But the unopened letter reveals to her not merely her employer's indifference to the orphans in her care but to herself. Like the reproof given to Lucy R., it shatters her hope of some sort of intimacy with her employer, and the shock of that experience produces from her the senseless charges against little Miles (pp. 24–26) [10]. Finally, we are given the broadest possible hint that the governess is ill, for her all important interview takes place in "Harley Street" (pp. 10, 17) [4, 7]—the conventional "physicians' row" of London. Thus, like T. S. Eliot, James has provided us with a sort of "objective correlative" for reading the story.

* * *

Prior to any knowledge of *Studien über Hysterie* was Henry James's personal acquaintance, of course, with the illness of his sister and with the delusions and fantasies of that illness.[7] * * * In the fortitude of Alice James facing her destiny James may have got the inspiration for making the governess the heroine of his tale and the confessor of her own terrible burden to her lover. But he noted other things in Alice's *Journal*: her lively curiosity for sexual anecdotes, such as the premarital chastity of her previous doctor, Sir Andrew Clark, and the vices of the Eton boys. When she sets down as fact Kate Loring's *always* coming, at a turn of the stairs, upon a waiter and a chambermaid, in "osculatory relaxations," Henry could have regarded that as a shared fantasy, but it may have suggested to him the relations of Peter Quint and Miss Jessel as imagined by the governess.[8] One of the tiniest hints in Alice's *Journal* may be seen as richly fertile in relation to *The Turn of the Screw*: Alice notes, "I can't read anything suggestive, or that survives, or links itself to experience, for it sets my silly stomach fluttering, and my flimsy head skipping so that I have to stop."[9] The governess had been reading Fielding's *Amelia* with great excitement (it having been denied her at home) at a "horribly late" hour when she becomes aware of "something undefinably astir in the house" (pp. 95–96) [38–39]; she rises, has an hallucination of Quint on the stair, and later sees little Miles on the lawn staring up at—she assumes—Quint on the tower, but really at his sister (pp. 99–106) [40–43]. Now the pertinence of the forbidden book is this: because her husband is frequently cast into prison, the beautiful Amelia, pursued by two ardent would-be seducers through a series of exciting adventures, is the sole protectress of two little children, a boy and a girl, Billy being "a good soldier-like Christian."[1] James put *Amelia* into the governess' hands because she could identify with the heroine: Amelia suffers early in the novel from what "some call a fever on the spirits, some a nervous fever, some the vapours, and some the hysterics," but which her husband pronounces "a sort of complication of all the diseases together, with almost madness added to them."[2] James's own interest in *Amelia* was probably aroused because one of the tenacious seducers was named "Colonel James" whereas the other remains unnamed throughout and is simply referred to as "the noble peer." When Douglas of *The Turn of the Screw* fails to reveal the name of the governess, that might be regarded as the protection a lover might offer, but

7. "She [Madame de Mauves] was not striving to balance her sorrow with some strongly flavored joy; for the present, she was trying to live with it peaceably, reputably, and without scandal, —turning the key on it occasionally, as you would on a companion liable to attacks of insanity." *Madame de Mauves, The Great Short Novels of Henry James*, ed. Philip Rahv (New York, 1944), p. 27. This story was published in the Galaxy, XVII (Feb.–Mar. 1874.), 216–233, 354–374.
8. [Alice James, *Alice James: Her Brothers—Her Journal*. New York: Dodd, Mead & Company, Inc., 1934], pp. 246–248, 215, 181.
9. A. J. . . . *Her Journal*, p. 105. Note that Alice had just been reading *Clarissa Harlowe* by Richardson.
1. *Amelia* (3 vols., London, 1871). III, 5–6. Not a prototype of Miles, but a suggestion for the latter's name.
2. I, 136–137.

the failure of Mrs. Grose or anyone else ever to call the governess by name, suggested by Fielding's omission possibly, can only be looked upon as an unconscious revelation of how deeply fixed was James's caution to avoid suspicion that his narrative had its source in Alice's illness.

T. J. LUSTIG

"The Turn of the Screw" and "Gabrielle de Bergerac"†

Is the governess right to jump to the conclusion that Quint is a corrupt and malevolent figure?[1] Since the question is not susceptible of absolute proof it may be a meaningless one, but the possibility gains added plausibility in the light of one of James's earliest tales. In 'Gabrielle de Bergerac' (1869), M. de Bergerac recalls how, as a nine-year-old child, he witnessed the developing relationship between his twenty-two-year-old sister Gabrielle and Pierre Coquelin, who has been employed by his father the Baron as a tutor. Marked with 'the genuine plebeian stamp', Coquelin possesses 'a certain masculine freshness and elasticity' (*CT*, II, 114, 115). He is a disciple of Rousseau's ideas on education and takes his charge on long walks, during which, 'without perverting my signorial morals or instilling any notions that were treason to my rank and position, he kindled in my childish breast a little democratic flame' (p. 130). Part way through the tale, the young M. de Bergerac is taken on a visit to a castle by Gabrielle and Coquelin. The castle has 'two great towers', and the boy watches his tutor climb one of them and stand 'on the summit of the edifice, waving his hat' (pp. 142, 148). When Coquelin and Gabrielle eventually confess their feelings for each other the latter recognizes the 'criminality' of her love and has 'no desire to realize her passion' (pp. 157, 156). Feeling that he could only remain 'on the footing of a thief and impostor', Coquelin decides to leave his employer's family (p. 156). Shortly afterwards the Baron forces his son to reveal the truth about the relations between Gabrielle and Coquelin (p. 159). Gabrielle finds herself rejected by her family and is accused of having tried to 'pollute' her younger brother (p. 166). She marries Coquelin, moves to Paris, and is executed alongside her husband during the Reign of Terror.

A young boy; a transgressive relationship between a woman and a socially inferior man; a castle with two towers: a number of elements

† From *Henry James and the Ghostly* (Cambridge: Cambridge University Press, 1994), pp. 109–11, 269–70. [Lustig's references are all to *The Complete Tales of Henry James*, edited by Leon Edel. 12 vols. (London, 1962–64). Page references to this Norton Critical Edition are given in brackets following the author's original citations.]

in 'Gabrielle de Bergerac' anticipate 'The Turn of the Screw'. The resonances between the two tales (both frame stories) are at their most intense in the resemblances between Pierre Coquelin and Peter Quint. One is a tutor; the other, according to Mrs Grose, used to behave as if he were a tutor (see *CT*, x, 64) [35]. One accuses himself of being a virtual thief; the other, again according to Mrs Grose, may well have been an actual thief (see p. 47) [23]. The governess remarks that Quint looks 'like an actor' (p. 47) [23]. The name 'Coquelin' itself belonged to an actor that James had known as a boy.[2] Both Quint and Coquelin are seen on the tops of towers and there is a suggestive echo which plays between French 'Pierre' and English 'Peter', between 'Coquelin' and 'Quint'. M. de Bergerac tells Coquelin that he is 'not a gentleman' (*CT*, II, 103) and when Mrs Grose asks the governess whether Quint 'was . . . a gentleman?', she replies in the negative (*CT*, II, 103; x, 45) [23].

Imagine that at the end of 'Gabrielle de Bergerac' the scene shifts to England. M. de Bergerac, now ten years of age, acquires a younger sister. The Baron dies and his brother, who lives in Harley Street, engages a governess to bring up his potentially polluted wards. Extended in this admittedly fanciful way, 'Gabrielle de Bergerac' begins to look like an account of what happened at Bly before the arrival of the governess. Read through 'Gabrielle de Bergerac', Miss Jessel's departure from Bly, like Coquelin's initial decision to rectify his false position by leaving the de Bergeracs, could be read as an attempt to avoid the criminality of a continued liaison. Far from being 'infamous', Miss Jessel would become a sad victim of class barriers (*CT*, x, 59) [31]. Read through 'Gabrielle de Bergerac', Quint might be a type of 'masculine freshness and elasticity' and not a 'horror' (*CT*, II, 115; x, 45) [22]. The relationship between Quint and Jessel would become an example not of corruption and depravity but of what Coquelin calls the 'tragedies, sorrows, and cruelties' which constitute 'the ghost of the past' (*CT*, II, 144). The time that Miles has spent with a social inferior like Quint would not in the least have perverted his 'signorial morals' but might instead have kindled a 'democratic flame' (*CT*, II, 130).[3] If the governess can be seen as a reader of 'Gabrielle de Bergerac' then she is an extremely unsympathetic one. Unlike Coquelin she is no devotee of Rousseau and describes the fact that Miles has lied and been impudent as an outbreak of 'the little natural man' (*CT*, x, 66) [36].[4] Coquelin's democratic beliefs would not have been attractive to the governess, who finds the very idea of freedom deeply suspicious. Quint's hatlessness is a 'strange freedom' (p. 37) [16]. His presence on the tower suggests that he has taken 'a liberty rather gross' (p. 39) [18]. When Mrs Grose tells her that Quint was 'much too free', the governess experiences 'a sudden sickness of disgust' (p. 50) [25]. On this basis, Miles's attempt to gain 'more freedom' will later confirm her worst fears

(p. 95) [55]. Read through 'Gabrielle de Bergerac', the governess's attitude to past events at Bly as well as her attempts to extract a confession from Miles begin to resemble the actions of the inflexible Baron and the self-interested Gaston de Treuil who, by forcibly drawing a confession from the young M. de Bergerac and then attacking a perceived source of pollution in Gabrielle and Coquelin, effectively force the young lovers together, making inevitable the transgression they had sought to avert.

To read a later work in terms of an earlier one is, of course, almost always to simplify both and often to use the original text as an improvised key to pick the lock of the later.[5] 'The Turn of the Screw' is by no means a straightforward extension of 'Gabrielle de Bergerac', and naturally there are numerous differences, deviations and mismatchings between one tale and the other. Neither the reader nor the governess can ever say with certainty that things at Bly did or did not happen in the way they happen in 'Gabrielle de Bergerac'. What is significant is that the governess's awareness is only of corruption and her response only one of horror. The governess is unique amongst James's ghost-seers in viewing the apparitional as a manifestation of unmitigated evil.[6] The uncanny and semi-ghostly encounters of 'Travelling Companions' or *The Portrait of a Lady* inspire in Brooke and Isabel a fear not so much of evil but of limitation, an awareness not so much of corruption but of the failure of imagination and desire. 'Sir Edmund Orme' and 'Owen Wingrave' go much further, presenting the ghostly encounter as a potential privilege. Even the narrator of 'The Way it Came', who closely resembles the governess in her determination to enforce a univocal reading of events, accepts that ghostly experience is 'a rare extension of being' (*CT*, IX, 396, 400).

NOTES

1. O'Gormon raises but finally rejects the idea that the ghosts are not evil (see 'Henry James's Reading of "The Turn of the Screw" ' pp. 239–40).
2. For James's reminiscences of the French actor, see 'Coquelin'; *Autobiography*, pp. 228, 607.
3. Sheppard argues that Quint and Jessel could be seen as 'godless revolutionaries' and that Quint is a revival of Paul Muniment in *The Princess Casamassima* (*Henry James and 'The Turn of the Screw'*, p. 100).
4. On this point, see O'Gorman, 'Henry James's Reading of "The Turn of the Screw" ', p. 238; Firebaugh, 'Inadequacy in Eden', p. 63.
5. This strategy is not unprecedented in accounts of the Jamesian uncanny. In 'The Ghost of Henry James', Rosenzweig reads 'The Jolly Corner' as a revised version of 'The Story of a Year'. Rosenzweig's 'The Ghost of Henry James: Revised' extends the theory of origins to 'A Tragedy of Error'.
6. See Briggs, *Night Visitors*, p. 151.

WORKS CITED

Briggs, Julia. *Night Visitors: The Rise and Fall of the English Ghost Story*. London: Faber, 1977.

Firebaugh, Joseph J. "Inadequacy in Eden: Knowledge and 'The Turn of the Screw.' " *Modern Fiction Studies* 3 (1957): 57–63.

James, Henry. "Coquelin" 1887. *The Scenic Art: Notes on Acting and the Drama, 1872–1901*. Ed. Allan Wade. London: Rupert Hart-Davis, 1949. 198–218.
——. *Autobiography*. Ed. Frederick W. Dupee. London: W. H. Allen, 1956.
O'Gorman, Donal. "Henry James's Reading of 'The Turn of the Screw.'" *Henry James Review* 1 (1979–80): 125–38, 228–56.
Rosenzweig, Saul. "The Ghost of Henry James." *Partisan Review* 11 (1944): 436–55.
——. "The Ghost of Henry James: Revised, with a Postscript, 1962." *Modern Criticism: Theory and Practice*. Ed. Walter Sutton and Richard Foster. New York: Odyssey Press, 1963, 401–16.
Sheppard, E. A. *Henry James and "The Turn of the Screw."* Auckland: Auckland University Press, 1974.

CRITICISM

Early Reactions: 1898–1921

When *The Two Magics* was published in England and America in 1898 reviewers practically ignored the second tale, *Covering End*, in favor of *The Turn of the Screw*. The following selection makes no attempt to cover all of the early criticism but does try to show the diversity of opinion which the tale aroused.

THE NEW YORK TIMES

Magic of Evil and Love†

AN EXTRAORDINARY NEW VOLUME FROM HENRY JAMES

* * * "The Turn of the Screw," is . . . a deliberate, powerful, and horribly successful study of the magic of evil, of the subtle influence over human hearts and minds of the sin with which this world is accursed, as our language has not produced since Stevenson wrote his "Jekyll and Hyde." * * * The work is not horrible in any grotesque or "realistic" sense. The strongest and most affecting argument against sin we have lately encountered in literature (without forcing any didactic purpose upon the reader) it is nevertheless free from the slightest hint of grossness. Of any precise form of evil Mr. James says very little, and on this head he is never explicit. Yet, while the substance of his story is free from all impurity and the manner is always graceful and scrupulously polite, the very breath of hell seems to pervade some of its chapters, and in the outcome goodness, though depicted as alert and militant, is scarcely triumphant. The most depraved "realist" (using that word in its most popular sense, for, correctly speaking, the artistic method of Mr. James is realism as opposed to idealism) could surely not be more powerful, though he might, in his explicitness, defeat his supposed purpose. Mr. James's present purpose, as we understand it, is amply fulfilled.

† From *The New York Times Saturday Review of Books and Art,* III (October 15, 1898), 681–82.

NEW YORK TRIBUNE

A Masterpiece by Mr. Henry James†

If "The Turn of the Screw" had appeared at the beginning instead of toward the close of Mr. James's career, his critics would have prophesied for him, we think, a bright immortality. The volume before us provokes mingled joy and resentment—joy because the first story is a masterpiece; resentment because the author should have seen fit to associate with it a piece of his most forced and infelicitous work, a tale trashy in itself and tragic in its implication of long years spent upon similarly fruitless tasks. Why Mr. James should have hidden his light under a bushel so long, no man, we suppose, will ever know. It is deplorable that no one was at his side at the start to show him wherein his genius resided, to set him on the right track. With some such mentor directing his early efforts who knows but what "The Turn of the Screw" might have been one of a great company of brilliant works instead of a belated triumph? In conception the story is one of those weird things which might have descended from Hawthorne in a fortunate moment. In respect to execution it has a perfection which he would not have disdained. In fact, it is with him, and with him alone, that Mr. James upon this occasion may be compared. At one leap the author of "What Maisie Knew" and "In the Cage" and a dozen other fatuities takes his place among the creators of literature. We know now for what high tasks that sinuous style of his was destined—only to be wasted upon themes ignobly small. We realize now that Mr. James, if he had known and had cared, could have been great.

"The Turn of the Screw" is great because it crystallizes an original and fascinating idea in an absolutely appropriate form. There is not a word which could be spared, and that art of suggestion which Mr. James has employed before so fantastically that it has been more irritating than a flood of words could be here plays its part with consummate effect. There is no plot. This is rather the notation of a weird experience, with ramifications that now touch the action of the figures involved, and now touch their innermost thoughts, emotions and divinations. Instead of watching the drama, one becomes part of it, and passes with the supposititious narrator and her two young charges through unprecedented spiritual adventures. The governess who tells the tale sets it down from day to day as the events or the reflections brought about by her situation impel her to write. On one side she and an old family servant fight as they can to save two beautiful children from themselves. On the other are the two powers of evil who have

† From *New York Tribune Illustrated Supplement* (October 23, 1898), 14.

half entered into Miles and Flora and are seeking to wreak all their malignant desires upon the pair. Mr. James wisely introduces us into the combat by degrees. This is no vulgar ghost story, with sudden shocks, with clanking chains and veiled ladies in white, and clammy atmospheres. It is rather a picture of spiritual states, so subtly and yet so poignantly observed that all the usual paraphernalia of ghostliness recede in to the background as irrelevant. The only concession to that spectacular element inseparable from the literature of ghosts which the author makes is noted in the sharp contrast drawn between the mortals and the evil spirits. The latter choose two astonishingly beautiful children for their victims, a boy and a girl so radiant and charming that an apparition from the grave becomes, in their presence, trebly awful; and the scene of the tragedy is laid in a sleepy old English country house, surrounded by a peaceful and beautiful landscape. Even here, however, Mr. James displays impressive tact. The contrast is sharp, as we have said, but it is never excessive, never theatrical. "The Turn of the Screw" is one of the most thrilling stories we have ever read, and at the same time one of the most natural. * * *

THE OUTLOOK

["The Story * * * Is Distinctly Repulsive"]†

Mr. Henry James has written nothing more characteristic in method and style than "The Turn of the Screw," the first of the two stories which make up his latest volume, *The Two Magics*. This story concerns itself with the problem of evil, from which men of Puritan ancestry seem never able entirely to detach themselves. It is a ghost story, psychologically conceived, and illustrating a profound mortal law. It is, in fact, an account of the possession of two children by two evil spirits. This statement seems very bald, and will remind the reader of the ordinary clumsy, materialistic ghost story. It is hardly necessary to say that Mr. James's tale has nothing in common with the ordinary ghost story; it is altogether on a higher plane both of conception and art. The story itself is distinctly repulsive.

† From *The Outlook*, LX (October 29, 1898), 537.

HENRY HARLAND

Academy Portraits: Mr. Henry James†

* * * To tell the story of two little English children pursued to their destruction by two particularly hideous and evil ghosts, and not to make the story ugly, not to make it horrible, sinister, repulsive, not to make it ridiculous either, but to make it beautiful, simply and entirely beautiful, might well strike one as a performance requiring supernatural aid. Analysed, however, "the third magic" will perhaps turn out to be just a finer, intenser insight than that of other artists, served by a technique nearer to perfection. Mr. James sees with a larger, clearer, and more considerate imagination. He sees his subject not as a spot, detached, isolated; he sees it in its place, as part of a whole, of a system. And the dimmest thing, seen thus, becomes suddenly vivid, because its meaning is seen, because it illuminates the meaning of the whole. The slightest incident or accident, the most trifling accessory, seen thus, becomes essential, and therefore impressive. And things which, detached, isolated, would seem ugly, become beautiful, seen thus, because they are seen as a part of what Mr. James himself has called "the figure in the carpet."[1] When the story of "The Turn of the Screw" was first revealed to Mr. James, he saw the beauty in it, the beauty that would have remained invisible to most of us, because he saw the story not as an episode, separated from the rest of life, but as an instance, illustrative of the rest of life; and he presents it to us not as an anecdote, but, tacitly, as an illustration. He presents it to us as a moment in a continuity, related to the life that had gone before it, that went about it, that came after it. And so he succeeds in making us see it as beautiful too —as all saturated and suffused with beauty.

An intenser, finer insight, served by a technique nearer to perfection, a freer, firmer, more accomplished hand, and guided, restrained by a more exacting, a more sensitive literary conscience—that is the word one first feels impelled to speak, when asked to speak a word about Mr. Henry James. It is by no means the only word, it is by no means the last word. The last word of all, in speaking of any artist, must of course be *temperament*. But the temperament, golden and generous, human and sympathetic, exalted, fastidious, chivalrous, that glows through every page of Mr. James's writing, that warms every sentence, that gives to every syllable the ring of the living voice—that would be the theme for another and a far more ambitious study than the present.

† From *The Academy* (November 26, 1898), 339–40.

1. Harland, of course, refers to James's story, "The Figure in the Carpet," which appeared almost two years before "The Turn of the Screw" (in *Cosmopolis* January/February 1896) [*Editors*].

THE BOOKMAN

Mr. James's New Book†

Mr. James is in a queer mood. Nearly all his later stories have been tending to the horrible, have been stories of evil, beneath the surface mostly, and of corruption. * * * The circumstances, the conditions, in "The Turn of the Screw," all make for purity, beauty, and joy; and on the surface these are resplendent. But underneath is a sink of corruption, never uncovered, but darkly, potently hinted. * * * We have never read a more sickening, a more gratuitously melancholy tale. It has all Mr. James's cleverness, even his grace. The plottings of the good governess and the faithful Mrs. Grose to combat the evil, very gradually discovered, are marvellously real. You cannot help but assist at their interviews, and throb with their anxiety. You are amply convinced of the extraordinary charm of the children, of the fascination they exercise over all with whom they come in contact. The symbolism is clumsy; but only there in the story has Mr. James actually failed. It is not so much from a misunderstanding of child nature that he has plunged into the deep mistake of writing the story at all. Here, as elsewhere in his work, there are unmistakable signs of a close watchfulness and a loving admiration of children of the more distinguished order. A theory has run away with him. It is flimsily built on a few dark facts, so scattered and uncertain that they cannot support a theory at all. He has used his amiable knowledge of child life in its brighter phases to give a brilliant setting to this theory. His marvellous subtlety lends his examination of the situation an air of scientific precision. But the clever result is very cruel and untrue.

DROCH

Henry James as a Ghost Raiser††

Henry James has frequently given his readers shivers by the coldness with which he treats intense emotions. But it is a new thing for him to create a semblance of terror by a genuine story of "uncanny ugliness and horror and pain." In his latest volume, "The Two Magics" (Macmillan), he has shown what he can do with a tale of the Poe sort—and

† From *The Bookman*, XV (November, 1898), 54.

†† From *Life* XXXII, no. 831 (November 10, 1898), 368. "Droch" is the pseudonym of Robert Bridges, who wrote many literary reviews for *Life* throughout the 1890s.

he does it extremely well. He calls the story "The Turn of the Screw," and he does not hesitate to give the extra twist that makes the reader writhe under it. And when you sift the terror to its essential facts, there does not seem to be anything in it to make a fuss about. That two supremely beautiful children should be under the evil spell of the ghosts of a dead governess and a wicked valet is not, on the face of it, a very awe-inspiring situation. Indeed, the ludicrousness of it, in these enlightened days, is always in danger of breaking through the hedge which the author has ingeniously constructed around it.

But right there is the place for the literary artist to show what he can do—and Henry James does it in a way to raise goose-flesh! He creates the atmosphere of the tale with those slow, deliberate phrases which seem fitted only to differentiate the odors of rare flowers. Seldom does he make a direct assertion, but qualifies and negatives and double negatives, and then throws in a handful of adverbs, until the image floats away upon a verbal smoke. But while the image lasts, it is, artistically, a thing of beauty. When he seems to be vague he is by elimination creating an effect of terror, of unimaginable horrors.

While his art is present in every sentence, the artist is absolutely obliterated. His personality counts for nothing in the effect. He is like a perfect lens which focuses light, but is itself absolutely colorless.

JOHN D. BARRY

On Books at Christmas†

* * * Equally involved [as *In the Cage*] is the style of his second autumn book, "The Two Magics," which consists of two long tales, one of which is a very up-to-date and absorbing ghost-story. Henry James, I ought to add by way of caution, is by no means a safe author to give for a Christmas gift.

† From *Ainslee's Magazine*, II (December, 1898), 518.

THE AMERICAN MONTHLY REVIEW OF REVIEWS†

Two Volumes from Henry James

* * * ["The Turn of the Screw"] shows the mysterious legacy of evil that may continue in force after death. * * * The introduction to "The Turn of the Screw" seems a needlessly awkward method of starting the story. In spite of any criticisms that may be made, it is impossible to read this horribly absorbing narrative without recognizing that it is a notable achievement. It is in an entirely new vein for Mr. James and one in which his delicate, subtle psychology shows to best advantage, for the foul breath of the bottomless pit itself, which strikes the reader full in the face as he follows the plot, puts to shame by its penetrating force and quiet ghastliness the commonplace, unreal "horrors" of the ordinary ghost-story: it does indeed give an extra "turn of the screw" beyond anything of the sort that fiction has yet provided. There is something peculiarly against nature, something indescribably hellish in the thought of the beautiful little children holding unholy communion with the wraiths of two vile servants who had, when alive, corrupted them; and it would be difficult to find anything so unpretentious capable of producing such a living, indelible impression upon the mind. Let us hope that Mr. James will soon again give his unique gifts another chance in a field so congenial. To my mind it is the finest work he has ever done: there is a completeness, a finish, a sense of easy mastery and boundless reserve force about this story which are entirely fascinating. Looking back upon the tale when one has finished it, one instinctively compares it to a beautiful pearl: something perfect, rounded, calm, unforgettable. It would not require a rash prophet to predict that *The Two Magics* (Macmillan) will outweigh a score of such books as *In the Cage* in the future estimate of later nineteenth century literature.

† From *The American Monthly Review of Reviews* 18 (December 1898), 732–33. The review's title refers to *In the Cage* and *The Two Magics*, both of which appeared in 1898, the latter containing "Covering End" and "The Turn of the Screw."

THE INDEPENDENT

["The Most Hopelessly Evil Story"]†

* * * "The Turn of the Screw" is the most hopelessly evil story that we have ever read in any literature, ancient or modern. How Mr. James could, or how any man or woman could, choose to make such a study of infernal human debauchery, for it is nothing else, is unaccountable. It is the story of two orphan children, mere infants, whose guardian leaves them in a lonely English country house. The little boy and little girl, at the toddling period of life, when they are but helpless babes, fall under the influence of a governess and her lover who poison the very core of their conscience and character and defile their souls in a way and by means darkly and subtly hinted rather than portrayed by Mr. James. The study, while it exhibits Mr. James's genius in a powerful light, affects the reader with a disgust that is not to be expressed. The feeling after perusal of the horrible story is that one has been assisting in an outrage upon the holiest and sweetest fountain of human innocence, and helping to debauch—at least by helplessly standing by—the pure and trusting nature of children. Human imagination can go no further into infamy, literary art could not be used with more refined subtlety of spiritual defilement.

THE CHAUTAUQUAN

["Psychic Phenomena"]††

* * * [In *The Turn of the Screw*] Henry James again displays his skill as a delineator of psychic phenomena. In this particular story the theme is the continued influence on two children of a disreputable governess and her accomplice after their disappearance and the discovery of this influence by another governess who is keenly sensitive to psychic impulses. The intangible is here painted with a skill little short of the supernatural, and in dealing with these subtleties of the mind the author has produced a tale whose suggestiveness makes the blood bound through the veins with unusual rapidity.

† From *The Independent*, LI (January 5, 1899), 73.
†† From "Talk about Books," *The Chautauquan*, XXVIII, old series (March, 1899), 630.

OLIVER ELTON

["Facts, or Delusions"]†

Mr. James has put still more force into *The Turn of the Screw*, one of the hideous stories of our language. Is any limitation placed on the choice of an artist by the mere measure of the pain he inflicts upon the nerves? If not, then the subject is admissible. It is a tale where sinister and spectral powers are shown spoiling and daunting the innocence of the young. There is * * * the doubt, raised and kept hanging, whether, after all, the two ghosts who can choose to which persons they will appear, are facts, or delusions of the young governess who tells the story. * * * The whole visitation comes to us through its play upon the nerves, its stimulus to the courage of the young English lady who, desperate and unaided, vainly shelters the children. The tension is heightened by the distrust with which others regard her story, and the aversion towards her inspired by the ghosts in the children themselves.

WILLIAM LYON PHELPS

[The "Iron Scot" Stenographer]††

* * * I did not dream until the year 1898 that our author could draw a winsome, lovable, charming little boy, who would walk straight into our hearts. That year was a notable year in our writer's career; because it saw the publication of "The Turn of the Screw," which I found then and find again to be the most powerful, the most nerve-shattering ghost story I have ever read. The connoting strength of its author's reticence was never displayed to better advantage; had he spoken plainly, the book might have been barred from the mails; yet it is a great work of art, profoundly ethical, and making to all those who are interested in the moral welfare of boys and girls an appeal simply terrific in its intensity. With none of the conventional machinery of the melodrama, with no background of horrible or threatening scenery, with no hysterical language, this story made my blood chill, my spine curl, and every individual hair to stand on end. When I told the author exactly how I felt while reading it, and thanked him for giving me

† From "The Novels of Mr. Henry James," *Modern Studies* (Edward Arnold: London, 1907), pp. 245–289, 255–256.

†† From "Henry James," *The Yale Review*, V (July, 1916), 794. Later versions of this anecdote appeared in *Howells, James, Bryant, and Other Essays* (New York, 1924), and in *Autobiography with Letters* (New York, 1939).

sensations that I thought no author could give me at my age, he said that he was made happy by my testimony. "For," said he, "I meant to scare the whole world with that story; and you had precisely the emotion that I hoped to arouse in everybody. When I wrote it, I was too ill to hold the pen; I therefore dictated the whole thing to a Scot stenographer. I was glad to try this experiment, for I believed that I should be able to judge of its effect on the whole world by its effect on the man who should hear it first. Judge of my dismay when from first to last page this iron Scot betrayed not the slightest shade of feeling! I dictated to him sentences that I thought would make him leap from his chair; he short-handed them as though they had been geometry, and whenever I paused to see him collapse, he would enquire in a dry voice, 'What next?' "

A. R. ORAGE

Henry James, and the Ghostly†

* * *

The surprising thing about Henry James's novels is that one approaches them as stories and leaves them having assisted at a piece of life. One begins to read him as a diversion and finds at the end of him that one has had real experiences. He is, in fact, the magician of psychology, who not only describes—who, indeed does not describe, but portrays,—but reveals. * * * And as his readers look at the figures through Henry James's eyes, they are aware of a strange transformation in the ordinary people before them. While still remaining ordinary, extraordinary manifestations begin to be visible among them. They arouse wonder, they arouse pity, they arouse admiration, they arouse horror or fear. * * *

* * * If Henry James drew our attention to the sub-conscious "double" or psychic penumbra of living figures, he was almost certain in the end to present his figures as doubles without a body, in a word, as ghosts. And I was among the critics who, long before Henry James had written his *Two Magics* prophesied that he would shortly be writing of shadows directly. No student of his works can fail to observe how imperceptibly his method of dealing with real persons shades into his dealing with ghosts. There is a little more quietness, a little more mystery, a little more holding of the breath in the process of observation; but fundamentally the method is the same. His stories of the unembodied are, I think, the flower of his art. In these Henry James rose to

† From *The Little Review* 5:4 (August 1918), 41–43.

the perfection of his observation. In them he examined the subconscious, as it were, face to face.

I have remarked on another occasion that Henry James would be happy among the dead, for he understood them while he was still living. But let me supplement the remark here by the observation that Henry James did not commune with the disembodied alone, but aloud and in the hearing and in the experience of all his intended readers. His mission (if I may use the word and grieve for it) was to act as a kind of Charon to ferry the understanding over the dark passage of the Styx and to show us that we are such stuff as ghosts are made of.[1]

VIRGINIA WOOLF

["Henry James's Ghosts"]†

Henry James's ghosts have nothing in common with the violent old ghosts—the blood-stained sea captains, the white horses, the headless ladies of dark lanes and windy commons. They have their origin within us. They are present whenever the significant overflows our powers of expressing it; whenever the ordinary appears ringed by the strange. The baffling things that are left over, the frightening ones that persist—these are the emotions that he takes, embodies, makes consoling and companionable. But how can we be afraid? As the gentleman says when he has seen the ghost of Sir Edmund Orme for the first time: "I am ready to answer for it to all and sundry that ghosts are much less alarming and much more amusing than was commonly supposed." The beautiful urbane spirits are only not of this world because they are too fine for it. They have taken with them across the border their clothes, their manners, their breeding, their band-boxes, and valets and ladies' maids. They remain always a little worldly. We may feel clumsy in their presence, but we cannot feel afraid. What does it matter, then, if we do pick up "The Turn of the Screw" an hour or so before bedtime? After an exquisite entertainment we shall, if the other stories are to be trusted, end with this fine music in our ears, and sleep the sounder.

Perhaps it is the silence that first impresses us. Everything at Bly is so profoundly quiet. The twitter of birds at dawn, the far-away cries of children, faint footsteps in the distance stir it but leave it unbroken. It accumulates; it weighs us down; it makes us strangely apprehensive of

1. In Greek mythology, Charon is the old man who ferried the spirits of the dead across the rivers Styx and Acheron. The Styx is the river of hate that flows around the infernal regions [*Editors*].

† From "Henry James's Ghost Stories," *Granite and Rainbow* (The Hogarth Press, London), pp. 71–72; originally published in the *Times Literary Supplement*, December 22, 1921.

noise. At last the house and garden die out beneath it. "I can hear again, as I write, the intense hush in which the sounds of evening dropped. The rooks stopped cawing in the golden sky, and the friendly hour lost for the unspeakable minute all its voice." It is unspeakable. We know that the man who stands on the tower staring down at the governess beneath is evil. Some unutterable obscenity has come to the surface. It tries to get in; it tries to get at something. The exquisite little beings who lie innocently asleep must at all costs be protected. But the horror grows. Is it possible that the little girl, as she turns back from the window, has seen the woman outside? Has she been with Miss Jessel? Has Quint visited the boy? It is Quint who hangs about us in the dark; who is there in that corner and again there in that. It is Quint who must be reasoned away, and for all our reasoning returns. Can it be that we are afraid? But it is not a man with red hair and a white face whom we fear. We are afraid of something unnamed, of something, perhaps, in ourselves. In short, we turn on the light. If by its beams we examine the story in safety, note how masterly the telling is, how each sentence is stretched, each image filled, how the inner world gains from the robustness of the outer, how beauty and obscenity twined together worm their way to the depths—still we must own that something remains unaccounted for. We must admit that Henry James has conquered. That courtly, worldly, sentimental old gentleman can still make us afraid of the dark.

Major Criticism: 1921–70

HAROLD C. GODDARD

A Pre-Freudian Reading of *The Turn of the Screw*†

* * *

Consider the second governess for a moment and the situation in which she finds herself. She is a young woman, only twenty, the daughter of a country parson, who, from his daughter's one allusion to him in her story, is of a psychically unbalanced nature; he may, indeed, even have been insane. We are given a number of oblique glimpses into the young woman's home and early environment. They all point to its stifling narrowness. From the confinement of her provincial home this young and inexperienced woman comes up to London to answer an advertisement for a governess. That in itself constitutes a sufficient crisis in the life of one who, after one glimpse, we do not need to be told is an excessively nervous and emotional person. But to add to the intensity of the situation the young woman falls instantly and passionately in love with the man who has inserted the advertisement. She scarcely admits it even to herself, for in her heart she knows that her love is hopeless, the object of her affection being one socially out of her sphere, a gentleman who can never regard her as anything other than a governess. But even this is not all. In her overwrought condition, the unexplained death of the former governess, her predecessor, was enough to suggest some mysterious danger connected with the position offered, especially in view of the master's strange stipulation: that the incumbent should assume *all* responsibility, even to the point of cutting off all communication with him—never writing, never reporting. Something extraordinary, she was convinced, lurked in the background. She would never have accepted the place if it had not been for her newborn

† From *Nineteenth-Century Fiction*, XII, No. 1 (June, 1957), 6–10, 11–13, 19–20, 22–24, 28, 32–33. Copyright © 1957 by the Regents of the University of California. Used by permission. Goddard's essay was discovered posthumously. Though he never made any attempt to have it published, Goddard delivered his remarks in course lectures from the early 1920s onward. Goddard's daughter forwarded the essay to Edmund Wilson, who sent it on to Leon Edel, who agreed that it should be published. Thus, despite its 1957 publication date, Goddard's essay is credited as the first to put forward the theory that James's governess suffers hallucinations.

passion; she could not bring herself to disappoint him when he seemed to beg compliance of her as a favor—to say nothing of severing her only link with the man who had so powerfully attracted her.

So she goes down to Bly, this slip of a girl, and finds herself no longer a poor parson's daughter but, quite literally, the head of a considerable country establishment. As if to impart the last ingredient to the witch's broth of her emotions, she is carried away almost to the point of ecstasy by the beauty of the two children, Miles and Flora, who have been confided to her care. All this could supply the material for a nervous breakdown in a girl of no worldly experience and of unstable psychical background. At any rate she instantly becomes the victim of insomnia. The very first night she fancies that she hears a light footstep outside her door and in the far distance the cry of a child. And more serious symptoms soon appear.

But before considering these, think what would be bound to happen even to a more normal mentality in such a situation. When a young person, especially a young woman, falls in love and circumstances forbid the normal growth and confession of the passion, the emotion, dammed up, overflows in a psychical experience, a daydream, or internal drama which the mind creates in lieu of the thwarted realization in the objective world. In romantic natures this takes the form of imagined deeds of extraordinary heroism or self-sacrifice done in behalf of the beloved object. The governess' is precisely such a nature and the fact that she knows her love is futile intensifies the tendency. Her whole being tingles with the craving to perform some act of unexampled courage. To carry out her duties as governess is not enough. They are too humdrum. If only the house would take fire by night, and both children be in peril! Or if one of them would fall into the water! But no such crudely melodramatic opportunities occur. What does occur is something far more indefinite, far more provocative to the imaginative than to the active faculties: the boy, Miles, is dismissed from school for no assigned or assignable reason. Once more, the hint of something evil and extraordinary behind the scenes! It is just the touch of objectivity needed to set off the subconsciousness of the governess into an orgy of myth-making. Another woman of a more practical and common sense turn would have made inquiries, would have followed the thing up, would have been insistent. But it is precisely complication and not explanation that this woman wants—though of course she does not know it. The vague feeling of fear with which the place is invested for her is fertile soil for imaginative invention and an inadvertent hint about Peter Quint dropped by the housekeeper, Mrs. Grose, is just the seed that that soil requires. There is no more significant bit of dialogue in the story. Yet the reader, unless he is alert, is likely to pass it by unmarked. The governess and the housekeeper are exchanging confidences. The former asks:

"What was the lady who was here before?"

"The last governess? She was also young and pretty—almost as young and almost as pretty, Miss, even as you."

"Ah then I hope her youth and her beauty helped her!" I recollect throwing off. "He seems to like us young and pretty!"

"Oh he *did*," Mrs. Grose assented: "it was the way he liked everyone!" She had no sooner spoken indeed than she caught herself up. "I mean that's *his* way—the master's."

I was struck. "But of whom did you speak first?"

She looked blank, but she coloured. "Why, of *him*."

"Of the master?"

"Of who else?"

There was so obviously no one else that the next moment I had lost my impression of her having accidentally said more than she meant.

The consciousness of the governess may have lost its impression, but we do not need to be students of psychology to know that that inveterate playwright and stage manager, the subconscious, would never permit so valuable a hint to go unutilized.

Mrs. Grose, as her coloring shows and as the governess discerns, is thinking of some one other than the master. Of what man would she naturally think, on the mention of Miss Jessel, if not of Miss Jessel's running mate and partner in evil, Peter Quint? It is a momentary slip, but it is none the less fatal. It supplies the one character missing in the heroic drama that the governess' repressed desire is bent on staging: namely, the villain. The hero of that drama is behind the scenes: the master in Harley Street. The heroine, of course, is the governess herself. The villain, as we have said, is this unknown man who "liked them young and pretty." The first complication in the plot is the mysterious dismissal of the boy from school, suggestive of some dim power of evil shadowing the child. The plot itself remains to be worked out, but it will inevitably turn on some act of heroism or self-sacrifice—both by preference—on the part of the heroine for the benefit of the hero and to the discomfiture of the villain. It is a foregone conclusion, too, that the villain will be in some way connected with the boy's predicament at school. (That he really was is a coincidence.) All this is not conjecture. It is elemental human psychology.

Such is the material and plan upon which the dreaming consciousness of the governess sets to work. But how dream when one is the victim of insomnia? Daydream, then? But ordinary daydreams are not enough for the passionate nature of the governess. So she proceeds to act her drama out, quite after the fashion of a highly imaginative child at play. And the first scene of her dramatic creation is compressed into the few moments when she sees the stranger on the tower of Bly by twilight.

Whence does that apparition come? *Out of the governess's unconfessed love and unformulated fear.* * * *

* * * The governess feels her sudden vibration of duty and courage as the effect of the apparition, but it would be closer to the truth to call it its cause. Why has the stranger come for the children rather than for her? Because she must not merely be brave; she must be brave for someone's sake. The hero must be brought into the drama. She must save the beings whom he has commissioned her to protect. And that she may have the opportunity to save them they must be menaced: they must have enemies. That is the creative logic of her hallucination.

"Hallucination!" a dozen objectors will cry, unable to hold in any longer. "Why! the very word shows that you have missed the whole point of the story. The creature at the window is no hallucination. It is he himself, Peter Quint, returned from the dead. If not, how was Mrs. Grose able to recognize him—and later Miss Jessel—from the governess's description?"

The objection seems well taken. The point, indeed, is a capital one with the governess herself, who clings to it as unshakable proof that she is not mad; for Mrs. Grose, it appears, though she seems to accept her companion's account of her strange experiences, has moments of back-sliding, of toying with the hypothesis that the ghosts are mere creatures of the governess' fancy. Whereupon, says the latter, "I had only to ask her how, if I had 'made it up,' I came to be able to give, of each of the persons appearing to me, a picture disclosing, to the last detail, their special marks—a portrait on the exhibition of which she had instantly recognized and named them." This retort floors Mrs. Grose completely, and she wishes "to sink the whole subject."

But Mrs. Grose is a trustful soul, too easily floored perhaps. If we will look into the matter a bit further than she did, we will perceive that it simply is not true that the governess gave such detailed descriptions of Peter Quint and Miss Jessel that Mrs. Grose instantly recognized their portraits. In the case of Miss Jessel, indeed, such a statement is the very reverse of the truth. The "detailed" description consisted, beyond the colorless fact that the ghost was pale, precisely of the two items that the woman who appeared was extremely beautiful and was dressed in black. But Mrs. Grose had already told the governess explicitly, long before any ghost was thought of, that Miss Jessel was beautiful. Whether she had been accustomed to dress in black we never learn. But that makes little difference, for the fact is that it is *the governess herself and not Mrs. Grose at all who does the identifying*:

> "Was she someone you've never seen?" asked Mrs. Grose.
>
> "Never," the governess replies. "But some one the child has. Some one *you* have." Then to show how I had thought it all out: "My predecessor—the one who died."
>
> "Miss Jessel?"
>
> "Miss Jessel," the governess confirms. "You don't believe me?"

And the ensuing conversation makes it abundantly plain that Mrs. Grose is still far from convinced. This seems a trifle odd in view of the fact that Peter Quint is known to be haunting the place. After having believed in one ghost, it ought not to be hard for Mrs. Grose to believe in another, especially when the human counterparts of the two were as inseparable in life as were the valet and the former governess. Which makes it look as if the housekeeper were perhaps not so certain after all in the case of Quint. Why, then, we ask, did she "identify him"? To which the answer is that she identified him because the suggestion for the identification, just as in the case of Miss Jessel, though much more subtly, come from the governess herself. The skill with which James manages to throw the reader off the scent in this scene is consummate.

* * *

It is solely on the governess' say-so that we agree to the notion that the two specters have returned in search of the *children*. Again it is on her unsupported word that we accept for fact her statement that, on the occasion in the garden when Miss Jessel first appeared, Flora *saw*. The scene itself, after Miss Jessel's advent, is not presented. (Time enough to present his scenes when James has "suggested" to his readers what they shall see.) What happened is narrated by the governess, who simply announces flatly to Mrs. Grose that, "Two hours ago, in the garden, Flora *saw*." And when Mrs. Grose naturally enough demands, ". . . how do you know?" her only answer is, "I was there—I saw with my eyes," an answer valuable or worthless in direct proportion to the governess' power to see things as they are.

In the case of Miles the method is the same except that James, feeling that he now has a grip on the reader, proceeds more boldly. The scene is not narrated this time; it is presented—but only indirectly. The governess, looking down from a window, catches Miles out at midnight on the lawn. He gazes up, as nearly as she can figure, to a point on the building over her head. Whereupon she promptly draws the inference: "There was clearly another person above me. There was a person on the tower." This, when we stop to think, is even "thinner" than in the case of Flora and Miss Jessel, for this time even the governess does not see, she merely infers. The boy gazes up. "Clearly" there was a man upon the tower. That "clearly" lets the cat out of the bag. It shows, as every tyro in psychology should know, that "clear" is precisely what the thing is not.

These two instances are typical of the governess' mania. She seizes the flimsiest pretexts for finding confirmation of her suspicions. Her theories swell to such immense dimensions that when the poor little facts emerge they are immediately swallowed up. She half admits this herself at the very beginning of the story. "It seems to me indeed, in raking it all over," she says of the night following the appearance of Quint at the dining room window, "that by the time the morrow's sun was high I had restlessly read into the facts before us almost all the meaning they were to receive from subsequent and more cruel occurrences." Scarcely ever was the essence of mania better compressed into a sentence than in her statement: "The more I go over it the more I see in it, and the more I see in it the more I fear. I don't know what I *don't* see, what I *don't* fear!"

* * *

Fear is like faith: it ultimately creates what at first it only imagined. The governess, at the beginning, imagines that the actions and words of the children are strange and unnatural. In the end they become strange and unnatural for the good and sufficient reason that the children gradually become conscious of the strangeness and unnaturalness of her own attitude toward them. They cannot put it into words: they have never heard of nervousness, still less of insanity. But they sense it and grow afraid, and she accepts the abnormal condition into which their fear of *her* has thrown them as proof of their intercourse with the two specters. Thus do her mania and their fear feed and augment each other, until the situation culminates—in a preliminary way—in two scenes of shuddering terror.

The first of these is the occasion when the governess comes at night to Miles's bedside and tries, without mentioning the dreaded name of Quint, to wring from the child a confession of the infernal intercourse which, she is convinced, he is guilty of holding. Forget, for the moment, the governess' version of the occurrence and think of it as it must have appeared in the child. A little boy of ten, who has for some time felt something creepy and uncanny in the woman who has been placed in charge of him and his sister, lies awake in the dark thinking of her and of the strangeness of it all. He hears steps outside his door. At his call the door opens, and there, candle in hand, is this very woman. She enters and sits beside him on the edge of the bed. For a moment or two she talks naturally, asking him why he is not asleep. He tells her. And then, quite suddenly, he notices in her voice the queer tone he has felt before, and the something in her manner, excited but suppressed, that he does not like. As they go on talking, this excitement grows and grows, until in a final outburst she falls on her knees before him and begs him to let her *save* him! Visualize the scene: the hapless child utterly at a loss to know what the dreadful "something" is from which she would "save" him; the insane woman on her knees almost clasping him in her hysterical embrace. Is it any wonder that the interview terminates in a shriek that bursts from the lips of the terror-stricken boy? Nothing could be more natural. Yet, characteristically, the governess interprets the boy's fright and outcry as convincing proof of the presence of the creature she is seeking to exorcise. Utterly unconscious of the child's fear of *her*, she attributes his agitation to the only other adequate cause she can conceive.

The corresponding scene in the case of Flora occurs the next day by the lake. Once more, think of it from the angle of the child. A little girl, too closely watched and confined by her governess, seizes an opportunity for freedom that presents itself and wanders off for half an hour in the grounds of the estate where she lives. A little later, the governess and the housekeeper, out of breath with searching, come upon her. A half-dozen words have hardly been exchanged when the governess, a tremor in her voice, turns suddenly on the child and demands to know where her former governess is—a woman whom the little girl knows perfectly well is dead and buried. The child's face blanches, the housekeeper utters a cry, in answer to which the governess, pointing across the lake and into vacancy cries out: "She's there, she's there!" The child stares at the demented woman in consternation. The latter repeats: "She's there, you little unhappy thing—there, there, *there*, and you know it as well as you know me!" The little girl holding fast to the housekeeper, is frozen in a convulsion of fear. She recovers herself sufficiently to cry out, "I don't know what you mean. I see nobody. I see nothing. I never *have*," and then, hiding her head in the housekeeper's skirts, she breaks out in a wail, "Take me away, take me away—oh take me away from *her*!"

"From *me*?" the governess cries, as if thunderstruck that it is not from the specter that she asks to be delivered.

"From you—from you!" the child confirms.

Again, is not the scene, when innocently taken, perfectly natural? Yet again the governess is incapable of perceiving that the child is stricken with terror not at all at the apparition but at *her* and the effect the apparition has had upon her.

* * *

If on your first reading of *The Turn of the Screw* the hypothesis did not occur to you that the governess is insane, run through the story again and you will hardly know which to admire more, James's daring in introducing the cruder physical as distinguished from the subtler psychological symptoms of insanity or his skill in covering them up and seeming to explain them away. The insane woman is telling her own story. She cannot see her own insanity—she can only see its reflection, as it were, in the faces, trace its effect on the acts, of others. And because "the others" are in her case children and an ignorant and superstitious woman, these reflections and effects are to be found in the sphere of their emotions rather than in that of their understandings. They see and feel her insanity, but they cannot comprehend or name it.

The most frequent mark of her disease is her insane *look* which is mirrored for us in the countenances and eyes of the others.

Mrs. Grose first sees this look in something like its fullness when the governess gazes through the window of the dining room after she has seen Peter Quint. So terrible is the sight of her face that Mrs. Grose draws back blanched and stunned, quite as if it were a ghost that she had seen. "Did I look very queer?" the governess asks a moment later when the housekeeper has joined her. "Through this window?" Mrs. Grose returns. "Dreadful!"

There are a dozen other passages that strike the same note.

* * *

* * * Surely the human brain is as solid a fact as the terrestrial globe, and inhabitants of the former have just as authentic an existence as inhabitants of the latter. Nor do I mean by that to imply, as to some I will seem to have implied all through, that Peter Quint and Miss Jessel exist *only* in the brain of the governess. Perhaps they do and perhaps they don't. Like Hawthorne in similar situations—but with an art that makes even Hawthorne look clumsy—James is wise enough and intellectually humble enough to leave that question open. Nobody knows enough about insanity yet to be dogmatic on such a matter. Whether the insane man creates his hallucinations or whether insanity is precisely the power to perceive objective existences of another order, whether higher or lower, than humanity, no open-minded person can possibly pretend to say, however preponderating in the one direction or the other present evidence may seem to him to be. Whoever prefers to, then, is free to believe that the governess sees the actual spirits of Peter Quint and Miss Jessel. Nothing in the tale, I have tried to show, demands that hypothesis. But nothing, on the other hand, absolutely contradicts it. Indeed, there is room between these extremes for a third possibility. Perhaps the governess' brain caught a true image of Peter Quint straight from Mrs. Grose's memory via the ether or some subtler medium of thought transference. The tale in these respects is susceptible of various readings. But for one theory it offers, I hold, not an inch of standing ground: for the idea, namely, that the children *saw*.

* * *

EDNA KENTON

Henry James to the Ruminant Reader: *The Turn of the Screw*†

* * * Critical appraisement of *The Turn of the Screw* has never, indeed, pressed beyond the outer circle of the story where the children and ghosts dance together, toward any discerned or discernible inner ring where another figure may be executing some frantic dance of terror, toward any possible story behind the "story," toward any character protected by its creator to the very top of his sardonic, ironic bent. * * *

It is as if, wearied of devoted readers who boasted of their "attention of perusual" and their consequent certainties of perception—certainties, by the way, which James was never wont to disturb—he determined to write, in *The Turn of the Screw*, a story for "the world." He would write it of course primarily for himself and for that reader for whom he must always write—the reader not content to have the author do all of the work—but he would make this particular work a supreme test, of attention and of inattention alike. He would have his own private "fun" in its writing, his own guarded intention, his own famous centre of interest. But he would put about this centre, not only traps set and baited for the least lapse of attention, but lures—delights and terrors mingled—calculated to distract or break off short any amount of alert intentness. Let some singularly astute reader avoid one and yet another of these—others would lie hidden or beckon invitingly ten steps ahead. It would be, as he said ten years later, "an *amusette* to catch those not easily caught." But to make the amusement more complete, he would see how far he might go, this single time, in catching not only the cunning but the casual reader, the latter too often not his prey, in the maze of an irresistible illusion. He would make a deliberate bid, not only for as much attention as possible, but for as little. Illusion, if it were based on some denominator common to mankind, could be irresistible, if the right emotional spring were only rightly touched. It would be amusing to see how far he might work on the cunning and the casual alike; it would be the very essence of irony if their reactions to the story were identical. As a little matter of critical history they were. And Henry James narrowly escaped writing a best seller.

* * * The children hounded by the prowling ghosts—this is the hard and shining surface story of *The Turn of the Screw*; or to put it more accurately, it is the traditional and accepted interpretation of the story as it has come down through a quarter of a century of readers' reactions

† From *The Arts* 6 (November 1924), 245–55.

resulting from "a cold, artistic calculation" on the part of its highly entertained author. As a tiny matter of literal fact, no reader has more to go on than the young governess's word for this rather momentous and sidetracking allegation. As a rather large matter of literal fact, we may know, with but a modicum of attention paid to her recital of these nerve-shattering affairs at Bly, that it is she—always she herself—who sees the lurking shapes and heralds them to her little world. Not to the charming little Flora, but, behind Flora and facing the governess, the apparitional Miss Jessel first appeared. There are traps and lures in plenty, but just a little wariness will suffice to disprove, with a single survey of the ground, the traditional, we might almost call it lazy version of this tale. Not the children, but the little governess was hounded by the ghosts who, as James confides with such suave frankness in his Preface, merely "helped me to express my subject all directly and intensely." * * *

So, on *The Turn of the Screw*, Henry James has won, hands down, all round; has won most of all when the reader, persistently baffled, but persistently wondering, comes face to face at last with the little governess, and realizes, with a conscious thrill greater than that of merely automatic nerve shudders before "horror," that the guarding ghosts and children—what they are and what they do—are only exquisite dramatizations of her little personal mystery, figures for the ebb and flow of troubled thought within her mind, acting out her story. If the reader has won for himself a blest sense of an extension of experience and consciousness in the recognition that her case, so delicate, so complicated, so critical and yet so transparent, has never in its whole treatment been cheapened or betrayed; if he has had, in the high modern sense, all of his "fun," he has none the less paid; he has worked for it all, and by that fruitful labor has verified James's earliest contention that there was a discoverable way to establish a relation of work shared between the writer and the reader sufficiently curious to follow through.

EDMUND WILSON

The Ambiguity of Henry James†

* * *

Observe that there is never any evidence that anybody but the governess sees the ghosts. She believes that the children see them but there

† From *Hound & Horn* 7 (1934), 385–406. Excerpts from "The Ambiguity of Henry James" originally appearing in *Hound & Horn* Magazine and revised for publication in *The Triple Thinkers* by Edmund Wilson.

is never any proof that they do. The housekeeper insists that she does not see them; it is apparently the governess who frightens her. The children, too, become hysterical; but this is evidently the governess's doing, too. Observe, also, from the Freudian point of view, the significance of the governess's interest in the little girl's pieces of wood and of the fact that the male apparition first appears on a tower and the female apparition on a lake. There seems to be only a single circumstance which does not fit into the hypothesis that the ghosts are hallucinations of the governess: the fact that the governess's description of the first ghost at a time when she has never heard of the valet should be identifiable by the housekeeper. But when we look back, we see that even this has been left open to a double interpretation. The governess has never heard of the valet, but it has been suggested to her in a conversation with the housekeeper that there has been some other male somewhere about who "liked every one young and pretty", and the idea of this other person has been ambiguously confused with the master and with the master's interest in her, the present governess. The master has never been described; we have merely been told that he was "handsome." Of the ghost, who is described in detail, we are told that he has "straight, good features," and he is wearing the master's clothes.

The governess continues to see the spirits, and the atmosphere becomes more and more hysterical. She believes that the children get up at night to meet them, though they are able to give plausible explanations of their behavior. The children become obviously uncomfortable; they begin to resent the governess. The boy begs to be sent to another school and threatens to write to his uncle, and the girl, under the governess's pressure to make her admit that Miss Jessel is haunting her, breaks down and demands to be sent away.

The governess is now left alone with the boy. A gruesome scene ensues. "We continued silent while the maid was with us—as silent, it whimsically occurred to me, as some young couple who, on their wedding-journey, at the inn, feel shy in the presence of the waiter." When the maid has gone, and she presses him to tell her why he was expelled from school, the boy seems suddenly afraid of her. He finally confesses that he "said things"—to "a few", to "those he liked". It all sounds very harmless: there comes to her out of her "very pity the appalling alarm of his being perhaps innocent. It was for the instant confounding and bottomless, for if he *were* innocent, what then on earth was *I*?" The valet appears at the window—it is "the white face of damnation". (But is the governess condemning the spirits to damnation or is she becoming damned herself?) She is aware that the boy does not see it. "No more, no more, no more!" she shrieks to the apparition. "Is she *here*?" asks the boy in panic (he has heard from his sister the incident of the governess's trying to make her admit she has seen Miss Jessel). No, she says, it is not the woman; "But it's at the window—straight before us. It's *there*!" . . . "It's *he*?" then. Whom does he mean by "he"? " 'Peter Quint—you devil!' His face gave again, round the room, its convulsed supplication. 'Where?' " "What does he matter now, my own?" she cries. "What will he *ever* matter? *I* have you, but he has lost you forever!" Then she shows him that the figure has vanished: "There, *there*!" she says, pointing toward the window. He looks and gives a cry; she feels that he is dead in her arms. From her point of view, the disappearance of the spirit has proved too terrible a shock for him and "his little heart, dispossessed, has stopped"; but if we study the dialogue from the other point of view, we see that he must have taken her "There, *there*!" as an answer to his own "*Where?*" She has finally made him believe either that he has actually seen something or that he is on the point of seeing something. He gives "the cry of a creature hurled over an abyss". She has literally frightened him to death.

When one has once been given this clue to *The Turn of the Screw*, one wonders how one could ever have missed it. There is a very good reason, however, in the fact that nowhere does James unequivocally give the thing away: everything from beginning to end can be taken equally well in either of two senses. * * * The whole thing has been primarily and completely a characterization of the governess: her visions and the way she behaves about them become as soon as we look at them from the obverse side, a solid and unmistakable picture of the poor country parson's daughter, with her English middle-class class-consciousness, her inability to admit to herself her sexual impulses and the relentless English "authority" which enables her to put over on inferiors even purposes which are totally mistaken and not at all to the other people's best interests.

The Turn of the Screw, then, on this theory, would be a masterpiece—not as a ghost story, there are a great many better ones of the ordinary kind—but as a study in morbid psychology. It is to this psychological value of the ghosts, I believe, that the story owes its fascination: it belongs with *Moby Dick* and the *Alice* books to a small group of fairy tales whose symbols exert a peculiar power by reason of the fact that they have behind them, whether or not the authors are aware of it, a profound grasp of subconscious processes.

And when we examine the story in this light, we understand for the first time its significance in connection with Henry James's other fiction—for the first time, because on any other hypothesis *The Turn of the Screw* would be, so far as I remember, the only story James ever wrote which did not have some more or less serious point. We see now that it is simply a variation on one of James's familiar themes: the frustrated Anglo-Saxon spinster; and we remember that he presents other cases of women who deceive themselves and others about the sources and character of their emotions.[1] * * *

* * * Even after we have made out the case for the hallucinated governess in *The Turn of the Screw,* the ambiguity still remains. Did James really ever intend us to find the clue? See his curious replies in his letters to people who write him about *The Turn of the Screw*: to what seem to have been leading questions, he seems to have given evasive answers, dismissing the story as a mere "pot-boiler", a mere "jeu d'esprit". Is the governess nice or is she horrid? Olive Chancellor in *The Bostonians*, though tragic perhaps, is horrid, and she is vanquished by Basil Ransom. There is, however, always the possibility in the case of *The Turn of the Screw* that James may be deliberately amusing himself at the expense of the mystification of his readers. * * *[2]

KATHERINE ANNE PORTER, ALLEN TATE, MARK VAN DOREN

A Radio Symposium†

* * *

PORTER: When I first read this story, I accepted the governess's visions as real, that is, the ghosts were real in themselves, and not only the governess, perhaps, but others might have seen them; they had a life of their own. But as I went on reading the story and studying it through the years, and I read Henry James's notes on it, I decided that the ghosts were a projection of the governess's imagination and were part of her plot.

TATE: It is evident, Miss Porter, isn't it, that nobody actually sees these people but the governess?

PORTER: Nobody.

TATE: James is very adroit in convincing the readers that perhaps they can be seen by other people, or have been, but if you look closely it is perfectly evident that nobody sees them as physical existences but the governess. I don't say that that destroys their reality.

PORTER: Not at all.

1. Wilson refers to Olive Chancellor, from James's *The Bostonians,* as the strong-willed spinster who is blind to her own sexual motives [*Editors*].
2. Wilson's essay was substantially revised and reissued in 1948. In this second version, Wilson attenuates his original reading of the governess's neurosis. In 1959, Wilson added a note in which he once again endorsed his original 1934 position [*Editors*].

† From *The New Invitation to Learning,* edited by Mark Van Doren, pp. 223–35. Broadcast May 3, 1942, on "Invitation to Learning."

VAN DOREN: And, of course, there's no possible doubt that she does see them. The statement "the governess sees the ghosts" is a true statement.

TATE: Oh, there's no question of that.

VAN DOREN: Not only does she have no doubt herself, but it never occurs to her that anyone else could question their presence.

TATE: She has a momentary doubt of a certain kind, Mr. Van Doren. Doesn't she say toward the end that if Flora goes out into the world and people come in from outside—for example, her employer, the uncle of the children—and look at the situation and find that the apparitions don't visually exist, then she will have to say: "Where am I?" Those are her exact words.

VAN DOREN: Yes, and there is one moment when Mrs. Grose, the housekeeper, the plain and simple woman of the story, fails to see Miss Jessel, the evil governess who has died.

TATE: That is one of the most interesting moments in the whole story.

VAN DOREN: The present governess even then, as you say, seems to understand that she may be lost if she can't make Mrs. Grose see this woman who is "as big as a blazing fire," for then she has no case. She does seem, at that moment, to think of herself as one having a case.

TATE: She has been so hard-pressed that she feels she must build the case herself even at the expense of the children. That is the sinister note which enters the second half of the story.

* * *

VAN DOREN: Well, this is the question then that frames itself in my mind: are we to take the story as a piece of psychology, as an exploration of a peculiar temperament, namely, the governess', suffering under illusions and hallucinations? I prefer not to take it that way. It seems to me that the story would shrink a great deal in power and significance if it were merely a story which psychoanalyzed an old maid.

TATE: I think we've got to take it that way and the other way, too—both at once—and perhaps if we take it both ways, we've got to take it in a third way which will explain the fact that the story is a unified thing, a single thing which is neither psychological wholly nor a mere naive attempt on the part of this governess to protect her children.

* * *

TATE: * * * It seems to me that given the time in which James lived and the growing interest then in the processes of the mind, we have to see James as taking that peculiar interest as a medium through which to set forth the reality of evil; because the reality of evil in this story is not destroyed, or made a false issue, by explaining it psychologically. In James's time the psychological basis was necessary. In the past, treatment of ghosts, the material projection of evil in earlier literature, didn't follow a psychological bent; it wasn't done psychologically; the evil creatures were presented in their full physical body and the public accepted them at their face value. We have become more sophisticated, and perhaps a little more decadent in our literature—certainly more critical. Don't we demand that all of these allegorical effects, all of these realities of evil, be set forth on some level that will also satisfy the critical point of view?

PORTER: Yes, that is important. James himself confessed that he wished to catch those not easily caught.

* * *

VAN DOREN: * * * I quite agree that the children are in some sense innocent, beautiful and clear. But so is the governess. We are suggesting that she is more sinister than she ever, at any rate, knows herself as being.

TATE: She never knows herself as being sinister.

VAN DOREN: We almost have imputed to her a plot to corrupt the children herself. Now I'm willing to believe that it is she who corrupts the children and brings about the death of the little boy. Nevertheless, that is precisely my way of understanding how potent the evil in this story is. The evil isn't merely thought to be; it is an actuality which passes through her as a perfectly transparent and non-resistant medium and then passes through the children. The evil is somehow there.

PORTER: And finally it is projected to an immense distance.

VAN DOREN: Yes, for she has great power. If it were merely a story of what she thought, of what she could fool herself into seeing, she wouldn't have the power she has over us as readers; she wouldn't be able, as you say, to project Quint and Miss Jessel to great distances, across lakes; to the tops of towers, and so on.

TATE: Mr. Van Doren, couldn't we put it this way? The governess doesn't invent these apparitions; they merely use her as a medium. Because, obviously, the monstrous proportions of the evil are so great that they are beyond the power of any individual imagination to invent. There is something much stronger than the governess operating through her. She has her own innocent later existence, as is proved, I think, by the prologue of the story, where we learn that after this terrible incident had passed, she went on to other posts and nothing like it occurred again. It was some peculiar conjunction of forces which permitted this evil to emerge through her here.

VAN DOREN: That is extremely interesting, Mr. Tate. You suggest to me another reason why James is a great writer. Living as he did in our time, which usually does not take stock in either good or evil, he was able to construct in the governess a creature almost like Cassandra, through whom evil tears its way without any instigation on her part at all—without, so to speak, her permission.

* * *

PORTER: The popular psychological explanation is too superficial.

VAN DOREN: Otherwise we should be aware that an explanation is ready and easy as we read along, whereas the truth is—we all grant this—that as we read along we're not explaining anything to ourselves at all. We're not saying: Well, a dreadful, dreadful thing is happening, yet we know the reason. In a very important sense we don't know the reason. Something is loose here in the world, if only in the mind of a woman. Something is loose in the world which is very powerful and beyond the control of any human being.

PORTER: I would say quite beyond the Freudian explanation.

VAN DOREN: Oh, decidedly.

PORTER: Here is one place where I find Freud completely defeated.

TATE: James knew substantially all that Freud knew before Freud came on the scene.

PORTER: All major artists do.

VAN DOREN: Any great story-teller has to, because a great story-teller has for his subject good and evil.

TATE: * * * Isn't it true that one trouble with the first-person narrative, the story told by somebody in the story, is that the authority of that person is usually not quite established? We say usually of such a person: she is participating in it, you can't expect her to give us an unbiased version of it; she's not sufficiently detached; she's not disinterested. But, while that's a liability in most first-person narratives, it seems to me that James's triumph consists in the fact that he has been able to take the defect of the method and use it for a positive purpose. The very fact that the governess is biased becomes a dramatic factor. The bias becomes a part of the story.

PORTER: Yes, and because she has no understanding at all of her real motive, she gives herself away completely and constantly.

TATE: Constantly. There are two levels: the level at which she sees the action and the level at which the reader can see it, and this creates an irony of which the governess is not aware.

* * *

TATE: Isn't that a wonderful scene in Miles's room at night? The governess comes—it bears out just what you were saying, Mr. Van Doren—she comes to have a talk with him, as you will remember, and to try to get out of him what he did at school. It's a general stock-taking of Miles's situation. It is one of the most powerful pieces of irony I've ever read, because the governess is actually making love to the little boy and she doesn't know it. But he knows it in a curious instinctive way; he blows the candle out to get rid of her.

PORTER: And the scene is wonderfully written—his terror at this visit in the night, with what for him was ghost or devil, all evil in fact, everything he had reason to be terrified of, coming into his room with that unpardonable invasion of his privacy—this is all projected with such admirable simplicity and directness that the reader forgets the words and shares the impression.

VAN DOREN: His very childish understanding of the fact that she is in love with him comes out, it seems to me, in the conversation in which he suggests that he should be going back to school now, because, after all, he's just a "fellow," and has no right to spend all of his time with a lady.

TATE: He shows something perfectly wonderful there. It is so simple that the implications are sometimes lost on the reader. He is sitting with her and there's a silence. The governess says, "Well, here we are." And Miles says, "Yes, we're here." Just like that.

VAN DOREN: That's right. But again it seems to me that the fame of this story among all of James's stories is justified by the fact that the evil in it somehow remains pure and general, remains undefined. All of the attempts on the part of the governess to find out what it is, after all, are frustrated. There is never any danger that evil will shrink here into vice, into misdemeanor.

TATE: James says that evil is never credible in fiction if it is presented in "weak specifications."

VAN DOREN: We have all had the experience of reading a story about some villain whom we can believe to be unspeakable—we like to believe in unspeakable villains—and then of being shocked by the discovery that all he did was murder his grandmother. That never is enough.

PORTER: Yes, nearly always the specific act, the crime, does seem inadequate compared to the great force of evil which produces it.

* * *

ROBERT B. HEILMAN

The Freudian Reading of *The Turn of the Screw*†

The Freudian reading of Henry James' *The Turn of the Screw*, which has had some currency in recent decades, does violence not only to the story but also to the Preface, which, like the story, demands scru-

† From *Modern Language Notes* 62:7 (November 1947), 433–45. Page references to this Norton Critical Edition are given in brackets following the author's original citations.

pulous attention. The Freudian reading was first given public expression by Edna Kenton in 1924; her view is that the ghosts and the attendant horrors are imagined by the neurotic governess, "trying to harmonize her own disharmonies by creating discords outside herself."[1] Miss Kenton, however, adduces almost no evidence to sustain her interpretation, but simply enjoys a gracefully gleeful revel in the conviction that James, by permitting the ghosts to seem real, has utterly fooled all the other readers of the story. * * *

* * * Indeed, the sly Freudian readers of the Preface—who ignore the letters entirely—seem to miss its whole tone and import: James speaks continually of the ghosts as if they are objective manifestations, and there is no sign whatever of a knowing wink to the rationalists.[2] He is concerned almost entirely with defining his technical problems and with observing, almost gaily, how satisfactorily they have been met.

The Freudians misread the internal evidence almost as valiantly as they do the external. In the story, of course, there are passages that it is possible to read ambivalently; but the determining unambiguous passages from which the critic might work are so plentiful that it seems hardly good critical strategy to use the ambiguous ones as points of departure, to treat them as if they were *un*ambiguous, and to roughride over the immitigable difficulties that then arise. We cannot examine all the passages to which Wilson does violence, but a consideration of several of them will show how wobbly his case is.

Wilson supposes the governess to be seeing ghosts because she is in a psychopathic state originating in a repressed passion for the master.[3] In view of the terrible outcome of the story, we should at best have to suspect the fallacy of insufficient cause. But the cause does not exist at all: the governess's feelings for the master are never repressed: they are wholly in the open and are joyously talked about: even in the opening section[4] which precedes Chapter 1, we are told that she is in love with him. There is no faint trace of the initial situation necessary to produce the distortion of personality upon which Wilson's analysis depends. But

1. Henry James to the Ruminant Reader, *The Arts*, VI (1924), 254.
2. What happens in the story is exactly described by Graham Greene's shrewd general remark on James: "James believed in the supernatural, but he saw evil as an equal force with good," in *The English Novelists: A Survey of the Novel by Twenty Contemporary Novelists*, ed. Derek Verschoyle (New York: Harcourt, Brace, 1936), p. 245. [Heilman refers specifically to James's December 1898 letter to H. G. Wells (see pp. 116–17). Here, Heilman argues, James states that the governess is not his subject and insists that the phenomena that she records are objective. *Editors.*]
3. [Heilman refers to Edmund Wilson's 1934 essay "The Ambiguity of Henry James," revised rpt. in *The Triple Thinkers* (New York: Harcourt, Brace, 1938), 122. Wilson's essay is excerpted on pp. 170–73 of this Norton Critical Edition. *Editors.*]
4. [*The Novels and Tales of Henry James*, New York Edition (1922)] pp. 150 ff [2ff]. Cf. also the outright admission of Chapter 1 (p. 162) [8]; and the clear implications of the phrase "in the right quarter" (p. 199) [27] and of the governess's self-analysis at the end of Chapter 12 (pp. 239–240) [48]. She can even be laughingly, not tensely, ironic about the uncle's inattentiveness to her (p. 287) [72–73].

Wilson does compel us to consider one point: why does James emphasize the governess's fascinated devotion to the master? For an important technical reason: it is the only way of motivating—although it is probably not quite successful—the governess's stubborn refusal to take the logical step of over-riding the master's irresponsible wish not to be bothered and of calling him in.[5] * * *

When the governess describes the ghost to Mrs. Grose, Mrs. Grose identifies it with Quint, the dead valet, whom the governess had never so much as heard of; and Mrs. Grose gives him—and later Miss Jessel—a character which is entirely consistent with what the governess has already inferred about the moral quality and intentions of the ghost.[6] There can be no firmer dramatic evidence of the objectivity of the apparition, and Wilson acknowledges the difficulty: but in order to sustain his contention that the hallucination grows out of the repressed passion for the uncle, he advances the incredible hypothesis that the governess has got master and man confused—which is inconsistent with her obviously having a sharp eye for distinctions—and that Quint and the uncle may look alike.[7] Even at his most unsubtle, James would hardly be found thus trafficking in coincidence. But if he were, it can hardly be supposed that Mrs. Grose, who in such matters is very observant, would not at some time comment upon the strange resemblance of master and man.

Like Miss Kenton, Wilson infers the unreality of the ghosts from the fact that *only* the governess acknowledges seeing them; he does not stop to consider that this fact may be wholly explicable in aesthetic terms. Of course Mrs. Grose does not see the ghosts: she is the good but slow-witted woman who sees only the obvious in life—for instance, the sexual irregularity of Quint and Miss Jessel—but does not unassisted detect the subtler manifestations of evil. She is the plain domestic type who is the foil for the sensitive acute governess—Cassandra-like in the insight which outspeeds the perceptions of those about her—whose ideal function is to penetrate and shape the soul. James's fondness for allegorical names is commonplace knowledge: Mrs. Grose is not called Mrs. *Grose* for nothing[8] (just as the governess is not the governess for nothing: the narrator exhibits the ideal function of the tutorial type). But as, little by little, the tangible evidence, such as that of Flora's

5. See Chapters 12 and 13. James's honesty with his reader appears in his presenting so fully the governess's unwillingness to call the uncle. In order to strengthen our impression of the uncle's power to fascinate, James even suggests that Mrs. Grose has felt that power: *she* too had not informed him of former goings-on at Bly (p. 261) [59]. Compare a further comment of hers (p. 162) [8].
6. Chapters 5, 6, and 7. The breakdown of the Wilson theory at this point has already been discussed by A. J. A. Waldock, "Mr. Edmund Wilson and 'The Turn of the Screw,' " *MLN*, 331–334 (May, 1947).
7. [Wilson] pp. 125–26.
8. "But she was a magnificent monument to the blessing of a want of imagination, . . ." (p. 230) [43].

language, corroborates the racing intuitions of the governess, Mrs. Grose comes to grasp the main points of the issue as it is seen totally by the governess and to share her understanding of the moral atmosphere. The acceptance by Mrs. Grose is unimpeachable substantiation. We ought to observe here, also, how carefully the governess records all the initial doubts felt by Mrs. Grose in each new crisis—doubts which at times shake her belief in her own mental soundness.[9] This is one of James's ways of establishing the reliability of the governess.

As for the children's appearing not to see the apparitions: this is one of the author's finest artistic strokes. James says that he wants to evoke a sense of evil: one of his basic ways of doing it is the suggestion, by means of the symbolic refusal to acknowledge the ghosts, of a sinisterly mature concealment of evil. But almost as if to guard against the mistaking of the denial of the ghosts for the non-existence of the ghosts, James takes care to buttress our sense of the reality of evil from another direction: he gives us the objective fact of the dismissal of Miles from school—a dismissal which is unexplained and which is absolutely final.[1] This dismissal Wilson, in plain defiance of the text, must attempt to put aside as of no consequence; of such a situation he says, indeed frivolously, that the governess "colors [it], on no evidence at all, with a significance somehow sinister."[2] James invests the letter from the school with further significance by the fact that, despite her real shock, which is elaborated later, Mrs. Grose finds a private meaning in the dismissal—"She gave me a look that I remarked at the moment; then, visibly, with a quick blankness, seemed to try to take it back";[3] so, unless we are to repudiate the governess's testimony entirely, the letter gains dramatic value through what it intimates to Mrs. Grose. Further, Wilson cannot deal with the fact that at the end of the final scene Miles, without hearing them spoken by anyone else, speaks the names of Miss Jessel and Quint and indicates his belief that they may be present. Again in plain defiance of the text Wilson says that Miles has managed to see Flora before her departure and thus to find out what the governess is thinking about.[4] Wilson says they met; James clearly indicates that they did not. But even if they had met, their meeting would not help Wilson especially. From Flora Miles might have learned the name "Miss Jessel"; but his spontaneous bursting forth with "Peter Quint" would still have to be explained.

Wilson admits that one point is inexplicable: the "gust of frozen air" felt by the governess when, at Miles's bedside, her effort to break down his moral resistance to her is interrupted by his shriek, a shaking of the

9. Note pp. 168–69, 204, 230–231, 278 (". . . so I was neither cruel nor mad"), 280–81, 290–91 [12–13, 30, 43–44, 68, 69–70, 74–75].
1. Pp. 165–66 [10].
2. [Wilson] P. 123.
3. P. 165 [10].
4. [Wilson] P. 129.

room, and sudden darkness.[5] Despite her feeling a strong blast, no window is open. Wilson takes literally Miles's statement that he turned out the light and suggests that the motive is shame at having to tell about his disgrace at school. But, for one thing, Miles *does not tell* about his disgrace, and, more important, his turning out the light of his own accord is absolutely incompatible with the theory that the governess is unbalanced. If she is unbalanced we must assume, at this stage of the story, that the children sense her disorder and are humoring her and treating her very carefully, not engaging in violent pranks that might be expected to be dangerously aggravating.

There are still other parts of the story that, on the Freudian hypothesis, are wholly inexplicable. First, as we have seen, is the fact that Mrs. Grose always comes into agreement with the governess—an agreement that is especially forceful because it usually follows upon doubt and hesitation.[6] Further—and this is a very large point—the Freudian hypothesis fails completely to deal with the conduct of the children. In the first place, their night-time escapades[7] are, for an eight- and a ten-year-old, virtually beyond the bounds of physical possibility. Wilson says blandly that the children "are able to give plausible explanations of their behavior"[8] but the fact is that children of that age simply are not wide awake, imaginatively alert, and capable of strategic maneuvering in the middle of the night. The fact that they are earnestly and imperturbably plotting in the middle of the night, and that they are sophisticatedly evasive in their gay response to questioning, is one of James's subtlest ways of suggesting moral disorder. What Wilson takes to be their "plausibility" is an index of their corruption. Second, the children's daytime conduct makes sense only in the light of the ostensible meaning of the story—the entertainment of the governess by one of them while the other escapes, Flora's difficult solitary trip on the final Sunday afternoon, her crossing the pond in a boat and hiding the boat apparently unaided ("All alone—that child?" exclaims Mrs. Grose),[9] her majestically noncommittal manner when she is found strangely alone at a considerable distance from the house.[1] Wilson simply ignores all these matters—ignores them as facts, and of course as the brilliant dramatic symbols they are of something unchildlike and inexplicably wrong. Third, there is the vulgarity of Flora's language after the gov-

5. [Wilson] Pp. 127–28. The scene discussed is at the end of Chapter 17.
6. The corroborative value of Mrs. Grose's information on the past and of her establishing of connections between past and present cannot be questioned at all in terms of the theory of ambiguity. To dispose of her evidence, the psychological critic must impugn the veracity of the governess from beginning to end. But such a method would completely dissolve the story by leaving us no dependable facts for investigation. Moreover, it would ignore the sense in which James gives the governess "authority."
7. Chapter 10.
8. [Wilson] P. 126.
9. P. 275 [66].
1. Chapters 18, 19, and 20.

erness has openly asked her about Miss Jessel—important evidence which can be intended only to show a temporarily concealed deterioration of character coming at last to the surface. Notably, too, it is Mrs. Grose who tells about this language and who, what is more, initiates the subject: "horrors," she calls what she has heard, showing no sign of suggestive pressure from the governess.[2] Further, the whole manner of the children is incompatible with their being terrified and perverted by the "authority" of the governess. What is inescapable in them, despite the admirable subtlety with which all this is conveyed, is precisely their freedom, their skill in spending their time as they wish without open challenges, their marvelously disciplined catering to the governess—or appearing to do so—while doing exactly what they please. After Flora's departure what the governess especially feels is the slenderness of her personal, and the disappearance of her official, hold upon the boy.[3] At no time do the children show any sign of unwillingness, compulsion, or fright—except in the final scene, in which Miles's fright, it seems logical to suppose, proceeds from the causes which the story says it does. In fact, James emphasizes strongly the falseness of Flora's apparent fear of the governess at the end by giving her a "grand manner about it" and having her ask "every three minutes" whether the governess is coming in and express a desire "never again to so much as look at you."[4] These are signs of artifice, not fright; they indicate self-conscious acting, righteous indignation strategically adopted, the truculence of the guilty person who still seeks loopholes.

Such evidence suggests that a great deal of unnecessary mystery has been made of the apparent ambiguity of the story. Actually, most of it is a by-product of James's method: his indirection; his refusal, in his fear of anti-climax, to define the evil; his rigid adherence to point of view; his refusal—amused, perhaps?—to break that point of view for a reassuring comment on those uncomfortable characters, the apparitions. This theory seems to come very close to James's own view of the ambiguity, upon which, it conveniently happens, he commented in the year of the story's appearance.[5] The disturbing ghosts, of course, are to be taken as symbolic,[6] a fact which the modern critic might easily grasp if he did not have to wrestle with another problem peculiarly uncon-

2. P. 289 [74].
3. See especially paragraph two of Chapter 22 (pp. 294–95) [76–77].
4. Pp. 286–87 [72].
5. To F. W. H. Myers, one of the founders of the Society for Psychical Research, James writes that he cannot give "any coherent account of my small inventions 'after the fact.' . . . The one thing and another that are questionable and ambiguous in them I mostly take to be conditions of their having got themselves pushed through at all" (*Letters*, I, 300) [see pp. 117–18 of this Norton Critical Edition].
6. In *The Supernatural in the Writings of Henry James* (Unpublished Thesis, Louisiana State University, 1939), Benjamin Carroll acutely discusses the use of the symbolic ghost as a general practice of James, and the kind of "authority" which James gives to his narrators—the authority of the observing and recording consciousness which is central in his method.

genial to modernity—the drama of salvation. The retreat into abnormal psychology is virtually predictable.

There is a final irony, however: if he does not break the chosen point of view, James at least does not adopt it until his main story is under way. At the start, then, we see behind the curtain and find important objective evidence for use in interpreting the governess's narrative. Now Miss Kenton, with considerable amusement at less observant readers, has discovered what she calls "the submerged and disregarded foreword,"[7] and what she has got from it is that the governess is in love with the master. Hence her whole interpretation. But had Miss Kenton herself read the foreword more observantly, she would have found the evidence that makes her interpretation untenable. For this initial section tells us what the governess was like some years later.

The governess, Wilson assures us,[8] "has literally frightened him [Miles] to death": the neurotic approaches criminal insanity. For such an individual, only the gravest kind of prognosis could be made. We might expect progressive deterioration, perhaps pathetic, perhaps horrible. We might barely conceive of a "cure," but we could hardly expect that it would obliterate all traces of the earlier disastrous tensions. What, then, does happen to the governess who at twenty is supposedly in so terrible a neurotic state? The prologue tells us explicitly: at the age of thirty or so she is still a spinster, still a governess, and therefore still heir, we may assume, to all psychic ills which Wilson imputes to her at the earlier stage. But at this age she seems, to a Cambridge undergraduate whom, ten years her junior, we may expect to be thoroughly critical, a fine, gracious woman who can elicit liking and respect. * * * James's unqualified initial picture of the governess, then, is wholly irreconcilable with the Freudian interpretation of her. The conclusion is obvious: at twenty the governess was, aside from her unusual sensitiveness and charm, a perfectly normal person.

The Turn of the Screw may seem a somewhat slight work to call forth all the debate. But there is something to be said for the debate. For one thing, it may point the danger of a facile, doctrinaire application of formulae where they have no business and hence compel either an ignoring of, or a gross distortion of, the materials. But more immediately: *The Turn of the Screw* is worth saving. Wilson turns the story into a commonplace clinical record, at the same time feeling—in one of the loveliest ironies of contemporary criticism—that he is giving it stature. He complacently announces that "the story, on any other hypothesis, would be, . . . the only thing James ever wrote which did not have some more or less serious point."[9] But his interpretation is, in the words

7. P. 251.
8. [Wilson] P. 130.
9. [Wilson] P. 131.

of Philip Rahv, a "fallacy of rationalism";[1] for the story has a very serious point indeed. *The Turn*, F. O. Matthiessen says, illustrates James's "extraordinary command of his own kind of darkness, . . . the darkness of moral evil."[2] The darkness is not obvious: Miss Kenton has fittingly laughed some of the simpler didacticisms out of court. How it is to be defined is another problem, at least part of the answer to which may be found in James's extraordinarily suggestive use of language.

* * *

R. P. BLACKMUR

["Her Ghosts, Her Other Selves, Those Parts of Ourselves"]†

* * *

The economy, the essential housekeeping, of James's talent could not reach the outward concentration of the theater where the action commands the meaning. He was at home only where the meaning, closely grasped, specifically interwoven, commanded the action. This economy he found in his late work where life was testing the artist and where he enlarged his role of the historian of fine consciences and became the creator of conscience itself and, what is even more remarkable in this largely unmotivated world, the creator of genuine motive as well. In the three great novels conscience and motive unite. Considered in this way Lambert Strether in *The Ambassadors*, Maggie Verver in *The Golden Bowl*, and Milly Theale in *The Wings of the Dove* are conscience and motive for everybody else taken separately and, taken together, for the human action as well. Each, naturally, is destroyed.

* * *

The Turn of the Screw (1898), which for years has been the puzzle-piece in James for Freudians to play with (it would be more intelligent to apply the drama of the psyche as construed in Jung), is rather a magnificent creation of a bad conscience—a conscience vitally deprived, but vitally desperate to transform its hallucinations into reality.

1. *The Great Short Novels of Henry James* (New York: Dial, 1944), p. 624. Mr. Rahv also makes the excellent point that the Freudian interpretation is so commonplace as to make the story less than interesting, that it "reduces the intention to a minimum."
2. *Henry James: The Major Phase* (New York: Oxford, 1944), p. 94. For a series of similar comments see the already quoted essay by Graham Greene in *The English Novelists*, pp. 231–46 *passim*.

† From "The Wings of the Dove," from *Studies in Henry James* by R. P. Blackmur. 1958 (New York: New Directions, 1983) 166, 168–69.

It is by that conscience and its vision of evil that the governess destroys the two children, and having done so escapes into another life. The ghosts she sees are the agents of her conscience, and their malevolence is her motive. In chapter twelve, the very center of the story, the current of evil begins to flow not only from the general outside in, as in the beginning, or just through Quint and Jessel (the ghosts) where it had seemed to concentrate for outlet, but also and spontaneously from the souls of the children themselves. Our heroine feels the evil in their unnatural goodness, which she had herself invented, along with the evil, and is therefore prone to feel it as everywhere developing. It is as if innocence is the looking glass for evil. It is only for her to tell *them*, the children, that they are possessed, and so to tell them that they will believe it; and indeed that is what happens. Meanwhile our heroine has begun to show herself quite above any merely primary infatuation, whether with herself or her bachelor employer remote in London. She is now driven by an energy which is suited to this solitary and friendless place and which mustn't be interfered with. She has taken hold; she has pushed along; she has dragged everything; nothing must stop the energy within her, for that energy is creative. So she goes on until she creates "the white face of damnation" and by it succeeds in killing the little boy—but not before he has identified the governess as the Devil. The abyss over which he fell at the moment of death is that of the intolerable consciousness which may often be brought best to us by human cruelty become conscience and motive in a personality driven, possessive, possessed.

Either James's tale is frivolous and the ghosts are "real," or they are actual, the governess's other selves, actual hallucinations by which the moral depravity of the unnaturally "good" parson's daughter is exacerbated and enacted, to the mutilation of one life and the demolition of another. Or it may be that there is a combination of the light-hearted gruesome and the dark-hearted moral apologia, with the second running away with the first, and the first covering up the worse inner cysts of the second. We have in any case the record of the governess's gradual damnation. She reabsorbs her specters, and any respectable servant a hundred and fifty years ago would have known her as a witch and have called on the vicar to exorcise her if not hang her. For us she is as near as the evil conscience can come to creating and enacting the motives of a witch. Yet, either way or both, at the end some part of our heroine, our twenty-year-old girl, should have tumbled after the little boy into the abyss: her ghosts, her other selves, those parts of ourselves.

MAURICE BLANCHOT

The Turn of the Screw†

Reading Henry James's *Notebooks* one cannot fail to be impressed by the care with which he planned his novels down to the last detail, and by the fact that, though he sometimes altered these plans in the course of writing, by and large he followed them punctiliously.

* * *

Needless to say, James' case is less straightforward than it seems. In his *Notebooks* he collects the anecdotes he picks up in the drawing rooms he frequents. These are sometimes interesting and sometimes trivial. But he must have a plot. For him the subject is everything. He realises more and more intensely that it is on the solidity of the subject, its significance, its ability to move the reader, on that and on that alone that he must concentrate. All else crumbles, collapses, becomes dry, feeble, worthless, betrays him utterly. * * *

But what after all is a plot? It does not say much for the *genre* if all a novel has to offer is the excitement we derive from a well planned plot. Indeed this would imply that it owes nothing to character, to psychological or descriptive realism, that it is not by mirroring the world, society or nature that it stands or falls. It seems to suggest that a story based on a plot is something mysterious and almost immaterial—a story without protagonists and unrelated to that readily available commodity: unhistorical everyday life, uneventful personal existence. And what happens in such a story does not simply occur in an indifferent, random order—one episode following another as in the picaresque novel—but constitutes a coherent whole whose meticulous organisation corresponds to some unspoken law—eminently significant precisely because it is unspoken—to a sort of invisible core.

* * *

* * * Borges cites *The Turn of the Screw* as a story that seems to grow out of the significant, beautiful plot on which it is based.[1] It so happens that three years before writing the novella, James noted in his diary the anecdote which inspired it. It was told him by the Archbishop of Canterbury in the form of a vague, jumbled, uncircumstantial outline the

† From *The Siren's Song: Selected Essays by Maurice Blanchot*, ed. Gabriel Josipovici, trans. Sacha Rabinovitch (Bloomington: Indiana University Press, 1982), 79–86. The essay originally appeared in French in *Le Livre à Venir* (Paris: Gallimard, 1959), 155–64. Reprinted by permission of the publisher.

1. Jorge Luis Borges (1899–1986), Argentinian short-story writer, essayist, and poet [*Editors*].

latter had heard from an acquaintance who was gifted neither with fluency nor perspicacity:

> The story of the young children (indefinite number and age) left to the care of servants in an old country house through the death, presumably, of parents. The servants, wicked and depraved, corrupt and deprave the children; the children are bad, full of evil, to a sinister degree. The servants *die* (the story vague about the way of it) and their apparitions, figures, return to haunt the house *and* the children, to whom they seem to beckon, whom they invite and solicit, from across dangerous places, the deep ditch of a sunk fence, etc.—so that the children may destroy themselves, lose themselves, by responding, by getting into their power. So long as the children are kept from them, they are not lost; but they try and try, these evil presences, to get hold of them. It is a question of the children 'coming over to where they are'.[2]

James adds that all this is vague and insubstantial but that it contains a suggestion of 'strangely gruesome effect'. He notes that it should be told by an outside observer.

Is this the plot of *The Turn of the Screw*? It is all there, and especially the essentials: the children dominated by presences which haunt them and which try, by reviving memories of evil, to draw them to the place of their undoing. Yes, it is all there, even the worst: that the children are corrupt while innocent ('so long as the children are kept from them [the presences] they are not lost'). This is the blueprint from which James was to draw one of his most cruel effects: the ambiguity of innocence, of an innocence which is pure of the evil it contains; the art of perfect dissimulation which enables the children to conceal this evil from the honest folk amongst whom they live, an evil which is perhaps an innocence that becomes evil in the proximity of such folk, the incorruptible innocence they oppose to the true evil of adults; or again the riddle of the visions attributed to them, the uncertainty of a story which has perhaps been foisted upon them by the demented imagination of a governess who tortures them to death with her own hallucinations.

* * *

Is this then the plot of a story to whose authorship the Archbishop of Canterbury can no longer lay any claim? Is this really the plot? Is it even the plot James consciously chose? The editors of the *Notebooks* quote this anecdote as proof that recent interpretations are mainly un-

2. *The Notebooks of Henry James*, (eds) F. O. Matthiesson & Kenneth B. Murdock, OUP, New York, 1961 [112]. All further references are to this edition. [Page references to this Norton Critical Edition are given in brackets following the author's original citations. *Editors.*]

founded and that James really intended to write a ghost story with the corruption of children and the reality of apparitions as postulates. Doubtless the supernatural is only evoked indirectly and the story is gruesome and disturbing less on account of its ghostly apparitions than for the strange consequences they provoke. But this is a law James himself defines when, in the preface to his tales of fantasy he stresses the importance of presenting the strange and the wonderful by showing almost exclusively their effects on a given sensitivity, and of remembering that their main interest consists in the violent reactions they provoke.

* * *

After entering the anecdote in his diary James writes: 'The story to be told—tolerably obviously—by an outside spectator, observer' (p. 179) [112]. Thus it could be said that he still lacked the most important ingredient: the *plot*, this narrator who is the essence of the story, an alien essence admittedly, a presence seeking to penetrate the heart of the story where she is an intruder, an outsider forcing her way in, distorting the mystery, perhaps creating it, perhaps discovering it, but certainly breaking in, destroying it and only revealing the ambiguity which conceals it.

Which is tantamount to saying that the plot of *The Turn of the Screw* is quite simply James' talent, the art of stalking a secret which, as in so many of his books, the narration creates and which is not only a real secret—some event, thought or fact which might come to light—nor a simple case of intellectual duplicity, but something which evades elucidation because it belongs to a realm beyond light.[3] * * *

Why then did such a talent, which is nothing if not movement, discovery, exploration, folding and unfolding, sinuosity and reticence a talent which never deciphers but is the cipher of the indecipherable, instead of flowing from its own source have to take its impetus from a plan—and a most unsophisticated plan for the most part, all broad outline and disconnected items? Why did he have to start from a story to be told which was already a story before he had begun to tell it?

There are a number of possible answers to this question. For instance that the American novelist belonged to a period when novels were not written by Mallarmé, but by Flaubert and de Maupassant; that he was mainly concerned with the content of a work, or that moral conflicts

3. One is tempted to see this as an unconscious allusion to the accident James suffered when he was about eighteen, of which he rarely spoke and then only in the vaguest possible terms, referring to it as to an event which had mysteriously and exhilaratingly handicapped him. It has naturally been suggested that this spinal trauma had made him unfit for a normal existence (he took great pleasure in female company yet never married and we possess no indisputable evidence of his having ever had any sexual relationships). And the theory has also been advanced that he wilfully provoked this accident (which occurred while he was helping extinguish a fire in Newport), as a means of evading active service in the Civil War. We think we have said the last word when we talk of 'self-inflicted psychological trauma'.

interested him inordinately. But there is more to it than that. Obviously James mistrusted his talent, was wary of his tendency to prolixity and tried to resist his inclination to say everything, to 'say and describe too much' and be too longwinded. For he admired above all the perfection of a concise style. (James always wanted to be a popular novelist; he had also had hopes of becoming a successful playwright, taking as his model the worst of French theatrical productions. Like Proust, he had a taste for tableaux, for dramatic situations, and this ambivalence probably enabled him to keep his balance.) There is something excessive, almost pathological, in his natural style, against which he tried to react—because all artists profoundly mistrust themselves: 'Ah, just to let one's self go—at last' (p. 187). 'The upshot of all such reflections is that I have only to let myself *go*! So I have said to myself all my life. . . . Yet I have never fully done so' (p. 106). Though elsewhere he refers to the nervous dread of letting go which has always paralysed him.

And James dreaded beginning—that moment when a work is still unaware of itself, inconsistent because weightless, unreal, nonexistent, and yet already necessary, vacantly, unavoidably necessary. And because of this dread he required, before submitting to the story's will, a reliable outline, a means of clarifying and sifting his material, praying that he should, though not naturally thus inclined, never relax his faithful observance of that strong, salutary method which consists in having a solid framework, well structured and jointed. This dread of beginning is responsible for the time he wastes in a series of increasingly extended and circumstantial preliminary sketches where his talent for minutiae and circumvolution is already manifest, while all the time urging himself to begin and not spend his time talking about it; all he has to do is hold on and string one word to another!

But does this suffice to make everything clear? As the years go by and James comes to accept himself more willingly, he discovers the true significance of this preliminary chore—which in fact is no chore. He keeps referring to the time thus spent as 'blessed hours', 'wonderful, ineffable, secret, pathetic, tragic moments', or as a 'sacred' time when his pen exerts a magic pressure, becomes the deciphering pen, the enchanted signpost whose ever changing direction suggests the numberless routes which have not yet been mapped. He thinks of the plot as a 'divine light cast on holy little virtualities', talks of the 'sacred primaeval joy of the plot' which makes his arteries throb with its holy, irrepressible little emotions. Why such joy, such emotion, this impression of a life so wonderful he cannot think of it without tears, so that his *Notebook*, that patient, passionate little notebook, becomes the most important thing in his life? Because in these moments when he is at one with himself he confronts the perfection of the yet unstarted narrative, the still indeterminate work, motionless and limitless, mere potentiality. And we know the dangerous, almost pathological attraction which the possible—that ghostly, unreal existence of what might have been, of those presences we are always waiting for—exerted on James, and which perhaps only art enabled him to explore and exorcise. Indeed he grew more and more convinced that the one consolation, the one refuge, the real solution to the terrible problem of living is in that rapid, fruitful, profound struggle with the particular idea, the plot, the possibility, the scene.

If the time of this preliminary work is so necessary to James, and appears so wonderful in retrospect, is it not perhaps because it stands for a time when the work, near at hand yet inaccessible, is that secret core he cautiously dissects with an almost perverse relish and eminently conscious of the fact that, while it gradually yields the story, he is still uncommitted? Quite often the anecdotal details he has worked out in his plans do not merely disappear from the finished text but turn up as incidents he refers to as precisely what has not occurred. Thus James experiences the negative of the story he has to write rather than the actual story, its wrong side, the side which writing conceals; as though, seized by an agonising curiosity, both childish and moving, he has to know what lies behind what he writes while he writes it.

Paradoxically, James is obsessed with his plots because they constitute the guarantee for a given work and at the same time they represent the chanciness of creativity, the pure *indeterminacy* of a work. They are a means of testing the plot without depreciating it or reducing its potentialities—such perhaps is the essence of James' talent: to make the work present at every moment and to suggest, behind the structured determined work, different structures, the limitless, weightless space of the narrative as it might have been, as it was before all beginnings. And to this pressure he exerts on the work—not to restrict it, but on the contrary to extract everything from it so that it speaks without reticence while still maintaining its reticent privacy—to this firm, gentle pressure, this pressing incitement, what name does he give? The very name he chose as the title of his ghost story: *The Turn of the Screw*! 'What then do I see my K. B. case, under the pressure and the screw, as susceptible of giving?' (346–7) [108]. This is indeed a revealing statement; for it proves that James was certainly not unaware of the 'subject' of this story: the pressure the governess exerts on the children to extract their secret from them, which the supernatural too, doubtless, exerts upon them, but which primarily is the pressure of narration itself, the wonderful, terrible pressure exerted on reality by the act of writing—that anguish, torture, violence, finally conducive to death where everything seems to be revealed, yet where everything reverts to uncertainty, void and darkness. 'We work in the dark—we do what we can—we give what we have. Our doubt is our passion and our passion is our task. The rest is the madness of art.' Such is the proud and pathetic confession of the old writer in 'The Middle Years' when he realises simultaneously that he is dying without having achieved anything and that all the same he has wonderfully achieved all that of which he was capable.

LEON EDEL

Introduction to *Tales of the Supernatural*†

* * *

Critics have not been able to agree in their interpretations of "The Turn of the Screw" but they are in full agreement that, of its kind, it is a masterpiece. James said that in this tale (which has been transposed into all the modern media, including opera) he wanted to make the air "reek" with evil. The story is told by a young governess in a manuscript she has left behind after her death. What is at stake is the credibility of this young woman as a witness. James gives us a hint when he speaks in his preface of his having had to keep her record "crystalline" because she was describing so many ambiguities and anomalies. However, he promptly adds these significant words: "by which I don't of course mean her explanation of them, a different matter." There is no question that the young woman sees the ghosts of Peter Quint and of Miss Jessel. We recognize also that she is making an extraordinary effort to keep calm in the face of the evil she fears. The evil, however, is in her own mind; when she has the "certitude" that her ghosts have come for the children, the reader must decide whether she is stating a fact or enunciating a theory. Looking back over her story, we discover that her circumstantial account of the behavior of the children establishes them as "normal." Little Miles wants to know when he is going back to school; little Flora's escapade with the boat is perfectly in character for an eight-year-old. Yet the governess makes the behavior of the children seem sinister. The real "turn of the screw"—the particular twist of pain in the tale—resides in what the governess is doing to the children. They, on their side, try constantly to accommodate themselves to her vision.

James said he wanted to convey the "communication to the children of the most infernal imaginable evil and danger—the condition on their part, of being as *exposed* as we can humanly conceive children to be." Exposed, we may judge, not to the ghosts, which they do not even see, but to the governess, who does see them. In the final scene, horrible in its intensity and violence, the governess wins a strange victory. She believes she has succeeded in driving the evil spirit out of little Miles;

† From *Henry James: Stories of the Supernatural*, edited by Leon Edel (New York: Taplinger Publishing Company, 1970), x–xiii.

she has saved his soul. But, as in tales of demonic possession, "his little heart, dispossessed, had stopped." "The Turn of the Screw" is a powerful tale of "possession," as in the old fables of demons and dybbuks; and it is the governess who is possessed. Her demoniacal and malevolent imagination converts her anxieties and guilts, her romantic-sexual imaginings, which she considers "sinful," into demons and damned spirits. In seeking to cope with her own demons she infects those around her—as Hitler, raving and ranting, infected an entire nation with his hysteria. The contagion, indeed the epidemic quality of the malevolent imagination, is the ultimate horror of James's tale. This is perhaps why many have experienced it as the most frightening ghost story they have ever read.

Its effects are derived from James's theories of the supernatural. "So long as the events are veiled," James once explained, "the imagination will run riot and depict all sorts of horrors, but as soon as the veil is lifted, all mystery disappears." Everything in James's tale is ambiguous; every part of "The Turn of the Screw" seems to be concrete, and yet there is always a refusal on his part to specify. The story itself, we are told, is a printed version of a copy of the old manuscript. The governess has no name. She doesn't describe herself. We do not know what kind of clothes she wears. We have only the barest details of her background. We know only her daydreams. These are abundant and fanciful. In his preface, written ten years after publishing the story, James is explicit about what he has done. He tells us he has given each reader, so to speak, a blank check—told him to draw all the funds he needs out of his private bank of horror. "Only make the reader's general vision of evil intense enough . . . and his own experience, his own imagination . . . will supply him quite sufficiently with all the particulars. Make him *think* the evil, make him think it for himself, and you are released from weak specifications."

James spoke of the ghosts of Miss Jessel and Peter Quint as not being ghosts at all, in the usual sense, but "goblins, elves, imps, demons, as loosely constructed as those of the old trials for witchcraft." They represent any of the forms taken by the good and bad fairies of the mind —the witches bent on violence or the fairies "of legendary order, wooing their victims forth to see them dance under the moon." For James the ghostly tale was "the most possible form of the fairy-tale." In the fairy tale, great wonders are made real to children; ogres and giants are encountered; Cinderella finds her prince; carpets fly. So the wonders of the imagination, in the ghost story—the goblins and demons of man's inner world—take their shape and are spun into the wonders of the story-teller's art.

* * *

Recent Criticism: 1970–Present

TZVETAN TODOROV

The Fantastic†

* * * In a world which is indeed our world, the one we know, a world without devils, sylphides, or vampires, there occurs an event which cannot be explained by the laws of this same familiar world. The person who experiences the event must opt for one of two possible solutions: either he is the victim of an illusion of the senses, of a product of the imagination—and laws of the world then remain what they are; or else the event has indeed taken place, it is an integral part of reality—but then this reality is controlled by laws unknown to us. Either the devil is an illusion, an imaginary being; or else he really exists, precisely like other living beings—with this reservation, that we encounter him infrequently.

The fantastic occupies the duration of this uncertainty. Once we choose one answer or the other, we leave the fantastic for a neighboring genre, the uncanny or the marvelous. The fantastic is that hesitation experienced by a person who knows only the laws of nature, confronting an apparently supernatural event.

* * * The fantastic requires the fulfillment of three conditions. First, the text must oblige the reader to consider the world of the characters as a world of living persons and to hesitate between a natural and a supernatural explanation of the events described. Second, this hesitation may also be experienced by a character; thus the reader's role is so to speak entrusted to a character, and at the same time the hesitation is represented, it becomes one of the themes of the work—in the case of naive reading, the actual reader identifies himself with the character. Third, the reader must adopt a certain attitude with regard to the text: he will reject allegorical as well as "poetic" interpretations. These three

† From *The Fantastic* by Tzvetan Todorov (Cleveland: The Press of Case Western Reserve University, 1973), originally published in French as *Introduction à la Littérature Fantastique*.

quirements do not have an equal value. The first and the third actually constitute the genre; the second may not be fulfilled. Nonetheless, most examples satisfy all three conditions.

How are these three characteristics to take their place within the model of the work as we have articulated it in the preceding chapter? The first condition refers us to the *verbal* aspect of the text, more precisely, to what are called "visions": the fantastic is a particular case of the more general category of the "ambiguous vision." The second condition is more complex: it is linked on the one hand to the *syntactical* aspect, insofar as it implies the existence of formal units which correspond to the characters' estimation of events in the narrative; we might call these units "reactions," as opposed to the "actions" which habitually constitute the argument of the narrative; on the other hand, this second condition refers to the *semantic* aspect, since we are concerned with a represented theme, that of perception and of its notation. Lastly, the third condition has a more general nature and transcends the division into aspects: here we are concerned with a choice between several modes (and levels) of reading.

* * *

The fantastic, we have seen, lasts only as long as a certain hesitation: a hesitation common to reader and character, who must decide whether or not what they perceive derives from "reality" as it exists in the common opinion. At the story's end, the reader makes a decision even if the character does not; he opts for one solution or the other, and thereby emerges from the fantastic. If he decides that the laws of reality remain intact and permit an explanation of the phenomena described, we say that the work belongs to another genre: the uncanny. If, on the contrary, he decides that new laws of nature must be entertained to account for the phenomena, we enter the genre of the marvelous.

The fantastic therefore leads a life full of dangers, and may evaporate at any moment. It seems to be located on the frontier of two genres, the marvelous and the uncanny, rather than to be an autonomous genre. * * *

Yet it would be wrong to claim that the fantastic can exist only in a part of the work, for here are certain texts which sustain their ambiguity to the very end, i.e., even beyond the narrative itself. The book closed, the ambiguity persists. A remarkable example is supplied by Henry James' tale "The Turn of the Screw," which does not permit us to determine finally whether ghosts haunt the old estate, or whether we are confronted by the hallucinations of a hysterical governess victimized by the disturbing atmosphere which surrounds her. * * * Let us recall the *données* of the problem: in the universe evoked by the text, an event—an action—occurs which proceeds from the supernatural (or from the pseudo-supernatural); this action then provokes a reaction in the implicit reader (and generally in the hero of the story). It is this reaction which we describe as "hesitation," and the texts which generate it, as fantastic. When we raise the question of themes, we put the "fantastic" reaction in parentheses, in order to be concerned solely with the nature of the events that provoke it. In other words, from this viewpoint, the distinction between the fantastic and the marvelous is no longer of interest, and we shall be concerned with works belonging to one genre or the other without differentiation. Nonetheless the text may emphasize the fantastic (i.e., the reaction) so strongly that we can no longer distinguish the supernatural which has provoked it: the reaction makes it impossible to grasp the action, instead of leading us back to it. Putting the fantastic in parentheses then becomes extremely difficult, if not impossible.

In other words: concerned as we are here with the preception of an object, we may insist as much upon the preception as upon the object. But if the insistence on the perception is too strong, we no longer perceive the object itself.

There are very diverse examples of this impossibility of reaching the theme. Let us first consider Hoffmann, whose *oeuvre* constitutes a virtual repertory of fantastic themes.[1] What seems to matter to him is not what one is dreaming about, but the fact that one is dreaming and the joy that the dreaming provokes. The admiration to which he is provoked by the existence of the supernatural world often prevents us from seeing what this world consists of. The emphasis has shifted from the utterance to the act of uttering. The conclusion of "The Golden Pot" is revealing in this regard. After recounting the marvelous adventures of the student Anselm, the narrator himself appears and declares:

> But then I felt a sudden twinge and transport of pain. Ah happy Anselm, who has cast away the burden of ordinary life, who in the love of gentle Serpentina soars to Atlantis—While I, poor I, must soon, nay, at any moment, leave even this fair hall—which itself is far from an estate in Atlantis—and again be transplanted to my garret, where ensnared among the trifles of necessitous existence, my heart and my sight are so bedimmed with a thousand wiles, as with thick fog, that the fair Lily will never, never be beheld by me! At this moment the archivist Lindhorst patted me gently on the shoulder and said: "Soft, soft, my honored friend! Do not lament! Were you not even in Atlantis? And have you not at least cultivated a pretty little estate of lovely words there, the poetical possession of your inner self? And is Anselm's felicity anything more than living in Poetry? Can anything but Poetry reveal itself as the sacred Harmony of all Beings, as the deepest secret of Nature?"

1. Ernst Theodor Amadeus Hoffman (1776–1822), German Romantic writer and music critic [*Editors*].

This remarkable passage puts an equals sign between supernatural events and the possibility of describing them; between the purport of the supernatural and its perception. The happiness Anselm discovers is identical with that of the narrator who has been able to imagine it, who has been able to write his story. And because of this delight in the existence of the supernatural, it is all the more difficult to know it.

We find the converse situation in Maupassant, but with similar effects.[2] Here the supernatural provokes such anxiety, such horror, that we scarcely manage to distinguish what constitutes it. "Qui Sait?" is perhaps the best example of this method: the supernatural event which constitutes the tale's point of departure is the sudden and strange animation of the furniture in a house. There is no logic in the behavior of the furniture, and this phenomenon makes us wonder "what it means" less than it amazes us by the strangeness of the fact itself. It is not the animation of the furniture which counts so much, but the fact that someone could imagine such a thing and even experience it. Again the perception of the supernatural casts a heavy shadow over the supernatural itself and makes its access difficult to us.

Henry James's "Turn of the Screw" offers a third variant of this singular phenomenon, in which perception constitutes a screen rather than removes one. As in the preceding texts, our attention is so powerfully concentrated on the act of perception that we never know the nature of what is perceived (what are the vices of the discharged tutor and governess?). Anxiety predominates here, but it assumes a much more ambiguous character than in Maupassant.

SHOSHANA FELMAN

Henry James: Madness and the Risks of Practice (Turning the Screw of Interpretation)†

What does the act of turning a screw have to do with literature? What does the act of turning a screw have to do with psychoanalysis? Are these two questions related? If so, might their relationship help to define the status of literature? It is these rather odd questions that the present study intends to articulate, so as to give them a further turn, to

2. Guy de Maupassant (1850–1893), French naturalist short-story writer and novelist [*Editors*].

† From "Writing and Madness: (Literature/Philosophy/Psychoanalysis)," *Yale French Studies* 55–6 (1977): 94–113, 185–207. This reprint includes excerpts of Felman's study, which is available in its complete form in *Literature and Psychoanalysis: The Question of Reading—Otherwise*, edited by Shoshana Felman (Baltimore: The Johns Hopkins University Press, 1982), as well as in Shoshana Felman, *Writing and Madness: (Literature/Philosophy/Psychoanalysis)* (Ithaca: Cornell University Press, 1985). Reprinted by permission of *Yale French Studies* and the author. Page references to this Norton Critical Edition are given in brackets after the author's original citations.

investigate and interrogate them on the basis of Henry James's famous short novel, *The Turn of the Screw*.

I. An Uncanny Reading Effect

> I didn't describe to you the purpose of it (. . .) at all, I described to you (. . .) the *effect* of it—which is a very different thing.
>
> H. James, *The Sacred Fount*

> The mental features discoursed of as the analytical are, in themselves, but little susceptible of analysis: we appreciate them only in their effects.
>
> E. A. Poe, *The Murders in the Rue Morgue*

The plot of *The Turn of the Screw* is well known: a young woman answering a want ad in a newspaper goes to meet a "perfect gentleman," a "bachelor in the prime of life," who hires her to take charge of his niece Flora and his nephew Miles, two little orphans who live in a secluded country house belonging to him. The young woman is to become the children's governess, but under the strict condition set down by her employer—"the Master"—that she assume "supreme authority" for her two charges, that is, that she solve singlehandedly any problems concerning them, without at any time turning to him for help or even contacting him for any reason. This condition is no sooner accepted than it begins to weigh heavily upon the governess (who is also the narrator)—especially when a letter arrives informing her, without giving the reason, that little Miles has been expelled from school: this unexplained punishment makes the child's apparent innocence seem somehow mysterious, suspect, ambiguous. In addition, the governess discovers that the house is haunted: several times she finds herself confronted by strange apparitions, whom, with the help of information about the house's past history gleaned from the housekeeper, Mrs. Grose, she finally identifies as the ghosts of two servants, Peter Quint and Miss Jessel, now dead, but formerly employed by the Master in this very house, and whose shady intimacy had, it seems, "corrupted" the children. The governess becomes steadily more convinced that the ghosts have come back to pursue their nefarious intercourse with the children, to take possession of their souls and to corrupt them radically. Her task is thus to *save* the children from the ghosts, to engage in a ferocious moral struggle against "evil," a struggle whose strategy consists of an attempt to catch the children in the very act of communing with the spirits, and thereby to force them to admit that communion, to confess their knowledge of the ghosts and their infernal complicity with them. Total avowal, the governess believes, would exorcise the children. The results of this heroic metaphysical struggle are, however, ill-fated: Flora, the little girl, caught by the governess in presence of the phantom of Miss Jessel, denies seeing the vision and falls seriously ill following the vehement accusations directed at her by the governess, whom she thenceforth holds in abhorrence; Miles, the little boy, on the other hand, having seemingly "surrendered" by pronouncing—under the governess's pressure—the *name* of Peter Quint face to face with his ghost, at that very moment dies in the arms of the governess as she clasps him to her breast in moral triumph. It is with this pathetically ironical embrace of a corpse that the story ends.

If the strength of literature could be defined by the intensity of its impact on the reader, by the vital energy and power of its *effect, The Turn of the Screw* would doubtless qualify as one of the strongest—i.e., most *effective*—texts of all time, judging by the quantity and intensity of the echoes it has produced, of the critical literature to which it has given rise. Henry James was himself astounded by the extent of the effect produced on his readers by his text, the generative potency of which he could measure only *a posteriori*. Ten years after the first appearance of *The Turn of the Screw*, in his New York Preface (1908), he writes:

> Indeed if the artistic value of such an experiment be measured by the intellectual echoes it may again, long after, set in motion, the case would make in favour of this little firm fantasy—which I seem to see draw behind it today a train of associations. I ought doubtless to blush for thus confessing them so numerous that I can but pick among them for reference.[1]

Few literary texts indeed have provoked and "drawn behind them" so many "associations," so many interpretations, so many exegetic passions and energetic controversies. The violence to which the text has given rise can be measured, for example, by the vehement, aggressive tone of the first reactions to the novel, published in the journals of the period: "The story itself is distinctly repulsive," affirms *The Outlook* (LX, October 29, 1898, p. 537; Norton, p. 172 [151]). And *The Independent* goes still further:

> *The Turn of the Screw* is the most hopelessly evil story that we have ever read in any literature, ancient or modern. How Mr. James could, or how any man or woman could, choose to make such a study of infernal human debauchery, for it is nothing else, is unaccountable. . . . The study, while it exhibits Mr. James's genius in a powerful light, affects the reader with a disgust that is not to be expressed. The feeling after perusal of the horrible story is that one has been assisting in an outrage upon the holiest and sweetest fountain of human innocence, and helping to debauch-

1. Unless otherwise specified, all quotes from The New York Preface and from *The Turn of the Screw* are taken from the Norton Critical Edition of *The Turn of the Screw*, ed. Robert Kimbrough (New York: Norton, 1966); hereafter abbreviated "*Norton*." As a rule, all italics within the quoted texts throughout this paper are mine; original italics alone will be indicated.

> —at least by helplessly standing by—the pure and trusting nature of children. Human imagination can go no further into infamy, literary art could not be used with more refined subtlety of spiritual defilement. (*The Independent*, LI, January 5, 1899, p. 73; *Norton*, p. 175 [156])

The publication of *The Turn of the Screw* thus meets with a scandalized hue and cry from its first readers. But, interestingly enough, as the passage just quoted clearly indicates, what is perceived as the most scandalous thing about this scandalous story is that *we are forced to participate in the scandal*, that the reader's innocence cannot remain intact: there is no such thing as an innocent reader of this text. In other words, the scandal is not simply *in* the text, it resides in *our relation to the text*, in the text's *effect* on us, its readers: what is outrageous in the text is not simply that *of which* the text is speaking, but that which makes it speak *to us*.

The outraged agitation does not, however, end with the reactions of James's contemporaries. Thirty years later, another storm of protest very similar to the first will arise over a second scandal: the publication of a so-called "Freudian reading" of *The Turn of the Screw*. In 1934, Edmund Wilson for the first time suggests explicitly that *The Turn of the Screw* is not, in fact, a ghost story but a madness story, a study of a case of neurosis: the ghosts, accordingly, do not really exist; they are but figments of the governess's sick imagination, mere hallucinations and projections symptomatic of the frustration of her repressed sexual desires. This psychoanalytical interpretation will hit the critical scene like a bomb. Making its author into an overnight celebrity by arousing as much interest as James's text itself, Wilson's article will provoke a veritable barrage of indignant refutations, all closely argued and based on "irrefutable" textual evidence. It is this psychoanalytical reading and the polemical framework it has engendered that will henceforth focalize and concretely organize all subsequent critical discussion, all passions and all arguments related to *The Turn of the Screw*. For or against Wilson, affirming or denying the "objectivity" or the reality of the ghosts, the critical interpretations have fallen into two camps: the "psychoanalytical" camp, which sees the governess as a clinical neurotic deceived by her own fantasies and destructive of her charges; and the "metaphysical," religious, or moral camp, which sees the governess as a sane, noble savior engaged in a heroic moral struggle for the salvation of a world threatened by supernatural Evil. Thus, as John Silver astutely puts it, "If the ghosts of 'The Turn of the Screw' are not real, certainly the controversy over them is."[2]

Would it be possible to say, indeed, that the *reality of the debate* is

2. "A Note on the Freudian Reading of *The Turn of the Screw*," in: *A Casebook on Henry James's "The Turn of the Screw,"* ed. Gerald Willen, 2d ed. (New York: Thomas Y. Crowell, 1969), p. 239. This collection of critical essays will hereafter be abbreviated *Casebook*.

in fact more significant for the impact of the text than the reality of the ghosts? Could the critical debate itself be considered a *ghost effect*? Even more than the debate's content, it is its *style* which seems to me instructive: when the pronouncements of the various sides of the controversy are examined closely, they are found to repeat unwittingly—with a spectacular regularity—all the main lexical motifs of the text. Witness the following random examples, taken from a series of polemical essays:

—The motif of a danger which must be averted:

> The *danger* in the psychoanalytic method of criticism lies in its apparent plausibility.
>
> (Nathan Bryllion Fagin)[3]

—The motif of a violent aggression inflicted upon an object by an injurious, alien force:

> The Freudian reading of Henry James' 'The Turn of the Screw' (. . .) *does violence* not only to the story but also to the Preface.
>
> (Robert Heilman)[4]

—The motif of attack and defense, of confrontation and struggle: in a rebuttal to the Freudian reading, Oliver Evans proposes that Wilson's theory be

> *attacked* point by point.
>
> (Oliver Evans)[5]

—The motif of final victory, of the enemy's defeat:

> Here is one place where I find Freud completely *defeated*.
>
> (Katherine Anne Porter)[6]

It could perhaps be objected that a vocabulary of aggression, conflict, and maybe even danger is natural in a conflictive critical debate, and that it is just a coincidence that this vocabulary seems to echo and repeat the combative spirit that animates the text. Such an objection could not, however, account for some other, more specific, more peculiar stylistic echoes of the text which reemerge in the very language of the critics, in the very style of the polemic: the motif, for instance, of neurosis and of madness, of hysterical delusion. Robert Heilman thus accuses Wilson of alleged "hysterical blindness" (FR, *MLN*, p. 434), which alone would be able to account for the latter's errors in interpretation. Wilson, argues Heilman, is misreading James's use, in his New York Preface, of the word "authority." In Heilman's view, James's

3. "Another Reading of *The Turn of the Screw*," in *Casebook*, p. 154.
4. "The Freudian Reading of *The Turn of the Screw*," in *Modern Language Notes*, LXII, 7, Nov. 1947, p. 433 [177]. This essay will hereafter be referred to as: FR, *MLN*.
5. "James's Air of Evil: *The Turn of the Screw*," in *Casebook*, p. 202.
6. "James: *The Turn of the Screw*. A Radio Symposium," in *Casebook*, p. 167 [176].

statement that he has given the governess "authority" is referring but to her *narrative* authority, to the *formal* fact that the story is being told *from her point of view*, and not, as Wilson would have it, to "the relentless English 'authority' which enables her to put over on inferiors even purposes which are totally deluded." How is this misreading possible? "Once again," explains Heilman, "the word *authority* has brought about, in an unwary liberal, an emotional spasm which has resulted in a kind of hysterical blindness" (FR, *MLN*, p. 434). Wilson's reading is thus polemicized into a *hysterical* reading, itself viewed as a neurotic symptom. What is interesting—and seems to me instructive—about this is that it is the very critic who *excludes* the hypothesis of neurosis from the *story* who is rediscovering neurosis in Wilson's critical *interpretation* of the story, an interpretation which he rejects precisely on the grounds that *pathology as such cannot explain the text*:

> It is probably safe to say that the Freudian interpretation of the story, of which the best known exponent is Edmund Wilson, no longer enjoys wide critical acceptance. (. . .) We cannot account for the evil by treating the governess as pathological . . .[7]

But the hypothesis of madness, or "pathology," which is indeed brought up by the governess herself, is not nearly so easy to eliminate as one might think, since, expelled from the text, it seems to fall back on the text's interpreter, and thus ironically becomes, through the very critical attempt at its elimination, ineradicable from the critical vocabulary, be it that of the "Freudians" or that of the "metaphysicians."

Another textual motif which crops up unexpectedly in the very language of the critical controversy is that of *salvation*. While insisting on the fact that *The Turn of the Screw* is in truth a drama of salvation, that is, a rescue operation to save the children from the evil ghosts, Robert Heilman writes:

> *The Turn of the Screw* may seem a somewhat slight work to call forth all the debate. But there is something to be said for the debate. For one thing, it may point out the danger of a facile, doctrinaire application of formulae where they have no business and hence compel either an ignoring of, or a gross distortion of, the materials. But more immediately: *The Turn of the Screw* is *worth saving*. (FR, *MLN*, p. 443 [183; the italics are Felman's])

The rescue operation, the drama of salvation described by the text thus *repeats itself* in the critical arena. But *from what* must the text be saved? From being reduced, explains Heilman, to "a commonplace clinical record." But again, let us notice the terms of the objection, which associates the psychoanalytical reading's abuses with the more general abuses of science as such:

7. Robert Heilman, "*The Turn of the Screw* as Poem," in *Casebook*, p. 175.

> We run again into the familiar clash between scientific and imaginative truth. This is not to say that scientific truth may not collaborate with, subserve, and even throw light upon imaginative truth; but it is to say that the scientific prepossession may seriously impede the imaginative insight. (FR, *MLN*, p. 444)

Another critic, repeating and emphasizing the term "prepossession," agrees: "We must agree, I think, that Freudian critics of the tale are *strongly prepossessed*."[8] But what precisely is a "prepossessed" critic if not one whose mind is in advance in the *possession* of some demon, one who, like James's children, is himself *possessed*? Possessed—should we say—by the ghost of Freud? It is clear, in any case, that the urgency of rescuing, of *saving the text*, in a critical account like Heilman's, strongly resembles the exorcistic operations of the governess *vis-à-vis* her "possessed" charges, and that the critical confrontation appears itself as a kind of struggle against some ghost-effect that has somehow been awakened by psychoanalysis. The scene of the critical debate is thus a *repetition* of the scene dramatized in the text. The critical interpretation, in other words, not only elucidates the text but also reproduces it dramatically, unwittingly *participates in it*. Through its very reading, the text, so to speak, acts itself out. As a reading effect, this inadvertent "acting out" is indeed uncanny: whichever way readers turn, they can but be turned by the text, they can but *perform* it by *repeating* it. Perhaps this is the famous trap James speaks of in his New York Preface:

> It is an excursion into chaos while remaining, like Blue-Beard and Cinderella, but an anecdote—though an anecdote amplified and highly emphasized and returning upon itself; as, for that matter, Cinderella and Blue-Beard return. I need scarcely add after this that it is a piece of ingenuity pure and simple, of cold artistic calculation, an amusette to catch those not easily caught (the "fun" of the capture of the merely witless being ever but small), the jaded, the disillusioned, the fastidious. (*Norton*, p. 120 [125])

We will return later on to this ingenious prefatory note so as to try to understand the distinction James is making between naïve and sophisticated readers, and to analyze the way in which the text's return upon itself is capable of trapping *both*. Up to this point, my intention has been merely to suggest—to make explicit—this uncanny trapping power of Henry James's text as an inescapable *reading-effect*.

Taking such reading-effects into consideration, we shall here undertake a reading of the text which will at the same time be articulated with a reading of its readings. This two-level reading—which also must return upon itself—will be concerned with the following questions: What is the nature of a reading-effect as such? and by extension: what

8. Mark Spilka, "Turning the Freudian Screw: How Not to Do It," in *Norton*, pp. 249–250.

is a reading? What does the text have to say about its own reading? What is a "Freudian reading" (and what is it *not*)? What in a text *invites*—and what in a text *resists*—a psychoanalytical interpretation? In what way does literature *authorize* psychoanalysis to elaborate a discourse about literature, and in what way, having granted its authorization, does literature *disqualify* that discourse? A combined reading of *The Turn of the Screw* and of its psychoanalytical interpretation will here concentrate, in other words, not only on what psychoanalytical theory has to say about the literary text, but also on what literature has to say about psychoanalysis. In the course of this double reading, we will see how both the possibilities and the limits of an encounter between literature and psychoanalytical discourse might begin to be articulated, how the conditions of their meeting, and the modalities of their not meeting, might begin to be thought out.

II. What Is a Freudian Reading?

> The Freudians err in the right direction.
>
> Mark Spilka

I would like, as a starting point, to begin by subscribing to the following remarks by Mark Spilka:

> My concern (. . .) is with the imaginative poverty of much Freudian criticism, its crudeness and rigidity in applying valid psychological insights, its narrow conception of its own best possibilities (. . .) Over the past four decades Freudian critics have made James's tale a *cause célèbre*. The tale sustains the "*cause*" through erotic ambiguities. Since it also arouses childhood terrors, and perhaps arises from them, we may say that the Freudian approach works here or nowhere. Yet opponents charge that Freudian critics have reduced the tale to a "commonplace clinical record." Though they are perfectly correct, my own charge seems more pertinent: these Freudian critics have not been sufficiently Freudian. (*Norton*, p. 245)

These subtle, challenging remarks err only in the sense that they consider as resolved, non-problematic, the very questions that they open up: how Freudian is a Freudian reading? Up to what point can one be Freudian? At what point does a reading start to be "Freudian enough"? *What* is Freudian in a Freudian reading, and in what way can it be defined and measured?

The one characteristic by which a "Freudian reading" is generally recognized is its insistence on the crucial place and role of sexuality in the text. The focal theoretical problem raised by a psychoanalytical reading would thus appear to be the definition of the very status of sexuality as such *in a text*. Wilson's reading of *The Turn of the Screw* indeed follows the interpretative pattern of accounting for the whole story in terms of the governess's sexual frustration: she is in love—says Wilson—with the Master, but is unable to admit it to herself, and thus obsessively, hysterically projects her own desires upon the outside world, perceives them as exterior to herself in the hallucinated form of fantasmatic ghosts.

> The theory is, then, that the governess who is made to tell the story is a neurotic case of sex repression, and that the ghosts are not real ghosts but hallucinations of the governess.[9]

In order to reinforce this theory, Wilson underlines the implicitly erotic nature of the metaphors and points out the numerous phallic symbols:

> Observe, also, from the Freudian point of view, the significance of the governess's interest in the little girl's pieces of wood and of the fact that the male apparition first takes shape on a tower and the female apparition on a lake. (*Wilson*, p. 104)

What, however, was it in James's text that originally called out for a "Freudian" reading? It was, as the very title of Wilson's article suggests, not so much the sexuality as "the *ambiguity* of Henry James." The text, says Wilson, is ambiguous. It is ambiguous, that it, its meaning, far from being clear, is itself a *question*. It is this question which, in Wilson's view, calls forth an analytical response. The text is perceived as questioning in three different ways:

1) *Through its rhetoric*: through the proliferation of erotic metaphors and symbols *without* the direct, "proper" naming of their sexual nature.[1]

2) *Through its thematic content*—its *abnormal* happenings and its fantastic, strange manifestations.[2]

3) *Through its narrative structure* which resembles that of an enigma in remaining, by definition, elliptically incomplete.[3]

Solicited by these three modes of textual questioning—narrative, thematic, and rhetorical—the "Freudian" critic, in Wilson's view, is called upon to *answer*. In the case of the narrative question of the elliptical, incomplete structure of the enigma, he answers with the riddle's missing word, with the mystery's solution: the governess's sexual desire for the Master. In the case of the thematic question of uncanny

9. Edmund Wilson, "The Ambiguity of Henry James," in *The Triple Thinkers* (Penguin, 1962), p. 102. This essay will hereafter be referred to as *Wilson*. [Excerpts from the first version of Wilson's essay appear on pages 170–73. *Editors*.]

1. Cf., for example, *Wilson*, p. 126: "Sex *does* appear in his work—even becoming a kind of obsession," but we are always separated from it by "thick screens."

2. Cf. *ibid.*, "The people who surround this observer tend to take on the diabolic values of *The Turn of the Screw*, and these diabolic values are almost invariably connected with sexual relations that are always concealed and at which we are compelled to guess."

3. Cf. *ibid.*, p. 108: "When one has once got hold of the clue to this meaning of *The Turn of the Screw*, one wonders how one could ever have missed it. There is a very good reason, however, in the fact that nowhere does James unequivocally give the thing away: almost everything from beginning to end can be read equally in either of two senses."

strangeness, of fantastic happenings, he answers with a *diagnosis*: the ghosts are merely the symptoms of pathological, abnormal sexual frustration and repression. In the case of the rhetorical question of symbolic ambiguity, he answers with the "proper name," with the *literal* meaning of the phallic metaphors.

Considered from the "Freudian point of view," sexuality, valorized as both the foundation and the guidepost of the critical interpretation, thus takes on the status of an *answer* to the *question* of the text. Logically and ontologically, the answer (of sexuality) in fact pre-exists the question (of textuality). The question comes to be articulated (rhetorically, thematically, and narratively) only by virtue of the fact that the answer is as such *concealed*. Indeed the question is itself but an answer in disguise: the question is the answer's hiding place. The Freudian critic's job, in this perspective, is but to pull the answer out of its hiding place—not so much to give an answer *to* the text as to answer *for* the text: to be *answerable for* it, to answer *in its place*, to replace the question with an answer. It would not be inaccurate, indeed, to say that the traditional analytical response to literature is to provide the literary question with something like a reliably professional "answering service."

Such an operation, however, invites two fundamental questions: Does "James" (or James's text) authorize this way of answering *for* him? Does "Freud" (or Freud's text) authorize this way of answering *through* him?

The question of the possibility of answering for the text, as well as that of the status of such an answer, is in fact raised by James's text itself in its very opening, when Douglas, having promised to tell his dreadful story, intimates that it is a *love story*, which was confided to him by the heroine (the governess):

> Mrs. Griffin, however, expressed the need for a little more light. "Who was it she was in love with?"
>
> "The story will tell," I took upon myself to reply. (. . .)
>
> "The story *won't* tell," said Douglas; "not in any literal, vulgar way." (Prologue, *Norton*, p. 3 [3]; James's italics)

In taking upon himself "to reply," to make *explicit* who it was the governess was in love with, in locating the riddle's answer in the governess's repressed desire for the Master, what then is Edmund Wilson doing? What is the "Freudian" reading doing here if not what the text itself, at its very outset, is precisely indicating as that which it *won't* do: "The story *won't* tell; not in any literal, vulgar way." These textual lines could be read as an ironic note through which James's text seems itself to be commenting upon Wilson's reading. And this Jamesian commentary seems to be suggesting that such a reading might indeed be inaccurate not so much because it is incorrect or false, but because it is, in James's terms, *vulgar*.

If so, what would that "vulgarity" consist of? And how should we go about defining not only an interpretation's accuracy, but what can be called its *tact*? Is a "Freudian reading"—by definition—tainted with vulgarity? *Can* a Freudian reading, as such, avoid that taint? What, exactly, makes for the "vulgarity" in Wilson's reading? Toward whom, or toward what, could it be said that this analysis lacks tact?

"The difficulty itself is the refuge from the vulgarity," writes James to H. G. Wells (*Norton*, p. 111 [116]). And in the New York Preface to *The Turn of the Screw*, he elaborates further the nature of that difficulty, of that tension which underlies his writing as a question:

> Portentous evil—how was I to *save that*, as an intention on the part of my demon spirits, from the drop, the *comparative vulgarity*, inevitably attending, throughout the whole range of possible brief illustration, the offered example, the imputed vice, the cited act, the limited deplorable presentable instance? (*Norton*, p. 122 [127–28])

What is vulgar, then, is the "*imputed* vice," the "offered example," that is, the explicit, the specific, the unequivocal and immediately referential "illustration." *The vulgar is the literal*, insofar as it is unambiguous: "the story won't tell; not in any *literal, vulgar* way." The literal is "vulgar" because it *stops* the *movement* constitutive of meaning, because it blocks and interrupts the endless process of metaphorical substitution. The vulgar, therefore, is anything that misses, or falls short of, the dimension of the symbolic, anything that rules out, or excludes, meaning as a loss and as a flight—anything that strives, in other words, to eliminate from language its inherent silence, anything that misses the specific way in which a text *actively* "won't tell." The vulgarity that James then seeks above all to avoid is that of a language whose discourse is outspoken and forthright and whose reserves of silence have been cut, that of a text inherently *incapable* of silence, inherently unable to hold its tongue.

If vulgarity thereby consists of the *reduction of rhetoric* as such, of the elimination of the indecision which inhabits meaning and of the *ambiguity* of the text, isn't that precisely Wilson's goal? Isn't Wilson's critical and analytical procedure that, precisely, of a *literalization* (i.e., in James's terms, of a "vulgarization") of sexuality in the text? Wilson, in fact, is quite aware of the text's rhetorical, undecidable question:

> The fundamental question presents itself and never seems to get properly answered: What is the reader to think of the protagonist? (*Wilson*, p. 112)

But he only points out that question in order to *reduce* it, *overcome* the difficulty of the ambiguity, *eliminate* the text's rhetorical indecision by supplying a prompt *answer* whose categorical *literality* cannot avoid seeming rudimentary, reductive, "vulgar." What are we to think of the protagonist?

> We find that it is a variation on one of his [James's] familiar themes: the thwarted Anglo-Saxon spinster; and we remember unmistakable cases of women in James's fiction who deceive themselves and others about the origins of their aims and their emotions. (. . .)
>
> James's world is full of these women. They are not always emotionally perverted. Sometimes they are apathetic. (. . .)
>
> Or they are longing, these women, for affection but too inhibited or passive to obtain it for themselves. (*Wilson*, pp. 110–111)

Is this type of literalization of textual sexuality what a "Freudian point of view" is really all about? Invalidated and disqualified by James, would this "vulgarizing" literalization in truth be validated, authorized, by Freud? If for James the *literal* is *vulgar*, can it be said that from a Freudian point of view the *sexual* as such is *literal*? In order to investigate this question, I would like to quote, at some length, Freud himself, in a little-known text which appeared in 1910 under the title " 'Wild' Psychoanalysis":

> A few days ago a middle-aged lady (. . .) called upon me for a consultation, complaining of anxiety-states. (. . .) The precipitating cause of the outbreak of her anxiety-states had been a divorce from her last husband; but the anxiety had become considerably intensified, according to her account, since she had consulted a young physician in the suburb she lived in, for he had informed her that the *cause* of her anxiety was her *lack of sexual satisfaction*. He said that she could not tolerate the loss of intercourse with her husband, and so there were only three ways by which she could recover her health—she must either return to her husband, or take a lover, or obtain satisfaction from herself. Since then she had been convinced that she was incurable (. . .)
>
> She had come to me, however, because the doctor had said that *this was a new discovery for which I was responsible*, and that she had only to come and ask me to confirm what he said, and *I should tell her that this and nothing else was the truth* (. . .). I will not dwell on the *awkward predicament* in which I was placed by this visit, but instead will consider the conduct of the practitioner who sent the lady to me (. . .) connecting my remarks about "wild" psycho-analysis with this incident.[4]

It is tempting to point out the analogy between the rather comical situation Freud describes and the so-called "Freudian" treatment of the

4. " 'Wild' Psycho-Analysis," in *The Standard Edition of the Complete Psychological Works of Sigmund Freud*, Vol. XI (1910), pp. 221–222. This edition will hereafter be abbreviated *Standard*.

governess by Wilson. In both cases, the reference to Freud's theory is brutally and crudely literal, reducing the psychoanalytical explanation to the simple "lack of sexual satisfaction." Here therefore is Freud's own commentary on such procedures. Curiously enough, Freud, like James, begins with a reminder that the validity of an interpretation is a function not only of its truth, but also of its *tact*:

> Everyone will at once bring up the criticism that if a physician thinks it necessary to discuss the question of sexuality (. . .) he must do so with tact. (*Standard*, p. 222)

But tact is not just a practical, pragmatic question of "couchside manner"; it also has a theoretical importance: the reserve within the interpretative discourse has to allow for and to indicate a possibility of error, a position of uncertainty with respect to truth.

> Besides all this, one may sometimes make a wrong surmise, and *one is never in a position to discover the whole truth*. Psycho-analysis provides these definite technical rules to replace the indefinable "medical tact" which is looked upon as a special gift. (*Standard*, p. 226)

The analysis of the "wild psychoanalyst" thus lacks the necessary tact, but that is not all.

> Moreover, the physician in question was ignorant of a number of *scientific theories* [Freud's italics] of psycho-analysis or had misapprehended them, and thus showed how little he had penetrated into an understanding of its nature and purposes.
>
> (. . .) The doctor's advice to the lady shows clearly in what sense he understands *the expression "sexual life"—in the popular sense*, namely, in which by sexual needs nothing is meant but the need for coitus (. . .) *In psychoanalysis the concept of what is sexual comprises far more; it goes lower and also higher than its popular sense.*
>
> (. . .) Mental absence of satisfaction with all its consequences can exist where there is no lack of normal sexual intercourse (. . .)
>
> (. . .) By emphasizing exclusively the somatic factor in sensuality he undoubtedly simplifies the problem greatly. (*Standard*, pp. 222–223)

Sexuality, says Freud, is not to be taken in its literal, popular sense: in its analytical *extension*, it goes "lower and also higher" than its literal meaning, it extends both beyond and below. The relation between the analytical notion of sexuality and the sexual act is thus not a relation of simple, literal adequation, but rather a relation, so to speak, of *inadequation*: the psychoanalytical notion of sexuality, says Freud, comprises both *more* and *less* than the literal sexual act. But how are we to understand an *extension* of meaning which includes not only *more*, but also *less* than the literal meaning? This apparent paradox, indeed, points to the specific complication which, in Freud's view, is inherent in human sexuality as such. The question here is less that of the meaning *of* sexuality than that of a complex *relationship between sexuality and meaning*; a relationship which is not a simple *deviation* from literal meaning, but rather a *problematization of literality as such*.

The oversimplifying literalization professed by the "wild psychoanalyst" thus essentially misconstrues and misses the complexity of the relationship between sex and sense. It entails, however, another fundamental error, which Freud goes on to criticize:

> A second and equally *gross misunderstanding* is discernible behind the physician's advice.
>
> It is true that psycho-analysis puts forward *absence of sexual satisfaction* as the cause of nervous disorders. *But does it not say more than this?* Is its teaching to be ignored as too complicated when it declares that *nervous symptoms arise from a conflict between two forces*—on the one hand, the libido (which has as a rule become excessive), and on the other, a rejection of sexuality, or a repression (which is over-severe)? No one who remembers this *second* factor, which is *by no means secondary in importance*, can ever believe that sexual satisfaction in itself constitutes a remedy of general reliability for the sufferings of neurotics. A *good number of these people are, indeed,* (. . .) *in general incapable of satisfaction.* (*Standard*, p. 223)

Nervous symptoms, Freud insists, spring not simply from a "lack of sexual satisfaction" but from a *conflict between two forces*. Repression is constitutive of sexuality: the *second* factor is by no means *secondary* in importance. But the second factor as such is precisely the *contradiction* of the first. Which means not only that the literal meaning—the first factor—is not simply first and foremost, but also, that its *priority*, the very *primacy* in which its literality is founded, its very *essence of literality*, is itself *subverted* and *negated* by the second, but not secondary, meaning. Indeed, sexuality being constituted by these *two* factors, *its meaning is its own contradiction*: the *meaning* of the sexual as such is *its own obstruction*, its own deletion.

The "lack of satisfaction," in other words, is not simply an *accident* in sexual life, it is essentially inherent in it: "All human structures," says Lacan, after Freud, "have as their essence, not as an accident, the restraint of pleasure—of fulfillment."[5]

Here, then, is another crucial point which Wilson misses, *opposing*

5. Jacques Lacan, "Discours de elôture des journées sur les psychoses chez l'enfant," in *Recherches*, special issue on "Enfance aliénée," 11 décembre 1968, pp. 145–146; translation mine. Unless otherwise indicated, all quotations from Lacan's work in this paper are in my translation.

as he does sexuality to the "lack of satisfaction," considering the frustration of the governess (defined as the "thwarted Anglo-Saxon spinster") as an abnormal *accident* to be treated as pathogenic. What would "the abnormal" be, however, in Wilson's view, if not precisely that which is *not literal*, that which *deviates* from the *literal*? Literal (normal) sex being viewed as a simple, positive *act* or *fact*, it is simply inconceivable that it would constitutively miss its own aims, include its own negation as its own inherent property. For Wilson, sex is "simple," i.e., adequate to itself:[6] Wilson can thus write of *The Sacred Fount*, another enigmatic Jamesian story—"What if the hidden theme of *The Sacred Fount* is *simply sex* again?" (*Wilson*, p. 115). But for Freud, as we have seen, not only is the status of sexuality not *simple*: composed as it is by two dynamically contradictory factors, sexuality is precisely *what rules out simplicity as such*.

It is indeed because sexuality is essentially the violence of its own non-simplicity, of its own inherent "conflict between two forces," the violence of its own division and self-contradiction, that it is experienced as anxiety and lived as terror. The terrifying aspect of *The Turn of the Screw* is in fact linked by the text itself, subtly but suggestively, precisely to its *non-simplicity*. After promising to tell his story, Douglas adds:

> "It's quite too horrible." (. . .) "It's beyond everything. Nothing at all that I know touches it."
>
> "For sheer terror?" I remember asking. He seemed to say *it was not so simple as that*; to be really at a loss how to qualify it. (Prologue, p. 1 [1])

If, far from implying the simplicity of a self-present literal meaning, sexuality points rather to a multiplicity of conflicting forces, to the complexity of its own divisiveness and contradiction, its meaning can by no means be univocal or unified, but must necessarily be *ambiguous*. It is thus not rhetoric which disguises and hides sex; sexuality *is* rhetoric, since it essentially consists of ambiguity: it is the coexistence of dynamically antagonistic meanings. Sexuality is the *division and divisiveness of meaning*; it is meaning *as* division, meaning *as* conflict.

And, indeed, what is the *subject* of *The Turn of the Screw* if not this very conflict which inhabits meaning, the inherent conflict which structures the relationship between *sex* and *sense*? "The governess," John Lydenberg pertinently writes, "may indistinctly consider the ghosts as the essence of evil, and, as Heilman points out, she certainly chooses words which identify them with Satan and herself with the Saviour.

6. And if that adequation does not appear in James's work, it is, in Wilson's view, because James, too, like the governess, missed out on the simplicity of the normal status of normal sex and knew only the lack of satisfaction involved in its pathological manifestations: cf. *Wilson*, p. 125: "*Problems of sexual passion* (. . .) were beginning to be subjects of burning interest. But it is probable that James had by this time (. . .) come to recognize *his unfittedness for dealing with them* and was far too honest to fake."

But our vantage point is different from the governess's: we see her as one of the combatants, and as the story progresses we become even more uncertain who is fighting whom."[7]

In thus dramatizing, through a clash of meanings, the very functioning of meaning as division and as conflict, sexuality is not, however, the "text's meaning": it is rather that through which meaning in the text *does not come off*, that which in the text, and through which the text, *fails to mean*, that which can engender but a *conflict of interpretations*, a critical debate and discord precisely like the polemic that surrounds *The Turn of the Screw* and with which we are concerned here. "If analytical discourse," writes Lacan, "indicates that meaning is as such sexual, this can only be a manner of accounting for its *limits*. Nowhere is there a last word. (. . .) Meaning indicates only the direction, points only at the sense toward which it fails."[8]

* * *

IX. The Madness of Interpretation: Literature and Psychoanalysis

> "Do you know what I think?"
> "It's exactly what I'm pressing you to make intelligible."
> "Well," said Mrs. Briss, "I think you are crazy."
> It naturally struck me. "Crazy?"
> "Crazy."
> I turned it over. "But do you call that intelligible?"
> She did it justice. "No; I don't suppose it *can* be so for you if you *are insane*."
> I risked the long laugh which might have seemed that of madness. " 'If I am' is lovely." And whether or not it was the special sound, in my ear, of my hilarity, I remember just wondering if perhaps I mightn't be.
>
> H. James, *The Sacred Fount*

The indication that *The Turn of the Screw* is constructed as a *trap* designed to close upon the reader is in fact, as we saw earlier, explicitly stated by James himself:

> It is an excursion into chaos while remaining, like Blue-Beard and Cinderella, but an anecdote—though an anecdote amplified and highly emphasized and *returning upon itself*; as, for that matter, Cinderella and Blue-Beard return. I need scarcely add after this that it is a piece of ingenuity pure and simple, of cold artistic calculation, an *amusette** to *catch those not easily caught* (the "fun" of the *capture* of the merely witless being ever but small), the jaded, the disillusioned, the fastidious. (The New York Preface, *Norton*, p. 120 [125]; *James's italics; other italics mine)

7. J. Lydenberg, "The Governess Turns the Screws," in *Casebook*, p. 289.
8. J. Lacan, *Le Séminaire—Livre XX: Encore* (1972–73) (Paris: Seuil, 1975), p. 66. This work will henceforth be referred to as *Encore*.

What is interesting about this trap is that, while it points to the possibility of two alternative types of reading, it sets out, in capturing *both* types of readers, to eliminate the very demarcation it proposes.[9] The alternative type of reading which the trap at once elicits and suspends can be described as the *naïve* ("the capture of the merely witless") and the *sophisticated* ("to catch those not easily caught . . . the jaded, the disillusioned, the fastidious"). The trap, however, is specifically laid not for naïveté but for *intelligence* itself. But in what, indeed, does intelligence consist, if not in the determination to *avoid the trap*? "Those not easily caught" are precisely those who are *suspicious*, those who sniff out and detect a trap, those who refuse to be *duped*: "the disillusioned, the jaded, the fastidious." In this sense the "naïve reading" would be one that would *lend credence* to the testimony and account of the governess, whereas the "disillusioned" reading would on the contrary be one that would suspect, demystify, "see through" the governess, one that, in fact, would function very much like the reading carried out by Wilson, who in effect opens his discussion by *warning* us precisely against a *trap* set by the text, a "trick of James's":

> A discussion of Henry James's ambiguity may appropriately begin with *The Turn of the Screw*. This story (. . .) perhaps *conceals another horror behind the ostensible one*. (. . .) It is a not infrequent *trick of James's* to introduce sinister characters with descriptions that at first sound flattering, so *this need not throw us off*. (*Wilson*, p. 102)

Since the trap set by James's text is meant precisely for "those not easily caught"—those who, in other words, watch out for, and seek to avoid, all traps—it can be said that *The Turn of the Screw*, which is designed to snare *all* readers, is a text particularly apt to catch the *psychoanalytic* reader, since the psychoanalytic reader is, *par excellence*, the reader who *would not be caught*, who would not be made a *dupe*. Would it be possible then to maintain that *literature*, in *The Turn of the Screw*, constitutes *a trap for psychoanalytical interpretation*?

Let us return, one last time, to Wilson's reading, which will be considered here not as a model "Freudian reading," but as the illustration of a prevalent tendency as well as an inherent temptation of psychoanalytical interpretation as it undertakes to provide an "explanation,"

9. These two types of reading thus recall the illusory "two turns" which the mistaken reader in the frame attributes to the screw of the text's effect. (Cf. Prologue, p. 1 [1] * * *.) But we have seen [in Section VIII, "Meaning and Madness: The Turn of the Screw"] that the "two turns" in fact amount to the same: based on the symmetry implied by the "*two* children," the apparent *difference* between the "two turns" is purely *specular*. This is the final irony of the figure of the turn of the screw: while appearing to double and to multiply itself, the turn of the screw only *repeats* itself; while appearing to "turn," to *change* direction, sense, or meaning, the turning sense in fact does not change, since the screw *returns upon itself*. And it is precisely through such a "return upon itself" that the trap set by the text, says James, catches the reader.

or an "explication" of a literary text. In this regard, Wilson's later semi-retraction of his thesis is itself instructive: convinced by his detractors that for James the ghosts were real, that James's *conscious* project or intention was to write a simple ghost story and not a madness story, Wilson does not, however, give up his theory that the ghosts consist of the neurotic hallucinations of the governess, but concedes in a note:

> One is led to conclude that, in *The Turn of the Screw*, not merely is the governess self-deceived, but that James is self-deceived about her. (*Wilson*, note added 1948, p. 143)

This sentence can be seen as the epitome, and as the verbal formulation, of the desire underlying psychoanalytical interpretation: the desire to be a *non-dupe*, to interpret, i.e., at once uncover and avoid, the very traps of the unconscious. James's text, however, is made of traps and dupery: in the first place, from an analytical perspective, the governess is *self-deceived*; duping us, she is equally herself a *dupe* of her own unconscious; in the second place, in Wilson's view, James himself is self-deceived: the author also is at once our duper and the dupe of his unconscious; the reader, in the third place, is in turn duped, deceived, by the very rhetoric of the text, by the author's "trick," by the ruse of his narrative technique that consists in presenting "cases of self-deception" "from their own point of view" (*Wilson*, p. 142). Following Wilson's suggestions, there seems to be only one exception to this circle of universal dupery and deception: the so-called Freudian literary critic himself. By avoiding the double trap set at once by the unconscious and by rhetoric, by remaining himself *exterior* to the reading-errors that delude and blind both characters and author, the critic thus becomes the sole agent and the exclusive mouthpiece of the *truth* of literature.

This way of thinking and this state of mind, however, strikingly resemble those of the governess herself, who is equally preoccupied by the desire, above all, not to be made a dupe, by the determination to avoid, detect, demystify, the cleverest of traps set for her credulity. Just as Wilson is distrustful of James's narrative technique, suspecting that its rhetoric involves a "trick," i.e., a strategy, a ruse, a wily game, the governess in turn is suspicious of the children's rhetoric: " 'It's a game,' I went on, 'it's a policy and a fraud' " (chap. 12, p. 48 [47]). And just as Wilson, struck by the *ambiguity* of the text, concludes that the governess, in saying *less* than the truth, actually says *more* than she means—the governess herself, struck by the ambiguity of Mrs. Grose's speech, concludes in a parallel fashion that Mrs. Grose, in saying less than *all*, nonetheless says *more* than she intends to say:

> . . . my impression of her having accidentally said more than she meant. . . .

> I don't know what there was in this brevity of Mrs. Grose's that struck me as ambiguous. (chap. 2, pp. 12–13 [12])

> I was (. . .) still haunted with the shadow of something she had not told me. (chap. 6, p. 27 [26])

Like Wilson, the governess is *suspicious* of the ambiguity of signs and of their rhetorical reversibility; like Wilson, she thus proceeds to *read* the world around her, to *interpret* it, not by looking *at* it but by seeing *through* it, by demystifying and *reversing* the values of its outward signs. In each case, then, it is *suspicion* that gives rise as such to *interpretation*.

But isn't James's reader-trap, in fact, a *trap set for suspicion*?

> . . . an *amusette** to catch those not easily caught (. . .). Otherwise expressed, the study is of a conceived "tone," the tone of *suspected* and felt *trouble*, of an inordinate and incalculable sore—the tone of tragic, yet of exquisite, mystification. (New York Preface, *Norton*, p. 120 [125]; *James's italics; other italics mine)

The Turn of the Screw thus constitutes a trap for psychoanalytical interpretation to the extent that it constructs a trap, precisely, for suspicion. It has indeed been said of psychoanalysis itself that it is a veritable "school of suspicion."[1] But what, exactly, is suspicion? "Oran," reads the opening line of Camus' *The Plague*, "was a city without suspicion." Brought by "the Plague," suspicion will then signify, in this case, the awakening of consciousness itself through its mêlées with death, with fear, with suffering—the acquisition of a keen awareness of the imminence of a catastrophe of unknown origin, which has to be prevented, fought against, defeated. If it is thus the plague that brings about suspicion, it is well known, indeed, that Freud himself, at the historic moment of his arrival in the United States, said precisely that he had brought with him, ironically enough, "the plague" . . . Psychoanalysis, therefore, could very accurately be described as a "school of suspicion," a school that teaches an awareness of the Plague. What, however, is the alternative to suspicion? James's text can perhaps provide an answer. In the New York Preface, to begin with, the alternative to the suspicious reader was incarnated in the so-called "witless" reader ("the 'fun' of the capture of the merely witless being ever but small"); suspicion would thus seem to be equivalent to "wit," to the *intelligence* of the reader. In the text of *The Turn of the Screw* itself, moreover, the alternative to the suspicion of the governess is, symmetrically, the naïve *belief* of Mrs. Grose, who unsuspectingly lends credence to whatever the governess may choose to tell her. And, as if the very name of Mrs. Grose were not a sufficient clue to James's view of the attitude of *faith* that he thus opposes to suspicion, the fact that Mrs. Grose *does not know how to*

1. The formula is Paul Ricoeur's.

read ("my counselor couldn't read!" chap. 2, p. 10 [10]) clearly suggests a parallel with the "witless" reader that the New York Preface in its turn opposes to the suspicious, unbelieving reader, the one who is precisely difficult to catch. Psychoanalysis, therefore, is strictly speaking a "school of suspicion" to the extent that it is, in effect, a *school of reading*. Practiced by Wilson as well as by the governess, but quite unknown to Mrs. Grose, "suspicion" is directed, first and foremost, toward the non-transparent, arbitrary nature of the sign: it feeds on the discrepancy and distance that separate the signifier from its signified. While suspicion constitutes, thereby, the very motive of the process of interpretation, the very moving force behind the "wit" of the discriminating reader, we should not forget, however, that readers are here "caught" or trapped, not *in spite of* but *by virtue of*, *because of* their intelligence and their sophistication. Suspicion is itself here part of the mystification ("the tone of *suspected* and felt trouble . . . the tone of tragic, yet of exquisite, *mystification*"): the alert, suspicious, unduped reader is here just as "caught," as mystified, as the naïve believer. Like faith (naïve or "witless" reading), suspicion (the intelligence of reading) is here a *trap*.

The trap, indeed, resides precisely in the way in which these two opposing types of reading are themselves inscribed and comprehended in the text. The reader of *The Turn of the Screw* can choose either to *believe* the governess, and thus to behave like Mrs. Grose, or *not to believe the governess*, and thus to behave precisely *like the governess*. Since it is the governess who, within the text, plays the role of the suspicious reader, occupies the *place* of the interpreter, to *suspect* that place and that position is, thereby, *to take it*. To demystify the governess is only possible on one condition: the condition of *repeating* the governess's very gesture. The text thus constitutes a reading of its two possible readings, both of which, in the course of that reading, it deconstructs. James's trap is then the simplest and the most sophisticated in the world: the trap is but a text, that is, an invitation to the reader, a simple invitation to undertake its reading. But in the case of *The Turn of the Screw*, the invitation to undertake a reading of the text is perforce an invitation to *repeat* the text, to enter into its labyrinth of mirrors, from which it is henceforth impossible to escape.

It is in just the same manner as the governess that Wilson, in his reading, seeks to avoid above all being duped: to avoid, precisely, being the governess's dupe. Blind to his own resemblance to the governess, he repeats, indeed, one after the other, the procedures and delusions of her reading strategy. "Observe," writes Wilson, "from a Freudian point of view, the significance of the governess's interest in the little girl's piece of wood" (*Wilson*, p. 104). But to "observe" the *signified* behind the wooden *signifier*, to observe the meaning, or the significance, of the very *interest* shown for that signifier, is precisely what the governess herself does, and invites others to do, when she runs crying for Mrs. Grose, "They know—it's too monstrous: they know, they know!" (chap. 7, p. 30 [29]). In just the same manner as the governess, Wilson equally *fetishizes* the phallic simulacrum, delusively raises the mast in Flora's boat to the status of Master-Signifier. Far from following the incessant slippage, the unfixable movement of the signifying chain from link to link, from signifier to signifier, the critic, like the governess, seeks to *stop* the meaning, to *arrest* signification, by a grasp, precisely, of the Screw (or of the "clue"), by a firm hold on the Master-Signifier:

> What if the hidden theme (. . .) is *simply sex* again? . . . the *clue of experience* . . . (*Wilson*, p. 115)
> When one has once *got hold of the clue to this meaning* of *The Turn of the Screw*, one wonders how one could ever have missed it. (*Wilson*, p. 108)

Sharing with the governess the illusion of having understood *all*, of having *mastered* meaning by clutching at its clue, at its master-signifier, Wilson could have said, *with* the governess and *like* her, but *against* her: "I seemed to myself to have mastered it, to see it all" (chap. 21, p. 78 [76]). In Wilson's case as in the governess's, the move toward mastery, however, is an aggressive move, an "act of violence," which involves a gesture of repression and of *exclusion*. "Our manner of excluding," writes Maurice Blanchot, "is at work precisely at the very moment we are priding ourselves on our gift of universal comprehension." In their attempt to elaborate a speech of mastery, a discourse of *totalitarian* power, what Wilson and the governess both *exclude* is nothing other than the threatening power of rhetoric itself—of sexuality as *division* and as meaning's *flight*, as contradiction and as ambivalence; the very threat, in other words, of the unmastery, of the impotence, and of the unavoidable castration that inhere in *language*. From his very *grasp* of meaning and from the grasp of his interpretation, Wilson thus excludes, *represses*, the very thing that led to his analysis, the very subject of his study: the role of language in the text, "the ambiguity of Henry James":

> Henry James never seems aware of the amount of space he is wasting through the long abstract formulations that do duty for concrete details, the unnecessary circumlocutions and the gratuitous meaningless verbiage—the *as it were's* and *as we may say's* and all the rest—all the words with which he pads out his sentences and which themselves are probably symptomatic of a tendency to stave off his main problems. (*Wilson*, p. 129; Wilson's italics)

As Jean Starobinski puts it elsewhere, "The psychoanalyst, the expert on the rhetoric of the unconscious, does not himself wish to be a rhetorician. He plays the role that Jean Paulhan assigns to the terrorist as such: he demands that one speak in clear language."[2] In demanding that the text "speak in clear language," Wilson thus reveals the *terroristic status* of his psychoanalytic exegesis. But the governess as well demands "clear language": she terrorizes in effect the child into "surrendering the name," into giving, that is, to the ghost its *proper name*. Wilson's treatment of the text indeed corresponds point for point to the governess's treatment of the child: Wilson, too, forces as it were, the text to a *confession*. And what, in fact, is the main effort of the analytical interpreter as such, if not, at all events, to extort the *secret* of the text, to compel the language of the text—like that of the child—to confess or to avow: to avow its *meaning* as well as its *pleasure*; to avow its pleasure and its meaning to the precise extent that they are *unavowable*.

It is thus not insignificant for the text's subtle entrapment of its psychoanalytical interpretation that the governess ends up *killing the child*. Neither is it indifferent to the textual scene that the Latin word for child, *infans*, signifies precisely, "one incapable of speaking." For would it not be possible to maintain that Wilson, in pressing the text to confess, in forcing it to "surrender" its *proper* name, its explicit, literal meaning, himself in fact commits a *murder* (which once more brings up the question of *tact*), by suppressing within language the very silence that supports and underlies it, the silence *out of which* the text precisely speaks?

> . . . a stillness, a pause of all life, that had nothing to do with the more or less noise we at the moment might be engaged in making . . . (chap. 13, p. 53 [51])

As the figure of a *knowledge which cannot know itself*, which cannot reflect upon nor name itself, the child in the story incarnates, as we have seen, *unconscious* knowledge. To "grasp" the child, therefore, as both the governess and Wilson do, to press him to the point of suffocating him, of killing or of stifling the silence within him, is to do nothing other than to submit, once more, the silent speech of the unconscious to the very gesture of its *repression*.

Here, then, is the crowning aberration that psychoanalysis sometimes unwittingly commits in its mêlées with literature. In seeking to "explain" and *master* literature, in refusing, that is, to become a *dupe* of literature, in killing within literature that which makes it literature—its reserve of silence, that which, within speech, is incapable of speaking, the literary silence of a discourse *ignorant of what it knows*—the psychoanalytic reading, ironically enough, turns out to be a reading that *represses the unconscious*, that represses, paradoxically, the unconscious it purports to be "explaining." To *master*, then (to become the Master),

2. Jean Starobinski, *La Relation critique* (Paris: Gallimard, 1970), p. 271; my translation.

is, here as elsewhere, to *refuse to read* the letters; here as elsewhere, to "see it all" is in effect to "shut one's eyes as tight as possible to the truth"; once more, "to see it all" is in reality to *exclude*; and to exclude, specifically, the unconscious.

Thus repeated on all levels of the literary scene, by the governess as well as by her critics, in the story as well as in its reading, this basic gesture of repression, of exclusion, is often carried out under the auspices of a label which while naming that which is cast out, excluded, also at the same time sanctions the exclusion. That subtle label is the term "madness" used by the interpreter to mark what is repressed as indeed *foreclosed*, external to, shut out from, meaning. Wilson thus suggests that the governess is *mad*, i.e., that her point of view *excludes* her, and hence should be excluded, from the "truth" and from the meaning of her story. But the governess herself in her own reading, indeed, refers no less insistently to the question of insanity, of madness. She is preoccupied, as we have seen, by the alternative of madness and of sense as mutually exclusive; she is quite aware, in fact, that the possibility of her own madness is but the converse—the other side, the other turn—of her seizure and *control* of sense, of her "grasp" of and her firm "hold"[3] on meaning, a hold involving the *repression* of otherness as such, an exclusion of the Other. To "grasp," "get hold" of sense will therefore also be to *situate* madness—*outside*, to shut it out, to *locate* it—in the Other: to cast madness as such onto the other insofar as the Other in effect *eludes one's grasp*. The governess indeed maintains that the children are no less than *mad*;[4] when Mrs. Grose urges her to write to the Master about the children's strange behavior, the governess demurs:

> "By writing to him that his house is poisoned and his little nephew and niece *mad*?"
>
> "But if they *are*, Miss?"
>
> "And if I am myself, you mean? That's charming news to be sent him by a person (. . .) whose prime undertaking was to give him no worry." (chap. 12, pp. 49–50 [48])

It is thus *either* the governess *or* the children who are mad: if the children are *not* mad, the governess could well be; if the children *are* mad, then the governess is truly in the right, as well as in her right mind. Hence, to *prove* that the children *are* mad (that they are *possessed*

3. Cf. chap. 6, p. 28 [27; Felman's italics]: ". . . a suspense (. . .) that might well (. . .) have *turned* into *something like madness*. (. . .) It *turned* to *something else altogether* (. . .) from the moment I really *took hold*." Cf. also chap. 12, p. 48 [46; Felman's italics]: "I go on, I know, as if I am *crazy*, and it's a wonder I'm not. What I've seen would have made *you* so; but it only made me more lucid, made me *get hold* of still other things. . . ."

4. To begin with, she claims they are "possessed," that is, *unseizable*, possessed precisely *by the Other*: "Yes, *mad* as it seems! (. . .) They haven't been good—they've only been absent. (. . .) They're simply leading a life of their own. They're not mine—they're not ours. They're his and they're hers!" (chap. 12, pp. 48–49 [47; Felman's italics]).

by the Other—by the ghosts) is to prove that the governess is *not* mad: to point to the madness of the Other is to deny and to negate the very madness that might be lurking in the self. The Other's madness thus becomes a decisive proof and guarantee of one's own sanity:

> Miss Jessel stood before us (. . .). I remember (. . .) my thrill of joy at having brought on a *proof*. She was there, and I was justified; *she was there, so I was neither cruel nor mad.* (chap. 20, p. 71 [68; Felman's italics])

Thus, for the governess to be in *possession* of her *senses*, the *children* must be *possessed* and *mad*. The governess's very *sense*, in other words, is founded on the children's *madness*. Similarly but conversely, the story's very *sense*, as outlined by Wilson, by the *logic* of his reading, is also, paradoxically, *based on madness*—but this time on the madness of the *governess*. Wilson, in other words, treats the governess in exactly the same manner as the governess treats the children. It is the governess's madness, that is, the exclusion of her point of view, which enables Wilson's reading to function as a *whole*, as a system at once *integral* and *coherent*—just as it is the *children's* madness, the exclusion of *their* point of view, which permits the governess's reading, and its functioning as a *totalitarian* system.[5]

"It is not by locking up one's neighbor," as Dostoevsky once said, "that one can convince oneself of one's own soundness of mind." This, however, is what Wilson seems precisely to be doing, insofar as he is duplicating and *repeating* the governess's gesture. This, then, is what psychoanalytical interpretation might be doing, and indeed is doing whenever it gives in to the temptation of *diagnosing* literature, of indicating and of *situating madness* in a literary text. For in shutting madness up in literature, in attempting not just to explain the literary symptom, but to explain away the very symptom of literature itself, psychoanalysis, like the governess, only diagnoses literature so as to *justify itself*, to insure its own *control* of meaning, to deny or to negate the lurking possibility of its own madness, to convince itself of its own incontrovertible soundness of mind.

The paradoxical trap set by *The Turn of the Screw* is therefore such that it is precisely by proclaiming that the governess is mad that Wilson inadvertently *imitates* the very madness he denounces, unwittingly *participates in it*. Whereas the diagnostic gesture aims to situate the madness in the other and to disassociate oneself from it, to exclude the diagnosis from the diagnosed, here, on the contrary, it is the very gesture of exclusion that includes: to exclude the governess—as mad—from the place of meaning and of truth is precisely to repeat her very gesture of

5. Cf.: " 'It's a game,' I went on—'it's a policy and a fraud!' (. . .) 'Yes, *mad* as it seems!' The very act of bringing it out really helped me to trace it—follow it up and *piece it all together*" (chap. 12, pp. 48–49 [47; Felman's italics]).

exclusion, to *include oneself*, in other words, within her very madness. Unsuspectingly, Wilson himself indeed says as much when he writes of another Jamesian tale: "The book is not merely mystifying, but maddening" (*Wilson*, p. 112).

Thus it is that *The Turn of the Screw* succeeds in *trapping* the very analytical interpretation it in effect *invites* but whose authority it at the same time *deconstructs*. In inviting, in *seducing* the psychoanalyst, in tempting him into the quicksand of its rhetoric, literature, in truth, only invites him to *subvert himself*, only lures psychoanalysis into its necessary self-subversion.

In the textual mechanism through which the roles of the governess and of the children become reversible, and in the text's tactical action on its reader, through which the roles of the governess and of her critic (her demystifier) become symmetrical and interchangeable—the textual dynamic, the rhetorical operation at work consists precisely in the *subversion* of the *polarity* or the *alternative* that opposes as such analyst to patient, symptom to interpretation, delirium to its theory, psychoanalysis itself to madness. That psychoanalytical theory itself occupies precisely a symmetrical, and hence a specular, position with respect to the madness it observes and faces, is in fact a fundamental given of psychoanalysis, acknowledged both by Freud and by Lacan. Lacan as well as Freud recognize indeed that the very value—but equally the risk—inherent in psychoanalysis, its insightfulness but equally its blindness, its truth but also its error, reside precisely in this turn of the screw: "The discourse of the hysteric," writes Lacan, "taught [Freud] this other substance which entirely consists in the fact that such a thing as a signifier exists. In taking in the effect of this signifier, within the hysteric's discourse, [Freud] was able to give it that *quarter-turn* which was to turn it into analytical discourse" (*Encore*, p. 41). Freud, in turn, acknowledges a "striking similarity" between his own psychoanalytical theory and the delirious ravings of President Schreber: "It remains for the future to decide," writes Freud, "whether there is more delusion in my theory than I should like to admit, or whether there is more truth in Schreber's delusion than other people are as yet prepared to believe."[6]

It is doubtless no coincidence, therefore, that the myth of Oedipus —the psychoanalytical myth *par excellence*—should happen to recount not only the *drama of the symptom* but equally the very *drama of interpretation*. The tragedy of Oedipus is, after all, the story no less of the analyst than of the analysand: it is specifically, in fact, the story of the deconstruction, of the subversion of the polarity itself that distinguishes and opposes these two functions. The very *murder* that Oedipus commits is indeed constitutive in the story, just as much of the impasse of the interpreter as of the tragedy of the interpreted. For it is the murder

6. S. Freud, *Three Case Histories*, ed. Philip Rieff (New York: Collier Books, 1963), p. 182.

which founds the rhetorical movement of substitution as a *blind* movement, leading blindly to the commutation, or to the switch between interpreter and interpreted: it is by murdering that the interpreter takes the place, precisely, of the symptom to be interpreted. Through the blind substitution in which Oedipus unwittingly takes the place of his victim, of the man he killed, he also, as interpreter (as the detective attempting to solve the crime), and equally unwittingly, comes to occupy the place and the position of the very *target* of the blow that he *addresses to the Other*. But Wilson also is precisely doing this, unknowingly assuming the position of the target, when he inadvertently repeats the gesture of the governess at whom he aims his blow, thereby taking her *place* in the textual structure.

It is through *murder* that Oedipus comes to be *master*. It is by *killing literary silence*, by stifling the very silence that inhabits literary language as such, that psychoanalysis *masters* literature, and that Wilson claims to *master* James's text. But Oedipus becomes master only to end up *blinding himself*. To blind oneself: the final gesture of a master, so as to delude himself with the impression that he still is in control, if only of his self-destruction, that he still can master his own blindness (whereas his blind condition in reality preexisted his self-inflicted blindness), that he still can master his own loss of mastery, his own castration (whereas he in reality *undergoes* it, everywhere, from without); to blind oneself, perhaps, then, less so as to punish, to humiliate oneself that so as to persist, precisely, in *not seeing*, so as to deny, once more, the very truth of one's castration, a castration existing outside Oedipus's gesture, by virtue of the fact that his conscious mastery, the mastery supported by his consciousness, finds itself subverted, by virtue of the fact that the person taken in by the trap of his detection is not the Other, but he himself—by virtue of the fact that he *is* the Other. And isn't this insistence on not seeing, on not knowing, precisely what describes as well the function of the Master in *The Turn of the Screw*? In its efforts to master literature, psychoanalysis—like Oedipus and like the Master—can thus but blind itself: blind itself in order to deny its own castration, in order not to see, and not to read, literature's subversion of the very possibility of psychoanalytical mastery. The irony is that, in the very act of judging literature from the height of its masterly position, psychoanalysis—like Wilson—in effect rejoins within the structure of the text the masterly position, the specific place of the Master of *The Turn of the Screw*: the place, precisely, of the textual *blind spot*.

Now, to occupy a blind spot is not only to be blind, but in particular, to be blind to one's own blindness; it is to be unaware of the fact that one occupies a spot *within* the very blindness one seeks to demystify, that one is *in* the madness, that one is always, necessarily, *in* literature; it is to believe that one is on the *outside*, that one *can* be outside: outside the traps of literature, of the unconscious, or of madness.

James's reader-trap thus functions by precisely luring the reader into attempting to avoid the trap, into believing that there *is* an outside to the trap. This belief, of course, is itself one of the trap's most subtle mechanisms: the very act of trying to escape the trap is the proof that one is caught in it. "The unconscious," writes Lacan, "is most effectively misleading when it is caught in the act."[7] This, precisely, is what James suggests in *The Turn of the Screw*. And what James in effect *does* in *The Turn of the Screw*, what he undertakes through the performative action of his text, is precisely to mislead us, and to catch us, by on the contrary inviting us to *catch the unconscious in the act*. In attempting to escape the reading-error constitutive of rhetoric, in attempting to escape the rhetorical error constitutive of literature, in attempting to master literature in order *not to be its dupe*, psychoanalysis, in reality, is *doubly duped*: unaware of its own inescapable participation *in* literature and *in* the errors and the traps of rhetoric, it is blind to the fact that it itself exemplifies no less than the *blind spot* of rhetoricity, the spot where any affirmation of mastery in effect amounts to a self-subversion and to a self-castration. "*Les non-dupes errent*" [non-dupes err], says Lacan. If James's text does not explicitly make such a statement, it enacts it, and acts it out, while also dramatizing at the same time the suggestion that this very sentence—which entraps us in the same way as does the "turn of the screw"—this very statement, which cannot be affirmed without thereby being negated, whose very diction is in fact its own contradiction, constitutes, precisely, the position *par excellence* of *meaning* in the *literary utterance*: a rhetorical position, implying a relation of mutual subversion and of radical, dynamic contradiction between utterance and statement.

The fact that literature has no outside, that there is no safe spot assuredly outside of madness, from which one might demystify and judge it, locate it in the Other without oneself participating in it, was indeed ceaselessly affirmed by Freud in the most revealing moments of his text (and in spite of the constant opposite temptation—the mastery temptation—to which he at other times inevitably succumbed). Speaking of *The Sandman* and of Nathanael's uncanny madness—a madness textually marked, in Hoffmann's rhetoric, by the metaphor of Nathanael's distorted vision, due to the glasses bought from the Sandman (from the optician Coppola) and through which Nathanael at times chooses to behold the world which surrounds him; glasses through which he looks, at any rate, before each of his attacks of madness and of his attempts at murder—Freud emphasizes the fact that the reader is rhetorically placed *within* the madness, that there is no place from which that madness can be judged *from the outside*:

7. *Scilicet*, no. 1 (1968), 31 ("La Méprise du sujet supposé savoir").

> . . . We perceive that he [Hoffmann] means to *make us, too, look through the fell Coppola's glasses* (. . .)
>
> We know now that we are not supposed to be looking on at the products of a madman's imagination behind which we, with the superiority of rational minds, are able to detect the sober truth . . .[8]

In a parallel manner, *The Turn of the Screw* imposes the governess's distorted point of view upon us as the rhetorical *condition* of our perception of the story. In James's tale as in Hoffmann's, madness is uncanny, *unheimlich*, to the precise extent that it *cannot be situated*, coinciding, as it does, with the very space of reading. Wilson's error is to try to *situate* madness and thereby situate *himself outside it*—as though it were possible, *in* language, to *separate* oneself from language; as though readers, looking through the governess's madness and comprehended by it, could situate *themselves* within it *or* outside it with respect to it; as though readers could indeed know *where* they are, what their place is and what their position is with respect to the literary language which itself, as such, does not know what it knows. Thus it is that when, in another of James's novels, *The Sacred Fount*, the label "madness" is ironically applied to the narrator as the last word—the last judgment in the book, "You *are* crazy, and I bid you good night"[9]—the narrator, indeed, experiences this last word as the loss of his capacity to situate himself: "Such a last word," he remarks, "(. . .) put me altogether nowhere."[1]

"It's a game," says the governess of the behavior of the children that in her turn she claims to be "mad"—"It's a *game*, it's a *policy* and a *fraud*" (chap. 12, p. 48 [47; Felman's italics])—"It's all a mere mistake and a worry and a joke" (chap. 20, p. 72 [70]), answers, indirectly, Mrs. Grose, when she realizes that it is the governess who is mad, and that the children are but the victims of her delirium. The "mistake," the "worry" and the "joke," in Mrs. Grose's mouth, refer to, and affirm, the non-existence of the ghosts; they thus describe, accuse, excuse, the governess's madness. This ambiguous description of the error at the heart of *The Turn of the Screw* as at once tragic and comic, as both a "worry" and a "joke," is also implicit in James's statement in the New York Preface:

> The study is of a conceived "tone," the tone of suspected and felt trouble, of an inordinate and incalculable sore—*the tone of tragic, yet of exquisite, mystification*. (p. 120 [125; Felman's italics])

8. S. Freud, "The Uncanny," trans. Alix Strachey, in *Freud on Creativity and the Unconscious* (New York: Harper Torchbooks, 1958), p. 137.
9. H. James, *The Sacred Fount* (New York: Charles Scribner's Sons, 1901), p. 318.
1. *Ibid.*, p. 319.

The mystification is indeed exquisitely sophisticated, since it *comprehends* its very *de-mystification*. Since Wilson's gesture repeats the governess's, since the critic here participates in the madness he denounces, the psychoanalytical (or critical) *demystification*, paradoxically enough, ends up reproducing the literary *mystification*. The very thrust of the mystification was, then, to make us believe that there is a radical difference and opposition between the turn of the screw of mystification and the turn of the screw of demystification. But here it is precisely literature's mystification that demystifies and catches the "demystifier," by actively, in turn, *mystifying* him. Thus, paradoxically enough, it is mystification that is here demystifying, while demystification itself turns out to be but mystifying. The demystifier can only err within his own mystification.

"We could well wonder," writes Lacan of Poe's *Purloined Letter* but in terms applicable equally to *The Turn of the Screw*, "whether it is not precisely the fact that *everyone is fooled* that constitutes here the source of our pleasure."[2] If the literary mystification is, in James's term, "exquisite," it is indeed because it constitutes a source of pleasure. The mystification is a game, a joke; to play is to be played; to comprehend mystification is to be comprehended *in* it; entering into the game, we ourselves become fair game for the very "joke" of *meaning*. The joke is that, by meaning, everyone is fooled. If the "joke" is nonetheless also a "worry," if, "exquisite" as it may be, mystification is also "tragic," it is because the "error" (the madness of the interpreter) is the error of life itself. "Life is the condition of knowledge," writes Nietzsche; "Error is the condition of life—I mean, ineradicable and fundamental error. The knowledge that one errs does not eliminate the error."[3]

X. *A Ghost of a Master*

> The whole point about the puzzle is its ultimate insolubility. How skillfully he managed it (. . .) The Master indeed.
>
> Louis D. Rubin, Jr., *One More Turn of the Screw*

> Note how masterly the telling is (. . .) still we must own that something remains unaccounted for. Virginia Woolf, *Henry James's Ghosts* [160]

> The postbag (. . .) contained a letter for me, which, however, in the hand of my employer, I found to be composed but of a few words enclosing another, addressed to himself, with a seal still unbroken. "This, I recognize, is from the head-master, and the head-master's an awful bore. Read him, please; deal with him; but mind you, don't report. Not a word. I'm off!"
>
> H. James, *The Turn of the Screw* [10]

2. J. Lacan, "Séminaire sur *La Lettre volée*," *Ecrits*, p. 17.
3. F. Nietzsche, *The Will to Power*.

Thus it is that within the space of a joke that is also a worry, within the space of a pleasure that is also a horror, Henry James, Master of ceremonies, himself takes pleasure in turning the screw, in tightening the spring of our interest:

> That was my problem, so to speak, and my *gageure*—(. . .) to work my (. . .) *particular degree of pressure on the spring of interest.* (Preface to "The Golden Bowl," AN, p. 331)

> —"You almost *killed* me,"

protests, in Mozart's opera *Don Giovanni*, the valet of Don Giovanni, Leporello;

> —"Go on,—You are mad,
> It was only a *joke*."

replies his Master with a laugh. If the joke in *The Turn of the Screw* is equally a deadly, or a ghostly one, it is because the author—the master-craftsman who masters the "turns" of the game—has chosen indeed to *joke with death* itself. It is in his capacity as master of letters that James turns out to be a master of ghosts. Both ghosts and letters are, however, only "operative terms": the operative terms of the very movement of death within the signifier, of the capacity of *substitution* that founds literature as a paradoxical space of pleasure and of frustration, of disappointment and of elation:

> What would the operative terms, in the given case, prove, under criticism, to have been—a series of *waiting satisfactions* or an array of *waiting misfits*? The misfits had but to be positive and concordant, in the special intenser light, to represent together *(as the two sides of a coin show different legends)* just so many *effective felicities* and *substitutes*. (. . .) Criticism after the fact was to find in them arrests and surprises, emotions alike of disappointment and of elation: all of which means, obviously, that the whole thing was a *living** affair. (Preface to "The Golden Bowl," AN, pp. 341–342; *James's italics; other italics mine)

If death is but a joke, it is because death is, in a sense, as Georges Bataille has put it, "an imposture." Like the ghosts, death is precisely what cannot die: it is therefore of death, of ghosts, that one can literally say that they are "a *living* affair," an affair of the living, the affair, indeed, of living.

Master of letters and of ghosts alike, James, in contrast to his interpreters, lets himself become as much as possible a *dupe*, precisely, of their literality. It is as the dupe of the very letter of his text that James remains the Master, that he deflects all our critical assaults and baffles all our efforts to master him. He proclaims to know nothing at all about the content—or the meaning—of his own letter. Like the letters in the very story of *The Turn of the Screw,* his own letter, James insists, contains precisely *nothing.* His text, he claims, can, to the letter, be taken as

> a poor pot-boiling *study of nothing* at all, *qui ne tire pas à conséquence.** It is but a monument to my fatal technical passion, which prevents my ever giving up anything I have begun. So that when *something that I have supposed to be a subject turns out on trial to be none, je m'y acharne d'autant plus.** (Letter to Paul Bourget, August 19, 1898; *Norton,* p. 109 [114]; *James's italics; other italics mine)

> As regards a presentation of things so fantastic as in that wanton little tale, I can only blush to see real substance read into them. (Letter to Dr. Waldstein, October 21, 1898; *Norton,* p. 110 [115])

> My values are positively all blanks save so far as an excited horror, a promoted pity, a created expertness (. . .) proceed to read into them more or less fantastic figures. (New York Preface, *Norton,* p. 123 [128])

Master of his own fiction insofar as he, precisely, *is* its dupe, James, like the Master in *The Turn of the Screw,* doesn't want to *know* anything about it. In his turn, he refuses to read our letters, sending them back to us unopened:

> I'm afraid I don't quite *understand* the principle question you put to me about "The Turn of the Screw." However, that scantily matters; for in truth I am afraid (. . .) that I somehow can't pretend to give any coherent account of my small inventions "after the fact." (Letter to F. W. Myers, December 19, 1898, *Norton,* p. 112 [117–18])

Thus it is that James's very mastery consists in the denial and in the deconstruction of his own mastery. Like the Master in his story with respect to the children and to Bly, James assumes the role of Master only through the act of claiming, with respect to his literary "property," the "license," as he puts it, "of disconnexion and disavowal" (Preface to "The Golden Bowl," *AN,* p. 348). Here as elsewhere, "mastery" turns out to be self-dispossession. Dispossessing himself of his own story, James, more subtly still, at the same time dispossessed his own story of its master. But isn't this precisely what the Master does in *The Turn of the Screw,* when, dispossessing the governess of her Master (himself), he gives her nothing less than "supreme authority"? Is it with "supreme authority" indeed that James, in deconstructing his own mastery, vests his reader. But isn't this gift of supreme authority bestowed upon the reader as upon the governess the very thing that will precisely *drive them mad*?

> That one should, as an author, *reduce one's reader* (. . .) *to such a state of hallucination* by the images one has evoked (. . .)—nothing could better consort than *that* (. . .) with the desire or the pretension to cast a literary spell. (Preface to "The Golden Bowl," AN, p. 332)

It is because James's mastery consists in knowing that mastery as such is but a *fiction*, that James's law as master, like that of the Master of *The Turn of the Screw*, is a law of flight and of *escape*.[4] It is, however, through his escape, through his *disappearance* from the scene, that the Master in *The Turn of the Screw*, in effect, *becomes a ghost*. And indeed it could be said that James himself becomes a phantom master, a Master-Ghost *par excellence* in terms of his own definition of a ghost:

> *Very little appears to be [done]—by the persons appearing*; (. . .) This *negative quantity* is large—(. . .). Recorded and attested "ghosts" are in other words (. . .), above all, *as little continuous and conscious and responsive*, as is consistent with their taking the trouble—and an immense trouble they find it, we gather—to appear at all. (The New York Preface, *Norton*, p. 121 [127; Felman's italics])

Now, to state that the Master has become himself a ghost is once again to repeat the very statement of *The Turn of the Screw*: there are *letters* from the moment there is no Master to receive them—or to *read* them: letters exist because a Master ceases to exist. We could indeed advance this statement as a definition of literature itself, a definition implicated and promoted by the practice of Henry James: literature (the very literality of letters) is nothing other than the Master's death, the Master's transformation into a ghost, insofar as that death and that transformation define and constitute, precisely, *literality* as such; literality as that which is essentially impermeable to analysis and to interpretation, that which necessarily remains unaccounted for, that which, with respect to what interpretation does account for, constitutes no less than *all the rest*: "All the rest is literature," writes Verlaine.[5] "The rest," says the dying artist in James's novel *The Middle Years*, "the rest is the madness of art": the *rest*, or literality, that which will forever make us *dupes* insofar as the very knowledge it conveys but cannot know, the knowledge which *our* knowledge cannot integrate, *dispossesses* us both

4. Cf. "Our noted behaviour at large may show for ragged, because it perpetually *escapes our control*; we have again and again to consent to its appearing in undress—that is, in no state to brook criticism." "It rests altogether with himself [the artist] not to (. . .) 'give away' his importances." (AN, p. 348.)
5. "Il faut aussi que tu n'ailles point / Choisir tes mots sans quelque méprise / Rien de plus cher que la chanson grise / Où l'Indécis au Précis se joint / (. . .) Et tout le reste est littérature." (P. Verlaine, *Art poétique*.)

of our mastery and of our Master. "That all texts see their literality increase," writes Lacan, "in proportion to what they properly imply of an actual confrontation with truth, is that for which Freud's discovery demonstrates the structural reason" (*Ecrits*, p. 364). To quote James again:

> It's not that the muffled majesty of authorship doesn't here *ostensibly** reign; but I catch myself again shaking it off and disavowing the pretence of it while I get down into the arena and do my best to live and breathe and rub shoulders and converse with the persons engaged in the struggle that provides for the others in the circling tiers the entertainment of the great game. There is no other participant, of course, than each of the real, the deeply involved and immersed and more or less bleeding participants. (Preface to "The Golden Bowl," *AN*, p. 328; *James's italics)

The deeply involved and immersed and more or less bleeding participants are here indeed none other than the members of the "circle round the fire" which we ourselves have joined. As the fire within the letter is reflected on our faces, we see the very madness of our own art staring back at us. In thus mystifying us so as to demystify our errors and our madness, it is we ourselves that James makes laugh—and bleed. The joke is indeed on us; the worry, ours.

HENRY SUSSMAN

James: Twists of the Governess†

The central actor in Henry James's *The Turn of the Screw* and his other ghost stories may well be the human nervous system.[1] As the narrative moves through a sequence of sudden reversals of readerly expectations and toward the vertiginous plateau where none of its frames of reference hold fast or provide perspectival consistency, it is the nerves, our own as well as the governess's, which pay for the groundless footing. Our suspicions may dart from Flora and Miles to Mrs. Grose and may even alight upon the governess and Douglas, the final authorities to which the story grants us appeal, yet the narrative's demonic shifts are finally inscribed upon the organic system of the affections itself.

† From *The Hegelian Aftermath: Readings in Hegel, Kierkegaard, Freud, Proust, and James* by Henry Sussman (Baltimore and London: The Johns Hopkins University Press, 1982) 230–39, 254–55. Page references to this Norton Critical Edition are given in brackets after the author's original citations.

1. Citations refer to Henry James, *The Turn of the Screw*, ed. Robert Kimbrough, Norton Critical Edition (New York: Norton, 1966).

The story was composed at a time when Freud was supplementing his neurological account of consciousness with metaphysical and psychological constructs.[2] While the sources of stimulation, narrative as well as physiological, may be infinite, considerable coordination is required to marshal a set of facts and possibilities to the point where they effect a discharge of the nerves in anxiety. Yet it is precisely toward this effect that *The Turn of the Screw* is directed. The story is a meticulously constructed generator of a shock closely akin to the one that Walter Benjamin underscored as the insignia of the Modern age. Just as the Freudian trauma penetrates the psyche's own shield of defenses, the shocks almost tangentially disclosed in the course of the story undermine the reassurances that the text itself has volunteered.

The Turn of the Screw hovers in the uncertainties entertained by the too fertile imagination of a governess. The story, to whatever extent a jarringly abrupt narrative allows for one, concerns the degree to which the governess's suspicions as to the apparitions that she witnesses at Bly infect her relations with her charges, two children, her colleague, and herself. The basic unit of the story's momentum and force is the intellectual gesture in which an idle speculation becomes a conclusion, in which a precipitous determination predicates subsequent beliefs and actions. Through the repetition of this reflexive gesture on the part of the governess, the story becomes a vertiginous fabulation of hastily (if not falsely) drawn conclusions.[3]

Although the governess, as the story eventually and cruelly reveals, *governs*, she is initially cast in the role of an exemplary reader. Like Hegel's Antigone and Kierkegaard's women, at first she occupies the passive position of the observer and receptor. If the governess's hallucinations evolve from privately witnessed aberrations to actual personages in collusion with the children, if her anxieties progress beyond her psyche to the point where one of her charges dies of fright, this may be easily dismissed as a distinctly feminine hysteria. The core of the story, consisting of the governess's own written account of her stay at Bly and interactions with the children, Mrs. Grose, and the apparitions, is surrounded in a double narrative frame. Apart from serving as a setting for the governess's text, this framework provides the background and conditions of what might be considered a fictive case history of hysteria.

One element of the narrative framework concerns the rather practical question of how the governess's tale is to reach the hands of Douglas, host of a Christmas Eve gathering at which the story's narrator is a

2. The first edition of Breuer and Freud's *Studies on Hysteria* appeared in 1895. *The Turn of the Screw* was published both whole and as a serial in England and the United States in 1898.
3. For a fine discussion of "reading in" as it is dramatized and examined by the story, see Walter Benn Michaels, "Writers Reading: James and Eliot," *MLN*, 91 (1976), 834–37. Michaels also elaborates the "political" implications of the various choices that the story imposes upon the reader.

guest, so that he may read it aloud. Nothing could be more intimate than a story, even a ghost story, told around a fire at the most familial moment of the year, radiating a trust and warmth that would seemingly extend to the rapport between a governess and her charges. Yet at every turn the governess's narrative undermines the Kierkegaardian intimacy of this initial setting.

The story's first suspense is the waiting the guests must tolerate until the governess's manuscript arrives in the London post. Douglas informs his audience that the woman in question was his sister's governess, a tangential fact of some consequence, since it places him in the position of little Miles. It is Douglas who forges the central tale's setting in a second sense. By virtue of his "personal connection" to the governess, he can fill in other incidental but decisive details, specifically those relating to the circumstances and motives surrounding the governess's original acceptance of her position. It is from Douglas that we learn how "handsome and bold and pleasant, offhand and gay and kind" Bly's absent master was (p. 4) [4]; the condition "that she should never trouble him—but never, never: neither appeal nor complain nor write about anything; only meet all questions herself" (p. 6) [6]; and that having seen the master "only twice" and receiving only one handshake in thanks "for the sacrifice, she already felt rewarded" (p. 6) [6]. Apart from performing narrative groundwork, the story's frame thus qualifies all that follows by a specific symptomology, the pathology of hysteria. Hopelessly in love with an absent master, deprived not only of sexual gratification with him but even of words, the governess seems a textbook case of hysteria. The textbook, by Freud and Breuer, appeared in 1895, three years before James's story. The governess's visions, her hypnotic moments when time seems to stop, her machinations in winning Mrs. Grose to her point of view, and the ultimate transference of her anxiety to the children she ostensibly protects all seem to be hysterical manifestations that arise in the place of the master. In this regard, it would seem possible to dismiss both the governess and her narrative as mere onsets of "female trouble," a generically marked exaggeration to be deflated through the application of some measure and restraint.

To be sure, the parallels between the governess's experiences at Bly and the symptoms of hysteria set out in Breuer and Freud's *Studies on Hysteria* are nothing less than uncanny. In their treatise, the first major code of psychoanalytical research, Breuer and Freud settle on a group of recurrent hysterical symptoms, including "surplus excitation," "hypnoid states," and "splitting of the mind" or "double conscience," which they ascribe to sexual repression. In a striking number of instances, the governess's conditions at Bly correspond to ones characterizing the cases of the seminal patients of psychoanalysis, such as Fraüleins Anna O. and Elisabeth von R. By her own account, the governess's visions are hypnotic and marked by division. The repressively unselfish role of guardian (or nurse) is regarded by both Breuer and Freud as one particularly conducive to anxiety. The child-care situation was, for the progenitors of psychoanalysis, the breeding ground for premature sexual activity in children, another of the standard preconditions for adult neurosis. In this regard, the governess is more the cause than the sufferer of hysteria, yet Freud observes that child molestation often repeats abuses suffered earlier by the perpetrator. Not a case history in the formal sense, James's story stops at introducing material from the governess's past in explanation of her behavior.

Yet if we wish to write off the governess as a repressed hysteric, James offers us literary aids for this task beyond the aims and institution of psychoanalysis.[4] The arbitrary manner in which the governess forces interpretations upon both the phenomena she observes and the words she hears comprises a kind of inferential hysteria. The rigidity of her conclusions often far exceeds the uncertainty that prompted them, suggesting a logical hyperexcitability installed within her character. In her only promiscuity, the governess entertains a wide array of possibilities while she is at Bly: that the place is haunted altogether, who the apparitions are, that the children are their victims or their allies. Yet her logical point of departure at any given moment, her temporary working assumption, is almost invariably reached through this process of reading in, which is analogous to *projection* in psychoanalytical theory. The formative role of this inferential leap in her psyche has even penetrated her *conscious*: "by the time the morrow's sun was high I had restlessly read into the facts before us almost all the meaning they were to receive from subsequent and more cruel occurrences" (pp. 27–28) [27]. "I only sat there on my tomb and read into what my little friend had said to me the fulness of its meaning" (p. 57) [55]. It is on the basis of this projective mode of reading that the governess *decides* that Mrs. Grose speaks of someone *beside* the master (p. 12) [12], that the apparition known as "Quint" is after Miles (p. 25) [25], and that the children are in collusion with the ghosts that only she sees (pp. 52–53) [51].

On the basis of this literary instance of hypersuggestibility and the affinities between the governess's conditions and those outlined in the Freudian textbook, it would seem perfectly appropriate to dismiss both the governess and the story as illustrations or caricatures of the theory of hysteria. Yet such an application terminates with an abruptness be-

4. By far the most comprehensive treatment of *The Turn of the Screw* and its ramifications in terms of psychoanalytical and critical theory to date is Shoshana Felman's "Turning the Screw of Interpretation," *Yale French Studies*, 55–56 (1977), 94–207 [excerpted on pp. 196–228.] Felman anticipates many of the key concerns of my reading, including the application of Freudian theory to the story (Felman, pp. 103–11, 115–18) and the displacements within the narrative framework (p. 144). It is indicative of the critical controversy posed by the story that Felman and I would diverge at the point of placement. Having attempted to isolate a moment of irreparable stress in Hegel, I inscribe James's story back within a continuous Hegelian-Freudian tropological tradition. Felman finds in the text and its interpretations an occasion for delineating the systematic limits of precisely that tradition.

lying the prolonged indeterminacy that the story sustains. Even deeper than the governess's tendencies to hysteria are the roots of its uncanny moments of "visitation" in the matrix of Hegelian operations also underlying Freudian neurosis. When we turn to those horrifying and still scenes that serve as the "episodes" in her disease and as strategic turning points in her conquest of Bly, we see that they are catalogues of long-established reflexive and speculative operations.

> It was plump, one afternoon, in the middle of my very hour: the children were tucked away and I had come out for my stroll. . . . Someone would appear there at the turn of a path and would stand before me and smile and approve. . . . What arrested me on the spot—and with a shock much greater than any vision had allowed for—was the sense that my imagination had, in a flash, turned real. He did stand there! but high up, beyond the lawn and at the very top of the tower. . . . This tower was one of a pair—square, incongruous, crenelated structures—that were distinguished, for some reason, though I could see little difference, as the old and the new. They flanked opposite ends of the house and were probably architectural absurdities. . . . I admired them, had fancies about them . . . yet it was not at such an elevation that the figure I had so often invoked seemed most in place.
>
> It produced in me, this figure, in the clear twilight, I remember, two distinct gasps of emotion. . . . My second [surprise] was a violent perception of the mistake of my first: the man who met my eyes was not the person I had precipitately supposed. . . . It was as if, while I took it in—what I did take in—all the rest of the scene had been stricken with death. I can hear it again, as I write. . . . The rooks stopped cawing in the golden sky and the friendly hour lost, for the unspeakable minute, all its voice. The gold was still in the sky . . . and the man who looked at me over the battlements was as definite as a picture in a frame. . . . He was in one of the angles. . . . He turned away; that was all I knew (pp. 15–17) [15–17]

The governess's first horror, a specifically reflexive nightmare, takes place amid the benign plumpness of the afternoon, at her own special hour, when the children are "tucked away." The warmth of this golden "friendly hour" recalls the governess's first images of Bly: the "bumping, swinging coach" that brings her there, the "most pleasant impression" she has of "the broad, clear front, its open windows and fresh curtains . . . the lawn and the bright flowers" (p. 7) [7]. The harbinger of horror in the story is often an emotional release figured in intimacy and breadth, a relaxation of the defenses.

And yet, what exactly is the terror of this episode? On one level, the trauma is described as one that takes place on the border between the outside and the inside. And this particular shock allows for no exit. At first the governess is shaken by the uncanny *correspondence* between her sexual fantasy of the handsome "someone" and what she actually sees. Yet no sooner does this fright take place, of the imagination's "turning real," than it is compounded by an awareness of the discrepancy between the projection and the actuality: "he" stands not at the expected elevation. In both of its possible ramifications, then, the discrepancy between the outside and the inside upsets the governess. A reality that confirms fantasy is horrifying, and this shock is only aggravated when the correspondence begins to unravel. One dimension of the governess's terror, then, is the unmitigated unsettling caused by the compulsive displacement that transpires between the outside and the inside, among the most fundamental momentums of the Hegelian text.

Accompanying this compulsive and fatal comparison between the interior and the exterior are the fantastic symmetry and division that prevail within both the scene and the governess's reactions to it. The double towers flank the house symmetrically. The triggering of the hallucination provokes "two distinct gasps of emotion" in the governess. Yet this pronounced doubling or bifurcation dominates the scene not by virtue of its status as a formal category so much as in the relations of reciprocity that it initiates. In the sense that the male figure in this scene is a projection of the governess's, he exists as her double. More unsettling than this hypothesis are the implications, noted by the passage, that as a double of the governess, the apparition usurps her claims to "reality," becomes exactly as actual as she is. The ornamental doubling in the landscape underscores a much less palatable speculation: that the figment of the imagination has become as "real" as the "person," the thinking subject, the governing governess.

The schizoid mutuality of the relationship between the subject and the image is what gives the consummating horror to those moments in the visitations when the apparitions *stare back*. Shortly after the above citation ends, we read: "So I saw him as I see the letters I form on this page; then . . . as if to add to the spectacle, he . . . passed, looking at me hard all the while. . . . Yes, I had the sharpest sense that during this transit he never took his eyes from me" (p. 17) [16]. It is the imagistic autonomy attained by the governess's projections when they stare back that endows her visions with their fullest horror. And the reciprocity most succinctly abbreviated in the figure of the simultaneous and mutual regard of entities that may or may not share the same status, this sustained parity forms an economy governing the entire story. The story is calibrated according to a calculus of uncanny reciprocities, in love, communication, dissimulation, and protection. At several moments in the text, the governess assumes that Mrs. Grose and the children are concealing something from her. But the governess's suspicions that Mrs. Grose camouflages the apparitions at Bly (pp. 11–12, 27) [11, 26] and that the children conspire with the visitors (p. 52) [51] do not preempt her own dissimulations (pp. 38–39) [37–38]. In a similar vein, the governess stifles any attempted contact between her companions and the absent master (p. 54) [52], just as by contract she must repress her communicative urges. A final irony of the story is that little Miles, having been fatally influenced by the governess's projections, assumes the same protective stance toward her that comprises only one limited facet of her relation to the children (p. 66) [63–64]. And why should the reciprocal scrutiny that is a constitutive element of the governess's visitations not extend into every aspect of a story that *she* composes?

Doubling—in the above passage of towers, gasps, figures, and regards—is the basic unit of repetition, its primary instance. And the passage we read certainly harbors the seeds of the story's compulsive repetitions. The strange figure appears before the governess "at the turn of a path," and in recording the scene, in writing it, she can "hear" its sounds "again." The governess's horror accumulates in the persistence of scenic repetition. As in the case of Kierkegaardian repetition, the scenes vary as they transpose certain basic elements. As the first visitation, the scene we presently scan may contain the fullest vocabulary of elements: doubles, reciprocal regards, stillness, scaffolding and other frameworks, angles, and distortions. Subsequent scenes supplement this vocabulary; they also edit out certain of the elements. Quint's second visitation, for example, takes place indoors, enabling the implicit rhetoric of reflection in the first to become overt. Quint peers at the governess through a window (a "glass," also suggesting a mirror) situated near a staircase, an addition to the earlier external scaffolding (p. 20) [19–20]. In the third visitation, the apparition's participation is so intense that he becomes the scene's "spectator" (p. 29) [28]. It is in this episode that the story's imagistic *mise en scène* expands. Not only does the governess suffer the agonizing tension of her parity with an uninvited voyeur: she begins to measure the impact of the scene of a third party, in this case Flora. The governess awaits "what a cry from her, what some innocent sign either of interest or alarm, would tell me" (p. 30) [29]. Expanded to its full complexity, the visitation scene places the governess midway in a specular quandary. Simultaneously, she must mark both the unwanted visitor already gazing at her and the impact of the scene, whether "real" or invented on another audience, comprising Mrs. Grose and the children.

These scenes are divided off from the rest of the narrative by framing devices as effective as the scaffolding that often becomes part of the stage props. Specifically, it is the sudden hush that comes over these moments, their unbearable stillness, that separates them from the overall narrative flow. In fashioning a narrative that fluctuates between intimate storytelling and rigorously autonomous scenes, the governess experiments in that imagistic tradition synthesized in Kierkegaard's *The Concept of Irony*. The story's ample rhetoric of *fixing*, in the sense both of staring and of holding fast (pp. 3, 41) [2, 39], is indicative of the power of the stasis that prevails within the image. For James as for Kierkegaard, the self-enclosure of the image precludes the possibility of progress by bringing it to a halt.

Time stops during the scenes of visitation because they are so totally *absorbing*. For the governess, their fascination is itself a trespass, ending "the general high propriety" that rules at Bly when she first arrives (p. 15) [15]. The stoppage of time effected by the visitation scenes is in direct proportion to the degree to which the governess is captivated by her charges. In her attempts to definitively know and fix the children, the governess is in a position similar to Winterbourne's in relation to Daisy Miller. Daisy Miller so fascinates Winterbourne that he surveys her from every angle, but most of what he finds, by virtue of the standards he applies, is impropriety. Miles and Flora pose a similar riddle to the governess. In her attempts to resolve her interpretative problem, the governess treats the children as an imagistic surface to be *filled in* by projection: "They had nothing but me, and I—well, I had *them*. . . . This chance presented itself in an image richly material. I was a screen—I was to stand before them. The more I saw, the less they would. I began to watch them in a stifled suspense . . ." (p. 28) [27]. As in the case of Daisy Miller, the blank image under scrutiny is to be not only filled in by the observer but stifled and abused.[5] The children are eventually pushed out of the picture and blinded. Miles's beauty places the governess "under the spell" (p. 20) [19], and for this reason, perhaps, he does not escape her. The girl-child is more vigorous. By virtue of either extreme innocence or depravity, Flora refuses to be shaken and thus denies the governess confirmation of her uncanny experiences. In the line of Daisy Miller, Flora "absolutely declined to be puzzled" (p. 43) [41], to her warden's desperation. Not only, then, does the governess's experience break down with a sequence of imagistic moments, episodes informed by the Romantic tradition of the image. The governess's interactions take the form of imagistic activities: interpretation, projection, captivation, enclosure.

In James's vocabulary as in Hegel's, turning is the basic metaphor for repetition. James's screw may penetrate deeper (or tighten); its threads may move. But the activity of revolution characterizes the story's compulsive recurrences. And yet, not only do the story's apparitions turn their backs on the observer (pp. 17, 41) [17, 40]; not only does a reciprocal, reflexive vocabulary of fright *re*turn. The turns of the screw are upheavals, unmaskings, and debunkings of the presuppositions that

5. Cf. Henry James, *Daisy Miller*, in *The Bodley Head Henry James* (London: Bodley Head, 1972–), XI (1974), 45: "He [Winterbourne] had perhaps not definitely flattered himself that he had made an ineffaceable impression upon her heart, but he was annoyed at hearing of a state of affairs so little in harmony with an image that had lately flitted in and out of his own meditations; the image of a very pretty girl looking out of an old Roman window and asking herself urgently when Mr Winterbourne would arrive."

the text offers as givens. The turns of the screw effect a series of fictive negations that are all the more bewildering because the assumptions undermined are not abstract philosophical terms but items derived from a language of consciousness and life. It is in the sense of such turns that the governess passes from an intimate colleague and protectress to an author, the author of Mrs. Grose's unhinging and Miles's death as well as of the narrative. The governess *speaks* a language of nurturing and salvation (pp. 28, 65, 79, 81) [27, 62–63, 76, 78], but she composes one of bewilderment and wild suggestion. By the same token, Mrs. Grose and the children *turn* from dissimulations and conspirators to victims of a master, not an absentee one but an authoring one. In its vacillations between threat and protection, vulnerability and abuse, the story explores the potentials released by the Hegelian dialectic of the master and the slave.

As writer and author, the governess offers an alternate mastery to the one to which she initially subordinates herself. As the orchestrator of scenes of reciprocal indeterminacy and the impetus for the story's turns of the screw, she composes a world that supersedes the conventions from which it is derived. We have already cited some of the evidence that suggests the *story's* grounding in operations of internalization and externalization, bifurcation, reciprocity, and circularity. As we have seen, this matrix underlies not only the story but also the Freudian constructs according to which it may be read. Yet as an author, as a writer in the text, the governess composes a domain unified by no center or consistency. The story is a collage of mutually untenable logical conditions.

In the story's third and fourth sections, the narrative transcribes the voice of a governess who regards herself as the victim of strange visitations. In section 7 we witness a governess who assumes that the children know of the visitations. In sections 10 and 11 we read a narrative voice assuming the children to be in treacherous collusion with the visitors. In section 20, the governess sees figures that no one else sees; in the very next section we find Flora in absolute terror of her protectress. And in the final section, the governess embraces Miles with clutches as deadly as they are affectionate. These logically incongruous pictures come to us via the medium of a voice consistent in its intimacy. But this vocal steadiness betrays us, as the children are betrayed.

Rather than a narrative transcribing the presence of a *centered* self or personality, what we have in this text is a story without a center. This story shifts between assumptions so incongruous as to suggest either the absence of any central personality or authorship or, if some origin be required, the presence of a subject so fragmented and split as to be held together by no logic other than madness. The story becomes a recording of a decentered voice, hence one with no master, a narrative beyond control.

But the governess *is* the story's author. In fabulating a story beyond consistency and logic which nonetheless appropriates the Hegelian matrix of speculative operations, she removes the text from the space of mastery and inscribes it within the problematic of writing. To the extent that the governess does suffer from hysteria, it is not as a psychological category but as a condition of writing. It is the implicit hysteria of writing that imprisons the author in a self-enclosed domain and fabulates a miasma of repetitive yet shifting details.[6] The governess authors the story in the absence of the master's love, phallus, protection, and control. That the text replaces the dominant orders of reflection and hysteria with its own economics of writing in no way denies its debt to Hegelian operations. This, in a word, is the locus of the seminal works of modernism, moving toward a problematic of writing from within a framework of reflexive gestures.

The moments of textual violence that break out within Kafka's novels, as well as the intricate Proustian artifacts, are also situated in the transition charted by *The Turn of the Screw*. These and other distinctively modern experiments benefit from the dual possibilities afforded by the governess's story. The resources of fiction can move toward an explicit acknowledgement of the dynamics of writing without relegating the discursive activities here associated with "Hegel" to some closed and rigid otherness or past. Too much exuberance surrounds the groundbreaking explorations of modern literature to warrant a decisive threshold separating the outside and the inside of systematic thought. As both Hegel and Kierkegaard demonstrate, too much play and inefficiency are accommodated within philosophical speculation to definitively close it off from the textual activity of the artifacts that have recourse to it.

The impelling question facing modernism at the beginning of the twentieth century concerns the relation between the outside and the inside of the system of speculative thought. While within the field of critical theory this question has been specifically posed since 1967, with the appearance of three groundbreaking works by Jacques Derrida, the problem and its ramifications continue to undergo refinement.[7] If we follow the lead of such modernists as Proust and James, who examined the nature of language and the literary text from within the Hegelian aftermath, the border between the outside and inside can continue to be a threshold of *ouverture* and discovery.

6. It is in this regard that despite all superficial contrasts, the governess is a close relative of the frenetic subterranean rodent in Franz Kafka's story "The Burrow." For a close reading of this text, see Henry Sussman, "The All-Embracing Metaphor: Reflections on 'The Burrow,' " in *Franz Kafka: Geometrician of Metaphor* (Madison: Coda Press, 1979), pp. 147–81.
7. The works in question are *La Voix et le phénomène* (Paris: Presses Universitaires de France, 1967); *De la Grammatologie* (Paris: Minuit, 1967); and *L'Ecriture et la différence* (Paris: Seuil, 1967).

BRUCE ROBBINS

Recognition: Servant in the Ending†

* * *

One text where this reintroduction of collective social entities into the dynamics of the psyche can be tested is what has been, from Edmund Wilson to Shoshana Felman, the classical locus of Freudian exegesis: James' *The Turn of the Screw*. In the New York Preface, James states his intention not to specify the evil of the ghosts but to leave it to the reader's imagination. "I cast my lot with pure romance," he says. "There is not only from beginning to end of the matter not one inch of expatiation, but my values are positively all blanks."[1] Yet it is hard not to fill these blanks with the open secret of trans-class sexuality. Love between the classes is of course precisely what the governess discovers in the earthly paradise at Bly. The corruption she perceives has to do with the children's knowledge of sexual relations between their former governess and one of the servants, who was "dreadfully below." It is clear that her horror has as much to do with the sexual and class transgression as with their ghostly reappearing act. Even before she hears about them, each ghost provokes in her thoughts of a servant exceeding his or her station; later, each makes a carefully staged entry "below" her on the staircase, that ready-made icon of vertical social difference. In conversation with Mrs. Grose, the governess as much as admits to conflating supernatural evil with social anomaly: " 'But if he isn't a gentleman—' 'What *is* he? He's a horror' " (p. 22 [22]). To occupy a gentleman's place without being a gentleman is sufficient to become a horror, without further need of supernatural props or special effects. The novella's systematic confusion of ghosts with servants—both categories impalpable, alien, and threatening, both filling the house with noises and mysteries—comes to a head in the final confrontation. Miles, accused of excessive intimacy with a "base menial," wonders about the "others" with whom they've been left "alone," or "not absolutely alone": "they don't much count, do they?' " (p. 82 [79]).

To say that for the governess the supernatural otherness of the ghosts coincides with the class otherness of the servants is not to fall back into the sort of politicized Freudianism in which the governess would be charged with projecting her class ambivalence along with her repressed

† From *The Servant's Hand: English Fiction From Below* by Bruce Robbins (New York: Columbia University Press, 1986), 200–203, 238. Page references to this Norton Critical Edition are given in brackets after the author's original citations.

1. James, *The Turn of the Screw*, Kimbrough, ed., pp. 121, 123 [127, 128]. Further page numbers will be given in the text.

sexuality. Just as Marx extracted the labor theory of value as a sort of utopian kernal from political economy's apologies for capitalism, so we can extrapolate from her otherwise sordid "romance" of sexual transgression a final recognition that puts love between the classes in a different light. In *The Political Unconscious* Fredric Jameson describes romance, the genre that James asks to carry the weight of his blank, motiveless malignity, as a

> symbolic answer to the perplexing question of how my enemy can be thought of as being *evil* (that is, as other than myself and marked by some absolute difference), when what is responsible for his being so characterized is simply the *identity* of his own conduct with mine, the which—challenges, points of honor, tests of strength—he reflects as in a mirror image. Romance "solves" this conceptual dilemma by producing a new narrative, the "story" of a semic evaporation. The hostile knight, in armor, exudes that insolence which marks a fundamental refusal of recognition and stamps him as the bearer of the category of evil, up to the moment in which, defeated and unmasked, he asks for mercy and *tells his name* . . . at which point . . . he becomes one knight among others and loses all his sinister unfamiliarity. (pp. 118–119)

There is of course no moment at the end of *The Turn of the Screw* when "the antagonist *ceases* to be a villain," as Jameson says, when the mask of otherness is lifted and evil evaporates from the world. But to judge from the critical controversy surrounding this text, much of it builds toward just such a missing scene. The multiple mirror images, duplications, reenactments, and superimpositions between the governess and the servant-ghosts have been assembled as evidence, mainly by the anti-ghost party, in order to undermine the governess' narrative authority. Yet these parallels can also be interpreted as continual, unanswered beckonings to a recognition that would convert these threatening aliens into mere versions of herself.

Here it is helpful to remember * * * that the collapse of class otherness is erotically charged with pleasure as well as negatively charged with threat. What the governess herself desires is of course nothing but the erotic transgression of class. Her love for the Master requires that at some future point she herself must repeat the ghosts' transgression and indulge a love prohibited by the social hierarchy. Though the text does not follow her romance script, its unrealized happy end—victory over the ghosts and union with the Master—develops a utopian motif that is present from the outset. On her arrival at Bly, the governess describes it as a "castle of romance" (p. 10 [9]). As the pro-ghost party has observed, much emphasis is given to the aspect of a fallen Eden, an earthly paradise. Her terms for the innocence of the children are borrowed from the golden age. Miles, the governess says, has an "indescribable little air of knowing nothing in the world but love" (p. 13 [13]). In a sense, all the evil she later finds in this paradise does not dislodge this initial view. Miles *has* known love, the governess decides—the love between governess and valet. The hypothesis can thus be formulated that if his innocence seems not of this world, it is precisely *because* he, unlike most earthly children, has known love that triumphs over class in a house without a master. And this hypothesis returns upon the governess herself. One reviewer called *The Turn of the Screw* "a study of infernal human debauchery."[2] But this debauchery could better be seen as a sort of deconstruction of the human, as its etymology (perhaps fancifully) suggests: "ébaucher" is to lay the foundation, construct the skeleton; to debauch is to remove it, to deconstruct. In expressing its desire, the self exposes an identity or an identification—not upon which it is built, but toward which it is projected. Whether the governess loves the children's innocence or participates in their debauchery, her desire projects her toward the servant-ghosts.

Recall how far the text goes not only to show that evil is defined in class terms but also to remind us that the governess herself is a servant. As one example among many, there is her cross-examination of Mrs. Grose concerning Miles and his intimacy with Quint:

> "If Quint—on your remonstrance at the time you speak of—was a base menial, one of the things Miles said to you, I find myself guessing, was that you were another." Again her admission was so adequate that I continued: "And you forgave him that?"
>
> "Wouldn't *you*?"
>
> "Oh yes!" And we exchanged there, in the stillness, a sound of the oddest amusement. (p. 37 [36])

Mrs. Grose's "Wouldn't *you*?" suggests to the governess, in a mode approaching that of stage comedy, what so many critics of *The Turn of the Screw* have suggested in the mode of scholarly irony: her resemblance to the servant-ghosts, from which we can deduce the fragility of an "evil" that depends for its existence on nothing more than the illusion of otherness. In this sense it can be maintained that *The Turn of the Screw* projects an unrealized "happy end": the return of Bly to the (classless) Edenic state in which the governess first found it, the evaporation from her world of the "evil" that she added to it, which would result from her recognition of what so many voices are trying to tell her—her identity with "the others."

2. Kimbrough, ed., p. 175 [156].

NED LUKACHER

"Hanging Fire": The Primal Scene of *The Turn of the Screw*†

An obscure revelation of a referentiality that no longer refers to anything more than the evidentiality of an event that is no longer an event.

JACQUES DERRIDA, "Préjugés"

Of the critics of Henry James's *The Turn of the Screw*, Shoshana Felman writes: "In repeating as they do the primal scene of the text's meaning as division, the critics can by no means master or exhaust the very meaning of that division, but only act the division out, perform it, be part of it."[1] Here indeed is a text whose "polytonality" cannot be mastered. Like the governess herself, the critic is thwarted whenever he or she tries to grasp the real and tries to wrest from the unmasterable tone of *The Turn of the Screw* a determinant or univocal meaning. At every "turn" James invites his readers to make a construction and to attempt a solution. But as Felman's essay "Turning the Screw of Interpretation" definitively establishes, there is simply no way to avoid repeating the text's fundamental division between the uncanny ghostliness of the governess's visions and the hysterical mechanisms that inform them.

The point I would like to make here, however, does not directly concern the difference between the psychic and the sexual. While Felman is quite right to demonstrate how James implicates the reader in every effort by the governess to construct the primal scene, and to demonstrate that the governess's dilemma as analyst is that of every reader, she does not pose the question of the precise nature of the governess's constructions. It is one thing to say that, try as they may, critics can never demystify the governess's mystification and are condemned to repeat it; it is quite another thing to say, as I shall, that James's interest is as much in the specific nature of the governess's process of construction as it is in the indeterminacy of the finished product. What neither Felman nor any other critic of *The Turn of the Screw* has analyzed is the specificity of the governess's visions/hallucinations. Numerous details and many of the most extraordinary scenes in the story have gone

† From *Primal Scenes: Literature, Philosophy, Psychoanalysis* by Ned Lukacher (Ithaca: Cornell University Press, 1986), 116–121, 127–128. Page references to this Norton Critical Edition are given in brackets after the author's original citations.

1. Shoshana Felman, "Turning the Screw of Interpretation," in *Literature and Psychoanalysis: The Question of Reading Otherwise*, ed. Shoshana Felman (Baltimore, Md.: Johns Hopkins University Press, 1980), 113 [Felman's article is excerpted on pp. 196–228 of this Norton Critical Edition].

unnoticed, or at least unexplained, because the critical focus has been on the governess's state of mind rather than on the particularity of the vision in question.

* * *

The critical history of *The Turn of the Screw* reveals that there has been more interest in James's figure of the analyst than in the constructions she makes. Like the critics Freud describes in *From the History of an Infantile Neurosis,* who believe that the fact that the analyst proposes the primal scene and the patient does not remember it decides the whole question, critics of James's text have focused so myopically on either the hysterical projections of the governess or the possibility of psychic phenomena that they never consider the fundamental question posed by Freud's construction of the primal scene: What is the relation of the phantasy to reality? Without forgetting that the real remains out of our grasp, I will attempt here to relate the governess's constructions to the analyst's construction of the primal scene, to determine what primal scene or *fabula* lies behind the *sjuzet* that is her narrative. Her narrative, like the wolf dream, contains within itself a *fabula* that, while not constituting the real, nevertheless brings us closer to it than we could otherwise reach.

The question, therefore, is not whether the governess's visions involve sex or the supernatural but whether they compose an account of the events prior to her arrival at Bly House which, though still concealing the real, at least approximates it. In effect we are shifting what Felman calls "the text's meaning as division" from the *sjuzet* to the *fabula.* Through her visions the governess is trying to remember something that everyone else is trying to forget. But like an intemperate analyst, she comes to believe too vehemently in her own constructions of an event that remains rigorously unknowable. Because of the extent of her mystification, critics have focused solely upon her inability to distinguish reality from phantasy but have forgotten to consider the possibility that those phantasies are nevertheless related to the real. Even Felman, in the course of her otherwise brilliant Lacanian reading of the story, has omitted all reference to the real, which is a profoundly non-Lacanian reading strategy. The concealment of the real and one's inability to grasp it are never for Lacan reasons to forget the real. The critics of *The Turn of the Screw* have forgotten the story's temporality, which is the pathway to the real. Only by reconstructing that temporality will we be able to move beyond mere indeterminacy. Like the ghosts of ontotheology, the ghosts of Peter Quint and Miss Jessel pose the question of the origin through the medium of the question of time. James's "tone" is an achievement that must be placed in conjunction with the Freudo-Heideggerian notion of the temporality of the non-originary "event."

"In so far as the analyst is supposed to know," writes Lacan, "he is also supposed to set out in search of unconscious desire."[2] The governess errs in setting out on this search with perhaps a little too much determination, though we might as easily say too much self-righteousness or prurience: "What it was least possible to get rid of was the cruel idea that, whatever I had seen, Miles and Flora saw more—things more terrible and unguessable and that sprang from dreadful passages of intercourse in the past."[3] While an analyst would be concerned with the neuroses that might have developed in the children as a result of having witnessed the primal scene, the governess is concerned that the spectacle of *coitus flagrante* has placed the children within the diabolical power of the returning spirits of Quint and Jessel. (As we will see, for the governess the primal scene is literally a *flagrant* spectacle in the etymological sense of the word *flagrante*, "blazing.") Though these "things" are still "unguessable" at this early point in the text, the governess will soon be making quite a few guesses, which Freud would call "suppositions" *(Annahmen)*. Like the analyst, the governess cannot expect corroboration except for an occasional slip of the tongue from Mrs. Grose. Finally, like an analyst who succeeds only in driving the patient away, the governess will lapse from this salutary skepticism with regard to the limits of her knowledge into a grotesque certitude that will no longer admit any interdictions barring the way to the primal scene.

Suddenly confronted, in broad daylight, with the vision of the ghost of Miss Jessel at the writing desk—which reminds us that in this story the primal scene is always one of writing—the governess tries to grasp the vision in its entirety, to take it all in, only to discover that "even as I fixed and, for memory, secured it, the awful image passed away" (59) [57]. "Fixing" her gaze and "securing" an image in her memory are emblematic of the governess's behavior. Convinced that the children, whether unconsciously or not, have been "fixed," or rather fixated, upon the primal scene, the governess turns all her attention to their fixation, which in turn becomes her fixation and thus that of the reader. In the following passage James goes out of his way to fix our attention on "fixing." Mrs. Grose and the governess are discussing Miss Jessel:

> Mrs. Grose, at this, fixed her eyes a minute on the ground; then at last raising them, "Tell me how you know," she said.
> "Then you admit it's what she was?" I cried.
> "Tell me how you know," my friend simply repeated.
> "Know? By seeing her! By the way she looked."
> "At you, do you mean—so wickedly?"

2. Lacan, *The Four Fundamental Concepts of Psycho-Analysis*, 235.
3. Henry James, *The Turn of the Screw*, ed. Robert Kimbrough (New York: Norton, 1966), 53 [51]. All subsequent page numbers cited in the text refer to this edition.

> "Dear me, no—I could have borne that. She gave me never a glance. She only fixed the child."
>
> Mrs. Grose tried to see it. "Fixed her?"
>
> "Ah with such awful eyes!" (32) [31]

Mrs. Grose's response to this report of Jessel's "awful eyes" renders this scene a repetition and displacement of the very scene it describes: "She stared at mine as if they might really have resembled them." Mrs. Grose sees in the governess what the governess sees in her vision of Miss Jessel. She sees the same "fury of intention" and the same desire "to get hold of" the children. In Jessel's desire to possess the souls of the children, the governess sees her own desire to seize upon the children's unconscious desire. This is indeed an allegory of the analyst's desire to know. It is the task of the Jamesian "tone" to mark the diacritical point where analysis becomes a kind of possession.

* * *

Miss Jessel is at the heart of the governess's construction of the primal scene. From Mrs. Grose she learns that Miss Jessel became pregnant with Quint's child and was sent home, where she presumably died, as the result of either a miscarriage or an abortion: "She couldn't have stayed. Fancy it here—for a governess! And afterwards I imagined—and I still imagine. And what I imagine is dreadful" (33) [32]. These revelations by Mrs. Grose enable the governess to rationalize her strange predisposition to depise her precursor. Her aggressive detestation of a woman she has never met is one of the most disturbing features of her illness. She even speaks, again by way of rationalization, of the ability of women to "read one another." Her propensity to believe the worst of Miss Jessel is in marked contrast to Douglas's characterization of Jessel in the prologue to the story as "a most respectable person":

> So far had Douglas presented his picture when someone put a question. "And what did the former governess die of? Of so much respectability?"
>
> Our friend's answer was prompt, "That will come out. I don't anticipate."
>
> "Pardon me—I thought that was just what you are doing." (15) [5]

Is Douglas misleading us in the very act of letting us in on the secret? If he is not, then he is undermining one of the governess's major themes and in effect suggesting that her bitter recriminations against Miss Jessel are utterly delusional. Clearly, he is anticipating, despite his disclaimer. But that still does not make us any more or less certain of the reliability of his assurances of Jessel's respectability. Here indeed is an exemplary instance of the Jamesian "tone" at work: it directs us to a particular problematic at the same time that it calls into question both its own reliability and the significance of the very thing toward which it turns our attention. It is precisely by virtue of the hermeneutic interference it generates that the Jamesian "tone" calls attention to itself. James questions Miss Jessel's respectability by first establishing that this is a question that can never be resolved, a question whose answer will remain concealed, a question that both must be and cannot be answered.

* * *

In "The New York Preface" to *The Turn of the Screw*, James describes his achievement in terms of a tone that seems a precursor to Derrida's "apocalyptic tone": "The study is of a conceived 'tone,' the tone of suspected and felt trouble, of an inordinate and incalculable sore—the tone of tragic, yet of exquisite, mystification" (120) [125]. Notice the care with which James calculates the effect of the "incalculable." On the one hand there is the tone of suspicion, the tone that speaks of "an inordinate and incalculable sore"; on the other hand there is a tone of tragic mystification. In other words, the event remains "incalculable" because it can only be approached in terms of a mystified tone. The governess's tragic airs, her lurid Gothic imagination, become for James a synecdoche for the work of unconscious phantasy in general, which is always already at work in the determination of an event.* * *

PAUL B. ARMSTRONG

History and Epistemology: The Example of *The Turn of the Screw*†

* * *

The history of *The Turn of the Screw* provides classic evidence of why the goal of achieving a single right reading is elusive and misconceived. But it also shows that debates between conflicting communities of readers are governed by various constraints and tests for validity and are therefore not exercises in solipsism. I will develop a theory of interpretation by examining how *The Turn of the Screw* has been construed, and I will then argue that this epistemology is essentially the same in structure as historical understanding. Critics engaged in historical research related to *The Turn of the Screw* duplicate the epistemological processes involved in interpreting the work, and this is one of the rea-

† From "History and Epistemology: The Example of *The Turn of the Screw*." *New Literary History* 19 (1987–88): 694, 696–708, 710–12. Copyright © 1988 by *New Literary History*, The University of Virginia, Charlottesville. Reprinted by permission of The Johns Hopkins University Press. Page references to this Norton Critical Edition are given in brackets after the author's original citations.

sons why different interpreters of James's text offer different versions of its reception. This variability, in turn, is evidence that history is not neutral, bias-free description, but depends on the presuppositions of the interpreter.

* * *

The history of the reception of *The Turn of the Screw* suggests that accurate representation is a less useful model for describing understanding than variable conversations concerned with shifting, often incommensurable, problems. But it also demonstrates that there are fundamental epistemological reasons for these developments and discontinuities which we cannot understand if we stop asking theoretical questions about knowledge. And it shows as well that the process of validation has certain constant forms across different communities, including responses to otherness which cannot be collapsed into social agreement.[1]

The debate about *The Turn of the Screw* supports Rorty's claim that making the mind a mirror to its object will not end hermeneutic conflict.[2] The object's characteristics are precisely what are in dispute, and they can seem radically different to different minds. To take a classic example: for Edmund Wilson "there is never any reason for supposing that anybody but the governess sees the ghosts," and she is "self-deceived," while for Wayne Booth "the ghosts are real, the governess sees what she says she sees."[3] Attempts to mediate or resolve such conflicts by pointing to what is really there in the text extend the debate instead of stopping it. One of the earliest of such attempts is Leon Edel's claim that examining "the technique of the story-telling . . . would have made much of the dispute unnecessary." Because we are confined to the point of view of the first-person narrator, he argues, "the reader must establish for himself the credibility of the witness."[4] But that, of course, is exactly what Booth, Wilson, and many others have argued about—whether the governess's vision is to be trusted or suspected, believed or demystified. If anything, Edel shows one reason why the dispute occurred, not why it was superfluous. Appealing to the structure

1. I am contesting the skeptical claim of Dieter Freundlieb that the controversies surrounding James's novella show questions about interpretive correctness to be unanswerable and irrelevant. See Freundlieb, "Explaining Interpretation: The Case of Henry James's *The Turn of the Screw*." *Poetics Today*, 5 (1984), 79–95.
2. Armstrong refers to Richard Rorty (1931–), American philosopher. According to Armstrong, in *Philosophy and the Mirror of Nature* (Princeton: Princeton University Press, 1979), Rorty argues that understanding is not a matter of accurate or objective mental representation [*Editors*].
3. Edmund Wilson, "The Ambiguity of Henry James" (1938; rev. 1948, 1959), in *A Casebook on Henry James's "The Turn of the Screw,"* 2nd ed., ed. Gerald Willen (New York, 1969), pp. 117, 147 [the 1934 version of Wilson's essay is excerpted on pages 170–73 of this Norton Critical Edition]; and Wayne Booth, *The Rhetoric of Fiction* (Chicago, 1961), p. 314.
4. Leon Edel, "The Point of View" (1955), in the Norton Critical Edition of Henry James, *The Turn of the Screw*, ed. Robert Kimbrough (New York, 1966), pp. 228, 233.

beneath a conflict is sometimes a useful strategy for making sense of an unresolvable controversy, but it still leaves the interpreter with the decision of how he or she will participate in the discussion—either by choosing one of the opposing views, or by trying to oscillate back and forth between them (as one does with those figures where one first sees a rabbit and then a duck, first an urn and then two faces), or by developing yet another alternative not yet part of the conversation.

An appeal to objective textual features is often made in an effort to stop a debate which, it is felt, has become tedious. For how long, many readers have asked, can we argue about the existence of ghosts without losing interest? Even before their reality was questioned by Wilson, however, the conversation about the novella had begun to lag. Early reviewers wondered whether so harrowing a tale about such abominable evil should ever have been written. "The story itself is distinctly repulsive," one critic complained, and another reported that "we have never read a more sickening, a more gratuitously melancholy tale."[5] Only twenty years later, however, the work's gruesome effects seem to have worn off, and Virginia Woolf finds James's ghosts too domestic and worldly to be frightening. "What does it matter, then," she asks, "if we do pick up *The Turn of the Screw* an hour or so before bedtime?"[6] Wilson's hypothesis about the governess's madness—so familiar as to seem boring to readers in the 1960s and 70s—originally had the function of revivifying interest in a text which was losing its impact.

When readers grew tired of arguing about the governess's sanity, the reason was not that through this unresolvable controversy they had lost touch with the text itself, but that suggestions for reading which had at first given new impulses to discussion had eventually become conventional and incapable of opening new interpretive possibilities. This dilemma can only be resolved not by trying to cut beneath the controversy to reach the object which gave rise to it, but by developing new interpretive strategies to get the conversation out of its rut—by shifting suspicion to Mrs. Grose or the absent master, for example (Eric Solomon's and John Rowe's suggestions), or by introducing a new theme like interpretation as the play of differences (Shoshana Felman's way of turning the screw), or by transforming the discussion itself into the object of discussion (a tactic currently popular among many).[7]

In order to understand why interpreters of *The Turn of the Screw* have disagreed, we must ask epistemological and even metaphysical

5. Reviews from *The Outlook* (29 Oct. 1898) and *The Bookman* (Nov. 1898) in Norton, pp. 172, 173 [151, 153].
6. Virginia Woolf, "Henry James's Ghost Stories" (1921), in Norton, p. 179 [159].
7. See Eric Solomon, "The Return of the Screw" (1964), in Norton, pp. 237–45; John Carlos Rowe, *The Theoretical Dimensions of Henry James* (Madison, 1984), pp. 119–46; and Shoshana Felman, "Turning the Screw of Interpretation," in *Literature and Psychoanalysis: The Question of Reading: Otherwise*, ed. Shoshana Felman (Baltimore, 1982), pp. 94–207 [excerpted on pp. 196–228].

questions about their procedures and assumptions. (These are consequential questions because answering them can give us guidance about how to behave in the conversation even if it will not settle the disputes.) If, as Rorty claims, different partners in a discussion may not see eye to eye because they are concerned about different problems, such divergences occur because the interpreters have conflicting beliefs about what the object is and how best to engage it.* * *

* * * An appeal to either interpreter to reflect the text more transparently will have no effect, because what they see the work as—the typological hypothesis through which they fit its pieces together—is a consequence of convictions which do not derive from this text alone and which are incommensurable with the beliefs of the opposing camp.

This conflict is evidence of the inherent circularity of interpretation. Understanding is circular, according to classic hermeneutic theory, because we must project a sense of the whole in order to construe a text's parts even if we must also work through its various elements in order to achieve an overall view of their relations. * * *

* * *

The conflicts over how best to understand *The Turn of the Screw* suggest that the process of validation is at least to some extent responsible to the object interpreted, even if the relation between reading and text is not an empirical bond or a mirrorlike correspondence. In addition to intersubjective acceptability, an interpretation must demonstrate internal coherence and effectiveness in meeting unexpected challenges. Wilson's critics unwittingly but powerfully invoked these criteria when they thought they could prove him wrong on his facts, and their charges proved so embarrassing that he partially retracted his original reading. A. J. A. Waldock accused Wilson of ignoring "two stubborn facts of the story"—"details within the story itself that decisively negative" the hallucination theory. These "facts" are the governess's accurate, detailed description of Peter Quint and her previous ignorance of how he looked.

The language of Waldock's attack is interesting, however, because his empirical rhetoric of correct reflection alternates with images which acknowledge the circular interdependence of parts and wholes. Unless these details are "accounted for," he argues, "Mr. Wilson's whole case collapses like a house of cards."[8] These two small items can only have such destructive power if interpretation entails the projection of a pattern in which every piece depends on all the others. A single failure to fit may thus have devastating repercussions for the entire interpretive configuration—as it would not if knowing were a point-by-point process of correspondence in which the fuzziness of the mirror in one place

8. A. J. A. Waldock, "Mr. Wilson and *The Turn of the Screw*" (1947), in *Casebook*, pp. 171–72.

might not impugn its transparency elsewhere. Waldock's charges posed difficulties for Wilson because they suggested anomalies which undermine the internal coherence of his reading, and they were thus a challenge to his theory's effectiveness in producing new hypotheses to assimilate new materials. The dispute between Waldock and Wilson involves processes of validation which are object-related and not reducible to the epistemic rules of either opposing interpretive community, although their quarrel is also not an empirical question of accurate reflection.

Wilson's response suggests that even when criteria for validity are object-related they can be satisfied in incommensurable ways. He first acknowledged the importance of these anomalies by shifting the charge of self-deception from the governess to James. If Waldock is right, then he has pointed out flaws in the story's design which suggest that James was not fully aware of the kind of narrative he was writing.[9] This is an awkward tactic, however, because instead of removing anomalies, it only shifts responsibility for them in order to convert an embarrassment for the interpreter into one for the writer. Their status as inconsistencies remains unquestioned. Several years later, however, John Silver came to the rescue and pointed out several places where the governess could have learned about Quint, including a trip to the nearby village which she mentions in explaining why she is sure the figure on the tower was not a local resident: "I didn't tell you," she says to Mrs. Grose, "but I made sure."[1] Wilson could then proudly retract his retraction, and in doing so he gave as further evidence that James knew all along what he was up to in the placement of *The Turn of the Screw* in the New York Edition between two works with similarly unreliable narrators. Once again, validation is not a process of correspondence but an attempt to suggest coherent patterns—here viewing the text itself as part of a larger whole.

This crucial, well-known episode in the history of James's novella is worth telling in some detail because of its implications for the epistemology of validation. On the one hand, the dispute between Waldock and Wilson shows that interpretive communities are neither self-enclosed nor irresponsible to their objects. An antagonist in hermeneutic conflict not only has the option of questioning the opposing community's assumptions and procedures, but may also attempt to create embarrassing anomalies for it by pointing to textual details which its readings have not yet accounted for. On the other hand, however, these details are not simply empirical facts, inasmuch as an interpreter may defend the validity of his reading by assimilating anomalous evidence through ingenious hypotheses which his opponent refuses to ac-

9. See Wilson's 1948 postscript to "The Ambiguity of Henry James," pp. 145–53.
1. John Silver, "A Note on the Freudian Reading of 'The Turn of the Screw' " (1957), in *Casebook*, p. 243.

cept. The much discussed visit to the village has different meanings for the conflicting interpretive camps. For the governess's defenders, it is an occasion where she confirms Quint's menacing strangeness. For her detractors, it is a source of the information with which she browbeats Mrs. Grose into believing her wild fantasy. This interpretive disagreement suggests that an appeal to "facts in the text" cannot adjudicate correctness, because interpreters attribute different meanings to details by placing them in different overall patterns. But the way that the conflict unfolded until it reached this new deadlock calls into question Rorty's reduction of validation to a purely intracommunal exchange, because the disputants grappled with each other across epistemic boundaries by debating about the qualities of an object.

The general implication of the story I have been relating is that turning to history will not get us away from the epistemological questions about interpretive conflict which trouble contemporary theory. Rather, the history of the reception of a controversial text like *The Turn of the Screw* is one place where those questions have been most dramatically enacted. * * *

The dispute about *The Turn of the Screw* suggests that the "realist/idealist question" cannot be muted in the history of reception but turns up there again when critics with incompatible beliefs give incommensurable readings of "the facts of the text." The argument between Waldock and Wilson shows that a literary work is neither totally subordinate to nor completely autonomous of interpretation but is paradoxically both dependent and independent at once—"heteronomous," as I have elsewhere called it.[2] Wilson finds Waldock's objections troublesome because they call attention to seemingly independent features in the text which resist his hypotheses, but Wilson's solution does not satisfy the governess's defenders because they do not accept the typological pattern by which he constructs the text—a text which is self-evidently "there" only to those who share his beliefs about it. *The Turn of the Screw* is independent of either camp to the extent that both groups are pointing to and arguing about something other than themselves. But this otherness also depends for its very meaning and structure on how it is interpreted, inasmuch as each group's way of configuring the text excludes the other's. One reason why texts have histories is that they are indeed heteronomous in this manner—transcending any individual community's way of interpreting them as they are taken up again and again by different groups of readers, but varying in their shape according to the shifting patterns of coherence attributed to them.

* * * Although historians must arrange evidence in patterns which are coherent and acceptable to others, this is an imaginative act of consistency-building which can be done in many different ways. As a

2. See my essay "The Multiple Existence of a Literary Work," *Journal of Aesthetics and Art Criticism*, 44 (1986), 321–30.

result, according to Hayden White, "historical explanations are bound to be based on different metahistorical presuppositions about the nature of the historical field, presuppositions that generate different conceptions of the *kind of explanations* that can be used in historiographical analysis."[3] This interdependence of "metahistorical presuppositions" and acceptable explanations suggests that, as in the interpretation of a literary text, there are two levels of belief at work in historical understanding—metaphysical assumptions about the being of the entities under scrutiny which then sanction a certain range of interpretive hypotheses about their relations in any particular case.

* * *

I have been arguing that historical understanding and literary interpretation have the same epistemological structure.[4] One consequence of this homology is that different ways of construing a text lead their adherents to write different histories of its reception. The interdependence of textual interpretation and critical history can be seen, for example, in the conflict between two recent, theoretically sophisticated readings of *The Turn of the Screw*. For Shoshana Felman, the novella refuses to mean in a "vulgar," "literal" way which would stop "the *movement* constitutive of meaning" by "block[ing] and interrupt[ing] the endless process of metaphorical substitution." Despite the apparent differences between Wilson and his opponents, they are thus guilty of the same kind of misreading because they try to master and reduce the text's signifying power. The text defies its readers' attempts to contain and control it by enacting a conflict of interpretations which dramatizes, "through a clash of meanings, the very functioning of meaning as division and as conflict."[5] Where Felman finds in the text an absence of meaning which encourages play and resists mastery, John Carlos Rowe argues that the novella masters the reader for its own ends by playing the game of absent authority. Rowe argues that the governess's employer dominates the scene by removing himself and displacing the signs of his rule onto others so as to disguise and thereby secure his power. In the history of the tale's reception, James repeats the strategy which his

3. Hayden White, *Metahistory: The Historical Imagination in Nineteenth-Century Europe* (Baltimore, 1973), p. 13.
4. This claim might seem confusing if "history," "literary criticism," and "epistemology" are regarded as different kinds of writing, governed by different conventions and practiced by different communities. My argument is that the hermeneutic circle characterizes the operation of all three fields, whatever their surface differences. How we know (the main concern of epistemology) is a circular process of fitting together parts and wholes. This circularity can be seen in the stories we tell about the past (history) as well as in the readings we give to novels or poems (literary criticism). Radical differences can divide kinds of historical analysis or modes of interpretation, depending on what configurations of elements they typically expect to discover or what presuppositions lie behind the hypotheses through which they group parts together. But if opposing historical methods or critical schools have different epistemologies in the sense that they are different ways of knowing, they have the same epistemological basis inasmuch as they manifest the universal circularity of understanding.
5. Felman, "Turning the Screw of Interpretation," pp. 107, 112 [206, 210]

text dramatizes—preserving his power by pretending to give it up, withdrawing himself and handing authority over to the reader with the result that his own name is ever resounded in the conflicts among his agents.[6] The play which Felman finds semantically liberating seems to Rowe part of a ploy to gain dominance and authority.

Felman and Rowe narrate the work's history of reception differently because they have different beliefs about the text. Configuring the text and emplotting its heritage are correlative acts. She finds refusals to specify in the work which open up possibilities of meaning in its reception. He sees a strategy for winning power enacted in the story which is duplicated in the author's relation to his readers. History cannot settle or bypass their dispute, because writing different narratives of the work's hermeneutic past is a crucial way in which they argue about its present meaning.

Contesting the interpretation of a work may mean not only writing different histories of its reception but also suggesting different originating contexts for it. Defenders of the ghosts have expended much energy and ingenuity in tracking down parallel reports of apparitions in the nineteenth-century annals of the Society for Psychical Research.[7] Their argument is that the reality of the ghosts will be vindicated if it can be shown to match the behavior of supernatural beings in the historical record which James might have known. Those who doubt the governess's sanity have been equally zealous, but their hypotheses about the text lead them to discover its sources elsewhere. They differ among themselves as well, in ways which reflect subtle but important differences about how to construe the tale. To add credence to Wilson's psychoanalytic diagnosis of the governess, Oscar Cargill suggests that William James's Continental connections and his and Henry's concern about the psychological health of their sister Alice could have brought to the novelist's attention an early case history from Freud's *Studies in Hysteria* which has remarkable parallels to *The Turn of the Screw*. Mark Spilka agrees that repressed sexuality provides the necessary clue for reading the story, but he calls the tale an appeal to the Victorian reader's prurient interest in the erotic qualities of children. Citing pornographic literature from the time, however, Bruce Robbins calls attention to the Victorian fascination and fear about "love between the classes" to suggest that the sexual exploitation of servants is the tale's original social context.[8]

6. Rowe, pp. 123–28, 135, 145–46.
7. See Francis X. Roellinger, "Psychical Research and 'The Turn of the Screw' " (1949), in Norton, pp. 132–42, and Miall, "Designed Horror," pp. 308–22. See also Martha Banta, *Henry James and the Occult* (Bloomington, 1972), pp. 9–36, 116–21.
8. Oscar Cargill, "*The Turn of the Screw* and Alice James" (1963), in Norton, pp. 145–65 [138–43]; Mark Spilka, "Turning the Freudian Screw: How Not to Do It" (1963), in Norton, pp. 245–53; and Bruce Robbins, "Shooting Off James's Blanks: Theory, Politics, and *The Turn of the Screw*," *Henry James Review*, 5 (1984), 192–99.

In each of these instances, the historical frame of reference proposed would serve as a larger whole in which the text would fit as an intelligible part. Disagreements about the kind of coherence which internally unifies the text mirror themselves in the critics' hypotheses about the type of context to which it belongs. An appeal to origins cannot settle disputes about interpretation because in both arenas suppositions about part-whole relations are at stake. These are inherently contestable, as I have argued, not only because parts and wholes can be mutually confirming, but also because no single belief about coherence is ever immediately self-evident. Such a belief is only a guess—a wager about how pieces will probably fit together, and a gamble that other available hypotheses will not work better. A historical source seems self-evident to the critic only because it corroborates his sense of the whole which is the type of the story. To look for a work's source is to search for how its history begins, and a choice about how to start a narrative is always circularly dependent on the configuration which one anticipates will develop as the story unfolds. Where the history of *The Turn of the Screw* begins for any interpreter depends on where he thinks it ends—which, at least for the moment, is with his present reading of the work.

* * * The "Preface" calls the novella "a fairy-tale pure and simple" designed "to rouse the dear old sacred terror." But James also describes the work as a study "of a conceived 'tone,' the tone of suspected and felt trouble, of an inordinate and incalculable sore—the tone of tragic, yet of exquisite, mystification"—and this reference to the governess's confused emotional state seems to some an invitation to psychological demystification. The "Preface" credits the tale with "a perfect homogeneity"—with "being, to the very last grain of its virtue, all of a kind."[9] But because James gives conflicting signals about what this kind is, critics with opposing hypotheses about its type could and did quote him in their defense.

When James's *Notebooks* were published in 1947, however, Wilson's antagonists thought their battle was won. In a famous entry, James gives as the germ of the work a ghost story heard from the Archbishop of Canterbury, E. W. Benson.[1] The authority of this ascription was almost immediately contested, however, because Benson's sons had already declared it unlikely their father was James's source; they had never heard the story and doubted it belonged to their father's repertoire.[2]

9. James, "Preface," in *The Turn of the Screw* (1908), in Norton, pp. 119, 118, 120, 117 [124, 123, 125, 123].
1. The notebook entry, dated "Saturday, January 12th, 1895," can be found in Norton, pp. 106–7 [112].
2. James alludes to Benson in his "Preface" and wrote to one of the brothers, A. C. Benson, as early as 1898 to credit their father with the tale. These references, and not the notebook entry, prompted their denials. See A. C. Benson, *Memories and Friends* (New York, 1924), pp. 216–17, and E. F. Benson, *As We Were: A Victorian Peep Show* (London, 1930), p. 278. The publication of James's notebooks did not refute these denials but instead called attention to them and made them even more interesting.

Are they wrong, or did James's memory fail him, or is the notebook entry an attempt to send source hunters down the wrong track? James's intention seemed settled only to become unsettled again with the possibility he might have been lying. What is curious, however, is that both sides in the dispute have accused James of planting deceptive clues.* * *James seems to have anticipated this controversy in one "Preface" where he writes: "One's notes, as all writers remember, sometimes explicitly mention, sometimes indirectly reveal, and sometimes wholly dissimulate, such clues and such obligations."[3]

We have here a classic instance of the unreliability of documentary evidence about intention for settling interpretive disputes. Such evidence typically displaces rather than resolves arguments about the text's meaning by providing the combatants with more material to contest. Intention is never directly given, but must always be construed, even in such documents as notebooks and prefaces. A construal of intention is necessarily at least in part the product of the interpreter's choices, not only because he must decide whether to trust or suspect the evidence, but also because to attribute an intention to a work is to select one of a number of possible ways of typing it. Some have argued that meaning is identical with intention because to interpret a text entails adopting a characterization of the speaker.[4] If so, then the question of what intention an utterance expresses is not merely empirical but epistemological and theoretical, because it rests on a choice about classification. Do I believe that speakers typically deceive, so that I should type the text as a lie, or do I guess that the speaker deserves credence, which would give his utterance a different kind of designation? Here as before, the decision about how to interpret is epistemologically contestable because it is a matter of making a wager about what it is better to believe. Classifying the speaker's intention and typing the work are interdependent choices, and an appeal to one cannot justify the other.

* * *

3. Henry James, "Preface" to "The Altar of the Dead" in James, *The Art of the Novel*, ed. R. P. Blackmur (New York, 1934), p. 258 [107].
4. See Steven Knapp and Walter Benn Michaels, "Against Theory," *Critical Inquiry* 8 (1982), 725–26, 729.

T. J. LUSTIG

Henry James and the Ghostly†

If 'The Turn of the Screw' is concerned with slippages and turns of meaning, it is also deeply preoccupied with gaps and voids: James wrote in his Preface that the 'values' of the story were 'positively all blanks' (*LC*, II, 1188)[1] [128]. Shlomith Rimmon has argued that 'The Turn of the Screw' constructs its ambiguity around 'a central informational gap' (*The Concept of Ambiguity*, p. 51).[2] But this notion of an absent core, a single and central enigma, seems to secure its lucidity by avoiding any explication of the teeming voids which haunt 'The Turn of the Screw'. Few fictions deploy such extensive and disparate lacunae, and 'The Turn of the Screw' uses its blanks to undermine all attempts to establish relations and to join references into a coherent pattern. * * *

'The Turn of the Screw' is repeatedly concerned with the act of telling. More often than not, however, its predicament is that of not being able to tell. Fragmented and vestigial, the existing text looks like the ruined remains of a fuller story. The introductory chapter of 'The Turn of the Screw' begins just after a story has been told and ends just before a story is about to begin. It occupies a space between two acts of telling, framing and mediating a narrative which, as Douglas points out, takes up the tale 'at a point after it had, in a manner, begun', and which ends in the air, with a death whose consequences are not registered in the narrative of the governess, except in the sense that her narrative is the effect of that death (*CT*, x, 19)[3] [4]. * * *

The frame chapter serves to mediate a further mediation, since it seems that the events at Bly do not constitute a complete and discrete story so much as a border between a past defined in terms of social relations and a future made up of literary or textual relations. Miles and Flora are passed from their dead parents to their disappearing uncle and on to Quint and Jessel, who die to make way for an evanescent nursemaid, a temporary school, Mrs Grose and the governess herself.[4] Some time after the events of the main narrative the governess tells her story directly to Douglas. The story is subsequently written down by the governess and sent to Douglas before her death. Douglas reads the governess's narrative to the circle gathered in the old house and in turn transmits it, before his own death, to the narrator of the introductory chapter, who finally makes an 'exact transcript' of the manuscript (*CT*,

† From *Henry James and the Ghostly* by T. J. Lustig (Cambridge: Cambridge University Press, 1994), 115–18, 125–27, 172–73, 177–78, 187–89, and 271–77. The author's notes have been edited. Page references to this Norton Critical Edition are given in brackets after the author's original citations.

x, 19) [4]. The events at Bly thus form the mid-point in a sequence of transmissions, each of which begins and ends in death or absence, all of which lead away from genetic sources and reproductive pairs to single parental substitutes and from primary spoken narratives to written, read and copied ones.[5]

The spaces which intervene between the separate events of this skeletal history are complete blanks—mere spaces of time—but the events themselves are almost equally shadowy, permeated and punctured by the voids which they supposedly separate. * * *

* * *

Naturally no fiction is required to take out a stop-watch and calendar to account for its chronological lapses and transitions. Nor is a novel bound to represent time as a smooth linear succession of events: in *The Ambassadors*, as both Ian Watt and Charles Thomas Samuels have shown, James repeatedly employs proleptic and analeptic shifts.[6] One would be tempted to dismiss the temporal discrepancies in the frame chapter as oversights on James's part were it not for the fact that he rarely made such errors and for the far more important fact that the frame chapter seems to act as a small-scale model of the temporal uncertainties of the governess's own narrative. * * *

* * *

If the governess does wait ten years after the events at Bly to tell Douglas her story and another twenty years before writing it down, if Douglas indeed keeps her manuscript under lock and key for a further two decades, it is only to present a sequence of absences which invite, without rewarding, speculation. To map the uncertain edges of these blank areas is simply to secure the border of nothing—of a mere interval, a lapse. The blanks do not offer significance so much as pierce it; to the extent that they signify at all, they are signs only of the disappearance of forthright meanings. Yet the blanks do not only shatter, riddle or impair the narrative. They also permit an extraordinary multiplication of references to the impossibility of reference. Faced with the unrepresentable, the governess does not simply stop: she begins to elaborate, to find terms which describe the state of being unable to describe. Although the blanks in her narrative blot sense they also reiterate its absence, and one's impression is not of emptiness and silence but rather of a voluble swarm of surrogates and replacements. One of the most notable absences in the narrative of the governess is that of the word 'ghost'. The only use of the word in the text occurs when Douglas speaks cautiously, and with reference only to Griffin's story, of a 'ghost, or whatever it was' (p. 15) [1]. Instead of 'ghosts', the governess offers a host of variously suggestive or euphemistic terms: apparitions (see pp. 55, 71, 75, 88) [29, 39, 42, 51], demons (see pp. 82, 114, 133) [47, 68, 82], fiends (see p. 84) [48], figures (see pp. 55, 57, 71, 76, 116) [28, 30, 40, 43, 70], horrors (see pp. 45, 138) [22, 85], others (see pp. 82, 88) [47, 51], outsiders (see p. 88) [51], presences (see pp. 71, 74, 86, 115, 133, 138) [39, 42, 50, 69, 82, 85], spectres (see p. 96) [57], visitants (see pp. 62, 137) [33, 84] and visitors (see pp. 55, 72, 87) [28, 40, 51].

'The Turn of the Screw' is a matter of circles as well as blanks. Whereas the word 'ghost' is virtually excluded from the text, the word 'turn' is repeatedly and markedly present. 'Ghost' gives way to a play of alternative words; 'turn', on the other hand, remains verbally intact but instead seems to open a proliferation of alternative senses. Characters are said simply to turn (see pp. 71, 78, 83) [40, 44, 47] but they also turn their backs (see pp. 32, 55, 95, 105) [13, 29, 56, 62], turn away (see pp. 46, 76, 136) [22, 43, 84], turn in (see p. 41) [19], turn into (see p. 23) [6] and turn out of (see p. 85) [49]. They turn faces on each other (see p. 137) [84] and expressions at each other (see p. 114) [69]. They turn pale (see pp. 43, 58) [20, 31], turn things over in their minds (see pp. 38, 39, 83, 92, 104, 124, 137) [17, 48, 54, 62, 75, 84], take 'noiseless turns' (p. 74) [41], have 'quick turns' (p. 29) [11] and 'dreadful' turns (p. 115) [69]. They are turned out, both in the sense of being clothed (see p. 90) [53] and of being expelled (see p. 136) [83]. Staircases have turns (see p. 70) [39] and paths also have turns which one might approach whilst taking 'a turn into the grounds' (p. 35) [14]. 'Matters' are liable to turn (see p. 86) [50] and events to occur 'in turn' (p. 113) [68]. Corners and pages are turned (see pp. 42, 70) [20, 39], summers turn (see p. 86) [50] and Peter Quint dies on 'turn mistaken at night' (p. 52) [27].[7]

* * *

To a large extent the narrative of the governess records her attempts to master the logic of the turn. Although the inference that Miles has been an injury to others is temporarily abandoned because he is 'incredibly beautiful', it is not long before his manifest charms—with reflection, with suspicion—suggest the absent; and the absent, in turn, suggests the opposite (p. 32) [13]. Miles's beauty no longer testifies against the original hypothesis of his evil but actually confirms it. The governess argues that the children's beauty is 'more than earthly' and that their apparent goodness is 'absolutely unnatural' (p. 82) [47]. Miles must have been expelled for 'wickedness . . . what else—when he's so clever and beautiful and perfect?' (p. 100) [59]. The boy is 'exquisite —so it can be only *that*' (p. 100) [59]. To assume that beauty and goodness are identical is perhaps no more but certainly no less disquieting a procedure than to argue that they are incompatible. To turn from one strategy to the other, however, is to have one's interpretative cake and eat it, to read the same sign in two quite different ways.

* * *

What then on earth is the governess? To conclude that she is guilty and reverse her reading at every point would inevitably be to adopt her own dangerous logic, and maintaining that the blanks are never suspect is as doubtful a strategy as asserting that they always are. The governess turns the screw with such effect that the distinctions and oppositions on which she relies lose their integrity. If the divine and the infernal are not discriminable, then the question of whether the governess is 'good' or 'evil' no longer makes sense in the usual ways. One could very well give a further turn to the interpretative turns of the governess. But it may be more useful to examine how and with what effect the screw can be turned.

In the introductory chapter, Douglas comments on the way in which the child in Griffin's story 'gives the effect another turn of the screw' (*CT*, x, 15) [1]. The expression 'turn of the screw' seems to describe the results brought about by literary artifices, which in this case make use of the vulnerable figure of a child in order to solicit the reader's involvement and to intensify feelings of suspense, uncertainty and so on. Towards the end of the tale, the governess feels that her situation requires her to make 'another turn of the screw of ordinary human virtue' (p. 127) [77]. The repetition of the expression is accompanied by a turn in its sense, since the governess is not talking about the artifices of narrative but about her attempts 'to supply . . . nature' (p. 127) [77]. The governess's (oddly mechanistic) metaphor details an active moral manifestation rather than a passive aesthetic response. In spite of these differences, however, both Douglas's and the governess's turns of the screw are essentially centripetal. The turn of the screw connotes various forms of restriction, intensification, enclosure, enforcement or constraint. * * *

James's ghosts had always been infectious figures; time and again they had converted ghost seers into ghosts. 'You see a man who has seen a ghost!', proclaims the jubilant Clement Searle in 'A Passionate Pilgrim' (*CT*, II, 287). Yet the narrator will always feel 'that I, too, have seen a ghost' and Searle has himself already exclaimed that 'I *am* a ghost!' (pp. 287, 272). Hovering around Captain Diamond's house, the narrator of 'The Ghostly Rental' feels 'very much like a restless ghost myself' (*CT*, IV, 68). In 'Sir Edmund Orme', Mrs Marden's 'white face' leads the narrator to think for a second that she is 'an apparition' (*CT*, VIII, 125). James's stage directions for *The Saloon* emphasize that Owen Wingrave should present 'a startling apparitional effect'.[8] In 'The Third Person', the ghost of Cuthbert Frush converts Susan and Amy Frush, his living witnesses, into 'wandering ghosts' (*CT*, xi, 153). By embroidering the 'strange and sinister' on the 'normal and easy' (*LC*, II, 1264), James discovered that the strange often led back to ancient stories, hushed family secrets, originary traumas—things 'known of old and long familiar', to use Freud's expression (*SE*, XVII, 220).[9] Unlike Freud, however, James knew that this relation was a circular one and that the normal was itself often strange. 'The Turn of the Screw' is his most developed dramatization of this rotation, and the tale makes it clear that there is no just measure, no impermeable border between the dead and the living, between the familiar and the unfamiliar. Such categories fuse in a characteristically uncanny way even in the name 'Quint', which suggests both the odd, the quaint, and also the 'queynte'—the place which Freud in 'The "Uncanny" ' describes as 'the entrance to the former *Heim* [home] of all human beings' (p. 245).[10] Quint is certainly a strangely familiar presence, and the governess feels that it is 'as if I had been looking at him for years and had known him always' (*CT*, X, 42) [20]. She is 'inexplicably' but also 'intimately' connected with the master's dead servant (p. 39) [18]. 'Hideous' and simultaneously 'human', Quint is a 'detestable, dangerous presence' but also a 'living' one (p. 71) [39].

If the dead resemble the living, then the living may also resemble the dead. The governess, Mrs Grose and Miles repeatedly display white faces which resemble the 'pale face' of Quint and the 'pale and dreadful' countenance of Miss Jessel (pp. 46, 57; see also pp. 43, 44, 133, 134) [23, 30; 20, 21, 81, 82]. The living characters at Bly are connected to the dead in a ring of hatlessness which begins with Quint and extends to Flora, Mrs Grose and the governess (see pp. 46, 108–9, 113) [23, 64–65, 68].[11] Miss Jessel too is 'always without' a hat, and although Miles does pick up his hat in the final scene he is never to put it on (p. 108; see p. 132) [64; 80]. Hawthorne had examined the difference between humanity and monsters, concluding that those who commit the unpardonable sin of detecting the monstrous in others themselves take on a degree of monstrosity. James shifts his predecessor's inquiry to the problem of the difference between people and ghosts. In 'The Turn of the Screw' he concludes that there is something spectral about the spectator, something haunting about the haunted and something appalling about the appalled. Doubting 'if even *I* were in life', the governess cannot separate herself or others from the dead (p. 71) [40]. On a number of occasions the governess quite literally stands in the place of the ghosts. By taking over Quint's position outside the dining-room window, she replicates the effect of a ghost, giving Mrs Grose 'something of the shock that I had received' (p. 43) [20]. The governess tells Mrs Grose that she saw Quint 'as I see you', that Miss Jessel 'might have been as close as you' and that Flora sees Miss Jessel 'even as I actually saw Mrs Grose herself' (pp. 46, 57, 62) [22, 30, 33]. She accuses Flora of being able to see Miss Jessel 'as well as you see me'

(p. 114) [69]. Spectral experience initiates a play of reflections in which Mrs Grose stares into the eyes of the governess 'as if they might really have resembled' those of Miss Jessel and the governess gazes back into the eyes of the housekeeper as if, within them, 'Miss Jessel had again appeared' (pp. 58, 60) [31, 32]. These mirrorings are the greatest threat to the governess's attempt to distinguish herself from the predecessor who was 'almost as young and almost as pretty' as herself (p. 30) [12]. Even if one leaves aside the alliance between the two governesses suggested by the ghostly echoes of *Amelia*, *Jane Eyre* and *The Scarlet Letter*, the resemblances between the governess and Miss Jessel are established at numerous other points.[12] The governess collapses on the stairs (see p. 96) [56–57] in the same place and posture as Miss Jessel on her second appearance (see p. 74) [42]. She covers her face with her hands (see p. 88) [51] exactly as Miss Jessel does on both her second and third appearances (see pp. 74, 97) [42, 57].

To see a ghost is to become a ghost. But 'The Turn of the Screw' gives a further twist to this insight. To see a ghost is also to become what one thinks ghosts are. Requiring a counterweight to found her own being and her own desire, the governess sees the apparitions in her image and then becomes the image of a ghost. She shares a 'common intensity' with Quint and in her 'fierce rigour of confidence' haunts Bly with something like the 'fury of intention' she attributes to Miss Jessel (pp. 71, 58) [39, 31]. I have already examined some of the reasons for and implications of the Jamesian frame * * * Yet perhaps the most significant effect of the device, certainly in 'Sir Edmund Orme', 'The Way it Came' and 'The Turn of the Screw', is that it establishes the fact that the narrator is dead. Both a violator and a victim of the turns in meaning, the governess speaks in her narrative as a voice from beyond the grave, from what Maurice Blanchot has called 'the imprecise space of narration—that unreal beyond where everything is apparition, slippery, evasive, present and absent.[13]

NOTES

1. James, *Literary Criticism*, referred to as *LC*, II.
2. Todorov has also argued that 'the Jamesian narrative is always based on *the quest for an absolute and absent cause*' (*The Poetics of Prose*, p. 145).
3. Henry James, *The Complete Tales of Henry James*, referred to as *CT*.
4. In the revised version of the tale James further multiplied the intervening stages in the children's history by inserting a reference to some grandparents, who take care of Miles and Flora after the death of their parents and before their uncle (see *NYE*, XII, 153).
5. On the problem of origins and the relation between narrative and death in 'The Turn of the Screw', see Felman, 'Turning the Screw of Interpretation', pp. 122, 128.
6. See Watt, 'The First Paragraph of *The Ambassadors*, pp. 257 8; Samuels, *The Ambiguity of Henry James*, p. 199.
7. For further discussion of the word 'turn' in 'The Turn of the Screw', see Caws, *Reading Frames in Modern Fiction*, pp. 146–7.
8. James, *The Saloon*, p. 671.
9. Freud, *The Standard Edition of the Complete Psychological Works*, referred to as *SE*.

10. As well as referring to the female genitals, Middle English 'queynte' means 'strange', 'curious', 'artful' and 'sly'. On the significance of the related French words *'quinte'* and *'quinteux'* ('vagary', 'crotchet', 'whimsical', or 'fantastic'), see Lind, 'The Supernatural Tales of Henry James', p. 337. For other suggestions about the sources for or connotations of Quint's name, see Roellinger, 'Psychical Research and "The Turn of the Screw" ', p. 411; Sheppard, *Henry James and 'The Turn of the Screw'*, pp. 27, 93, 98; O'Gorman, 'Henry James's Reading of "The Turn of the Screw" ', pp. 240–1. One might add that the rotary motifs in James's tale indicate a possible reference to 'quintain', a dummy figure or target used in medieval tournaments which, when hit incorrectly, revolved to strike the tilting knight. On Miss Jessel's name, see Sheppard, *Henry James and 'The Turn of the Screw'*, p. 28; O'Gorman, 'Henry James's Reading of "The Turn of the Screw" ', p. 241.
11. On the absence of hats in 'The Turn of the Screw', see Norrman, *Techniques of Ambiguity*, pp. 89–92; *The Insecure World*, pp. 170–1.
12. On the resemblances between the governess and the ghosts, see Edel's introduction to *CT*, X (p. 9); McMaster, ' "The Full Image of a Repetition" ', pp. 125–6; Banta, *Henry James and the Occult*, pp. 124–5; Mackenzie, *Communities of Honor and Love*, p. 79; Norrman, *Techniques of Ambiguity*, pp. 89, 160; *The Insecure World*, pp. 169–70; Brooke-Rose, *A Rhetoric of the Unreal*, pp. 168–9; Robbins, 'Shooting Off James's Blanks', pp. 196–7; Millicent Bell, ' "The Turn of the Screw" and the *Recherche de L'Absolu*', p. 72; Goetz, *Henry James and the Darkest Abyss*, p. 137; Poole, *Henry James*, pp. 142, 156.
13. Blanchot, ' "The Turn of the Screw" ', p. 82.

WORKS CITED

Banta, Martha. *Henry James and the Occult: The Great Extension.* Bloomington: Indiana University Press, 1972.

Bell, Millicent. " 'The Turn of the Screw' and the *Recherche de L'Absolu.*" *Henry James, Fiction as History.* Ed. Ian F. A. Bell. London: Vision, 1984. 65–81.

Blanchot, Maurice. " 'The Turn of the Screw.' " 1959. *The Sirens' Song: Selected Essays.* Ed. Gabriel Josipovici. Trans. Sacha Rabinovitch. Brighton: Harvester, 1982. 79–86. [See pp. 186–91 of this Norton Critical Edition for an excerpt of this essay.]

Brooke-Rose, Christine. *A Rhetoric of the Unreal: Studies in Narrative and Structure, Especially of the Fantastic.* Cambridge: Cambridge University Press, 1981.

Caws, Mary Ann. *Reading Frames in Modern Fiction.* Princeton: Princeton University Press, 1985.

Edel, Leon. Introduction. *The Complete Tales of Henry James.* Ed. Leon Edel. Vol. 10. London: Rupert Hart-Davis, 1962. 12 vols.

Felman, Shoshana. "Turning the Screw of Interpretation." *Yale French Studies* 55–56 (1977): 94–207. [See pp. 196–228 of this Norton Critical Edition for an excerpt from this essay.]

Freud, Sigmund. *The Standard Edition of the Complete Psychological Works of Sigmund Freud.* Trans. James Strachey. London: The Hogarth Press and the Institute of Psycho-Analysis, 1957. 24 vols.

Goetz, William R. *Henry James and the Darkest Abyss of Romance.* Baton Rouge: Louisiana State University Press, 1986.

James, Henry. *The Complete Tales of Henry James.* Ed. Leon Edel. London: Rupert Hart-Davis, 1962–64. 12 vols.

——. *Literary Criticism: French Writers, Other European Writers, The Prefaces to the New York Edition.* New York: The Library of America, 1984.

——. *The Novels and Tales of Henry James.* New York Edition. 26 vols. (vols. I–XXIV, London: Macmillan, 1907–9; vols. XXV–XXVI, London: Macmillan, 1917).

——. "The Saloon." *The Complete Plays of Henry James.* Ed. Leon Edel. London: Rupert Hart-Davis, 1949. 639–74.

Lind, Sidney Edmund. "The Supernatural Tales of Henry James: Conflict and Fantasy." Diss. New York University, 1948.

MacKenzie, Manfred. *Communities of Honor and Love in Henry James.* Cambridge, Massachusetts: Harvard University Press, 1976.

McMaster, Juliet. " 'The Full Image of a Repetition' in 'The Turn of the Screw.' " 1969. *Henry James*. Ed. Harold Bloom. New York: Chelsea House, 1987. 125–30.

Norrmann, Ralf. *The Insecure World of Henry James's Fiction: Intensity and Ambiguity*. London: Macmillan, 1982.

———. "Techniques of Ambiguity in the Fiction of Henry James, with Special Reference to 'In the Cage' and 'The Turn of the Screw.' " *Acta Academia Aboensis* 54:2 (1977).

O'Gorman, Donal. "Henry James's Reading of 'The Turn of the Screw.' " *Henry James Review* 1 (1979–80): 125–38, 228–56.

Poole, Adrian. *Henry James*. London: Harvester Wheatsheaf, 1991.

Rimmon, Shlomith. *The Concept of Ambiguity: The Example of Henry James*. Chicago: University of Chicago Press, 1977.

Robbins, Bruce. "Shooting Off James's Blanks: Theory, Politics, and 'The Turn of the Screw.' " *Henry James Review* 5 (1983–4): 192–9.

Roellinger, Francis X. "Psychical Research and 'The Turn of the Screw.' " *American Literature* 20 (January 1949): 401–12. [See pp. 135–38 of this Norton Critical Edition for an excerpt from this essay.]

Samuels, Charles Thomas. *The Ambiguity of Henry James*. Urbana: University of Illinois Press, 1971.

Sheppard, E. A. *Henry James and "The Turn of the Screw"*. Auckland: Auckland University Press, 1974.

Todorov, Tzvetan. *The Poetics of Prose*. Trans. Richard Howard. Oxford: Blackwell, 1977.

Watt, Ian. "The First Paragraph of *The Ambassadors*: An Explication." *Essays in Criticism* 10 (1960): 250–74.

Henry James: A Chronology

1843	Born April 15 in New York City, the second of five children of Henry James Sr. and Mary Robertson Walsh James. James's siblings: William James (older brother), Garth Wilkinson James, Robertson James, and Alice James.
1843–45	Family travels in France and England.
1845–55	Childhood spent in New York City and Albany, New York.
1855–58	Schooling in Switzerland, England, and France.
1858	Family settles briefly in Newport, Rhode Island. Schooling continues there.
1859–60	Family returns to Europe. Schooling in Geneva and Bonn.
1860–62	Moves to 13 Kay Street, Newport. Art training. Suffers a profoundly meaningful "obscure hurt," likely a back injury.
1862–63	A term at Harvard Law School. Family moves to Ashburton Place in Boston. Submits stories for magazine consideration. Younger brothers fight with the Union forces in the Civil War. Wilkinson injured, Robertson a hero.
1864	First anonymous story published: "A Tragedy of Error." Writing stories and literary reviews.
1865	First signed story in the *Atlantic Monthly*: "The Story of a Year." Writing anonymous reviews. Friendship with Oliver Wendell Holmes Jr.
1866	Develops an acquaintance with William Dean Howells that will grow into an enduring friendship.
1867	Meets Charles Dickens at the home of Charles Eliot Norton.
1869–70	Travels in Europe, meeting literary figures including George Eliot, William Morris, John Ruskin. Cousin Minnie Temple dies of tuberculosis at 23.
1870–71	Living in "exile" from Europe in Cambridge, Massachusetts. First novel serialized: *Watch and Ward*.
1872–74	Returns to Europe with sister and aunt. Writes newspaper sketches. Lives in Paris and Rome, where he falls in with American social circles.
1875	*Roderick Hudson*, *A Passionate Pilgrim and Other Tales*, *Transatlantic Sketches*. A brief winter in New York. Return to Europe.

1875–76 Moves to 29 Rue de Luxembourg, Paris. Friendship with Ivan Turgenev. Meets Gustave Flaubert, Emile Zola, and Guy de Maupassant. Meets Charles Sanders Peirce. Finds it increasingly difficult to satisfy his obligations as travel journalist for American newspapers.

1877 Moves to 3 Bolton Street, Piccadilly, London. *The American.*

1878 "Daisy Miller," *French Poets and Novelists.*

1879 *The Europeans*, *Confidence*, *Hawthorne*, and numerous tales. Becomes a feature of London's cultural life: friendships with Robert Louis Stevenson, Edmund Gosse, and Henry Adams; meetings with James McNeil Whistler, Frederic Leighton, William Holman Hunt, Alfred Tennyson, and Robert Browning.

1880–81 *Washington Square.* Trip to Florence where he composes *The Portrait of a Lady.* Close friendship with Constance Fenimore Woolson. Homecoming to Boston and New York.

1882 Mother and father die. Returns to London. Joins Athenaeum Club.

1883 Macmillan publishes 14-volume Collective Edition of James's works. *The Siege of London* and *Portraits of Places.*

1884 Friendships with Paul Bourget and Viola Paget. Alice James, now an invalid, settles in Bolton Row, London. *A Little Tour of France*, *Tales of Three Cities*, and "The Art of Fiction."

1885 Moves to 34 De Vere Gardens, London

1886 *The Bostonians* and *The Princess Casamassima* written during the previous year.

1887 In Italy with Constance Fenimore Woolson.

1888 *Partial Portraits*, *The Reverberator*, *The Aspern Papers.* Untimely death of friend Elizabeth Boott.

1889 *A London Life.*

1890 *The Tragic Muse.* Turns his attention to writing for the theatre.

1892 Alice dies.

1893 *Essays in London and Elsewhere.* Continues unsuccessful theatre writing.

1894 Constance Fenimore Woolson commits suicide in Italy.

1895 "The Altar of the Dead" and "The Figure in the Carpet." Theatrical hopes dashed by the sensational failure of *Guy Domville.* Abandons the theatre and begins writing scenarios for novels. Visits with Edward White Benson, Archbishop of Canterbury. *Terminations.*

1896 *Embarrassments* and *The Other House*. Relies on dictation.
1897 *The Spoils of Poynton* and *What Maisie Knew*. Meets Joseph Conrad.
1898 "The Turn of the Screw" serialized. Leases Lamb House, Rye, Sussex, which he later buys. "In the Cage." Friendship with Jonathan Sturges. Meets H. G. Wells and Stephen Crane.
1899 *The Awkward Age*. Employs James B. Pinker as his literary agent. Meets Norwegian-American sculptor Hendrik Andersen.
1900 *The Soft Side*. Begins *The Sense of the Past*, which he never finishes. Begins *The Ambassadors*. Meets Mark Twain.
1901 *The Sacred Fount*. Completes *The Ambassadors*. Begins *The Wings of the Dove*.
1902 *The Wings of the Dove*. Writes "The Beast in the Jungle."
1903 *The Ambassadors* and the biography of *William Wetmore Story and His Friends*. Meets Edith Wharton with whom he has corresponded for some time.
1904 *The Golden Bowl*. Sails for the United States.
1905 Lecture tour. "The Lesson of Balzac," *The Question of Our Speech*, and *English Hours*.
1906 "The Jolly Corner." Begins revising and writing prefaces for the collected New York Edition of his works.
1907 *The American Scene*. Hires Theodora Bosanquet as his amanuensis.
1907–09 The New York Edition in 24 volumes.
1909 *Italian Hours*.
1910 Illness. *The Finer Grain*. Returns to the United States with William James. William dies.
1911 *The Outcry*, James's last completed novel. Honorary degree from Harvard. Returns to England.
1912 Honorary degree from Oxford.
1913 *A Small Boy and Others*, first autobiographical volume. John Singer Sargent portrait marks seventieth birthday.
1914 *Notes of a Son and Brother*, autobiography's second volume. *Notes on Novelists*.
1915 British citizenship. Participates in war relief work. H. G. Wells's *Boon* critiques James.
1916 Awarded Order of Merit. Dies February 28. William's widow, Alice, smuggles James's ashes back to the United States. Buried in family plot in Cambridge, Massachusetts.
1917 *The Ivory Tower* and *The Sense of the Past* (unfinished novels). *The Middle Years* (unfinished autobiography).
1919 *Within the Rim*.
1920 *The Letters of Henry James*.

Selected Bibliography

For editions of *The Turn of the Screw* published in James's lifetime, see page 90.
•indicates those works included or excerpted in this Norton Critical Edition.

BIBLIOGRAPHIES AND CHECKLISTS

Bender, Claire E. and Todd K. *A Concordance to Henry James's "The Turn of the Screw."* New York: Garland, 1988.
Bradbury, Nicola. *An Annotated Critical Bibliography of Henry James.* Brighton: Harvester, 1987.
Budd, John, ed. *Henry James: A Bibliography of Criticism, 1975–1981.* Westport, Connecticut: Greenwood, 1983.
Edel, Leon, Dan H. Laurence, and James Rambeau. *A Bibliography of Henry James.* Oxford: Clarendon, 1982.
Fogel, Mark Daniel, ed. *A Companion to Henry James Studies.* Westport, Connecticut: Greenwood, 1993.
Foley, Richard N. *Criticism in American Periodicals of the Works of Henry James from 1866 to 1916.* Washington: The Catholic University of America Press, 1944.
Freedman, Jonathan, ed. *The Cambridge Companion to Henry James.* Cambridge: Cambridge University Press, 1998.
Funston, Judith E. *Henry James: A Reference Guide, 1975–1987.* Boston: G. K. Hall, 1991.
Gale, Robert L. *A Henry James Encyclopedia.* New York: Greenwood, 1989.
——. *Plots and Characters in the Fiction of Henry James.* [Cambridge, Mass.]: MIT Press, 1972.
Leeming, Glenda. *Who's Who in Henry James.* London: Elm Tree Books, 1976.
McColgan, Kristin Pruitt. *Henry James, 1917–1959: A Reference Guide.* Boston: G. K. Hall, 1979.
Scura, Dorothy McInnis. *Henry James, 1960–1974: A Reference Guide.* Boston: G. K. Hall, 1979.
Taylor, Linda J. *Henry James, 1866–1916: A Reference Guide.* Boston: G. K. Hall, 1982.

BIOGRAPHIES, NOTEBOOKS, LETTERS

Anesko, Michael, ed. *Letters, Fictions, Lives: Henry James and William Dean Howells.* New York: Oxford University Press, 1997.
Dupee, F. W. *Henry James.* New York: Doubleday, 1956.
Edel, Leon. *Henry James: A Life.* New York: Harper and Row, 1985.
——. *The Life of Henry James.* 5 vols. Philadelphia: J. B. Lippincott, 1953–72.
——, ed. *Henry James, Selected Letters.* Cambridge, Mass.: Belknap Press of Harvard University Press, 1987.
•——, ed. *Letters: Henry James.* 4 vols. Cambridge, Mass.: Belknap Press of Harvard University Press, 1974–84.
——, and Lyall H. Powers, eds. *The Complete Notebooks of Henry James.* New York: Oxford University Press, 1987.
Graham, Kenneth. *Henry James: A Literary Life.* New York: St. Martin's Press, 1995.

Kaplan, Fred. *Henry James: The Imagination of Genius, A Biography.* New York: Morrow, 1992.
Lewis, R. W. B. *The Jameses: A Family Narrative.* New York: Farrar, Straus and Giroux, 1991.
•Lubbock, Percy, ed. *The Letters of Henry James.* New York: Charles Scribner's Sons, 1920.
Matthiessen, F. O. *The James Family.* New York: Oxford University Press, 1947.
——, and Kenneth B. Murdoch, eds. *The Notebooks of Henry James.* New York: Oxford University Press, 1947.
Monteiro, George, ed. *The Correspondence of Henry James and Henry Adams, 1877–1914.* Baton Rouge: Louisiana State University Press, 1992.
Moore, Rayburn S., ed. *The Correspondence of Henry James and the House of Macmillan, 1877–1914: "All the Links In the Chain".* Baton Rouge: Louisiana State University Press, 1993.
——, ed. *Selected Letters of Henry James to Edmund Gosse, 1882–1915: A Literary Friendship.* Baton Rouge: Louisiana State University Press, 1988.
Novick, Sheldon M. *Henry James: The Young Master.* New York: Random House, 1996.
Powers, Lyall H., ed. *Henry James and Edith Wharton: Letters, 1900–1915.* New York: Charles Scribner's Sons, 1990.
Skrupskelis, Ignas K. and Elizabeth M. Berkeley, eds. *William and Henry James: Selected Letters.* Charlottesville: University Press of Virginia, 1997.

SELECTED TEXTUAL CRITICISM

Allott, Miriam. "Mrs. Gaskell's 'The Old Nurse's Story': A Link Between *Wuthering Heights* and 'The Turn of the Screw.' " *Notes and Queries* 206 (1961): 101–2.
Alvarez Amorós, José Antonio. "Possible-World Semantics, Frame Text, Insert Text, and Unreliable Narration: The Case of 'The Turn of the Screw.' " *Style* 25 (1951): 42–70.
•Armstrong, Paul B. "History and Epistemology: The Example of *The Turn of the Screw.*" *New Literary History* 19 (1987–88): 693–712.
Banta, Martha. *Henry James and the Occult: The Great Extension.* Bloomington: Indiana University Press, 1972.
Beidler, Paul G. *Frames in James: "The Tragic Muse," "The Turn of the Screw," "What Maisie Knew," and "The Ambassadors."* [Victoria], British Columbia: English Literary Studies, University of Victoria, 1993.
Beidler, Peter G. *Ghosts, Demons and Henry James: "The Turn of the Screw" at the Turn of the Century.* Columbia: University of Missouri Press, 1989.
——, ed. *"The Turn of the Screw."* Boston: Bedford Books of St. Martin's, 1995.
Bell, Millicent. *Meaning in Henry James.* Cambridge: Harvard University Press, 1991.
——. " 'The Turn of the Screw' and the *Recherche de L'Absolu.*" In *Henry James, Fiction as History,* ed. Ian F. A. Bell. London: Vision, 1984. 65–81.
Bengels, Barbara. "The Term of the Screw: A Key to the Imagery in Henry James's *The Turn of the Screw.*" *Studies in Short Fiction* 15 (1978): 332–37.
Benn Michaels, Walter. "Writers Reading: James and Eliot." *MLN* 91 (1976): 834–37.
Bersani, Leo. *A Future for Astyanax: Character and Desire in Literature.* Boston and Toronto: Little, Brown and Company, 1976.
•Blackmur, R. P. *Studies in Henry James.* Ed. Veronica A. Makowsky. New York: New Directions, 1983.
•Blanchot, Maurice. "The Turn of the Screw." *The Sirens' Song: Selected Essays by Maurice Blanchot.* Ed. Gabriel Josipovici. Trans. Sacha Rabinovitch. Bloomington: Indiana University Press, 1982. 79–86.
Bloom, Harold, ed. *Henry James's "Daisy Miller," "The Turn of the Screw," and Other Tales.* New York: Chelsea House Publishers, 1987.

Bontly, Thomas J. "Henry James's General Vision of Evil, in *The Turn of the Screw*." *Studies in English Literature, 1500–1900* 9 (1969): 721–39.

Booth, Wayne C. *The Rhetoric of Fiction*. Chicago: University of Chicago Press, 1961.

Brooke-Rose, Christine. *A Rhetoric of the Unreal: Studies in Narrative and Structure, Especially of the Fantastic*. Cambridge: Cambridge University Press, 1981.

———. "The Squirm of the True: An Essay in Non-Methodology." *Poetics and the Theory of Literature* 1 (1976): 265–94.

———. "A Structural Analysis of Henry James's *The Turn of the Screw*." *Poetics and the Theory of Literature* 1 (1976): 513–46.

•Cargill, Oscar. "*The Turn of the Screw* and Alice James." *PMLA* 78 (June 1963): 238–49.

Caws, Mary Ann. *Reading Frames in Modern Fiction*. Princeton: Princeton University Press, 1985.

Chase, Dennis. "The Ambiguity of Innocence: *The Turn of the Screw*. *Extrapolation* 27 (1986): 197–202.

Clair, John A. *The Ironic Dimension in the Fiction of Henry James*. Pittsburgh: Duquesne University Press, 1965.

Cook, David, and Thomas J. Corrigan. "Narrative Structure in *The Turn of the Screw*." *Studies in Short Fiction* 17 (1980): 55–65.

Costello, Donald P. "The Structure of 'The Turn of the Screw.' " *Modern Language Notes* 75 (1960): 312–21.

Cranfill, Thomas Mabry, and Robert Lanier Clark. *An Anatomy of "The Turn of the Screw."* Austin: University of Texas Press, 1965.

Eaton, Marcia M. "James's Turn of the Speech-Act." *British Journal of Aesthetics* 23:4 (Autumn 1983): 333–45.

•Edel, Leon, ed. *Henry James: Stories of the Supernatural*. New York: Taplinger Publishing Company, 1970.

———, and Gordon N. Ray, eds. *Henry James and H. G. Wells: A Record of Their Friendship, Their Debate on the Art of Fiction, and Their Quarrel*. London: R. Hart-Davis, 1958.

Evans, Oliver. "James's Air of Evil: 'The Turn of the Screw.' " *Partisan Review* 16 (1949): 175–87.

Faulkner, Howard. "Text as Pretext in *The Turn of the Screw*." *Studies in Short Fiction* 20:2–3 (Spring–Summer 1983): 87–94.

•Felman, Shoshana. *Writing and Madness: (Literature/Philosophy/Psychoanalysis)*. Ithaca: Cornell University Press, 1985.

•———. "Writing and Madness: (Literature/Philosophy/Psychoanalysis)" *Yale French Studies* 55–56 (1977): 94–207.

•———, ed. *Literature and Psychoanalysis: The Question of Reading—Otherwise*. Baltimore: The Johns Hopkins University Press, 1982.

Firebaugh, Joseph J. "Inadequacy in Eden: Knowledge and 'The Turn of the Screw.' " *Modern Fiction Studies* 3 (1957): 57–63.

Freud, Sigmund. "The Uncanny." 1919. *The Standard Edition of the Complete Psychological Works of Sigmund Freud*. Ed. and trans. James Strachey et al. Vol. 17. London: 1953–74. 219–52.

Freundlieb, Dieter. "Explaining Interpretation: The Case of Henry James's *The Turn of the Screw*." *Poetics Today* 5 (1984): 79–95.

Fussell, Edwin. "The Ontology of *The Turn of the Screw*." *Journal of Modern Literature* 8 (1980): 118–28.

Gargano, James W. "The Turn of the Screw." *The Western Humanities Review* 15 (Spring 1961): 173–79.

•Goddard, Harold C. "A Pre-Freudian Reading of *The Turn of the Screw*." *Nineteenth-Century Fiction* 12:1 (June 1957): 1–36.

Goetz, William R. "The 'Frame' of *The Turn of the Screw*: Framing the Reader In." *Studies in Short Fiction* 18 (1981): 71–74.

———. *Henry James and the Darkest Abyss of Romance*. Baton Rouge: Louisiana State University Press, 1986.

Hallab, Mary Y. "*The Turn of the Screw* Squared." *Southern Review* 13 (1977): 492–504.

Haskell, Barbara. *Charles Demuth.* New York: Whitney Museum of American Art in Association with Harry N. Abrams, Inc., 1987.

•Heilman, Robert B. "The Freudian Reading of *The Turn of the Screw.*" *Modern Language Notes* 57:7 (November 1947): 433–45.

——. " 'The Turn of the Screw' as Poem." *The University of Kansas City Review* 14 (1948): 277–89.

Heller, Terry. *The Turn of the Screw: Bewildered Vision.* Boston: Twayne, 1989.

Holland, Laurence Bedwell. *The Expense of Vision: Essays in the Craft of Henry James.* Princeton: Princeton University Press, 1964.

Hoople, Robin P. *Distinguished Discord: Discontinuity and Pattern in the Critical Tradition of "The Turn of the Screw."* Lewisburg, Pennsylvania: Bucknell University Press, 1997.

Jones, Alexander E. "Point of View in 'The Turn of the Screw.' " *PMLA* 74:1 (1959): 112–22.

•Kenton, Edna. "Henry James to the Ruminant Reader: *The Turn of the Screw.*" *The Arts* 6 (November 1924): 245–55.

Kimbrough, Robert, ed. *The Turn of the Screw.* Norton Critical Edition. New York: W. W. Norton, 1966.

Knox, George. "Incubi and Succubi in *The Turn of the Screw.*" *Western Folklore* 22 (1963): 122–23.

Krook, Dorothea. *The Ordeal of Consciousness in Henry James.* Cambridge: Cambridge University Press, 1962.

•Lukacher, Ned. *Primal Scenes: Literature, Philosophy, Psychoanalysis.* Ithaca: Cornell University Press, 1986.

•Lustig, T. J. *Henry James and the Ghostly.* Cambridge: Cambridge University Press, 1994.

Lydenberg, John. "The Governess Turns the Screws." *Nineteenth-Century Fiction* 12 (1957–58): 37–58.

MacKenzie, Manfred. "The Turn of the Screw: Jamesian Gothic." *Essays in Criticism* 12 (January 1962): 34–38.

McMaster, Juliet. " 'The Full Image of a Repetition' in 'The Turn of the Screw.' " 1969. In *Henry James,* ed. Harold Bloom. New York: Chelsea House, 1987. 125–30.

Matthiessen, F. O. *Henry James: The Major Phase.* London: Oxford University Press, 1944.

Miall, David S. "Designed Horror: James's Vision of Evil in 'The Turn of the Screw.' " *Ninetheenth-Century Literature* 39:3 (1984): 305–27.

O'Gorman, Donal. "Henry James's Reading of 'The Turn of the Screw.' " *Henry James Review* 1 (1979–80): 125–38, 228–56.

Pollak, Vivian R., ed. *New Essays on "Daisy Miller" and "The Turn of the Screw."* Cambridge: Cambridge University Press, 1993.

•Porter, Katherine Anne, Allen Tate, and Mark Van Doren. "James: 'The Turn of the Screw' A Radio Symposium." In *The New Invitation to Learning,* ed. Mark Van Doren. New York: Random House, 1942. 223–35.

Reed, Glenn A. "Another Turn on James's 'The Turn of the Screw.' " *American Literature* 20 (January 1949): 413–23.

Rimmon, Shlomith. *The Concept of Ambiguity: The Example of Henry James.* Chicago: University of Chicago Press, 1977.

•Robbins, Bruce. *The Servant's Hand: English Fiction From Below.* New York: Columbia University Press, 1986.

——. "Shooting Off James's Blanks: Theory, Politics, and 'The Turn of the Screw.' " *Henry James Review* 5 (1983–84): 192–99.

•Roellinger, Francis X. "Psychical Research and 'The Turn of the Screw.' " *American Literature* 20 (January 1949): 401–12.

Rowe, John Carlos. "Screwball: The Use and Abuse of Uncertainty in Henry James's

The Turn of the Screw." *Delta: Revue du Centre d'Etudes et de Recherche sur les Ecrivains du Sud aux Etats Unis* 15 (November 1982): 1–31.

Rubin, Louis D., Jr. "One More Turn of the Screw." *Modern Fiction Studies* 9 (Winter 1963–64): 314–28.

Schleifer, Ronald. "The Trap of the Imagination: The Gothic Tradition, Fiction, and *The Turn of the Screw.*" *Criticism* 22 (1980): 297–319.

Sheppard, E. A. *Henry James and 'The Turn of the Screw'.* Auckland: Auckland University Press, 1974.

Shine, Muriel G. *The Fictional Children of Henry James.* Chapel Hill: University of North Carolina Press, 1969.

Siebers, Tobin. "Hesitation, History, and Reading: Henry James's 'The Turn of the Screw.' " *Texas Studies in Literature and Language* 25 (1983): 558–73.

Silver, John. "A Note on the Freudian Reading of 'The Turn of the Screw.' " *American Literature* 29 (1957–58): 207–11.

Stone, Albert E. "Henry James and Childhood: *The Turn of the Screw.*" In *American Character and Culture in a Changing World: Some Twentieth-Century Perspectives.* ed. John A. Hague. Westport: Greenwood, 1979. 279–92.

•Sussman, Henry. *The Hegelian Aftermath: Readings in Hegel, Kierkegaard, Freud, Proust, and James.* Baltimore and London: The Johns Hopkins University Press, 1982.

Tintner, Adeline R. "Henry James's Use of *Jane Eyre* in 'The Turn of the Screw.' " *Brontë Society Transactions* 17:1 (1976): 42–5.

•Todorov, Tzvetan. *The Fantastic: A Structural Approach to a Literary Genre.* 1970. Trans. Richard Howard. Cleveland and London: The Press of Case Western Reserve University, 1973.

——. *The Poetics of Prose.* 1971. Trans. Richard Howard. Ithaca: Cornell University Press, 1977.

Tompkins, Jane P., ed. *Twentieth-Century Interpretations of "The Turn of the Screw" and Other Tales: A Collection of Critical Essays.* Englewood Cliffs N.J.: Prentice-Hall, 1970.

Tuveson, Ernest. "*The Turn of the Screw*: A Palimpsest." *SEL: Studies in English Literature, 1500–1900* 12 (1972): 783–800.

Van Peer, Willie, and Ewout van der Knaap. "(In)Compatible Interpretations? Contesting Readings of *The Turn of the Screw.*" *MLN* 110:4 (September 1995): 692–710.

Vicinus, Martha, ed. *Suffer and Be Still: Women in the Victorian Age.* Bloomington: Indiana University Press, 1972.

Ward, J. A. *The Imagination of Disaster: Evil in the Fiction of Henry James.* Lincoln: University of Nebraska Press, 1961.

West, Muriel. "The Death of Miles in *The Turn of the Screw.*" *PMLA* 79 (June 1964): 283–88.

——. *A Stormy Night with "The Turn of the Screw."* Phoenix: Frye & Smith, 1964.

Willen, Gerald. *A Casebook on Henry James's "The Turn of the Screw."* New York: Thomas Y. Crowell, 1960.

•Wilson, Edmund. "The Ambiguity of Henry James." *Hound & Horn* 7 (1934): 385–406.

•Wolff, Robert Lee. "The Genesis of *The Turn of the Screw.*" *American Literature* 13 (March 1941): 1–8.